Egalitarian perspectives

This book presents fifteen essays, written over the past dozen years, on egalitarianism. The essays explore contemporary philosophical debates on this subject, using the tools of modern economic theory, general equilibrium theory, game theory, and the theory of mechanism design.

Egalitarian Perspectives is divided into four parts: on the theory of exploitation, on equality of resources, on bargaining theory and distributive justice, and on market socialism and public ownership. The first part presents Roemer's influential reconceptualization of the Marxian theory of exploitation as a theory of distributive justice. The second part offers a critique of Ronald Dworkin's equality-of-resources theory, and puts forth a new egalitarian proposal based upon a specific method of measuring individual responsibility. The third part introduces a novel application of the theory of mechanism design to the study of political philosophy, and raises new concerns about the limitations of that application. The fourth part presents the author's views on market socialism and public ownership, and demonstrates that Professor Roemer is at the forefront of refining new theories and conceptions of market socialism.

Egalitarian perspectives
Essays in philosophical economics

John E. Roemer
University of California, Davis

CAMBRIDGE
UNIVERSITY PRESS

CAMBRIDGE UNIVERSITY PRESS
Cambridge, New York, Melbourne, Madrid, Cape Town, Singapore, São Paulo

Cambridge University Press
The Edinburgh Building, Cambridge CB2 2RU, UK

Published in the United States of America by Cambridge University Press, New York

www.cambridge.org
Information on this title: www.cambridge.org/9780521450669

First published 1994
Reprinted 1996
First paperback edition 1996

A catalogue record for this publication is available from the British Library

ISBN-13 978-0-521-45066-9 hardback
ISBN-10 0-521-45066-7 hardback

ISBN-13 978-0-521-57445-7 paperback
ISBN-10 0-521-57445-5 paperback

Transferred to digital printing 2006

To G. A. Cohen

Contents

Acknowledgments

Had I not encountered, in chronological order, the work of G. A. Cohen, Jon Elster, Amartya Sen, Ronald Dworkin, William Thomson, and Richard Arneson, and then been so lucky as to meet and talk with them, this book would not exist, at least in any form like its present one. I have also been most fortunate to have collaborated with David Donaldson, Roger Howe, Joaquim Silvestre, Hervé Moulin, Pranab Bardhan, and Ignacio Ortuño-Ortin. Some of the main ideas, and their final distilled form as mathematical theorems, would not have been found (or proved) without them.

In addition to countless referees and conference and seminar participants, I wish explicitly to acknowledge members of the "September Group," who have met annually during the period when these essays were written: Pranab Bardhan, Samuel Bowles, Robert Brenner, G. A. Cohen, Jon Elster, Adam Przeworski, Hillel Steiner, Philippe Van Parijs, Robert Van der Veen, and Erik Olin Wright. They have all read and discussed many of these essays in various versions over the years, and their influence upon me and this book is surely more than I can say.

I dedicate this book to Jerry Cohen, consummate socialist scholar, who, like no other in our generation, combines a passionate hatred for injustice with a most ruthless honesty and perspicuity in trying to understand it.

Sources

"Exploitation, alternatives and socialism," *Economic Journal* 92, March 1982, 87–104. Reprinted by permission.

"Property relations vs. surplus value in Marxian exploitation," *Philosophy & Public Affairs* 11, Fall 1982, 281–313. © 1982 by Princeton University Press. Reprinted by permission.

"Should Marxists be interested in exploitation?" *Philosophy & Public Affairs* 14, Winter 1985, 30–65. Reprinted by permission.

"What is exploitation? Reply to Jeffrey Reiman," *Philosophy & Public Affairs* 18, Winter 1989, 90–97. Reprinted by permission.

"Second thoughts on property relations and exploitation," *Canadian Journal of Philosophy,* Supplementary Volume 15, 1989, 257–66. Reprinted by permission.

"Equality of talent," *Economics and Philosophy* 1, 1985, 151–81. © 1985 Cambridge University Press. Reprinted by permission.

"Egalitarianism, responsibility, and information," *Economics and Philosophy* 3, 1987, 215–44. © 1987 Cambridge University Press. Reprinted by permission.

"A pragmatic theory of responsibility for the egalitarian planner," *Philosophy & Public Affairs* 22, 1993, 146–66. Reprinted by permission.

"The mismarriage of bargaining theory and distributive justice," *Ethics* 97, October 1986, 88–110. © 1986 by The University of Chicago. All rights reserved. Reprinted by permission.

"A challenge to Neo-Lockeanism," *Canadian Journal of Philosophy* 18, December 1988, 697–710. Reprinted by permission.

"Distributing health: Allocation of resources by an international agency," in M. Nussbaum and A. Sen (eds.), *The Quality of Life,* Oxford: Oxford University Press, 1992, 339–57. Reprinted by permission of Oxford University Press.

"The morality and efficiency of market socialism," *Ethics* 102, April 1992, 448–64. © 1992 by The University of Chicago. All rights reserved. Reprinted by permission.

An expanded version of "A future for socialism" is forthcoming from Harvard University Press as *A Future for Socialism*.

Introduction

The essays collected here were written between 1981 and 1992. They are organized into four parts, which follow a roughly, but not exactly, chronological order. (The most recently written essays are numbers 8 and 15.) The four parts also display the intellectual development of an author who began thinking about egalitarianism from a Marxian viewpoint and whose tools were those of a neoclassical economist. Some personal details of that development may help the reader discern a thread through these essays that is not, perhaps, readily apparent.

In 1979–80, while writing what was to become a book in Marxian economics (*A General Theory of Exploitation and Class* [Harvard University Press, 1982], hereafter referred to as *GTEC*), I came to realize that the political philosophy motivating the Marxian concept of exploitation was unclear. At the time I was reading G. A. Cohen's magisterial *Karl Marx's Theory of History: A Defence* (Oxford University Press, 1978), my first introduction to analytical philosophy. In my book and a previous one (*Analytical Foundations of Marxian Economic Theory* [Cambridge University Press, 1981]), I had examined Marx's economics from a modern and rigorous viewpoint;[1] Cohen's example showed me that it was possible and important to apply the same standards to Marx's philosophy. Essay 1 summarizes my version of exploitation theory as I had developed it in *GTEC*. As I presented the theory, the political philosophy which motivated the diagnosis of "exploitation" was an egalitarian one in which justice entailed the equal distribution of certain kinds of property among the population.

In the spring of 1981, with the help of a Guggenheim fellowship, I visited G. A. Cohen, then at University College, London, and began to learn from him the range of questions addressed by modern political philosophy. Emboldened, I pushed further against the classical Marxian conception of exploitation, and the result was Essay 2, in which I staked my claim that the "surplus value" approach to exploitation was wrongheaded, and that what Marx had "really meant" was better captured by

---

[1] I was inspired by Morishima (1973) in this project.

1

the property-relations approach. Essay 3, written several years later, went still further and argued that the Marxian definition of exploitation gave incorrect verdicts about who was really exploiting whom when people had different preferences.

The next landmark in my development was reading the pair of essays published by Ronald Dworkin in 1981 on egalitarianism ("What is Equality? Part 1: Equality of Welfare," and "Part 2: Equality of Resources," *Philosophy & Public Affairs*). Having come to the conclusion that the political philosophy justifying Marxism's condemnation of capitalism was a kind of resource egalitarianism, I decided I had to understand Dworkin's work, which was the state-of-the-art presentation on that subject. Dworkin proposed a kind of comprehensive resource egalitarianism, in which resources were specified to include internal talents that people possessed; thus, equalizing resources was not a conceptually simple task, because one had to decide what degree of compensation with transferable resources was due a person with a low endowment of nontransferable ones. I was completely in sympathy with Dworkin's approach, and was hopeful that his insurance mechanism would solve the problem. But, after experimenting with examples, I concluded that the insurance mechanism did not always do what it was supposed to do, that is, compensate those with low talent with more transferable resources. My studies on this question are summarized in Essay 6.

I had recently discovered the work of William Thomson,[2] who was using the tools of axiomatic bargaining theory to study egalitarianism. This gave me the idea of trying to salvage Dworkin's attempt at finding a way to equalize resources comprehensively by modeling the problem as one of mechanism design, after the methods of Thomson. But I soon discovered that axiomatic bargaining theory was inadequate for the task, as it possessed no language for representing "resources," but only "utility." This led to my efforts to model equality-of-resources by specifying axioms on resource allocation mechanisms, which, after quite a while, led to the work summarized in Essay 7, whose main mathematical idea, the CONRAD axiom, would not have been discovered without the insight of Roger Howe. Howe also developed a key theorem in the representation of concave functions that was used in the proof of the main theorem of that essay.

Although that theorem said that any comprehensive resource egalitarianism must dissolve into welfare egalitarianism, I did not put it forth as an ethical argument for the latter kind of equality, but rather as an argument for devoting more thought to how, precisely, one should distinguish

---

[2] Now available in Thomson and Lensberg (1989) and Thomson (1991).

a fortunate endowment of resources from a fortunate set of preferences. For that theorem was based upon a refusal to make such a distinction. After Richard Arneson's (1989) and G. A. Cohen's (1989) recent contributions, I came back to this problem and wrote Essay 8, which proposes how a society might distinguish between those aspects of a person's situation for which he is responsible, and those for which he is not, and is therefore due compensation under an egalitarian ethic.

During 1981, G. A. Cohen was formulating a rejoinder to Nozick's justification of capitalism, as follows. The Nozickian–Lockean presumption was that, before their private appropriation, resources in the world external to human beings were unowned. Why not, Cohen said, view them as having been, morally speaking, publicly owned? Perhaps *this* presumption would suffice to reverse the inegalitarian outcome that Nozick deduced as just, without challenging his relatively more appealing postulate that persons were owners of themselves and their labor. Thereby it would be shown that inegalitarian outcome requires more than a self-ownership postulate. I tried to model "the Cohen problem" in various ways, as reported in Essays 9 and 10. Essay 11 came about from thinking about the problems of representing the kind of information that ethical theories use in axiomatic models of resource allocation.

Thinking about the Cohen problem, and discussing it with Joaquim Silvestre, made us realize the lacuna there was in economics with respect to the articulation of a theory of public ownership. Our collaboration in an effort to construct such a theory led to the results that are reported in Essay 13. The proposals we made for a normative theory of public ownership were, however, with one exception, not easily implementable with markets. By 1988, I (finally) understood that any solution to the problems of socialism would require the massive introduction of markets, and that the formulation of a theory of market socialism was in order. The beginnings of such a theory are summarized in Essays 14 and 15. I have further pursued this undertaking elsewhere, with collaborators.[3]

To save the reader time, I will briefly describe what I think are the six principal ideas or claims of this book. The first five are substantive and the sixth is methodological. (1) We should not search for the cause of exploitation in the Marxian sense in the labor process or at the point of production, but in the distribution of property. The call for the abolition of exploitation is a call for an egalitarian distribution of resources in the external world (Part I). (2) Defensible egalitarianism is equality of opportunity; Ronald Dworkin's equality-of-resources theory is a major contemporary statement of such a theory. While Dworkin argued convincingly

---

[3] See Ortuño, Roemer, and Silvestre (1993), Bardhan and Roemer (1992), and Roemer (in press).

that equality of welfare should not be the egalitarian's goal, his own proposal for implementing equality of resources is flawed. Moreover, it was later work, by Richard Arneson and G. A. Cohen, which explained more clearly what a system ensuring equality of opportunity must do: fully compensate people precisely for that aspect of their situations for which they are not responsible. I propose how this may actually be done in Essay 8 (Part II). (3) Although a regime implementing full equality of opportunity, so defined, cannot respect self-ownership (because people are in large part not responsible for their inborn talents and characteristics and therefore the highly talented should be taxed to compensate those with low talent),[4] it is nevertheless of interest to ask how much equality of outcome would be achieved by a less radical egalitarianism, which held that resources in the external world were to be publicly owned while talents remained owned by those in whom they reside. Several answers to this question are offered (Parts III and IV). (4) Indeed, there is, in economic theory, no well-developed theory of public ownership. How should a society that wishes to respect public property rights in some resources but private ones in others allocate labor and output to its members? Several suggestions are offered (Part IV). (5) The egalitarian whose views are described here should, in our present world, advocate an economic mechanism that can be described as market-socialist. While the concept of market socialism is as old as the century, it has been thoroughly transformed by the experiences of the Soviet-type economies and advanced capitalist economies. There is a new generation of market-socialist ideas, which deserve the serious consideration of egalitarians (Part IV). (6) While the axiomatic theory of mechanism design (of which social choice theory and axiomatic bargaining theory are instances) is a major achievement of the social sciences, its application to political philosophy must be made with great care. Apparently compelling mathematical assumptions are sometimes philosophically unacceptable. One specific lesson from this approach to political philosophy is that there will be no simple statement of a theory of justice in the language of mechanism design (Part III).

To help place the essays of this book in the context of contemporary political philosophy, I will provide a thumbnail sketch of modern attempts to answer the question: What should an egalitarian wish to equalize? Attempts to address this question have engendered an exciting literature which, I believe, has made much more precise than heretofore our understanding of what distributive justice consists in. I take the frontier of the work on this question to be represented by the recent writings of

---

[4] This point is fully articulated by Rawls (1971), who states that the distribution of talents is "morally arbitrary."

Richard Arneson (1989, 1990), G. A. Cohen (1989, 1990, 1992), Ronald Dworkin (1981, 1981a), Amartya Sen (1980, 1985, 1985a, 1992), and, of course, John Rawls (1971).

The most prominent nineteenth-century theory of distributive justice was utilitarianism, the view that society should seek "the greatest good for the greatest number." The quoted phrase is ambiguous; the most obvious interpretation, I think, is to recommend, for any given population size, that distribution of resources which maximizes total welfare, and then to choose population size to maximize that number. (In other words, let $W(n)$ be the maximum total welfare that can be achieved in a world with n people; the ideal world has a population n^* that maximizes $W(n)$.) It is clear that this could lead to the advocacy of an extremely large population, where no individual was much better off than he would be at a starvation level. (Derek Parfit, 1984, describes a theory of justice closely related to this as leading to a "repugnant conclusion.") Nevertheless, utilitarianism was viewed by J. S. Mill and others as an egalitarian ethic. For if everyone had the same utility function, which we might express in a reduced form as a utility for money, and the quantity of money is fixed, then, for a given population size, the distribution of money which maximizes total utility would be the equal distribution.

If, however, utility functions are not identical across people, then utilitarianism recommends that distribution which equalizes the marginal utilities of persons, a distribution that can lead to extremely unequal utility *levels* for individuals.[5] In looking at only the total sum of utility, utilitarianism is in a sense indifferent to how individuals benefit: persons are viewed simply as machines for producing utility, and resources should be poured into them only insofar as they are effective at producing the desired output. In particular, a person who is handicapped in the sense of not being a good utility-producing machine fares very poorly under utilitarianism. Thus, twentieth-century egalitarians, who took seriously differences across people, viewed utilitarianism as recommending a potentially regressive social policy.

The modern debate between utilitarianism and egalitarianism began with Rawls (1971), who proposed a theory of justice in which distribution was determined by the difference principle, which stated that, first, one should look at "primary goods," instead of utility, and second, that justice requires the adoption of that economic mechanism which maximizes the bundle of primary goods that the group that is worst off (gets the fewest of them) receives. Rawls did not propose how to aggregate primary goods into an index that could be used to apply maximin; one cannot

---

[5] This assumes interpersonal comparisons of utility are possible. For a number of views on this question, see Elster and Roemer (1991).

maximize a bundle or a vector, and others have claimed that in trying to specify such an index, Rawls would inevitably be pulled back into evaluating primary goods with some sort of "welfarist" metric. The two salient points for the present discussion are that Rawls proposed that certain kinds of resources, presumably necessary for every conception of welfare (or for realizing any life plan) should be the equalisandum for egalitarians, not welfare itself, and that one should replace utilitarianism's concern for the total sum with a concern for equality across people.

Amartya Sen's rejoinder to Rawls was first broached in a paper entitled "Equality of What?" (Sen, 1980), in which he argues that Rawls's concern with primary goods was misplaced; what should be equalized are not the resources that all people need to carry out life plans, but rather the capabilities to function in various ways that resources engender. One should not, for example, equalize the amount of money (a primary good) that all receive, but rather the capabilities to function that money facilitates (e.g., the capabilities to be well nourished, well sheltered, well educated, well dressed, to move about freely, etc.). Thus, a paralyzed person would generally require more money than an able-bodied person to reach the same level of functioning as the latter. For Sen, a person's degree of well-being is some index of his levels of functioning (Sen, 1985, p. 25). Because levels of functioning are for the most part observable to an outsider, a person's level of well-being is therefore not a subjective matter – it may be independent of his degree of happiness, for instance, which is in part a subjective matter (though surely influenced by his levels of functioning).[6] If welfare is that thing which preferences maximize, then Sen, like Rawls, degrades welfare to be only one goal among many that people might have, and hence not the sole concern of a theory of just distribution. Both Sen and Rawls were reacting against using subjective utility, the level of a person's preference satisfaction, as the key attribute of a person insofar as distributive justice is concerned; they sought a more objective standard.

In 1981, Ronald Dworkin, in two papers I referred to earlier, offered a third proposal for what egalitarians should concern themselves with: resources. For Dworkin, resources include not only objects in the world external to people, but also their internal resources, their talents and handicaps. But how can one equalize all resources when some are inalienable in the physical sense? The originality in Dworkin's proposal rests in his answer to this question. Dworkin's ethical stance is that, although a person cannot be considered responsible for his inborn talents and their early nurture – these are, in Rawls's words, traits whose distribution is morally

---

[6] In later expositions of the view, Sen includes happiness as a functioning (1992, p. 39). This decreases the distinctiveness of Sen's approach.

arbitrary – a person is responsible for his preferences, including his attitude toward risk, so long as he identifies with these preferences, views them as an essential part of himself. Thus, although a person's preferences may be formed in large part by resources whose distribution is morally arbitrary – one's family, one's talents, one's culture – Dworkin asserts one can nevertheless be morally responsible for the choices that preferences direct one to make. A similar position is maintained by Thomas Scanlon.[7] Given this assumption, Dworkin asks us to consider a hypothetical experiment behind a thin veil of ignorance (although he does not himself call it that, and has indeed argued against Rawls's veil-of-ignorance formulation of contractarianism). Suppose each person knows her preferences behind the thin veil, but does not know what resources she will receive in the birth lottery, internal or external; she knows the distribution of resources that characterize the world she shall be born into, but not her place in it. (Think of the birth lottery as distributing places to souls behind the veil.) Suppose, behind the veil, each person is given the same number of clamshells (or vouchers) with which she can purchase insurance, whose price will be quoted in clamshells, against being born into certain places. If people have different goals and different attitudes toward risk, they will purchase different insurance policies. There will be an equilibrium in the market for insurance. Dworkin's proposal is essentially this: in the actual world, a tax scheme should be devised that implements the distribution of transfers that the hypothetical insurance market would have brought about. Thus, those who end up in a place they did not insure against pay net insurance premiums which are distributed to those who end up in places they did insure against, who receive net insurance payouts. In Dworkin's view, egalitarianism should seek to compensate people only for that bad luck that they would have insured against, had they had the opportunity. The cost of the insurance, moreover, is determined by the preferences of everyone, given that all start with equal purchasing power for insurance, in the sense that an equilibrium in the insurance market depends on those preferences. One can say that the hypothetical insurance market implements a distribution of resources in which people are held responsible for their preferences but not for their resource endowments.

Dworkin's contribution injected subjective preferences and choice back into the debate on egalitarianism, after the more minor role played by these features in the theories of Rawls and Sen. As I noted, both Rawls and Sen were seeking an objective basis on which to evaluate a given distribution. Dworkin, like Rawls and Sen, is opposed to equalizing welfare across persons, and his reason for opposing equality of welfare is similar

[7] See Scanlon (1988 and 1986).

to Rawls's, that people should be held responsible for their preferences, and hence their conception of welfare (the thing that preferences maximize). One's level of welfare is therefore not morally arbitrary.[8] Egalitarianism should only attempt to equalize "resources," those things that people are not responsible for. The example given (by both Rawls and Dworkin) to clarify the point is one involving expensive tastes. She who loves expensive French wine but detests beer, and identifies with those tastes, should not receive a money transfer from him who is satisfied with cheap beer, on the grounds that such a transfer would be necessary to equalize their welfares. She should receive the transfer if, in the hypothetical insurance scheme, she would have contracted to guarantee herself an income level sufficient to enable her to consume French wine.

Richard Arneson (1989) and G. A. Cohen (1989, 1990) both argue that Dworkin's and Rawls's arguments against equality of welfare do not hold against equality of opportunity for welfare, where welfare is the level of preference satisfaction. Arneson defines equality of opportunity for welfare as follows. A person with given resources can choose a number of life plans; each plan will yield an expected level of welfare. Call the set of such possible life plans a life-plan tree. Two persons are said to face equal opportunities for welfare if they face life-plan trees which are equivalent in the sense that the expected levels of welfare achieved by the branches in one person's tree equal the expected levels of welfare of the branches in the other's. A distribution of resources equalizes opportunities for welfare across persons if it renders the life-plan trees of all equivalent. (Actually, Arneson's definition of equivalence is too demanding, and will, in most cases, rule out the possibility of attaining equality of opportunity for welfare. But I suggest that no great harm is done to his proposal by weakening 'equivalence' to mean that the maximum expected welfare achievable on one tree is equal to the maximum expected welfare achievable on the other.) In general people will not all choose the life plan which maximizes their expected welfare, because, for instance, of lack of planning or lack of will power; those who are in one of these ways imprudent receive no further compensation. They are responsible for the shortfall. The problem of expensive tastes is handled: if a person is responsible for her taste for champagne, she could have trained herself to like beer; the "beer life plan" would have given her more welfare for the same money endowment. It follows that equality of opportunity need not compensate the champagne lover (at least, one with voluntarily cultivated

---

[8] Dworkin also opposes welfare egalitarianism on the grounds that people have such incommensurably different concepts of welfare that it is meaningless to talk about equality of it. But the reason that the previous sentence in the text gives for his opposition to welfare egalitarianism would hold even with commensurable welfare across persons.

expensive tastes) by transfering money to her from him who has chosen the beer life plan.[9]

Cohen makes an essentially similar proposal, to equalize "access to advantage"; his notion of access is somewhat different from Arneson's "opportunity" and he views "advantage" as a broader concept than welfare. The key point is that both accept Dworkin's main focus, that egalitarians must distinguish between those aspects of a person's condition for which he is responsible, and those for which he is not, and egalitarianism requires compensating people only in regard to welfare or advantage deficits for which they cannot be held responsible. They differ from Dworkin, however, in where to make the cut between these two sets of aspects: Dworkin says people are responsible for their preferences but not for their resources, while Arneson and Cohen say that people are responsible for outcomes, but not for the set of opportunities they face.

I hope that the essays that follow will be read with the rich intellectual tradition that I have hastily summarized in mind.

---

[9] It must be noted that, for Arneson, a person's choices do not necessarily maximize the satisfaction of his preferences. For if they did, then the choice of a life plan from one's tree would by definition maximize one's (expected) preference satisfaction (i.e., one's welfare), and hence equality of opportunity for welfare would deflate into equality of welfare.

Exploitation

Introduction to Part I

The essays in this part develop the claim that the Marxian concept of exploitation, defined as the extraction of surplus labor at the point of production, should be replaced by a definition which gives priority to property relations. The property-relations definition makes clear what the surplus-labor definition fails to, that the ethical condemnation of capitalism, from the Marxian viewpoint, is based on the unequal access to society's alienable means of production. This, at least, is the position that I take, although it is challenged by two types of criticism: those, like Allen Wood's (1981), that claim Marxism makes no ethical condemnation of capitalism (at least, not on grounds of exploitation), and those, like Jeffrey Reiman's, that claim that the ethical bad that exploitation diagnoses concerns social relations at the point of production, while my concept is entirely "distributional." I do not respond to the Wood criticism in these papers (though Geras, 1986, 1992, does, and lists many others who have). Essay 4 is included here because it responds specifically to criticisms of the Reiman variety.

The reader will note that my proposal for a property-relations definition of exploitation changes in these papers. Specifically, in Essay 1, the third clause of the definition is "the coalition S' is in a relation of dominance to S"; in Essay 2, the third clause of the definition states that "the [exploiting] coalition S' would be worse off if the [exploited] coalition S withdrew with its own endowments"; and in Essay 5, the third clause is that "the coalition S' gains by virtue of the labor of S." This variation was an attempt, never entirely satisfactory, to deal with pathological counterexamples. Probably the last formulation, in conjunction with the rest of the definition, best captures the Marxian intuitions (although, with complicated examples, people do not always agree on what those intuitions are). The fact that it is not possible to come up with a simple, abstract characterization of "exploitation" that coincides in all cases with intuition, or that commands universal agreement when those intuitions differ, does not suggest, to me, that the basic property-relations (or, more generally, game-theoretic) approach to exploitation is wrong-headed, but rather that the relationship between inequality and injustice is extremely

13

complex – more complex, in particular, than Marxism admits. My claim remains that, despite Marx's own ambivalence toward the use of his theory as a moral condemnation of capitalism, it does contain such a condemnation, that, *ceteris paribus,* the final allocation of resources is unjust because it flows from a prior unjustly unequal distribution of ownership rights in the alienable means of production. Under the *ceteris paribus* clause, many attributes of people – their preferences, attitudes toward risk, and capacities to take responsibility for their choices – are either held constant or left unfocused, which, in later twentieth-century theories of egalitarianism, become well focused and differentiated across people.

I do not find much in the following essays that I would now retract, with these exceptions. I would not now say that "justice entails incomes are deserved" (Essay 2, Section IV), or take the view that "democratic control of the economic surplus . . . is the real necessity for fundamental social transformation" (Essay 4). As I explain in Essay 15, I now think the latter view made a fetish of democratic control. The reason that the investment process should not be left entirely to the market is not because, for some deep ethical reason, people should collectively (democratically) decide upon the use of the economic surplus, but because the market fails to do a perfect job of it, due to specific market failures (externalities and incomplete markets).

Exploitation, alternatives and socialism

How can one understand the formation of inequality, strata and classes, and perhaps exploitation, in socialist society? Among Marxists there is no widely accepted materialist theory of the development of classes and inequality under socialism. Perhaps more noticeably, there is no widely accepted theory of the political behaviour of socialist states. Indeed, the response of many or most Marxists to wars between socialist states, for example, is that at least one of the countries involved is not socialist. This argument is tautological and not scientific: since two socialist countries could never fight each other, therefore the major premise (that they are both socialist) must be false.

The example of wars between socialist countries is given to point out the nature of a crisis in Marxian theory: that theory, formulated in the late nineteenth century to explain the development of nineteenth century capitalism, does not seem useful when applied to late twentieth century socialism (and capitalism, perhaps). Marxists cannot, for instance, agree on the nature of Soviet society. Is it socialist, capitalist, state capitalist, or transitional? What definitions might one give to decide? Taking a cue from the Marxian approach to capitalism, one might seek to define a notion of exploitation relevant to socialist society. From such a beginning could follow a theory of class, and finally a political theory of socialist society as corollary to the theory of class. This paper is an attempt to approach this set of problems in the way indicated, by proposing a general theory of exploitation, of which socialist exploitation will be a special case. The task of providing a theory of exploitation relevant to socialist economies has much in common with the problem Marx faced in providing a theory of exploitation for capitalist economies. The economic problem for Marx was to explain how the gross inequities of capitalism could be reproduced in an economy characterised by voluntary exchange. In feudal and slave economies, there was no mystery to the locus of surplus

This work has been carried out with support from the John Simon Guggenheim Memorial Foundation. Many people have given me valuable comments on this paper, in particular Zvi Adar, G. A. Cohen, Meghnad Desai, Jon Elster, Victor Goldberg, Serge-Christophe Kolm, Andreu Mas-Colell and Amartya Sen.

appropriation, since the institution of labour exchange was coercive: one could clearly speak of serf and slave labour as being forcibly expropriated due to those social relations. Under capitalism, where the institution for labour exchange is non-coercive, how could one speak of exploitation, or expropriation of any commodity, including labour power? Marx's effort was to resolve this paradox by providing a theory of value which claimed that *despite* the non-coerciveness of the institution of labour exchange, that exchange was exploitative. Thus, he claimed that exploitation was a phenomenon which was robust when one relaxes the requirement that institutions for labour exchange be coercive. It is at this point that neoclassical and Marxian theory part company, for as will be shown, neoclassical economics claims that competitive allocations are not exploitative precisely because market institutions are competitive and non-coercive.

In facing socialist society, we must relax the institutional dimension labelled 'private ownership of the means of production', just as Marx had to relax the institutional dimension labelled 'coerciveness of labour exchange'. A nineteenth century Marxist might have thought that when the means of production are no longer differentially (and privately) owned, then exploitation would be a meaningless concept. I wish to claim such is not the case: that, indeed, a generalisation of the Marxian theory of exploitation exists in which the phenomenon remains viable even when the means of production are socialised.

This paper proposes a general taxonomy of exploitation, which will have as special cases feudal exploitation, capitalist exploitation, and socialist exploitation. This taxonomy constitutes a general definition of exploitation. Although one intention is to apply the taxonomy to understand socialist development, as has been briefly described, there are several other applications. It provides a common language with which social scientists can contrast different conceptions of exploitation. Neoclassical economists often challenge Marxists to defend their notion of exploitation: granted, surplus value (if one wants to call it that) exists, but why should its existence entail exploitation? It is shown below how both the neoclassical conception of exploitation and the Marxian conception are special cases of the general taxonomy. The inherent normative disagreement between neoclassicals and Marxists on this issue can be stated precisely.

A third application of the general theory of exploitation is a characterisation of Marxian exploitation which, I believe, is in many ways superior to the classical approach via the labour theory of value. The key to the present approach is property relations, not labour value, and although the two are related, the property relations approach is more general and resolves many classical problems which have inflicted the labour theory of value approach to exploitation.

The outline of the paper is as follows. In section I, a game-theoretic formulation of the concept of exploitation is proposed. Sections II and III define the games which characterise feudal and capitalistic exploitation; it is argued that the form of inequality which neoclassicals consider exploitative is akin to feudal exploitation, while Marxian exploitation is equivalent to capitalist exploitation. Section IV defines another game which characterises socialist exploitation. Section V investigates the issue of socially necessary exploitation, and states some claims of the theory of historical materialism in the language of the theory of exploitation, although it does not argue for those claims. Section VI indicates briefly the application of the theory to inequality in existing socialist societies (which is a more subtle project than simply defining socialist exploitation), and section VII summarises.

I.   Exploitation and alternatives

In virtually every society or economic mechanism, there is inequality. Yet not all inequality is viewed by a society as exploitative; nor will all people agree whether a given form of inequality is exploitative. Certainly, however, the notion of exploitation involves inequality in some way. What forms of inequality does a particular society (or person) view as exploitative? The inequality of master and slave was viewed as just and non-exploitative by many in ancient society, as was the inequality of lord and serf in feudal society, although today most of us consider both of these relationships exploitative. Similarly, Marxists view the inequality in the capitalist–worker relationship as exploitative, although this inequality is conceived of as non-exploitative by many people in capitalist society today. I wish to propose a theoretical device for clarifying the criteria according to which a type of economic inequality is evaluated as exploitative or not so.

What is meant when one says a person or group is exploited in a certain situation? I propose a concept of exploitation which entails these conditions. A coalition S, in a larger society N, is exploited if and only if:

(1)   There is an alternative, which we may conceive of as hypothetically feasible, in which S would be better off than in its present situation;

(2)   Under this alternative, the complement of S, the coalition $N - S = S'$, would be worse off than at present.

The formal analysis in this paper will take exploitation to be characterised by (1) and (2), although a third condition is also necessary to rule out certain bizarre examples, namely:

(3) S' is in a 'relationship of dominance' to S.

Precisely how to specify the alternative is left open for the moment. The general claim is that this device can be applied whenever people use the word 'exploit' referring to the human condition. If two people disagree on whether a group is exploited in some situation, then the device leads us to ask: Are they specifying the alternative for the group differently? Different *specifications of the alternative* will be proposed which will define different concepts of exploitation.

What is accomplished by the conditions (1)–(3) above? Condition (1) has an obvious meaning. Conditon (2) is necessary for exploitation since it must be the case that the exploited coalition S is exploited by other people, not by nature or technology, for instance. (Thus, exploitation as here used is to be distinguished from the exploitation of natural resources.) Condition (3) is sociological, and is not formally modelled, nor will dominance be defined. It will be indicated in a footnote below why (3) is not redundant with (1) and (2).

Formally, we can model (1) and (2) by specifying a game played by coalitions of agents in the economy. To define the game, it is specified what any coalition can achieve on its own, if it 'withdraws' from the economy. The alternative to participating in the economy is for a coalition to withdraw, taking its payoff or dowry, under the definition of the game. If a coalition S can do better for its members under the alternative of withdrawing, and if the complementary coalition to it, S', does worse after S's withdrawal, then S is *exploited* under that particular specification of the rules of the game.[1]

To make this more concrete, consider as an example the usual notion of the core of a private ownership exchange economy. The core is the set of allocations which no coalition can improve upon by withdrawing under the following rule: that it can take with it the private endowments of its members. Under these particular withdrawal rules, there is a certain utility frontier available to any coalition, and we could say a coalition is exploited if it is receiving utilities which can be dominated by a vector of utilities achievable by the coalition acting cooperatively on its own, given those withdrawal rules. In addition, for exploitation to occur, it must be the case that the complementary coalition fares worse after the original coalition withdraws with its endowments. More generally, if we adopt a different rule of withdrawal, which is to say a different way of specifying the payoffs achievable by the various coalitions on their own, a different game with a different core will result. Our definition implies this: exploitation occurs, at a given allocation, if that allocation is not in the

---

[1] A formal definition of exploitation is given below.

core of the game defined by the particular withdrawal specification under consideration. That is, a coalition is exploited if and only if it can 'block' an allocation, under the rules of the game. This will be proved presently.

This device captures the idea that exploitation involves the possibility of a better alternative. My proposal for what constitutes feudal exploitation, capitalist exploitation, and socialist exploitation amounts to naming three different specifications of withdrawal rules, three different games. One can then compare different concepts of exploitation by comparing the different rule specifications which define their respective games. A particular concept of exploitation is exhibited in explicit or canonical form as it were, as the rules of a game.

A formal definition of the concept follows. Let an economy be sustaining an allocation $\{z^1, \ldots, z^N\}$. That is, z^ν is the payoff that the νth agent is receiving. (z^ν can be an amount of money, or a bundle of goods and leisure, or a utility level.) Suppose we specify a game for this economy by stipulating a *characteristic function* v which assigns to every coalition S of agents in the economy a payoff $v(S)$. The value $v(S)$ should, of course, be in the same space as the values z^ν. $v(S)$ is to be thought of as the payoff available to the coalition S should it choose to exercise its right to withdraw from the parent economy; it is the dowry assigned to it by society as a whole. We do not assume that institutional arrangements exist in the parent economy for actually giving S an amount $v(S)$ should it choose to withdraw; for instance, the function v may define what some observer considers the just entitlement to coalitions should be, were they to opt out of society. Given this structure, we say a coalition S is *exploited at an allocation* $\{z^1, \ldots, z^N\}$ *with respect to alternative* v if [2]

$$\sum_{\nu \in S} z^\nu < v(S), \tag{1}$$

$$\sum_{\nu \in S'} z^\nu > v(S'). \tag{2}$$

We assume at this point that the coalition can distribute the dowry to its members so that each member ν receives a share v^ν such that $z^\nu < v^\nu$, which is certainly algebraically possible if (1) holds. (Thus, there are no considerations of incentives and strategy within the coalition, an important complication avoided here. Within the coalition, there is cooperative behaviour.)

---

[2] From now on, reference to the dominance requirement is omitted. For the body of the paper, (3) is assumed to hold whenever (1) and (2) do. In a footnote below, a perverse example is given in which this would not be the case. For most practical purposes, however, (1) and (2) together are a satisfactory definition of exploitation. As well, it is assumed that we have transferable utility, so that payoffs can be treated additively within coalitions.

Notice exploitation is defined with respect to a *specific conception* of an alternative. The actual allocation is $\{z^1, ..., z^N\}$, the alternative is defined by the function $v(S)$. There are, of course, both interesting and silly ways of specifying v: the task will be to specify particular functions v which capture intelligible and historically cogent types of exploitation. For instance, one might wish to require of a specification v that it permit the possibility of no exploitation. That is, given v, is there an allocation of the economy at which no agent or coalition is exploited? If not, then v would seem to suggest the impossible, if we take as v's suggested ethical imperative the elimination of its associated form of exploitation. A sufficient condition that v permit a non-exploitative allocation is that the game v have a non-empty core (there should be an allocation $\{z^1, ..., z^N\}$ which no coalition S can block, according to (1)). The different games in characteristic function form v which are proposed in this paper all have non-empty cores.

We define the *exploiting* coalitions with respect to an alternative v as the complementary coalitions to the exploited coalitions. S is an exploiting coalition if and only if the inequalities (1) and (2) hold, but with the inequality signs reversed in each.

We now observe, under reasonable assumptions, the non-exploitative allocations are precisely the core of the game v:

Theorem 1: *Let v be a superadditive game, and let the allocation $\{z^1, ..., z^N\}$ be Pareto optimal: $v(N) \leq \sum_N z^\nu$. Then a coalition S is exploited if and only if $v(S) > \sum_S z^\nu$. Likewise a coalition T is exploiting if and only if $v(T') > \sum_{T'} z^\nu$. Hence the core of v is precisely the set of non-exploitative allocations.*

Proof: The necessity of the condition holds by definition. To prove sufficiency, suppose S is not exploited but:

$$v(S) > \sum_S z^\nu. \tag{4}$$

Then S's failure to be exploited can only be due to:

$$v(S') \geq \sum_{S'} z^\nu. \tag{5}$$

Adding (4) and (5) gives

$$v(S) + v(S') > \sum_N z^\nu \geq v(N). \tag{6}$$

But the superadditivity of v implies $v(S) + v(S') \leq v(N)$, for any coalition S. Hence S must be exploited if (4) holds.

The second statement follows since the complements of exploiting sets are exploited sets.

We remark further on why condition (2) is required for the definition of exploitation. As mentioned, it is to guarantee that when a coalition is exploited, it is exploited *by someone*. If we required only (1) for S to be exploited, then it would be possible for both S and its complement to be exploited. Symmetrically, if we required only $\sum z^{\nu} > v(S)$ for S to be exploiting, then both S and S' could be exploiting. Consider, for instance, an economy with increasing returns to scale, and let $v(S)$ be the income a coalition S would attain by withdrawing with its own assets. Because of the returns to scale, it is possible that both S and S' satisfy $\sum_S z^{\nu} > v(S)$: but we would not wish to consider them to be exploiting coalitions at the allocation $\{z^1, ..., z^N\}$. Rather, they are each benefitting from (or exploiting) the scale economies present. (Similarly, an economy with decreasing returns would identify many coalitions and their complements as exploited, if only inequality (1) were insisted upon.) Defining exploitation as consisting of (1) and (2) guarantees that every exploited coalition has as its complement an exploiting coalition, and conversely. Thus, exploitation must involve some coalition's benefitting at another coalition's expense – rather than benefits or expenses accruing from a purely natural or technological phenomenon, such as scale economies.[3]

Thus, the device for defining exploitation conceives of agents as exploited at a particular allocation, with respect to a particular alternative. The alternative is specified by a characteristic function which defines the entitlements of agents and coalitions of agents. The formulation ignores, for the time being, these sorts of problems: Is realisation of payoffs $v(S)$ in some way feasible? What are the costs of coalition formation? How will the coalition S arrange to distribute $v(S)$ among its members?[4]

II. Feudal exploitation

I will not be historically precise concerning the underlying model of feudal economy. Think of agents with various endowments, who are engaged in production and consumption under feudal relations. A coalition

---

[3] My first pass at a definition of exploitation involved requiring only inequality (1). I am indebted to Jon Elster and Serge-Christophe Kolm for criticising the lack of interaction between agents in that formulation. In the current formulation, interaction is necessary for exploitation to the extent that exploiting and exploited coalitions always appear as complements. Interaction is also assured by the dominance requirement (3).

[4] I now indicate why the dominance condition (3) is needed to eliminate certain perverse cases. Consider an invalid, supported with costly medical services by the rest of society. Suppose we specify the game as withdrawal with one's own assets. Then the invalid will be worse off and the rest of society better off (if, at least, we do not count the pain society may feel for the death of the invalid after his withdrawal). This might lead one to conclude, according to (1) and (2), that the invalid is exploiting the rest of society according to this specification of the alternative. The dominance condition (3) eliminates this perverse conclusion since the relation of dominance is the other way around. Despite this case, I think conditions (1) and (2) suffice to characterise economic exploitation for most practical purposes.

is *feudally exploited* if it can improve its lot by withdrawing under the following rule: the coalition can take with it its own endowments. Thus, feudally non-exploitative allocations are, in fact, precisely the usual core of the exchange game, as conventionally defined, for a private ownership economy. (See, for one of many references, Varian, 1978.) This withdrawal specification, it is claimed, is the correct one for capturing feudal exploitation as it gives the result that serfs are exploited and lords are exploiters, which is the result we wish to capture. Moreover, non-serf proletarians will not be an exploited coalition, under these rules, and so the definition captures *only* feudal exploitation.

To verify this claim, we will make a cavalier assumption, that the serf's family plot was part of his own endowment. Clearly demarcated property rights in these plots did not in general exist under feudalism, but the history will be simplified, for the sake of making a point, to say that the essence of feudalism was bondage which required the serf to perform labour on the lord's demesne and corvée labour, *in spite* of his access to the means of subsistence for his family which included the family plot. Thus, a crucial distinction between proletarians and serfs is that the former must exchange their labour to acquire access to their means of sustenance, while the latter must exchange their labour despite their access to the means of sustenance. This distinction accounts for the coerciveness of labour extraction relations under feudalism, as contrasted with the voluntary labour market under capitalism.[5]

Thus, were a group of serfs to be allowed to withdraw from feudal society with their endowments, in which we include the family plots, they would have been better off, having access to the same means of production, but providing no labour for the demesne and corvée. Withdrawal, under these rules, amounts to withdrawal from feudal bondage, and that only. There is, however, a counterargument, which could have been put forth by a feudal ideologue: serfs would not be better off, he might say, by withdrawing with their own endowments, because they receive various benefits from the lord which they cannot produce on their own, the most obvious being military protection. The argument concerning military protection is an important one, and it introduces the difficulties in analysing exploitation as here defined when non-convexities are present. These are treated at length elsewhere (Roemer, 1982); the essential point is that when non-convexities are present, it is not relevant to ask whether individuals (or small coalitions) are exploited. (Indeed, if one serf withdraws under rules of the feudal game, he may be worse off, and so will the complementary coalition. Thus, he is not feudally exploited.)

---

[5]   For discussion see Brenner (1977) and Marx, *Capital,* Volume III (1966, pp. 790–1), in the section on labour rent.

If sufficiently large coalitions of serfs had withdrawn with their plots, they could have provided for their own defence, and hence have been better off; clearly the complementary coalition would be worse off, not benefitting from the serfs' surplus labour. The serfs as a class were feudally exploited and the lords were feudal exploiters.[6]

Secondly, the feudal ideologue might assert the lord possessed certain skills or abilities to organise manor life, without which the serfs would have been worse off. This argument is put forth by North and Thomas (1973), who claim that the serf's demesne and corvée labour was the *quid pro quo,* and a fair one (or implicitly agreed upon), for access to the benefits of feudal society. The claim is rebutted by Brenner (1976), and will not be further discussed here. Suffice to say, the disagreement between North and Thomas and Marxists concerns the proper specification of the characteristic function: that is, what income would the serfs have enjoyed had they seceded from feudal society, even supposing the immediate costs of withdrawal need not be counted? This disagreement will be taken up briefly below, when the concept of *socially necessary exploitation* is discussed.

To say serfs would be better off were they to withdraw from bondage and preserve their access to technology and land is to invoke a static notion of welfare comparison, which is purposeful at this point. What should be conveyed is that the ex-serfs could enjoy a bundle of leisure and goods which strictly dominated the bundle they received under feudal bondage. If the problem is treated dynamically, one is forced to ask other questions. Suppose, after withdrawal from serfdom, the peasant eventually becomes a proletarian, after being impoverished by his ineffectiveness in competitive agricultural capitalism which develops after feudalism's demise. As a proletarian, is he now better off than he was on the manor?

The general definition of exploitation purposely ignores these dynamic issues in constructing the counterfactual against which to judge the current allocation. The alternative we pose to the feudal allocation of society's income is an allocation which agents could hypothetically realise for themselves, through cooperative agreement, in an economy where private property is respected, but no ties of bondage or coercive dues arising therefrom exist. Thus the inequality viewed as feudally exploitative is that inequality which is specifically feudal in origin – as opposed, for instance, to inequality which is capitalist in origin, discussed next.

[6] For the precise resolution of the treatment of exploitation in the presence of increasing returns the reader is referred to Roemer (1982), Chapter 7. In brief, the approach is this. An agent is considered *vulnerable* if he is a member of a minimal exploited coalition, and *culpable* if he is a member of a minimal exploiting coalition. With increasing returns, the minimal exploited coalitions will have many members. Vulnerability and culpability become the relevant characteristics of agents with non-constant returns.

III.   Capitalist exploitation

To test whether a coalition of agents is capitalistically exploited, a different set of withdrawal rules is specified to define the game. When a coalition 'withdraws', it takes with it the coalition's *per capita* share of society's alienable, non-human property, and its *own* inalienable assets. That is, a coalition can block a particular allocation if that allocation can be improved upon by the coalition, when the initial endowment of alienable assets is an equal-division, egalitarian endowment of property. While the test for feudal exploitation amounts to equalising every agent's access to personal freedom in constructing the alternative against which a current allocation is judged, the test for capitalist exploitation amounts to equalising every agent's access to society's alienable property (non-human means of production) in constructing the hypothetical alternative. Under feudalism, it is asked how well agents do if relations of feudal bondage are abolished; under capitalism, we ask how they fare if property relations in alienable property are changed so that each agent possesses the same amount. Given this phrasing of the alternative, it is not surprising that capitalist exploitation, as here defined, is equivalent to the usual Marxian definition of exploitation in terms of socially necessary labour time and surplus value.[7]

This is, indeed, a theorem, which space does not permit me to formulate precisely, as such formulation requires that Marxian exploitation be exhibited in explicit economic models. Suffice to say that in a variety of such models, Marxian exploitation is equivalent to capitalist exploitation as here defined. That is: the expropriation or transfer of surplus value from workers to capitalists occurs, in the Marxian framework, precisely because workers do not have access to alienable means of production. In the counterfactual posited by the game posed above, workers are imagined to withdraw with their proportionate share of society's alienable assets, thus eliminating the necessity to trade their 'surplus' labour for access to that capital. The coalitions which are Marxian-exploited are precisely the ones which are capitalistically exploited, i.e., which can block an allocation under the rules of the game assigning coalitions proportionate shares of society's aggregate alienable assets. Moreover, the game-theoretic definition of capitalist exploitation applies more generally than Marxian exploitation: the test for capitalist exploitation can be applied even if labour

---

[7] In the models for which capitalist exploitation is proved to be equivalent to Marxian exploitation, there are no externalities or public goods. Admitting these features, which complicate property relations, will surely complicate the game-theoretic test for exploitation, and consequently the theorem referred to. Nevertheless, some types of externality (such as increasing returns to scale) can be successfully handled as the previous footnote indicates.

is heterogeneous and other non-produced factors exist, a production environment in which the classical definition of Marxian exploitation, depending as it does on the labour theory of value, encounters severe if not intractable problems.[8]

In most summary form, the specification of the games which define feudal and capitalist exploitation capture what is meant when we say feudal exploitation is that inequality which comes about because of specifically feudal relations, and capitalist exploitation is that inequality which is the consequence of relations of private property in the alienable means of production (capitalist relations of property).

Just as the feudal ideologue argued that, in fact, serfs would not have been better off had they withdrawn with their own endowments, so a bourgeois ideologue might argue that those who are Marxian-exploited (that is, whose surplus value is appropriated by others) would not, in fact, be better off were they to withdraw with their per capita share of society's alienable assets. The surplus value which workers contribute to the capitalist is, perhaps, a return to a scarce *skill* possessed by him, necessary for organising production. The bourgeois ideologue's argument is in theory a correct one: if, in fact, equalisation of alienable assets would not be sufficient to make Marxian-exploited workers better off on their own, then they are not capitalistically exploited. This non-trivial bone of contention between Marxist and bourgeois thinkers will be called the subtle disagreement on the existence of capitalist exploitation under capitalism.

There is, however, a less subtle disagreement also. A common neoclassical position is that exploitation cannot be said to exist at a competitive equilibrium, because everyone has gained from trade as much as possible. How can one say μ is exploiting ν if ν has voluntarily entered into trade with μ? Now the models of Marxian-exploitation which have been referred to, show that *gains from trade and Marxian exploitation are not mutually exclusive.* (The proletarian gains from trading his labour power, since otherwise he cannot survive, but his surplus labour time is nevertheless transferred.) What is at issue here is precisely the difference between feudal and capitalist exploitation. The statement that no coalition can gain further from trade amounts to saying the allocation is in the core of the feudal game: no group of agents, withdrawing with *its endowments,* can trade to a superior allocation for its members. Hence, the neoclassical position says 'There is no feudal exploitation under capitalism', a

---

[8] The definitions of Marxian and capitalist exploitation are equivalent in the standard models which have been used to study Marxian exploitation in a formal way. There are, however, situations in which the two definitions render different judgements concerning the exploitation status of some coalitions. In these cases, I think the property relations definition is superior to the surplus labour definition, as its verdict on exploitation conforms more to the intuitive judgements of Marxists. See Essay 2.

statement which is true by the well-known fact that competitive equilibria lie in the private ownership core of the economy, that is, the core of the game defined by private ownership withdrawal rules.

It is not always obvious whether objections to the Marxian notion of exploitation are of the subtle form (in which case there is a substantial disagreement about the contribution of agents' inalienable assets to production), or of the non-subtle form (in which case there are two different varieties of exploitation under discussion). In the non-subtle case, the antagonists are adopting different specifications of the hypothetical alternative which they respectively view as normatively cogent for testing 'exploitation'. Although, in the case of the non-subtle disagreement, the difference between the two positions may be unambiguous, that does not mean it is simply resolved: there are still substantial disagreements concerning what kind of property entitlements are acceptable or just. I would argue that the non-subtle disagreement is quite prevalent. In particular, if both parties to the discussion agree to model agents as differing only in their ownership rights of produced goods, then the disagreement must be of the non-subtle variety. When the neoclassical party says that the proletarian is not exploited by the capitalist because the latter requires a return to his capital (being, we insist, alienable assets, not skills) for whatever reason, what is in fact being said is that ownership rights of produced means of production must be respected, and therefore the test for capitalist exploitation is not appropriate.

To be more precise in discussions of this nature, it is convenient to differentiate between *entrepreneurs* and *coupon-clippers* among the class of capitalists. Entrepreneurs presumably earn a high return to their inalienable endowments, while coupon-clippers earn a return only to their alienable endowments. If we conceive of the capitalist class as predominantly composed of the former, then the statement 'exploitation does not exist under capitalism' can be consistently interpreted as referring to *capitalist* exploitation; if the latter, then that statement can only refer to feudal exploitation.

There is, however, one most important piece of circumstantial evidence against the hypothesis that the prevailing disagreement about exploitation under capitalism is of the subtle variety. Prevailing norms of neoclassical (liberal, pluralist) social science respect private property in the means of production. (In contrast, they do not respect relations of personal bondage of either the slave or feudal type.) Consequently, prevailing liberal philosophy cannot accept the test for capitalist exploitation which has been proposed, for that test nullifies property relations. Note that a proponent of the existence of capitalist exploitation would not judge *all* inequality under capitalism as being of the capitalistically exploiting type but only that part of it which could be eliminated by an egalitarian distribution of endowments of *alienable* resources.

I therefore conclude that a fair summary of prevailing liberal opinion, which argues against applying the term exploitation to the idealised equilibria of a private ownership market economy, is, in terms of this taxonomy: 'There is no feudal exploitation under capitalism.' This is a true statement, at least of a competitive equilibrium. Marxists would argue, however, that there is capitalist exploitation under capitalism, although – and this is critical – not all inequality would be eliminated by abolishing private ownership of the means of production.

The implicit alternative against which neoclassical economists evaluate an allocation is the 'free trade' alternative, and agents or coalitions are exploited if they could be doing better under that alternative. The culprits in a neoclassically exploitative allocation are barriers to the competitive operation of markets. We can, indeed, link up another traditional neoclassical notion of exploitation with our characterisation of it as feudal exploitation. Joseph Ostroy (1980) has shown that in large economies, the allocations in the private ownership core of an exchange economy (i.e., feudally non-exploitative allocations) are precisely those allocations at which every agent is receiving his marginal product, properly defined.

On the other hand, the implicit alternative against which a Marxist evaluates an allocation is not one of free trade, but of 'free' alienable property.

I close this section by noting that the specification of the communal game, which defines capitalist exploitation, has the advantage of capturing the Marxian theory of exploitation without reference to the labour theory of value. It is property relations which occupy centre stage in the definition, not the transfer of labour. This immediately clarifies the different ethical positions which lie behind neoclassical and Marxist conceptions of exploitation, as they are exhibited transparently in the rules of the game which define the two concepts.[9]

IV.   Socialist exploitation

I now pose the rules of the game which define *socialist exploitation*. Some endowments were not hypothetically equalised in formulating the rules

[9] The confrontation between the surplus labour (Marxian) definition of exploitation and the property relations definition of capitalist exploitation can be made sharper, in this sense. There are situations in which the Marxian definition diagnoses certain coalitions as exploited who are not capitalistically exploited according to the property rights definition. In these cases, it is the property relations definition which renders the intuitively correct judgement. The surplus labour approach fails essentially because it takes too micro an approach, concentrating on what is happening in one market (the labour market) rather than evaluating the macro alternatives under different regimes of property.

of the game to test for capitalist exploitation: endowments of inalienable assets, skills. Let us picture an idyllic socialist economy where private property is not held in alienable assets which are accessible to all, but inalienable assets are still held by individuals. Under market arrangements, those with scarce skills will be better off than the unskilled. This inequality is not, however, capitalist exploitation, as all have equal access to alienable property, and so no coalition can improve its position by withdrawing with its per capita share of society's alienable means of production. We may, however, wish to refer to this inequality as socialist exploitation, characterised as follows. Let a coalition withdraw, taking with it its per capita share of *all* endowments, alienable and inalienable. If it can improve the position of its members, and if the complementary coalition is worse off under such an arrangement, then it is socialistically exploited at the allocation in question.

There are, of course, formidable incentive problems with carrying out this procedure, as has been discussed by parties to the Rawlsian debate over talent pooling. (See, for example, Kronman, 1981.) How can talents be pooled without destroying them, and so on? Although the potential *realisation* of the alternative is problematical, as a hypothetical test it can be specified. We can distribute *property rights* in one person's skills equally among all. This means, in a market economy, that each receives an equal share of the value that can be generated by that person's skills. This procedure enables us to define the appropriate alternative against which to test for 'socialist exploitation'.

Thus, if all individual endowments are of either the alienable or inalienable type, then an allocation is free of socialist exploitation precisely when it is in the equal-division core (the core of the game in which each receives an equal property share in all of society's alienable and inalienable endowments). One should note how a certain classical conception of socialism and communism is reflected in this definition. The historical task of the socialist revolution is to bring about a regime where each labours according to his ability and is paid according to his work, while the communist revolution (from socialism) transforms the formula so that each is paid according to his need. Thus, socialist exploitation is to be expected under socialism: the elimination of differential rewards to ability is not socialism's historical task, only the elimination of differential reward to alienable property ownership. The communist revolution is the one which eliminates socialist exploitation. This is as it should be, following the historical parallels of the demise of feudal exploitation in the capitalist revolution, and of capitalist exploitation in the socialist revolution.

Hence the rules of the latest game seem to fit classical definitions. The troublesome question is: To what extent can we attribute inequality in real socialist economies to 'socialist exploitation'?

V.   Socially necessary exploitation and historical materialism

From the names given to the various forms of exploitation – feudal, capitalist, socialist – it appears that history, according to the historical materialist conception, necessarily eliminates the various forms of exploitation, in a certain order, until communism is reached, a society whose distribution, according to the *Critique of the Gotha Program,* is characterised by 'from each according to his ability, to each according to his need.' There is a temptation to claim that, in the language of historical materialism, the historical task of a given epoch is to eliminate its concomitant form of exploitation, as here named. Yet a more careful reading of historical materialism shows this is not its claim: rather, the historical task of an epoch is to remove fetters on the development of the productive forces, which is not necessarily the same as producing a situation in which the direct producers are 'better off'.

To approach this question somewhat more carefully, socially necessary exploitation is now defined. It was assumed in the initial definition of exploitation that when a coalition withdraws, the incentive structure which its members face in the alternative economy set up by the coalition does not differ from the incentive structure in the original economy. In general, this would be false. Consider proletarians under early capitalism. Had they withdrawn with their per capita share of the produced assets of society, they may very well not have worked long enough to make the income that they had as proletarians; instead they might have chosen to take more leisure and less income. Assuming capitalist property relations were necessary to bring about accumulation and technical innovation in the early period of capitalism, then the coalition which has withdrawn will soon fall behind the capitalist society because of the absence of incentives to innovate. Even the proletarians under capitalism will eventually enjoy an income-leisure bundle superior to the bundle of independent utopian socialists who have retired into the hills with their share of the capital, assuming enough of the benefits of increased productivity pass down to the proletarians, as has historically been the case. Thus, a more precise phrasing of the criterion is: *were* a coalition able to preserve the same incentive structure, and, by withdrawing with its per capita share of produced assets thereby improve the lot of its members, then it is capitalistically exploited in the current allocation. If, however, the incentive structure cannot be maintained, and in addition, as a consequence, the coalition will immediately be worse off, then the capitalist exploitation which it endures is *socially necessary in the static sense*. Suppose, however, the coalition is initially better off after exercising its withdrawal option, even allowing for incentive effects, but then 'soon' it becomes worse off, due for instance to the lack of incentives to develop the forces of production. In this case, I will say the exploitation was *socially necessary in the dynamic sense*.

There are, in the Marxist reading of history, many examples of the implementation of regimes entailing dynamically socially necessary exploitation, which brought about an inferior income-leisure bundle for the direct producers. Two will be mentioned. Marx approved of the British conquest of India, despite the misery it brought to the direct producers, because of its role in developing the productive forces. Thus, the contention is proletarians in India would have been better off, statically, in the alternative without imperialist interference, but dynamically British imperialist exploitation was socially necessary to bring about the development of the productive forces, eventually improving the income-leisure bundles of the producers (or their children) over what they would have been. (For a discussion of this point, see Brenkert, 1979.) A second example is taken from Brenner's (1976) discussion of the development of capitalism in England as contrasted with France. In England, agrarian capitalists succeeded in breaking the power of the yeoman peasantry, and the productive forces in agriculture were developed under the capitalists' aegis. In France, the independent peasantry remained strong, did not develop the productive forces, and chose a bundle of leisure and income which was doubtless superior to that of their English counterparts, in the short run.[10] The development of productive forces in agriculture was not synonymous with the improved welfare of the peasantry. Eventually, the British agricultural proletarians were better off (in our sense) than their French counterparts.

Why does Marxism maintain capitalist exploitation was dynamically socially necessary in early capitalism – otherwise phrased, that capitalism was initially a progressive system, an optimal economic structure for furthering the development of the productive forces at a certain stage in their development.[11] First, it is claimed to be socially necessary only in the

---

[10] Perhaps 'doubtless' is not the word, for neoclassical interpreters such as North and Thomas (1973) would say that the English agricultural proletarians voluntarily contracted with their capitalists to enter into relations of wage labour, so that the capitalists would force them to work, prevent them from shirking, thereby improving their welfare. See Brenner (1976) for arguments against the neoclassical implicit contract interpretation.

[11] For discussion of what is meant by an economic structure being optimal for the level of development of productive forces, see Cohen (1978), especially chapter 6, and Elster and Hylland (1983).

dynamic sense: that without capitalist property relations, innovation and the development of labour productivity would have stagnated, and workers would consequently eventually have been worse off. Secondly, and worthy of note, it is relations of private property which were socially necessary, not particular individual capitalists as such. It is not the contention that private property was necessary to coax certain specific individuals in possession of scarce skills to employ them (entrepreneurial ability, inventiveness); rather, it was the *system* of private property in the means of production which stimulated innovation. Anyone could have played the role of capitalist, but someone had to. This is not to deny that the skills of capitalists may be somewhat scarce – it is just that they are not *that* scarce. Within the population of proletarians there are plenty of potential capitalists, that is, persons capable of performing that role, but who do not, because of their lack of access to the means of production.

There is a difference between maintaining that capitalist exploitation exists, but is socially necessary, and the argument of the bourgeois ideologue that capitalist exploitation does not exist. For he is maintaining that capitalists' profits are a return to scarce skills they possess, and hence the income losses workers would suffer in the coalition, when they withdraw with their per capita share of alienable assets, are not due to incentive problems, but rather to their lack of accessibility to the skills of capitalists. The bourgeois ideologue claims the workers under capitalism are experiencing *socialist* exploitation, not capitalist exploitation. This is quite different from maintaining that capitalists possess no skills which do not also exist in the large pool of proletarians (even though they may be scarce!), but that the regime of private ownership relations in the means of production produces certain behaviour (of competition leading to innovation) which would be absent without those relations. In the second view, it does not matter who the capitalists are, but the workers will be better off if someone is a capitalist. Capitalism is socially necessary, but particular individual capitalists are dispensable.

The social necessity of socialist exploitation in early socialism may appear to differ from this, in that the skills which are specially remunerated are embodied in particular people. Not only may socialist exploitation be necessary, but particular socialist exploiters may be. Viewed dynamically, however, this may not be (and I believe is not) the case. If skills are a consequence of nurture only, the result of prior status exploitation, perhaps, then anyone can be the vessel for them, although someone must be.[12] It is, again, not the particular person who must be discovered, and will so be with the offer of a special wage, but rather that the special wage

---

[12] Those with high status have access to educational facilities for their children. (See section VI.)

creates a system where a certain fraction of people will train themselves. Once trained, the particular skilled person will be of special value to society, but the same may be true of particular capitalists, like Henry Ford II, who acquire their class status by virtue of birth, but eventually do learn to run capitalist empires.

According to historical materialism, feudal, capitalist and socialist exploitation all exist under feudalism. At some point feudal relations become a fetter on the development of the productive forces, and they are eliminated by the bourgeois revolution. Feudal exploitation is outlawed under capitalism. Although the proletarians might not immediately appear to be better off than the serfs, because of the non-comparability of their income-leisure bundles, one can assert that quite rapidly (in a generation, perhaps) they are better off due to the rapid development of the productive forces and the increase in the real wage.[13] Thus, feudal relations were eliminated when they became *socially unnecessary in the dynamic sense.* Under capitalism, only capitalist and socialist exploitation continue to exist. Capitalist exploitation in the beginning is socially necessary, as discussed; eventually, however, it becomes a fetter on the development of productive forces. Large coalitions of proletarians could be (dynamically) better off by withdrawing with their per capita share of the produced means of production, and organising themselves in a socialist way, because capitalism no longer performs a progressive innovating function, compared to what society is capable of accomplishing under socialist organisation. Capitalist exploitation becomes socially unnecessary, and is eliminated by socialist revolution. Under socialism, capitalist exploitation is outlawed, but socialist exploitation exists and, most would argue, is socially necessary, at least in the early period.

Historical materialism, in summary, claims that *history progresses by the successive elimination of forms of exploitation which are socially unnecessary in the dynamic sense.*[14] It is important to reiterate this does not

---

13 Lindert and Williamson (1983) claim, on the basis of new statistical evidence, that workers in the cities of mid-nineteenth century England were better off, in terms of real wages, life expectancy and other quality-of-life indicators, than rural unskilled labourers of 1780. Their work challenges the conventional Marxist view that the 'satanic mills' were an unmitigated disaster for the working class over the period of the industrial revolution. It is nevertheless true that at any point in time until the 1880s or so life expectancy was lower for urban workers than rural workers. They also assert that at any point in time urban workers felt subjectively better off than they had as country dwellers, that is, the higher urban wage compensated for the disamenities of city life.

14 The precise claim is that history progresses by eliminating property relations which fetter the productive forces: but it is further claimed that the fettering of the productive forces makes the direct producers worse off than they would be with the further development of the productive forces, since enough of the benefits of increased productivity will return to them in the form of better living standards. These two claims together imply the statement to which this note is attached.

mean the exploited agents will immediately be better off (in terms of the income-leisure bundle) after the revolution. Nor has the historical mechanism been discussed here which might lead to this pattern. The above is a translation of the technological determinist aspect of historical materialist theory into the language of the theory of exploitation.

In summary, the purpose of this section has been to exhibit how some claims of historical materialism can be stated in the language of the taxonomy of exploitation. I must underscore it has not been my intention to argue for the theory of historical materialism, which would be a much more subtle undertaking.

VI.   Exploitation in existing socialism

I take up, briefly, the question posed at the end of section IV. The first relevant, important phenomenon is the existence of inequality in socialist countries which comes about by virtue of *status* such as Communist Party membership. To the extent that status is itself a 'competitive' remuneration to skill, it can be viewed as the conduit (or signal) which permits differential remuneration to skill. In principle, party members possess some scarce skills (the ability to lead the revolution, and so on), but there will be little debate here if I claim that not all (or even most) of the remuneration to status can be explained by remuneration to skill. How then, should we treat inequalities due to that part of status which is not a signal for skill? Formally, this is most appropriately viewed as feudal exploitation, which is precisely exploitation by virtue of status. If we ask whether a coalition under socialism could improve the position of its members if the rights of status were abolished, the test is the same as for feudal exploitation. (Some of the product of low-status individuals goes to high-status individuals; if the low-status ones could exempt themselves from their dues of status, they would be better off. If in fact the high-status people are not especially skilled, the low-status people will be better off simply by withdrawing with their own endowments.)

Why does status exploitation exist under socialism? A conjecture is because of the absence of markets in current socialist mechanisms. A long literature testifies to the belief that if the market is not used, bureaucratic power must replace it. (A pithy statement by Marx, albeit from another context: 'Rob the thing [money] of this social power, and you must give it to persons to exercise over other persons' (Marx, 1973, pp. 157–8).) Hence the question whether status exploitation must necessarily be concomitant with socialism is, under this conjecture, equivalent to the more familiar question of whether the practice of socialism conflicts with the use of a market mechanism.

Suppose status exploitation exists in socialist countries; it may nevertheless be socially necessary in the sense of section V, as follows. To eliminate status exploitation may entail the elimination of the bureaucracy, replacing it by the market. Under the market, capitalist exploitation may regenerate, thus making the coalitions who are status-exploited even worse off. Hence, the social necessity of status exploitation. Those who attack étatism (such as Branco Horvat) argue against the social necessity of status exploitation. The debate between self-management and central planning can be seen, in part, as concerning whether it is better to take the socially necessary dose of inequality in the form of status exploitation, or as capitalist exploitation which will accompany a system giving sufficient leeway to markets. (The inequalities between rich and poor firms in Yugoslavia are an example of capitalist exploitation, according to the game-theoretic criterion.)

A second important question, with respect to the applicability of the theoretical characterisation of socialist exploitation to current socialist inequality, is this: has socialism abolished capitalist exploitation? If a coalition of socialist workers were to withdraw, taking with them their *per capita* share of society's *alienable* assets, could they perhaps improve their position? The reason this question emerges forcefully is that alienable assets are not distributed in an egalitarian manner to individuals under socialism – as they would be under a syndicalist or anarchist mechanism – but are centralised in the hands of the state. This, indeed, is precisely the left-anarchist critique of socialism: in our terms, that capitalist exploitation will not be abolished so long as property is not in the hands of individual producers, because there is no guarantee that the state will follow the best interests of the direct producers. Proponents of the thesis that *state capitalism* is the proper way to describe the Soviet state are also saying that the state apparatus is controlled by a stratum which employs the means of production in its own interest. As with the previous question, it is beyond our scope to pursue this further.

The taxonomy of exploitation suggests a sense in which socialism is an inherently unstable arrangement. Under capitalism, agents are allowed to reap the benefits from all their assets. Under communism (hypothetically), agents are not allowed differential remuneration due either to alienable or inalienable assets which they possess. Socialism takes a compromise stance: it allows agents differential remuneration to skill, but it forbids the capitalisation of those rewards into alienable assets, for that would give rise to capitalist exploitation. The difficulty of maintaining this posture may explain, to some extent, the necessity for authority under socialism.

VII.   Concluding remarks

Some conclusions with respect to four questions will be indicated.

(1) With respect to the *debate between neoclassicals and Marxists* concerning exploitation, the taxonomy of exploitation proposed allows the antagonists to formulate the disagreements precisely. It is claimed that the neoclassical and Marxian conceptions of exploitation correspond to two different hypothetical alternatives, two different games. Neoclassicals pose feudal exploitation as the relevant concept, Marxians pose capitalist exploitation. (If, however, the antagonists disagree on the contribution of entrepreneurial skill to production, the disagreement is of another sort.)

(2) Concerning the *Marxian theory of exploitation,* the game-theoretic property relations approach allows a considerably more general definition than the labour-theory-of-value approach. I believe the property relations approach is superior for several reasons. First, it makes explicit the alternative of which Marxists are conceiving when they say surplus value is expropriated, is *unpaid* labour. Secondly, it is applicable with general production sets, while the labour-theory approach is not. Thirdly, it allows one to distinguish between different forms of 'expropriation of unpaid labour' – those resulting from feudalism, capitalism and socialism, as the labour-theory by itself does not.

(3) With regard to *historical materialism,* the taxonomy of exploitation allows a statement of its major claims in analytical terms. The link between two great Marxian theories is exhibited. An analytic statement of historical materialism should allow critical discussion of its claimed theorems to proceed.

With reference to *inequality in existing socialism,* the theory proposes a decomposition into three types of exploitation. Marxist theory has long recognised the social necessity of socialist exploitation in early socialism; capitalist exploitation in existing socialism can be more carefully discussed if the definitions here are applied; on the social necessity of status exploitation there has been the least theory, although the debate on the plan versus the market touches on that issue.

Perhaps the main influence this theory should have on our evaluation of existing socialist societies is to teach us not to expect too much of them, with respect to the elimination of inequality. In each epoch, revolutionaries have believed that the elimination of the major prevailing form of exploitation would bring about a free society. The French revolutionaries thought the ending of feudal exploitation would entail 'liberté, fraternité, égalité'; they underestimated the effects of capitalist exploitation. Socialist revolutionaries have believed that the elimination of capitalist exploitation would bring about the conditions for the free development of all, underestimating, perhaps, the significance of socialist and status exploitation. That these forms of exploitation exist in socialist countries should not necessarily be cause for condemning them. In particular, both socialist and status exploitation exist in capitalism also. While capitalism's advertisement has been that status exploitation does not exist as the market rewards only real contributions and ruthlessly casts aside all remnants of feudal privilege, this is clearly not the case. It seems quite possible that status exploitation in existing capitalism is more severe than in existing socialism.

Property relations vs. surplus value in Marxian exploitation

I.   Introduction

Marxian exploitation is defined as the expropriation of surplus labor, where the definition of surplus labor depends on the labor theory of value. Surplus labor is the excess of time labored by the worker over the amount of labor embodied in the bundle of goods the worker consumes, under the assumption that his entire wage is spent on that bundle. Thus, exploitation is said to exist because the amount of dead labor the worker can command through purchasing commodities with his income is less than the amount of labor he expends in production. If A is an exploited agent, then another agent B is said to exploit A if the surplus labor performed by A is embodied in goods which B appropriates. It is also generally assumed that this appropriation must occur as a consequence of A being hired by B. Expropriation is said to occur at the point of production.

Exploitation is a consequence of the private ownership of the means of production: the abolition of Marxian exploitation is supposed to be accomplished by eliminating this property relation in the means of production. Yet the definition of exploitation makes no explicit mention of this property relation. It is possible, however, to characterize Marxian exploitation using solely concepts of property relations, in particular, without reference to the concept of surplus labor and therefore to the labor theory of value. To be precise, it is possible to define a kind of exploitation which I will call *capitalist exploitation,* using only terms of property relations, and for the usual simple cases and models of economies the definitions of *Marxian* exploitation (in terms of the surplus labor concept) and capitalist exploitation (in terms of property relations) coincide. When we go beyond these simple models, however, examples can be constructed in which the two definitions do not coincide: that is, they may render different judgments concerning whether a particular agent or group of agents is exploited by other agents. This poses the question, Which definition better captures the notion of exploitation coinciding with the

I thank R. Brenner, G. A. Cohen, J. Elster, and A. K. Sen for stimulating discussions, and the John Simon Guggenheim Memorial Foundation for support.

Marxist intuition? In this article, I present the property relations definition of exploitation, and then argue that it is superior to the surplus labor theory definition – when the two definitions disagree, it is the property relations one which is correct. Furthermore, the property relations definition provides a clearer explanation of why Marxists consider the "transfer of surplus labor" to be exploitative.

There are a number of problems with the classical labor-theory-of-value definition of exploitation, which can motivate why a definition based directly on property relations might be desirable. These include the following. (1) Why should the transfer of surplus labor between worker and capitalist be considered exploitative? The neoclassical economist, and bourgeois thinker more generally, will object that the worker who owns no means of production himself is trading his labor power for access to the means of production owned by another. Both gain from the trade. Or, a different argument, the worker trades his labor power for access to the entrepreneurial skill of the capitalist, or the risk-loving nature of the capitalist which enables him to set up a business. In any case, the trade of labor power for access to capital or entrepreneurial skill is a quid pro quo, and should therefore not be viewed as exploitative; in the case of the risk-loving capitalist and risk-averse worker, the 'surplus' labor is an insurance premium the worker pays to protect himself against having to take those business risks himself. I will not reply to these arguments now. They are principled objections, because the definition of Marxian exploitation does not go beyond the definition of surplus labor; to answer the objections, one must reply at the level of property relations. For instance, one might say that the ownership of capital by the capitalist is unjust in the first place, and hence the worker should not have to give up anything to have access to it. From the formal point of view, however, invoking aspects of property relations is *ad hoc* if one adheres to the labor-theory-of-value definition of exploitation: if property relations must be invoked, they should either be built into the definition or implied by it. (2) The objection has been made that, so long as workers under socialism work more hours than are embodied in the goods they receive, they are exploited under socialism. Marxists reply, again, by saying that property relations are different under socialism, that workers have decided to work longer hours to produce a surplus, and so on. This reply again relies on a fact about underlying property relations which is not explicit in the surplus labor definition of exploitation. It demonstrates the necessity for defining exploitation more directly in terms of property relations. (3) The labor theory of value can be defined for only certain special models of an economy. If the production set is complicated in various ways, then it is not possible to give an unambiguous definition of what "labor-embodied" means. In the past decade, it has been shown that the Marxian definition of exploitation can be extended to apply to production sets in which fixed capital and joint production are allowed.[1] But I think there is no adequate definition of embodied labor time when we admit the existence of several nonproduced factors (such as land), other than labor. Moreover, if we admit that labor is heterogeneous, I believe the labor theory of value also evaporates. Defending these points is beyond the scope of this paper;[2] suffice to say, everyone will admit that at least extremely severe problems (if not insurmountable ones) are encountered when one seeks to generalize the labor theory of value, and hence the labor-theory-of-value definition of exploitation, to general production sets. This suggests the desirability of having a characterization of exploitation independent of the labor theory of value, and the property relations definition that will be proposed is just that.

With the property relations approach to exploitation, it cannot be said that expropriation takes place at the point of production. Exploitation can exist even when no agent sells labor power to any other agent; it can exist when agents trade only produced commodities. Conversely, situations exist in which it appears expropriation is taking place, from the classical point of view, but in fact it is not. The property relations approach implies that exploitation takes place because of the distribution of the means of production, not at the point of production. The relevant coercion, as concerns exploitation, is in maintaining property relations, not in the labor process.

The outline of the paper is as follows. In the next section I present the property relations definition of capitalist exploitation. In Section III, a number of examples are posed, in a simple model of an economy, which enable us to apply both the labor-theory-of-value definition of exploitation and the property relations definition; we see in which cases the two definitions render different judgments, concerning whether particular groups are exploited, and the anomalies are discussed. In the fourth section, some arguments against the Marxian theory of exploitation are addressed in the light of the property relations definition. The final section summarizes briefly.

II.   A property relations definition of exploitation

The property relations definition of exploitation can be applied to groups of agents (which are called coalitions, using the game-theoretic terminology),

---

[1] See Morishima (1973) and Roemer (1981), chap. 2.

[2] I pursue the problems with a labor-theory-of-value definition of exploitation when labor is heterogeneous in Roemer (1982), chap. 6.

or to individual agents (who are singleton coalitions). Imagine an economy in which agents each own some property, which can be used in production, and some labor power. Perhaps some agents own no alienable property but only labor power; perhaps there are many different types of labor power or skill; perhaps some property consists of other nonproduced goods. (The production environment is very general.) Under market arrangements, we imagine agents engaging in production and trading and ending up with certain incomes. To decide whether a coalition is exploited or exploiting (or neither), we compare how well the coalition is faring at the present distribution of income and labor with how well it would have fared under a certain alternative distribution of property. (One's original endowment of property and labor determines how well one fares with the market.) More generally, when one says that A is exploiting B, I think one is conceiving of an *alternative arrangement* of some sort under which A would be worse off and B better off than at present. The alternative arrangement embodies one's notion of what is ethically preferable and nonexploitative: and so, if A is better off and B worse off than in the ethically preferable alternative, that constitutes exploitation. This is not quite precise, but will be made so below. The alternative will be defined by posing an alternative distribution of the original endowments of property.

To make the discussion in the following pages simple, I will assume that production in this economy is characterized by constant returns to scale; there are no positive externalities to increasing scale. In particular, if a group of people one-tenth the size of the population withdraws with one-tenth of society's assets, and the group possesses the same skills as the population as a whole, then it can produce one-tenth the output of the whole population. (This assumption is not necessary for the theory here to work, but it is simplifying.) Consider a coalition S, and call its complement S'. Then, at the allocation or distribution of income in question, S will be said to be *capitalistically exploited* if the following three conditions hold:

Definition PR

(1) If S were to withdraw from the society, endowed with its per capita share of society's alienable property (that is, produced and nonproduced goods), and with its own labor and skills, then S would be better off (in terms of income and leisure) than it is at the present allocation;

(2) If S' were to withdraw under the same conditions, then S' would be worse off (in terms of income and leisure) than it is at present;

(3) If S were to withdraw from society with its *own* endowments (not its per capita share), then S' would be worse off than at present.

If (1)–(3) hold, then we say as well that S' is an *exploiting* coalition. Exploiting and exploited coalitions are always complements of each other.

Notice the definition of capitalist exploitation is entirely in terms of property relations: we compare how well a coalition is doing in the present distribution, where private property is being respected, to how well it would do in a situation where *differential* ownership of the alienable means of production is abolished. (That is what the per capita withdrawal test accomplishes.) If Marxian exploitation comes about because of differential ownership of the means of production, then it is not surprising that this definition captures Marxian exploitation. To say this definition and the labor-theory-of-value definition are *equivalent,* in certain cases, the following is meant: that both definitions identify the same coalitions as exploited (and the same coalitions as exploiting).[3]

How the definition works will become clearer by passing to some examples.

III. The labor-theory-of-value definition vs. the property relations definition of exploitation

Consider an economy which produces one good, called corn. There are two technologies available for producing corn: the farm technology and the factory. The farm technology produces corn using only labor as an input; the factory technology uses two inputs, labor and seed corn (capital).[4] (There is no land involved in producing corn, or, alternatively, land is used but is free and available to everyone.) Let us assume that each producer desires only to subsist, which requires consumption of b bushels of corn per day. Using the farm technology sixteen hours are required to produce b bushels of corn; using the factory technology, only eight hours are required to produce b bushels, and to reproduce the seed corn used up in the process. That is, the *labor embodied* in b bushels using the farm technology is sixteen hours, and it is eight hours using the factory technology. Suppose that society possesses in total just half the amount of seed corn which is required to equip every producer with enough seed so that he could reproduce himself using only the factory technology. We do not specify yet how this capital stock is distributed. Notice, however, that for society to reproduce itself the average time labored by agents must be twelve hours a day. For instance, if half the producers possessed

---

[3] The proof that the two definitions are equivalent for many standard economic models is presented in Roemer (1982). General equilibrium models are studied, in which it is shown that the exploited coalitions are identical under both definitions. Proving this theorem is beyond our scope here, although the intuition behind it should become clear from the examples in Section III.

[4] How could one produce corn without any capital (seed)? Perhaps by foraging in fields where wild corn grows, and cultivating these corn weeds.

all the seed corn, and it were equally divided among them, then they could each just reproduce themselves, using all the seed corn, in eight hours, using the factory technology, while the other producers will then each have to work sixteen hours a day on the farm. This sums to an average worktime of twelve hours. There is no way to do better than this, on the average, and there are arrangements (as we will see) which do considerably worse. Hence, in this case, twelve hours a day is the *socially necessary labor time:* it is the amount of time the producers must work on average to reproduce themselves, given the technologies and the capital stock available.

All the examples below are based on the economy described above. In particular, it is assumed that all producers have an identical unit of labor power. It is also assumed that producers can and will change over from using the farm technology to the factory technology, costlessly, if they can reduce their total labor expended, and still survive, by so doing. (There are no transaction costs, nor disamenities from working in the factory as opposed to the farm, although these can easily be added to the story.) The producers using the farm technology will be called peasants, and the producers using the factory will be called workers.

Example 1

Suppose the seed corn (capital) is distributed in an egalitarian manner – each producer owns his per capita share of the seed, which, by hypothesis, is just one-half what he needs to reproduce himself using the more favorable factory technology. The factory technology is more favorable, since agents in this economy desire only to subsist, and hence they wish to minimize the time they work subject to producing the bundle b of corn they need, and reproducing the seed they use up. Then the simplest arrangement is for each producer to work twelve hours: he works, first, four hours in the factory, producing $\frac{1}{2}b$ and engaging all his seed corn, and then he works eight hours on the farm, producing another $\frac{1}{2}b$. (One might object: why doesn't he take his seed corn, which emerges after the first four hours, and simply work again in the factory for another four hours? This would be a different technology. Time is of the essence in this model. To be precise, we must say that the corn, although requiring only four hours of labor to plant, cannot be harvested until twenty-four hours have passed. Thus, the producer gets his seed corn back, but he can only plant once a day.)

In this example everyone would agree there is no exploitation. No one is working for anyone else, the distribution of work times is egalitarian. One can easily verify that there is no exploitation under the property relations definition, since the original distribution of assets is already egalitarian, that is, seed corn is endowed on a per capita basis.

Example 2

Assume the same distribution of seed corn as in Example 1, but now arrange the equilibrium in another way. An equilibrium distribution of work exists in which there is complete social division of labor, by using a labor market; that is, some producers will work only on farms, and others only in factories, but each will work just twelve hours, as before. One part of the population, called coalition H, is going to hire the other part, called S. In fact, S will be a coalition comprising precisely one-third of the entire population. First, each producer Smith in S works up his own seed corn, in four hours, and receives $\frac{1}{2}b$ of corn he thereby produces. Then Smith goes to work for Jones, a member of H. He works up Jones's capital in four hours, for which Jones pays him a wage of $\frac{1}{4}b$. Jones takes the other $\frac{1}{4}b$ produced by Smith's labor as his profit from hiring Smith. Then Smith goes to work for Kaplan, another member of H, for the same wage. He works four hours on Kaplan's seed capital, producing $\frac{1}{2}b$, of which he is paid $\frac{1}{4}b$; Kaplan takes the other $\frac{1}{4}b$ as profit. Now Smith has worked twelve hours and has received precisely one bundle b of corn. This arrangement can be replicated throughout the economy, each agent in S hiring himself out to two agents in H. Thus the seed corn capital is all employed. This arrangement precisely exhausts the seed corn, since S and H are in a ratio of $1:2$ in size. Now, each producer in H has gotten $\frac{1}{4}b$ as his profits from the labor of his employee in S; everyone in H goes to the farm (for they have engaged all their seed corn with their hired workers, and have none left to work up on their own), and each works long enough on the farm to produce the other $\frac{3}{4}b$ he needs, which requires twelve hours' labor on the farm. This is the equilibrium. Each producer in S and H works twelve hours, exactly as in Example 1.

Why will agents in S agree to this deal? Because they are no worse off than under the alternative of being autarkic (Example 1). In fact, if there are savings from the social division of labor (such as no lost time in commuting from the farm to the factory), then the equilibrium in Example 2 can be arranged so that everyone works less time than in Example 1. (If commuting time is taken into account, perhaps it takes fourteen hours to reproduce oneself using the autarkic arrangement, and only twelve hours with the social division of labor.)

Is S exploited by H? Certainly H is profiting from S's labor; by the Marxian labor-theory-of-value definition, H appears to be exploiting S. (Each producer in S does produce $\frac{1}{2}b$ of surplus product, which is "expropriated" by two agents in H.) But I claim it is incorrect, intuitively, to view S as exploited by H, for the outcome of each producer working twelve hours is identical to Example 1, where clearly there is no exploitation. The initial distribution is egalitarian and the outcome is egalitarian – how can there be exploitation?

The answer lies in realizing that the essence of exploitation is in property relations and not in the use of the labor market or the apparent expropriation of surplus in the labor process. Usually, the production of surplus in the labor process is accompanied by exploitation, but this example illustrates that such need not be the case.

It is easily seen that, according to the property relations definition, there is no exploitation. Let us test if S is an exploited coalition. If S withdraws with its share of the assets, which in this model means its share of the seed corn, it will have precisely what it does in fact have, namely its original endowment of seed corn. Hence, each producer in S must work twelve hours, as has been verified. Thus, S will not be better off, and we need go no further to verify that S is not exploited, under the arrangement in Example 2.

The property relations definition of exploitation and the labor-theory-of-value definition yield different judgments concerning whether coalition S is exploited. The property relations definition renders the intuitively correct judgment in this case. Although S is trading some labor that is 'surplus' for access to H's capital, the arrangement does not constitute exploitation; the arrangement, for example, could just as well have been made the other way around, with some of the people in H forming the coalition of the hired, and the present workers in S becoming part of a new hiring coalition. Every producer is indifferent among these various arrangements, assuming no particular preferences for the country life over the city life.

Example 2a

We can perform exactly the same arrangement as Example 2 by using a credit market instead of a labor market. Instead of H hiring S, we can say H lends its capital to S, and each member of S pays interest in amount $\frac{1}{4}b$ to two members of H. Thus the credit market and the labor market are identical in allowing the social division of labor to be accomplished. This example is not important to the present story, but it is interesting in another context, in showing how exploitation (when it *does* exist) can be accomplished just as well with a credit market as with a labor market. The labor market is not necessary to generate exploitation.

Example 3

I now present an example that is the prototype of capitalism. Imagine, instead of an original equal division of seed corn assets, all the seed corn is owned by a few producers (say, comprising 1 percent of the population), each of whom owns a lot. What will the equilibrium look like? Here is a classical story in which the variable around which equilibration takes place is the length of the working day in the factory. The asset owners are going to offer to hire the assetless to work in the factory. The offer they make is a certain length of the working day in exchange for the subsistence wage b. Suppose they offer a working day of twelve hours, in return for a wage of b. Then all the peasants (the assetless) will flock to the factory gates, demanding work, as their next best alternative is to work sixteen hours on the farm, for the same income. (Recall, they own no seed corn.) The capitalists can raise the length of the working day to sixteen hours since there is a surplus population always willing to work in the factory if the terms are better than on the farm. (For this, invoke the relative scarcity of seed capital.) By hypothesis, there is still only enough seed corn to reproduce half the population using the factory. Since each worker works sixteen hours in the factory, there is just enough seed corn to hire one-fourth the peasants. The hirers pay these workers b, and keep the surplus for themselves. For each worker hired, a profit b is made. Notice the asset holders have become capitalists – that is, they are extracting surplus production, not just subsisting. (This is the only way they can keep the peasants from banging at their doors for employment, which is what would happen if they set the length of the working day at less than sixteen hours.) The other 74 percent of the population stay as peasants on the farm, and each works sixteen hours a day.

According to the labor-theory-of-value definition, the capitalists are exploiters, gaining from the surplus labor of the workers. This is true also by the property relations definition. For suppose the coalition S of workers and peasants were to withdraw with its *per capita* share of the capital; then, as we know from Example 1, each of them would have to work twelve hours a day to subsist, making them better off than at present. Similarly, the complementary coalition S' of capitalists, withdrawing with its per capita share, would have to work twelve hours a day, faring much worse. Thus (1) and (2) of the definition hold. Furthermore, (3) holds: for if S withdrew from this society with its own capital, the coalition S' would have to work each eight hours, faring worse, as there would be no workers without assets to hire. Although the capitalists would have excess capital it would do them no good, as there would be no assetless producers who would gain from trading their labor power with them.

Are the peasants exploited? According to the labor-theory-of-value definition, there is no question: they are not. No surplus labor is expropriated from them, as they do not work for the capitalists. The situation is somewhat trickier from the propery relations point of view. Examining the property relations definition, we see the peasants are *not* exploited, because of condition (3). Let S be the coalition of peasantry. Then (1) and (2) both hold, but (3) fails. That is, if S' withdraws with its own assets (which is to say, the capitalists and workers withdraw as they are, with all the assets), then S' will not be worse off, because the capitalists and workers do not depend on the peasantry. This assumes that the pressure of the peasantry on the wage, in their role as industrial reserve army, is not necessary to keep the length of the working day up to sixteen hours, an assumption which is acceptable at this level of abstraction, as we are dealing thus far with perfectly competitive models, not with bargaining models. Alternatively stated, the peasants are not exploited because they could disappear from the scene and the income of the others would not change. (This is exactly what (3) tests for.)

If, however, one insists that the 74 percent of the population who comprise the peasantry are a necessary industrial reserve army, without whom the real wage in the factory would be bargained up, one still cannot conclude the coalition S' of workers and capitalists would be worse off were S to withdraw with its own assets. (Indeed, part of the coalition would be better off and part worse off.) Without the peasants, there still exists a *feasible* solution in which each member of S' is exactly as well off as in the existing allocation – that is the point.

Although the peasants are not exploited, according to the property relations definition, they are, in some sense, being treated as unfairly by the system as are the workers – both they and the workers have to work sixteen hours a day, while the capitalists work not at all, by virtue of their ownership of the means of production. To capture this, I propose the following. If a coalition S satisfies (1) and (2) of the Definition PR at a particular allocation, then I say it is being *Marxian-unfairly treated*. (It may or may not be *exploited,* depending on whether or not (3) holds in addition.) Thus, a coalition is unfairly treated simply by virtue of property relations (in particular, the asset-poor are unfairly treated); it is only exploited, however, if the complementary coalition *depends* on it for its current income, in the sense that (3) assures. Some people may wish to drop the notion of unfair treatment, and drop requirement (3), and say that a coalition is exploited if (1) and (2) hold. In that case, one would say the peasants in Example 3 are exploited. I believe, however, the distinction between unfair treatment and exploitation is useful, as will become clearer below.

Example 4

Consider, now, another distribution of the seed corn assets, in which half the population owns all the seed corn, and it is distributed equally among the producers in that half. Then the obvious equilibrium is that everyone in the rich half (call it R) works eight hours and reproduces himself in the factory, and everyone in the poor half P works sixteen hours on the farm. The equilibrium is autarkic. According to the labor-theory-of-value definition, there is no exploitation. This is also true from the property relations definition, because condition (3) fails to hold with $S = P$. (If P withdraws with its assets, R is no worse off.) However, P is unfairly treated, since if each coalition were to withdraw with its per capita share of the assets, R would be worse off (having to work twelve hours each) and P would be better off (working twelve hours).

A sharper formulation of this example is to consider R to be a rich island, well-endowed with resources, and P to be a poor island. The populations on the two islands are identically skilled. Then the people on R work less long to subsist than those on P. The poor island is not exploited, but it is unfairly treated, according to Definition PR.

Example 5

The distribution of assets is the same as in Example 4, but we use a labor market, under which R hires P. In fact, R can set the length of the working day at sixteen hours in its factory, since as we have observed, the alternative for producers in P is to work sixteen hours on the farm. There are various equivalent ways of arriving at an equilibrium; here is one. Each person in R hires one person in P to work up his seed corn, in eight hours, and pays his employee $\frac{1}{2}b$, taking the other $\frac{1}{2}b$ himself as profit. Each person in P goes back to the farm, working another eight hours to produce his other $\frac{1}{2}b$, thus for a total of sixteen hours. Each person in R goes to the farm and works for eight hours to produce *his* other $\frac{1}{2}b$. Thus, at equilibrium, each person in R works eight hours and each in P sixteen hours, exactly the same as in Example 4, as is required for this to be an equilibrium.

Is R exploiting P? According to the Marxian labor-theory-of-value definition, surely yes. R is expropriating surplus value from P. But we agreed that in Example 4 R is not exploiting P from the Marxian point of view, and the two equilibria are identical as far as every producer is concerned! (Remember, there are no disamenities from working for another in this model – only the surplus labor itself counts as exploitation.) Thus, the Marxian definition falters, in that it changes its verdict concerning P's condition, when in fact there is no real change – only the market changes which is being used to arrange the equilibrium.

The property relations definition gives a better judgment. According to it, P is not exploited in Example 5. P continues to be unfairly treated, but condition (3) of Definition PR still fails to hold, and so P is not exploited. If P were to withdraw with its own assets, we know R can reproduce itself still with eight hours in the factory. *R does not depend on P at all* in Example 5, in the precise sense that it has an autarkic alternative in which it fares just as well.

The mechanisms of the labor-theory-of-value and property relations definitions are hopefully becoming clear. The surplus labor definition takes too micro an approach, by focusing only on what happens at the point of production, between worker and capitalist. The property relations definition ignores particular markets which are used to arrange equilibria, and examines only how well off agents would be under alternative distributions of property in the means of production.

Example 6

Until now, the models have been perfectly competitive. I now introduce an element of bargaining into the factory. Suppose, as in Example 3, a few producers (capitalists) own all the seed corn. The working day, however, does not equilibrate at sixteen hours in the factory, but at something less than that, because the workers form a strong union. Let us say they force the working day down to eleven hours, still receiving b as the daily wage. The capitalists can put up with this, as they still make a profit of $\frac{3}{8}b$ bushels of corn from each worker per day. The union must now keep the peasants, who are banging at the factory door wanting employment at eleven hours a day, from getting jobs. (This is the noncompetitive element.) Perhaps the peasants live in one country and the workers and capitalists in another, and so this problem is not too severe.

Are the workers exploited? According to the labor-theory-of-value definition, certainly. But according to the property relations definition they are not, for if they withdrew with their per capita share of the seed corn, they would have to work twelve hours a day, and be worse off!

I would argue that, although this may appear to be one strike in favor of the surplus labor definition against the property relations definition, in fact it is not. The reason Marxists intuitively feel the workers are exploited in this situation is that they view the coalition of workers and capitalists as the universe. If that is the case, then indeed the workers are exploited by the capitalists according to the property relations definition as well. That is, if by "taking their share" we mean their share of the assets, divided up among only the workers and capitalists (but not the peasants), then the workers are exploited according to the property relations definition. Within the coalition of workers and capitalists, the workers are exploited: but they are not exploited within the universal coalition which includes the peasants.

This is not an academic point, but has a political analog in revolutionary movements: I refer to the issue of proletarian internationalism. Suppose there is sufficiently little capital stock in the world that the length of the working day would be twelve hours, were that capital shared equally by all. Yet workers in the United States work eight hours a day. We say they are exploited by the capitalists in the United States, since within the U.S. coalition of workers and capitalists, that is the case. But U.S. workers would be worse off (at least in the sense described here) were there to be an international socialist revolution, abolishing differences in per capita distribution of capital internationally. It is because the workers of the advanced countries are not exploited in the international universal coalition that proletarian internationalism is an extremely difficult idea for Marxist political movements in relatively advanced industrial countries.

Although the workers of the United States are not exploited in the grand coalition consisting of the world (in this example), neither do they comprise an exploiting coalition. This can be seen by checking condition (2) of Definition PR. Let S' be the coalition of U.S. workers and S the rest of the world (including U.S. capitalists). Assume that U.S. workers possess less than their per capita share of international assets (since the capitalists have all the assets). Then if S withdrew with its per capita share of the assets, it would be taking with it fewer assets than it now has, making it worse off. Thus S is not an exploited coalition, so S' is not exploiting.

Although the U.S. workers are not an exploiting coalition, the international peasantry are being unfairly treated. Let S be the international peasantry, that is, the world minus the U.S. workers and capitalists, who are S'. Conditions (1) and (2) of Definition PR hold, but (3) fails. If S withdraws with its assets, the U.S. is no worse off. This, however, assumes there is no trade between the U.S. and the rest of the world. If there is such trade, and the U.S. benefits from it, then S is exploited by the U.S. coalition, although we cannot assert it is the U.S. workers which are exploiting the rest of the world. In fact, the definition can be applied to show that U.S. capitalists are an exploiting coalition and the U.S. workers and peasantry constitute an exploited coalition.

Example 7

This example shows that if a coalition is exploited, it is not necessarily worse off than another coalition which is unfairly treated but not exploited. Let there be capitalists who do not work, workers who work fifteen hours a day (more than socially necessary labor time) and peasants who work sixteen hours a day. There are, however, many fewer peasants than workers in this case. (This can be accomplished by increasing the total amount of seed corn which is originally available and owned by the capitalists.) Then the coalition S of workers is exploited: for if its complement, the capitalists and peasants, withdraw with their own assets, we can arrange initial conditions so that they will be worse off. As this situation is more ambiguous than the previous ones, we require a more precise definition of what it means for the coalition S' to be worse off in one situation than another, for these examples. I will say S' is worse off in state α than in state β if the total time worked by S' in α is greater than in β, while the same income is received. If there are sufficiently few peasants (in particular, fewer peasants than capitalists), then when S withdraws with its own assets S' will have to work longer hours in total than before. For suppose there are so few peasants that the seed corn in S' is abundant, rather than scarce relative to the labor supply. The working day in S' will then be bid down to eight hours for the peasants in S' when S withdraws, which means no capitalist earns any profit from hiring peasants. Consequently each capitalist must also work eight hours to reproduce himself. Thus average working time in S' is eight hours, but in the original situation the average working time in S' is less than eight hours, since by hypothesis there are more capitalists than peasants. This verifies that condition (3) holds under suitable initial conditions when we take S as the workers, and it is easily seen that (1) and (2) hold as well. So S is exploited.

However, the peasantry are unfairly treated but not exploited, as we know. Nevertheless, the peasantry are worse off than the workers, and the claim is demonstrated.

The moral: being exploited, as opposed to being unfairly treated, does not entail a welfare comparison, but only a difference in the relation of dependence of the exploiting coalition upon the exploited coalition. The capitalists depend on the workers but not on the peasants. An important example of an unfairly treated coalition which is worse off than an exploited one is the coalition of the unemployed, contrasted with the workers (see next example).

Example 8

It is perhaps worth remarking that we can reinterpret these examples to apply to situations which sound more like modern capitalism. Think of there being only one 'technology', the factory; the alternative to working in the factory is to be unemployed. When unemployed, one collects a wage smaller than when employed (a welfare payment or unemployment insurance). The unemployed are what were called, in previous examples, the peasantry. Hence, the unemployed are not exploited, by Definition PR, but are unfairly treated.[5]

Example 9

In the examples given thus far where a coalition S is unfairly treated but not exploited, there has been no relationship between S and S'. Moreover, when a coalition S has been exploited, it has always been in a relationship of being hired by (or of borrowing capital from) a subset of its complement. (Whenever a labor market has been used as the conduit for exploitation, a credit market could have been used as well. See Example 2a.) It might therefore seem necessary that there be a relationship of working for or borrowing from another for a coalition to endure exploitation. This, however, is not the case, although it is not possible to give an example of exploitation *in the absence of labor and credit markets* using the simple one-commodity market under discussion here. I will, however, outline such an example in a many-commodity world. (Only two commodities are required.) Each agent possesses some bundle of endowments of the different and several produced goods. Each agent knows the technology, which includes a method for producing every good. There is only one technology, unlike the previous examples. A producer, facing prices for the goods, chooses a production plan to operate which will enable him to produce goods worth, at going prices, just enough for him to purchase his subsistence bundle b, which now is a vector of goods (some of the various different commodities). He is constrained in his choice of production plan by his wealth, which is the value of his nonlabor endowments, priced at market prices. He must be able to advance the capital to finance the production plan he chooses from his own wealth, since there is no credit market on which he can borrow capital. Thus, poor

---

[5] To assure the unemployed are worse off than the employed we need to know that the wage differential between the two groups more than compensates for the disutility of working. In practical situations this is usually true, as there is also a disutility from being unemployed independent of the lower wage.

producers must concentrate in labor intensive production activities, and rich ones can concentrate in capital intensive activities. The objective of a producer, as before, is to minimize the labor he expends in production, subject to producing a net output which he can trade for his b (that is, which is worth as much as b at going prices). In this model, it can be shown that in general, at equilibrium prices, poor producers work longer than is socially necessary, in the Marxian sense, and rich producers work less time than is socially necessary. It can be shown, at equilibrium, that the society as a whole always works precisely socially necessary labor time. (That is, let t be socially necessary labor time, and let there be N producers. Then at equilibrium society works in total Nt. Thus if some producer works less than t, another must work more than t.) As a consequence, it is easily shown that the coalition of producers who work less long than socially necessary exploit the others, according to the property relations definition.

But notice there is no relationship of hiring or lending between the exploiters and exploited in this example! Only produced commodities are traded, and exploitation is mediated entirely through those markets. Hence the relation of dependence necessary for exploitation can exist with trade of produced commodities only.

According to the surplus value definition, however, it is questionable whether the producers who work longer than socially necessary labor time are exploited in this model, as every producer works only for himself: there is no relationship between the producers at the point of production in which surplus value is extracted. The 'extraction' of surplus value occurs entirely through trade of finished goods, not labor power or finance capital. In this case, again, I think the property relations definition renders a verdict which conforms much more closely to a Marxist's intuitive conception of exploitation. To make the example as clear as possible, let there be two producers in this example, called Friday and Robinson, who are poor and rich in capital, respectively. Socially necessary labor time, let us say, is eight hours. At the equilibrium Friday works twelve hours and Robinson four. There is no relationship between them except trade of initial inputs and final products, at equilibrium prices. If Friday withdraws with one-half of the total stock of produced goods, he can reproduce himself, with no trade, in eight hours. The same, of course, goes for Robinson. Indeed, if Robinson withdraws with his own stock (which is more than one-half the total), he must work eight hours to reproduce his bundle b. Thus Robinson benefits from Friday's presence, and is able to use his wealth as leverage, through the market, to get Friday to work "for" him, which Friday would not have to do if he had access to his per capita share of the produced capital. Should our definition of exploitation not render the verdict of exploitation of Friday by Robinson in this case from the Marxian point of view? If yes, one agrees with the property relations verdict and disagrees with the labor-theory-of-value verdict, if the labor-theory-of-value definition is taken to include a clause that exploitation occurs as a consequence of a direct relationship (as in employment or borrowing) between the agents.

This example is the prototype of 'unequal exchange' between countries. Imagine that country A and country B have different capital–labor ratios, due to their different endowments. Even if both countries have knowledge of the same technology, and even if there is no trade of labor or capital across national borders, country A (with the higher capital–labor ratio) can exploit country B, according to the property relations definition. The goods B can command with its national income embody less labor than its population expended, and the goods A commands with its national income embody more labor than its population expended. Thus what has been called unequal exchange in international trade is seen to be simply a type of capitalist exploitation. The counterfactual against which the present allocation of income is compared is one in which each country is endowed with its per capita share of international capital. Since both countries gain from trade, test (3) of Definition PR applies, and B is not only unfairly treated but exploited.[6]

Working through these examples will have given the reader an intuitive feeling for how Definition PR works, and it is now appropriate to comment further on the definition. It accomplishes two purposes. The first is to compare how well a coalition is doing with how well it would be doing in a counterfactual situation where differential ownership of the alienable means of production is abolished. This is what test (1) does. Test (2) says that capitalist exploitation can be said to exist only if one coalition is gaining at the expense of another.[7] (That is, if both S and S' were better off under the alternative per capita distribution of property, it would not be correct to say S' was gaining at the expense of S in the present situation – they would both be suffering due to some negative externality such as severe decreasing returns to scale.) Yet, as has been illustrated, (1) and (2) are not sufficient to capture the intuitive notion of exploitation, but only of what I have called unfair treatment, since (1) and (2) can both hold without S' depending on S for its good fortune. (See Examples 4 and 5.) I think this aspect of dependence is necessary for capitalist

---

[6] For a fuller treatment of unequal exchange between countries viewed as exploitation, see Roemer (1983b).

[7] In a general game-theoretic framework, it can be shown that if the game characterizing the counterfactual payoffs is superadditive and the allocation in question is Pareto optimal, then (1) implies (2) (but not conversely). See Roemer (1982), Theorem 7.1.

exploitation, and (3) tests for that dependence.[8] Nevertheless, (3) alone is not sufficient to guarantee that exploitation is occurring, since it is possible for (3) to hold, but for S to be worse off if it withdraws with its per capita share of property as well, that is, for (1) to fail. To see this, consider the next example.

Example 10

The economy differs from the ones discussed thus far; there is now a group of highly skilled producers, who also own more capital than the average, and a group of unskilled poor producers. Let S be the coalition of the poor unskilled. If S' withdraws with its own capital (and labor), S' will be worse off, not having access to the unskilled labor, but if S withdraws even with its per capita share of the capital, it too will be worse off, not having access to the skills of S'. Thus (3) holds but (1) fails; in this case, it should not be said, I believe, that S is capitalistically or Marxian exploited, since it is not by virtue of its lack of access to capital that it is badly off, but by virtue of its lack of skill.[9] This example will become important in the next section. Capitalist exploitation is that inequality in income produced by the unequal distribution of alienable means of production, not of skills. Socialism makes no claim to eliminating differential income due to skill or effort.

The property relations definition of exploitation not only renders better verdicts than the surplus-value definition, as I have tried to show, but it is far more general. It is clear one can perform the tests required in (1)–(3) regardless of how complicated the production specification is – that is to say, we do not require restrictions on the production set which are necessary to allow us to be able unequivocally to speak of embodied labor time. Thus the theory of exploitation is liberated from its dependence on the very *special* labor theory of value. The advantage of the labor-theory-of-value approach is that it presents a graphic picture of expropriation of something by one person from another; but I have argued that this advantage is only superficial, for to justify the description of expropriation requires providing a counterfactual situation against which one judges the fairness of the labor transfer, and that counterfactual situation

[8] Note there is a distinction in this usage between "A gaining at the expense of B," and "A depending on B." I use "gaining at the expense of" to mean A gains by virtue of having property which is "rightfully" B's under the counterfactual; I use "depending upon" to mean in the *current* situation A gains from trade with B.

[9] I call inequalities such as this one, which result from differential endowments of skill, socialist exploitation. It is not the "historical task" of the socialist revolution to eliminate socialist exploitation, but only capitalist exploitation. See Roemer (1982), chaps. 7 and 8, for further discussion, and Essay 1.

is one made explicit in (1) and (2) of the property relations definition. Furthermore, in taking too micro an approach, we have seen the labor-theory-of-value definition gets into trouble in judging when expropriation is taking place.

One reason that Marxists sometimes offer in defense of the labor-theory-of value is that exploitation of labor explains the ability of a capitalist economy to expand. Exploitation, it is argued, is not important as an ethical category, but only as an explanation of accumulation. It is maintained, following Marx, that the *labor* theory of value is necessary to accomplish this, because labor power is that unique commodity which has the capacity of creating more value than it itself contains, and hence one is directed to the choice of the labor numéraire to demonstrate the secret of accumulation. This argument is wrong. One can choose *any* commodity to be the value numéraire, and prove the following theorem: An economy is capable of producing a surplus if and only if, given any commodity k chosen as value numéraire, the embodied k-value of one unit of k is less than one.[10] Hence, one cannot explain accumulation on the basis of the exploitation of labor, uniquely. That can be explained using any commodity as numéraire. The choice of labor as the value numéraire commodity does, at least under certain assumptions, provide a theory of exploitation which classifies the poor proletarians as exploited and the rich capitalists as exploiters. This is attractive for two reasons: first, it conforms to the lines drawn (more or less) in class struggles under capitalism; second, it may have some ethical interest. It can be shown that, if all producers possess the same amount of a uniform kind of labor power, but producers possess different amounts of all other endowments, then labor is the unique commodity which will produce *this* division of society into exploiters and exploited. I would argue, then, that the Marxian theory of exploitation (by which I mean here either the labor-theory-of-value theory or the more general property relations theory) is of interest only for the two reasons stated above (and they are related to each other, I think, through the claims of historical materialism), and not as an explanation of accumulation or profits.

The property relations definition of exploitation is more general than the labor-theory-of-value definition. But furthermore, the property relations definition is itself a special case of an even more general definition of exploitation, in a natural way, while the labor-theory-of-value definition is not. In the property relations definition, one *special* counterfactual has been chosen against which to compare the present allocation – namely, the counterfactual where property in the means of production is distributed

---

[10] For a precise statement and proof of this theorem, see Roemer (1982), Appendix to chap. 6. See also Wolff (1981).

in an egalitarian manner. There are many other counterfactuals which could be chosen, each giving rise to a definition of a different kind of exploitation. In fact, this is done in *A General Theory of Exploitation and Class,* where other counterfactuals are chosen to specify what are called socialist, feudal, neoclassical, and status exploitation. More precisely, a given kind of exploitation is defined in a game-theoretic way, by specifying the characteristic function of a game which defines the payoffs available to coalitions in the alternative, counterfactual regime. (The payoffs available under an egalitarian distribution of the means of production are captured by one characteristic function.) Thus, the game-theoretic property relations approach embeds the Marxian theory of exploitation in a more general theory in a way which allows one to specify any given conception of exploitation in a canonical form, using the characteristic function of a certain game.[11] One can then compare the ethics which are associated with different conceptions of exploitation by examining their different underlying characteristic functions, or conceptions of alternative property distributions defining the counterfactuals which give rise to them.[12]

[11] A summary of how the game-theoretic approach can be used to define feudal, capitalist, socialist, and neoclassical exploitation can be found in Essay 1.

[12] An apparent defect in the property relations definition, and its resolution, must be mentioned. Suppose we drop the assumption of constant returns to scale, made early in Section II, and postulate the existence of positive externalities from scale and the social division of labor among large coalitions, as in fact exist in modern economies. Consider an individual proletarian, or a small coalition of proletarians. If they withdrew with their per capita share of the means of production, they (or he) would surely be worse off because of the great gains from increasing returns to size and scope which exist in the large economy. By the property relations definition, small coalitions and individuals are therefore not exploited, even if they are very poor. When increasing returns exist, it is not relevant to inquire whether individuals are exploited: rather, one asks if they belong to some minimal exploited coalition. An agent is called *vulnerable* if he is a member of some minimal exploited coalition. Essentially, when increasing returns exist, it is only relevant to inquire into the exploitation status of sufficiently large coalitions. All proletarians will be vulnerable, if not individually exploited. The relevance of vulnerability as the proper generalization of exploitedness in the presence of increasing returns is pursued in Roemer (1982).

Another defect of the game-theoretic approach to exploitation is pointed out by Jon Elster (1982), who claims that the conception of exploitation as "taking unfair advantage of someone" can never be precisely captured by the positing of counterfactuals. Consider, for example, an invalid who is supported by the rest of society, or children who are supported by adults. According to Definition PR, the invalid, and the children, are exploiting the rest of society. (Elster concocts a subtler example.) Thus, I cannot claim Definition PR really stands on its own as a definition, but rather characterizes exploitation more cogently than the labor theory of value. (Note, as well, there is a transfer of surplus value from society to the invalid, so some supradefinitional considerations must be invoked in the case of applying the labor-theory-of-value definition to that situation.) It appears the missing clause in the definitions of exploitation concerns the dominance of the exploiter over the exploited, for in the case of the invalid and the children, the relation of dominance is of the supposed exploited over the supposed exploiter. Dominance,

IV.   Some arguments against Marxian exploitation

The property relations approach to exploitation makes clear its ethical imperative: abolish differential ownership of the alienable means of production. This contrasts with the surplus labor approach, whose ethical imperative is unclear; it is certainly not to abolish surplus labor, which, for example, should exist under socialism. *Why* do Marxists consider exploitative a distribution of income which arises from differential ownership of the alienable means of production? That is the basic question which must be answered to justify the vituperative nomenclature of exploitation.

I cannot answer this question here, but I have made some attempts to elsewhere.[13] This section has a less ambitious task, to reply to some standard arguments which are proposed to counter the charge that what Marxists call exploitation should be called that.

There are, I think, two main arguments for why the differential ownership of the means of production is not wrong or unjust, and therefore why the resulting distribution should not be called exploitative, or, more weakly, what I have called unfair treatment. The first is that (I) the distribution of means of production is a consequence of inherent traits of agents, which are legitimate and worthy of respect: skills, including entrepreneurial talent; attitudes towards risk; rates of time preference. And (II) regardless of how the distribution came about, it is necessary for the good of all (or, one can say for the good even of the exploited, or the worst-off coalition) that there be private and differential ownership of the means of production; this is the incentive argument.

Notice that in the property relations definition of exploitation it is only alienable property, and not inherent traits such as skills, attitudes towards risk, and so forth, which are hypothetically equalized to test for the existence of exploitation. Recalling Example 10 from the last section, it is possible for a poor but unskilled coalition not to be capitalistically exploited, since if it withdraws with its share of the alienable assets, it is worse off, without access to the skills of the others, who are richer. This is, indeed, the first argument of opponents to Marxian exploitation: that if the proletarians withdraw with their per capita share of the transferable means of production they will be worse off, because the reason they are poor in the first place is that they lack the various inalienable traits necessary for successful production. Perhaps the most powerful opponent on this question is Robert Nozick; I shall address some (but not all) of his arguments.

---

however, is a term as demanding of definition as exploitation, and so it is inappropriate to append a dominance condition to the list of requirements in Definition PR. A completely satisfactory analytical definition of exploitation is an open question.

[13] Roemer (1982), chap. 9.

Nozick presents a clear property relations explanation of Marxian exploitation.[14] Nevertheless, he also believes that since the labor theory of value is not very general, the Marxian theory fails.[15] The argument of this paper has shown this to be an incorrect inference, since the Marxian theory can be resurrected independently of the labor theory of value. Nozick also raises an argument that it is essential for workers to be forced to work for capitalists for exploitation to be said to exist.[16] This is also incorrect, from the property relations vantage point: indeed, Example 9 of the previous section showed that exploitation can exist even when no one works for anyone else. Thus the labor theory of value and the question of whether or not workers are forced to work for capitalists are seen to be peripheral issues, once the property relations view of exploitation is adopted. The only question is, What is ethically wrong with the differential distribution of the means of production?

Despite these incorrect but peripheral inferences, Nozick's main arguments against the contention that the differential distribution of the means of production is unjust are that it came about because of different rates of time preference between workers and capitalists (see his footnote, p. 254), the lack of entrepreneurial ability of workers (p. 255), and the differential attitudes towards risk in the population, which result in people sorting themselves into capitalists and workers (p. 255). The argument based on different rates of time preference, applied to present-day capitalism, is almost facetious. Capitalists do not suffer from abstention when they put their capital into production and not consumption. The other two traits are more important, and Nozick's key evidence that entrepreneurial talent and risk are central, is that we do not observe more worker-

[14] Robert Nozick (1974), p. 253: "But at the bottom, Marxist theory explains the phenomenon of exploitation by reference to the workers not having access to the means of production. The workers have to sell their labor (labor power) to the capitalists, for they must use the means of production to produce, and cannot produce alone. A worker, or groups of them, cannot hire means of production and wait to sell the product some months later; they lack the cash reserves to obtain access to machinery or to wait until later when revenue will be received from the future sale of the product now being worked on." This is exactly my explanation of exploitation in the models of this paper.

[15] Nozick (1974), p. 253: "With the crumbling of the labor theory of value, the underpinning of its particular theory of exploitation dissolves. And the charm and simplicity of this theory's *definition* of exploitation is lost when it is realized that according to the definition there will be exploitation in *any* society in which investment takes place for a greater future product. . . ." This remark shows the importance of recasting the Marxian theory of exploitation in terms of property relations.

[16] Nozick (1974), p. 254: "Note that once the rest of the theory, properly, is dropped, and it is this crucial fact of nonaccess to the means of production that underlies exploitation, it *follows* that in a society in which the workers are *not* forced to deal with the capitalist, exploitation of the laborers is absent." Nozick is correct that the "rest of the theory" (namely the labor of value) should be dropped, but incorrect that exploitation cannot exist without forcing. Note Example 9.

owned firms under capitalism. Workers have access to capital, in pension funds; also, unless we assume some imperfection in capital markets, workers with good ideas should be able to get bank loans. If workers are similar to capitalists in their entrepreneurial ability and attitudes towards risk, why are there not more worker-owned firms?

I think this is an important question, which in the last instance can only be answered with empirical research. I would, however, like to offer several explanations for the absence of such firms which do not depend on workers being more risk averse than capitalists or less skillful. First, there are some worker-owned firms in modern capitalism; they tend to be firms which had been set up by capitalists, which went bankrupt, and the firms were bought by the workers. Indeed, this could be an additional piece of evidence for Nozick, in that one could infer that workers do not have the ability to set up a firm themselves, but once it is in place they can take it over. An alternative explanation is based on the scale economies in the *ownership* of capital. Even if workers do not differ from capitalists in their profiles of traits it is much more difficult to coordinate decisions and organization among 1000 small asset holders than for one large asset holder to do so. This scale economy in ownership with regard to decision making is in no way a trait that should be associated with the holder of the capital: it is a consequence of the technology of information, which redounds to the benefit of large holders of capital. That we observe only worker-owned firms in the case of takeovers is understandable if scale economies in capital ownership are important: for in that case, the apparatus for making decisions has already been set up, and can be easily transferred to the worker-owners. Indeed, once firms are set up, the ownership of capital typically becomes dispersed in any case (when the firm becomes a corporation). Yet firms are always organized by a small number of people.

Secondly, even if the risk profiles of workers and capitalists are the same, the capitalist is at a different point on his risk schedule from the worker, when risk preferences are viewed as a function of wealth. If the worker were as wealthy as the capitalist, he might also be willing to take large risks. It is one thing to gamble with one's pension, and another to gamble with wealth which is discretionary with respect to survival. It cannot be inferred that the worker is more risk averse than the capitalist from observing he does not invest in a business, because the consequence of failure is much more severe for him than for the capitalist. As in the rates-of-time preference argument, the risk-attitudes argument seems to be based on the imaginary situation that all agents start out with the same wealth, and hence their underlying utility functions can be compared by observing a point of behavior, rather than a whole schedule.

Concerning entrepreneurial ability, one need not argue that it is non-existent, or even common, to falsify the bourgeois claim. It need only exist in sufficient quantity in the large pool of proletarians for the workers to be able to take over the factories, and run them themselves. The fact that we do not observe worker-owned firms does not imply this entrepreneurial talent does not exist in the large pool of proletarians; rather, the scale economies in ownership of capital can be the responsible factor, or imperfections in the capital market. Also, much of what passes for entrepreneurial talent is knowledge of investment opportunities, which comes as a consequence of having capital and therefore cannot be used to explain why only some people become capitalists.

One argument of Nozick which has not been addressed is that the present unequal distribution of capital may be the consequence of fair transfer which occurred beginning from some state in the past when the initial unequal distribution of property was, indeed, a consequence of differential skills, risk aversion, rates of time preference, luck, and so on. At best, this defense of capitalist exploitation can only apply to a very singular history of a hypothetical capitalism, one which in all likelihood does not describe the actual history. Marx's attempt in his history of the original accumulation of capital was to deny these untainted initial conditions. I will not pursue this point here, nor discuss the principle of just transfers.

The argument (II), concerning the incentives associated with private property in the means of production, maintains that without differential and private ownership people would cease to work hard, and technological change would slow down or cease. Thus, even though differential ownership gives rise to inequality, everyone is better off than under an egalitarian regime. I take this to be, implicitly at least, a Rawlsian argument against calling certain inequalities exploitative which Marxists would call exploitative. In examining the counterfactual after a coalition's hypothetical withdrawal one must distinguish between what could transpire in the absence of changes in incentives, and what transpires if we admit the possibility of adverse productivity effects due to changes in incentives due to the new distribution of property. The counterfactual I propose makes a *ceteris paribus* assumption concerning the incentive structure. What income is feasible for the withdrawing coalition, if it takes its per capita share of the assets, assuming its members work as hard as before? Given a description of the assets and knowledge of a population, one can perform this calculation. If conditions (1)–(3) of Definition PR all hold for a coalition S under the *ceteris paribus* assumption then S is exploited. If, upon dropping the *ceteris paribus* assumption, the actual incentive changes upon withdrawal would be so adverse as to make S *worse* off than at present, then I say its exploitation is *socially necessary*. If capitalist exploitation is socially necessary, then the workers benefit under capitalism not because of any trait the capitalist possesses, but because the system of private and differential ownership of the means of production induces a favorable incentive structure. Although someone has to be a capitalist for the social product to be maximized, no particular person must be.

Thus certain inequalities may be to the benefit of the exploited, or the least well off. The Rawlsian theory views such inequalities as just. I think, however, justice entails that incomes to individuals are deserved. If it is the differential distribution of assets as such, rather than the skills of capitalists, which brings about incentives, competition, innovation, and increased labor productivity which benefit even the workers, then the capitalists do not deserve their returns. Although no particular person must be a capitalist, someone must be a capitalist to set in motion the system which renders the workers best off among possible alternatives.

The Marxian position on early capitalism is similar to this. Although it is not claimed that workers would have been worse off to withdraw with their per capita share of the capital in early capitalism, capitalism was responsible for innovation through competition, and so eventually future generations are better off than they would have been had capitalism not existed. We might say capitalist exploitation, although not socially necessary in a static sense, was dynamically socially necessary.[17] Thus the exploitation of workers in early capitalism was dynamically socially necessary.[18]

This brief discussion does not attempt to argue why differential ownership of the means of production is unjust, and therefore the consequent distribution of income is exploitative. More weakly, it only argues why some of the arguments against the Marxian contention are false. Indeed, I think the property relations definition of exploitation shows the depth of the question, obscured by the surplus value approach, which does not help us see why the transfer of surplus value should be viewed as an expropriation.

V.   Summary and implications

The property relations definition of exploitation gives a different explanation of the cause of exploitation from the labor-theory-of-value definition. Marxists have often maintained that production as opposed to distribution

---

[17] There is a more protracted discussion of socially necessary exploitation and its relation to some claims of historical materialism in Roemer (1982), chap. 9.

[18] However, the debate on the "paradox of future generations" (*Philosophy & Public Affairs* II, no. 2 [Spring 1982]) calls this statement into question. Although future generations are better off, because their ancestors endured capitalist exploitation, than future generations would be had they come from a yeoman peasantry ancestry, let us say, no particular individual is better off in the first history than the second. According to the 'paradox', dynamically socially necessary exploitation is extremely rare if not nonexistent.

is key in causing exploitation.[19] On the contrary, the property relations definition insists it is *distribution of the means of production* which is the cause of exploitation, not what goes on in production. Indeed, the same relations of production, of one agent hiring another and earning profits from his labor, can be either exploitative or not, depending on the underlying distribution of productive assets, as the examples in Section III showed. It is even possible to generate exploitation with no relationship in production between producers. Exploitation can be mediated entirely through the trade of produced goods.

In short, I have maintained that Marxists can give no justification describing exploitation as the expropriation of surplus labor or surplus value without making reference to the differential ownership of the means of production. The property relations definition makes explicit an otherwise implicit assumption. Indeed without invoking property relations explicitly in the definition of exploitation, one cannot distinguish between the forms of exploitation which existed under feudalism and capitalism, and perhaps continue to exist under socialism. Capitalist and feudal exploitation differ because different forms of property are legal in the two systems; specifically feudal property (the bond) can be parlayed into labor expropriation under feudalism, but that property does not exist under capitalism.

The change of locus (from the production process to property distribution) for the source of exploitation which the property relations definition posits has important implications for Marxian analysis. Marxists have often emphasized the coercion of the worker by the capitalist at the point of production, as it occurs at the locus of expropriation of surplus value. According to the property relations definition, the key locus of coercion is not at the point of production, but in the maintenance of property relations. The struggle at the point of production is, I think, of second order in importance; it is the struggle over the terms of a contract. As a first approximation to understanding capitalism, I follow Marx in assuming a model where all trades are 'fair', where all contracts can be costlessly enforced. Thus, assume the worker and capitalist agree precisely on the terms of the contract for wage labor. Assume the contract is costlessly enforceable. Then there is no struggle at the point of production between the two, but capitalist exploitation continues to exist, as has been shown. Indeed, it has been shown we can have capitalist exploitation with no relationship in production between exploiter and exploitee. The struggle at the point of production, pursuing this point, is not anticapitalist struggle, but trade union struggle. It is surely an important reformist struggle,

---

[19] Although Marxists are often unclear on this, Marx was clear. For evidence, see Cohen (1981), footnote 7.

but it is not necessarily the touchstone for judging the power of capitalists, which resides in the security of property rights in the means of production.[20]

As a tool in political philosophy, the property relations definition is superior. Since the property relations definition makes explicit the counterfactual against which the current regime or distribution of income is being judged, it renders transparent the comparison of different conceptions of exploitation, as the labor-theory-of-value definition does not. By comparing the counterfactuals of different theories of exploitation, one can compare their ethical presumptions in a standardized way. In game-theoretic terminology, the core of the game which characterizes a conception of exploitation consists of precisely the nonexploitative allocations with respect to that concept of exploitation. As an example of the usefulness of this procedure, it is possible to characterize the Rawlsian theory of justice as the core of a game,[21] thereby enabling its comparison to other concepts of exploitation which can be put in their canonical form, using the characteristic function of some game.

The labor theory of value has held a key place in Marxian economic theory, in which it has played two roles: one in the theory of equilibrium prices and exchange, the other in the theory of exploitation. Many writers have clarified, over the past decade, the irrelevance of the labor theory of value as a theory of exchange.[22] But most have adhered to the labor theory of value as useful in the theory of exploitation.[23] On the basis of the arguments presented here, I would claim that, although the labor theory of value is not incorrect as a theory of exploitation in certain special and simple cases, it is unnecessary for that theory. It is superseded by the property relations approach to exploitation. Moreover, when we pass beyond the simple cases (either because production sets become complicated or because of the problems brought out in the examples here), the labor theory of value fails to provide a good theory of exploitation, and the property relations is not only clearer, but necessary.[24] Hence, Marxian

---

[20] The contrast between exploitation viewed as a consequence of domination by the boss over the worker at the point of production, on the one hand, and of property relations, on the other, is further discussed in Roemer (1982b).

[21] See Howe and Roemer (1981).

[22] See Morishima (1973), Steedman (1977), Roemer (1981).

[23] I include myself; see Roemer (1981), chap. 7. Another recent example is R. P. Wolff's (1981) attempt to defend the labor theory of exploitation for reasons which I have criticized in Roemer (1983a).

[24] Note, however, that when we pass to examples that are 'noneconomic' in some sense, as described in the footnote at the end of Section III, the game-theoretic approach fails. It is perhaps more appropriate to say that within the domain of situations which involve unambiguously arms-length economic transactions, the property relations definition performs better than the labor-theory-of-value definition.

economic theory (both with respect to the study of price and exploitation) is liberated from the special labor theory of value. This nullifies the attacks on the Marxian theory that proceed by attacking its weak link, the labor theory of value. It does not, however, make obvious why one should view Marxian exploitation as *exploitative,* although it does make clearer what has to be justified (namely, an egalitarian distribution of property in the alienable means of production) for that claim to be cogent.

Should Marxists be interested in exploitation?

To work at the bidding and for the profit of another . . . is not . . . a satisfactory state to human beings of educated intelligence, who have ceased to think themselves naturally inferior to those whom they serve.

J. S. Mill, *Principles of Political Economy*

The capitalist mode of production . . . rests on the fact that the material conditions of production are in the hands of non-workers in the form of property in capital and land, while the masses are only owners of the personal conditions of production, of labour power. If the elements of production are so distributed, then the present-day distribution of the means of consumption results automatically.

Karl Marx, *Selected Works*

I. Motivations for exploitation theory

Marxian exploitation is defined as the unequal exchange of labor for goods: the exchange is unequal when the amount of labor embodied in the goods which the worker can purchase with his income (which usually consists only of wage income) is less than the amount of labor he expended to earn that income. Exploiters are agents who can command with their income more labor embodied in goods than the labor they performed; for exploited agents, the reverse is true. If the concept of embodied labor is defined so that the total labor performed by a population in a certain time period is equal to the labor embodied in the goods comprising the net national product (NNP), and if the NNP is parcelled out to the members of the population in some way, then there will be (essentially) two groups: the exploiters and the exploited, as defined above. (I say "essentially" because there may be some ambiguity; an agent may be able to purchase different bundles of goods, some bundles of which embody more labor than he worked, and other bundles of which embody less labor

I am indebted to the following individuals for many discussions, comments, and disagreements: G. A. Cohen, Jon Elster, Joseph Ostroy, Amartya Sen, Philippe Van Parijs, Erik Wright; and to participants in seminars where these ideas were presented, at the University of Oslo, the University of Copenhagen, Yale University, the University of Chicago, the 1983 Maison des Sciences de l'Homme Colloquium in London, and the 1984 Colloque Marx in Paris organized by the Ecole des Hautes Etudes en Sciences Sociales.

than he worked. This gives rise to a "gray area" of agents whom we might wish to consider neither exploited nor exploiting.)[1] Thus, exploitation theory views goods as vessels of labor, and calculates labor accounts for people by comparing the "live" labor they expend in production with the "dead" labor they get back in the vessels. Exploitation is an aspect of the pattern of redistribution of labor which occurs through the process of agents "exchanging" their current productive labor for social labor congealed in goods received. It may not always be easy or even possible to *define* the content of dead labor in the vessels, as when labor is heterogeneous or joint production of many goods from the same production process exists. There is a large literature on these questions, which shall not concern me here. For this article, I assume labor is homogeneous.

It is important to note that exploitation is not defined relationally. The statement "A exploits B" is not defined, but rather "A is an exploiter" and "B is exploited." Exploitation, as I conceive it, refers to the relationship between a person and society as a whole as measured by the transfer of the person's labor to the society, and the reverse transfer of society's labor to the person, as embodied in goods the person claims.

What are the uses of exploitation theory? Why is it considered the cornerstone of Marxian social science by many writers? More directly, what positive or normative conclusions might we draw about capitalism from observing that workers are exploited under capitalism? I can identify four main uses or justifications of exploitation theory:

(1) the accumulation theory: exploitation of workers explains profits and accumulation under capitalism; it is the secret of capitalist expansion.

(2) the domination theory: exploitation is intimately linked to the domination of workers by capitalists, especially at the point of production, and domination is an evil.

(3) the alienation theory: exploitation is a measure of the degree to which people are alienated under capitalism. The root of alienation is the separation of one's labor from oneself. If one's labor is put into goods which are produced for exchange (not for use by oneself or one's community), that constitutes alienation. Exploitation occurs because some people alienate more labor than others. It is differential alienation.

(4) the inequality theory: exploitation is a measure and consequence of the underlying inequality in the ownership of the means of production, an inequality which is unjustified.

[1] For a discussion of the gray area of agents, see Roemer (1982), chap. 4.

There is another theory which is, I think, a special case of (4), and so will be numbered:

(4′)   the expropriation theory: exploitation is a measure of expropriation, of one agent owning part of the product which should rightfully belong to another agent.

These four (or five) proposed explanations for our interest in exploitation theory are usually confounded. They should not be, however, because they constitute different claims. Adherents to exploitation theory tend to emphasize some of (1) through (4) when others of the list become subjected to embarrassments or counterexamples. I will argue that in the general case none of (1) through (4) can be sustained; there is, in general, no reason to be interested in exploitation theory, that is, in tallying the surplus value accounts of labor performed versus labor commanded in goods purchased. My arguments against (1) through (4) are, briefly, these: (1) all commodities are exploited under capitalism, not only labor power, and so the exploitation of labor does not explain profits; concerning (2), domination is an important issue under capitalism, but exploitation is irrelevant for its study; concerning (3), differential alienation can be measured using surplus value accounts, but I do not think such alienation is interesting unless it is a consequence of unequal ownership of the means of production. We are thus led to (4) which, I think, is the closest explanation for Marxists' interest in exploitation; but in the general case, I will show inequality in ownership of the means of production, even when ethically indefensible, is not properly measured by exploitation. In particular, it can happen in theory that those who own very little of the means of production are exploiters and those who own a lot are exploited. Hence exploitation (the transfer of surplus value) is not a proper reflection of underlying property relations.

There is an apparent similarity between this iconoclastic posture toward exploitation theory, and the attacks on the labor theory of value which have accelerated in the past decade.[2] In the final section, I evaluate this similarity, and claim it is quite shallow. While the labor theory of value almost always gives incorrect insights, exploitation theory in many cases coincides with a deeper ethical position – although on its own terms it does not provide a justification for that position. My verdict will be that exploitation theory is a domicile that we need no longer maintain: it has provided a home for raising a vigorous family who now must move on.

---

[2] See, for example, Robinson (1966), Morishima (1973), Steedman (1977), Roemer (1981), Samuelson (1971), Elster (1985).

The reader should bear in mind that throughout the article "exploit" has a technical meaning, the unequal exchange of labor. When I claim that exploitation theory is without foundation, I do not mean capitalism is just. I believe capitalism is unjust (or ethically *exploitative*) because of sharply unequal ownership of the means of production. What I show in Section V is that this inequality is not necessarily coextensive with the transfer of surplus value from workers to capitalists, and therefore it is inappropriate to ground an equality-based morality on the technical measure of exploitation. If I occasionally use "exploitation" in its ethical as opposed to technical sense, the word will be italicized as above.

II.   Definition of terms: a simple model

I have outlined above an identification problem with respect to the motivation for our interest in exploitation. In this section, this identification problem will be posed as starkly and schematically as possible, by exhibiting a simple model in which exploitation emerges simultaneously with accumulation, domination, differential alienation, and inequality in ownership of the means of production. This section, therefore, serves to define terms and to pose the problem more precisely.

Imagine an economy with 1,000 persons and two goods: corn and leisure. There are two technologies for producing corn, called the Farm and the Factory. The Farm is a labor-intensive technology in which no seed capital is required, but corn is produced from pure labor (perhaps by cultivating wild corn). The Factory technology produces corn with labor plus capital – the capital is seed corn. The technologies are given by:

Farm: 3 days labor → 1 corn output
Factory: 1 day labor + 1 seed corn → 2 corn output

Corn takes a week to grow (so the seed is tied up in the ground for that long). The total stock of seed corn in this society is 500 corn, and each agent owns $\frac{1}{2}$ corn. The agents have identical preferences which are these: each wants to consume 1 corn *net* output per week. After consuming his 1 corn, the agent will consume leisure. If he can get more than 1 corn for no more labor, he will be even happier: but preferences are lexicographic in that each wishes to minimize labor expended subject to earning enough to be able to consume 1 corn per week, and not to run down his stock of capital.

There is an obvious equilibrium in this economy. The typical agent works up his $\frac{1}{2}$ corn in the Factory in $\frac{1}{2}$ day, which will bring him 1 corn at the end of the week. Having fully employed his seed capital, he must produce another $\frac{1}{2}$ corn somewhere, to replace his capital stock: this he does by working in the Farm technology for $1\frac{1}{2}$ days. Thus he works 2 days and produces 1 corn net output. Every agent does this. Indeed, 2 days is the labor time socially necessary to produce a unit of corn, given that this society must produce 1,000 corn net each week. It is the labor embodied in a unit of corn. At this equilibrium there is no exploitation, since labor expended by each agent equals labor embodied in his share of the net output. Nor is there accumulation, for society has the same endowments at the beginning of next week; nor is there domination at the point of production, since no one works for anyone else; nor is there differential alienation of labor, since there is not even trade; and, of course, there is equality in initial assets.

Now change the initial distribution of assets, so that each of 5 agents owns 100 seed corn, and the other 995 own nothing but their labor power (or, to be consistent with our former terminology, nothing but their leisure). Preferences remain as before. What is the competitive equilibrium? One possibility is that each of the 995 assetless agents works 3 days on the Farm, and each of the 5 wealthy ones works 1 day in the Factory. But this is not an equilibrium, since there is a lot of excess capital sitting around which can be put to productive use. In particular, the wealthy ones can offer to hire the assetless to work in the Factory on their capital stock. Suppose the "capitalists" offer a corn wage of 1 corn for 2 days labor. Then each capitalist can employ 50 workers, each for 2 days, on his 100 seed corn capital. Each worker produces 4 corn in the Factory with 2 days labor. Thus each capitalist has corn revenues of 200 corn: of that, 100 corn replace the seed used up, 50 are paid in wages, and 50 remain as profits. Capital is now fully employed. But this may or may not be an equilibrium wage: only $5 \times 50 = 250$ workers have been employed, and perhaps the other 745 peasants would prefer to work in the Factory for a real wage of $\frac{1}{2}$ corn per day instead of slaving on the Farm at a real wage of $\frac{1}{3}$ corn per day. If so, the real wage in the Factory will be bid down until the assetless agents are indifferent between doing unalienated, undominated labor on the Farm, and alienated, dominated labor in the Factory. Let us say, for the sake of simplicity, this equilibrating real wage is one corn for $2\frac{1}{2}$ days Factory labor. (In the absence of a preference for Farm life over Factory life, the real wage will equilibrate at 1 corn for 3 days labor, that is, at the peasant's labor opportunity cost of corn, since in this economy there is a scarcity of capital relative to the labor which it could efficiently employ.) Now we have *accumulation* (or at least much more production than before, which I assume is not all eaten by the capitalists), since each capitalist gets a profit of $200 - 100 - 40 = 60$ corn net, and each worker or peasant gets, as in the first economy, 1 corn net. Hence total net product is $995 + (5 \times 60) = 1,295$ corn, instead of 1,000 corn as before. We also have *domination* since some agents are employed by others, and by hypothesis, this gives rise to domination at the point of production. *Differential alienation* has emerged, since some agents (the workers) alienate a large part of their labor to the capitalists, while the capitalists and the peasants alienate no labor (although they work different amounts of time). *Exploitation* has emerged since the workers and peasants all expend more labor than is "embodied" in the corn they get, while the five capitalists work zero days and each gets 60 corn.

Hence, the four phenomena in question emerge simultaneously with exploitation, in the passage from the "egalitarian" economy to the "capitalist" economy. With respect to expropriation, we might also say that it has emerged in the second economy.

III.   The accumulation theory

The unique positive (as opposed to normative) claim among (1) through (4) is the claim that our interest in exploitation is because surplus labor is the source of accumulation and profits. Explanation (1) uses "exploit" in the sense of "to turn a natural resource to economic account; to utilize," while theories (2), (3) and (4) use "exploit" in the sense of "to make use of meanly or unjustly for one's own advantage or profit."[3] A current in Marxism maintains that exploitation is not intended as a normative concept, but as an explanation of the *modus operandi* of capitalism; the production of profits in a system of voluntary exchange and labor transfers is the riddle which must be explained, and which Marx posed in *Capital,* Volume I. The discovery that exploitation of labor is the source of profits answers the riddle. (Even though all commodities exchange "at their values," a surplus systematically emerges at one point in the labor process. For the value which labor produces is greater than what labor power is worth, and hence what it is paid.) Indeed, the claim that exploitation theory should not be construed as normative theory has its source in Marx, as Allen Wood points out.[4]

The formal theorem supporting position (1) was first presented by Okishio and Morishima,[5] and the latter coined it the Fundamental Marxian Theorem (FMT). It demonstrates that in quite general economic models, exploitation of labor exists if and only if profits are positive. The FMT is robust; the error lies in the inference that its veracity implies that profits are *explained* by the exploitation of labor. For, as many writers have

---

[3] Definitions of exploitation are from *Webster's Dictionary* (1966).

[4] Wood (1981), chap. 9.

[5] Morishima (1973). Many authors have since studied and generalized the Fundamental Marxian Theorem.

now observed, *every* commodity (not just labor power) is exploited under capitalism. Oil, for example, can be chosen to be the value numeraire, and embodied oil values of all commodities can be calculated. One can prove that profits are positive if and only if oil is exploited, in the sense that the amount of oil embodied in producing one unit of oil is less than one unit of oil – so oil gives up into production more than it requires back.[6] Thus the exploitation of labor is not the explanation for profits and accumulation any more than is the exploitation of oil or corn or iron. The motivation for the privileged choice of labor as the exploitation numeraire must lie elsewhere, as I have argued elsewhere.[7] In trying to locate the specialness of labor which would justify its choice as the exploitation numeraire, one is inexorably led into arguments that labor is the unique commodity which can be "dominated" or "alienated" – the terrain of argument shifts to a defense of theories like (2) and (3). The dialogue goes something like this, where "Marxist" is defending theory (1):

Marxist: The exploitation of labor accounts for the existence of profits under capitalism. That's why we are interested in exploitation theory, not as normative theory.

Antagonist: But oil is exploited too under capitalism, and its exploitation is, as well, necessary and sufficient for profits. So labor's exploitation does not *explain* profits.

Marxist: No, you are not entitled to say oil is exploited, because oil is not dominated, oil is not alienated from its possessor in any interesting sense during production, one's oil is not a joint product with one's self, there are no problems in extracting the oil from the "oil power." Only labor has these properties and hence only labor is exploited.

Antagonist: Initially you claimed your interest in exploitation theory was as a positive theory only. But you rule out describing oil as exploited for reasons that can only imply exploitation has normative content. For surely the domination and alienation of labor and the attachment of labor to the self are germane not for evaluating whether labor is or is not used in the sense of "turning a natural resource to economic account," but only for deciding whether labor is "made use of meanly or unjustly for [one's own] advantage or profit." You claim to be interested in labor's exploitation only because labor is

---

[6] This Generalized Commodity Exploitation Theorem has been proved and/or observed by many authors, including Vegara (1979); Bowles and Gintis (1981); Wolff (1981); Roemer (1982), Appendix 6.1; Samuelson (1982).

[7] See Roemer (1983a).

exploited in the first sense, but rule out calling other commodities exploited because they are not *exploited* in the second sense. I take it, then, your *true* justification for describing labor as exploited must lie in one of the normative theories of exploitation.

I conclude position (1) cannot be supported as the reason for our interest in exploitation theory.[8] Despite his avowed lack of interest in a normative justification of exploitation theory, the Marxist in the dialogue can only rescue exploitation theory from the jaws of the Generalized Commodity Exploitation Theorem by appealing to a special claim labor has on wearing the exploitation mantle, a claim that seems only to be defensible on grounds of the unfairness or unjustness or nastiness of the conditions of labor's utilization. As G. A. Cohen writes, ". . . Marxists do not often talk about justice, and when they do they tend to deny its relevance, or they say that the idea of justice is an illusion. But I think justice occupies a central place in revolutionary Marxist belief. Its presence is betrayed by particular judgments Marxists make, and by the strength of feeling with which they make them."[9] And I would add, it is only by appealing to conceptions of justice that exploitation theory can be defended as interesting.

IV.   The domination theory

For the remainder of this article, my concern will be to investigate the possibility of defending an interest in exploitation theory for the light it sheds on the three issues of domination, differential alienation, and inequality in ownership of the means of production. My interest in these three issues is normative. If, for example, exploitation can be shown to imply domination of workers by capitalists, and if we argue independently that domination is unjust, then exploitation theory provides at least a partial theory of the injustice of capitalism. (Only a partial theory, since other practices besides domination might be unjust, which exploitation theory would not diagnose.) Identifying the main evil of capitalism as domination, and even extraeconomic domination, is a theme of some contemporary Marxist work.[10] It is not my purpose to evaluate this claim (with which I disagree), but rather to postulate an ethical interest in domination, and ask whether that justifies an interest in exploitation theory.

---

[8] Wolff (1981), while recognizing that the exploitation of labor cannot explain profits, offers a reason other than domination and alienation to be interested in exploitation; as I have argued against his proposal elsewhere (Roemer, 1983a), I will not repeat that discussion.

[9] Cohen (1981). For an opposite point of view, see Wood (1981).

[10] E. M. Wood (1981), Bowles and Gintis (1981), Wright (1982).

It is necessary to distinguish two types of domination by capitalists over workers, domination in the maintenance and enforcement of private property in the means of production, and domination at the point of production (the hierarchical and autocratic structure of work). The line between the two cannot be sharply drawn, but let us superscript the two types domination[1] and domination[2], respectively. I will argue that each of domination[1] and domination[2] implies exploitation, but not conversely. Hence if our interest is in domination, there is no reason to invoke exploitation theory, for the direction of entailment runs the wrong way. Domination may be a bad thing, but there is no reason to run the circuitous route of exploitation theory to make the point. In certain situations, exploitation requires domination[1], but since we cannot know these cases by analyzing the exploitation accounts alone, there is no reason to invoke exploitation if, indeed, our interest in exploitation is only as a barometer of domination[1]. Furthermore, our interest in domination[1] is essentially an interest in the inequality of ownership of the means of production, for the purpose of domination[1] is to enforce that ownership pattern. I maintain if it is domination[1] one claims an interest in, it is really inequality (however defined) in the ownership of the means of production which is the issue. Thus, an ethical interest in domination[1] shifts the discussion to the validity of position (4), while an interest in domination[2] has as its source the moral sentiments reflected in the epigraph from J. S. Mill, in the analogy implied by the term wage slavery.

Domination[1] enforces property relations in two ways. The obvious way is through police power protecting assets, preventing their expropriation by those not owning them. Clearly, since differential ownership of the means of production gives rise to exploitation, this form of domination implies exploitation. The second way domination[1] enters into property relations is to give property its value in the absence of perfect competition. A property right is not a physical asset, it is the right to appropriate the income stream flowing from a certain physical asset. (As C. B. MacPherson points out, it is peculiarly under capitalism that physical assets are confused with the property rights that are related to them.)[11] In the absence of perfect competition, the value of property is not defined by the market. Under perfect competition, all agents are price (and wage) takers, no one has power to bargain or to set the terms of trade. Prices in equilibrium clear markets. Assuming the equilibrium is unique (a heroic assumption), property values are then well-defined. But in the absence of perfect competition, there is room for bargaining, and the value of one's property rights may well be determined by extraeconomic

[11] MacPherson (1978), chap. 1.

domination.[12] (It is more accurate to say values are not defined by the traditional economic data, and at present there is no accepted theory of bargaining under imperfect competition which can determine them.) This is typically the case where markets for particular assets or commodities are thin. The state or landlord which (or who) controls the irrigation canal (an indivisible commodity, with a very thin market) can exact a monopolistic price for its use, giving rise to high peasant exploitation. Due to thin credit markets in rural areas of the underdeveloped countries, local landlords are able to charge usurious interest rates to peasants for consumption loans, increasing the rate of exploitation. To the extent that one thinks incomes from different types of labor under capitalism are politically determined, in order to assert control over the work force,[13] rather than as a reflection of relative scarcities, then domination[1] plays a role in determining exploitation. Domination[1] may determine what certificates people receive, through channeling them into different educational careers, and those certificates determine the value of the person's labor services.[14] In these cases, the peculiarity of domination[1], what contrasts it with feudal domination, is its effect on setting the value of services or assets in the *market* (and thereby influencing the degree of exploitation). Although the power relation inherent in domination[1] is finally realized through markets, contrasted with feudalism, it is similar to feudal exploitation, since one agent has *power* over another which he would not have in a fully developed, perfectly competitive market economy. Thus this exercise of domination[1] is not the essence of capitalism, if capitalism is essentially a competitive system. Certainly Marx's proclaimed task was to explain capitalism in its purest form: where the values of all commodities are explained by "fair trades," that is, values commanded on perfectly competitive markets.

In certain situations, conversely, exploitation implies domination[1]; I mean the trivial observation that exploitation is the consequence of differential ownership of the means of production which, in many cases, the exploited would alter were it not for police power preventing them from doing so. (Hence, if we observe exploitation, there must be domination[1].) It has been maintained, however, that exploitation need not imply domination[1]; Adam Przeworski argues that in some Western European countries workers have the power to expropriate capitalists, and hence they are not

---

[12] Samuel Bowles and Herbert Gintis (1983) claim that even in perfect competition, if there are multiple equilibria, then property values are not well-defined and there is room for domination[1] in determining which set of equilibrium prices will prevail. This is a dubious assertion. If indeed no agent has economic power, in the sense perfect competition postulates, then which of several multiple equilibria will rule is not due to domination[1] but is simply an unanswerable question, given the information in the model.

[13] See Edwards (1979).

[14] Bowles and Gintis (1976).

dominated[1], but they do not, because it is not in their perceived interests to do so.[15] Moreover, in Sections V and VI below I show that exploitation can exist without differential ownership of the means of production; therefore, presumably exploitation can exist even though all agents accept as just the property rights, and so domination[1] (police power to protect property) need not obtain. In summary, my claims concerning domination[1] are these: (a) with respect to the exercise of power under conditions of imperfect competition, domination[1] exists and is perhaps important in capitalism, and more so in less developed capitalism, but it is characteristically noncapitalist, that is, being due to imperfect competition and thin markets; (b) it implies exploitation, but that provides no reason to be interested in exploitation theory, if our concern is really with domination[1]; (c) in some cases, perhaps the archetypical case, exploitation implies domination[1] in the sense of police power protecting property, but in that case it is not the domination that concerns us but the unjust inequality in the distribution of the means of production. If (c) is our reason for justifying an interest in exploitation theory, we are invoking position (4) and not position (2), since domination[1] in this case is only the means to maintain the unequal distribution of assets which is the basis for our condemnation of capitalism.

The more usual conception of domination is the second one; domination[2] does not involve the protection or creation of value in capitalist property, but rather the hierarchical, nondemocratic relations in capitalist workplaces. Of course, this hierarchy presumably creates (additional) profits, and therefore leads to an increased valuation of capitalist property, and hence is similar to the role of domination[1]; but in discussing domination[2] I am specifically concerned with the domination of the worker's self, the relation of subordination he enters into with the capitalist when he enters the workplace. While our moral opposition to domination[1] shares its foundation with our moral opposition to feudalism, our opposition to domination[2] shares its foundation with our opposition to slavery. (The analogy is inexact, since many feudal practices involved domination[2] over the selves of serfs; for the sake of the analogy, I envisage "pure feudalism" as a system where feudal dues are paid because of extraeconomic coercion, but the serf never sees or interacts personally with the lord.)

Although domination[2] can create the conditions for profitability and therefore exploitation of labor, the converse is in general not the case. Exploitation does not imply the existence of domination[2]. I showed in my book that the class and exploitation relations of a capitalist economy using labor markets can be precisely replicated with a capitalist economy

[15] Przeworski (1980).

using credit markets,[16] where domination[2] does not exist. In Labor Market Capitalism, agents optimize, given their endowments of property, and end up choosing either to sell labor power, to hire labor power, or to produce for the market using their own labor power on their own account. Agents segregate themselves into five classes, based on the particular ways they relate to the labor market. The Class Exploitation Correspondence Principle demonstrates that everyone who optimizes by selling labor power is exploited, and everyone who optimizes by hiring labor is an exploiter. It was assumed in that analysis that agents make the decision to sell labor entirely on economic grounds; they do not calculate as part of their objective the disutility associated with being dominated[2], with working under a boss. In Credit Market Capitalism, there is no labor market, but a market for lending capital at an interest rate. At the equilibrium, some agents will lend capital, some will borrow capital, some will use their own capital for production. Again, agents segregate themselves into five classes defined by the particular ways they relate to the credit market. Again, the Class Exploitation Correspondence Principle holds: any agent who optimizes by borrowing capital will turn out to be exploited. Moreover, the Isomorphism Theorem states that these two hypothetical capitalisms are identical insofar as class and exploitation properties are concerned. An agent who, under Labor Market Capitalism, was a member of a labor-selling class, and was therefore exploited, will be a member of a capital-borrowing class in Credit Market Capitalism, and will be exploited. This result replays the Wicksell–Samuelson theme that it is irrelevant, for the distribution of income, whether capital hires labor or labor hires capital; the mild sin of omission of these writers was not to point out that propertyless agents are exploited in either case, whether they be the hirers or sellers of the factor. In Labor Market Capitalism there is domination[2], but in Credit Market Capitalism, there is not.[17]

Moreover, an even sharper example may be constructed of an economy possessing no labor or credit market, but only markets for produced commodities which are traded among individual producers. In such an economy exploitation will result at equilibrium, in general, if there is initial inequality in the ownership of means of production. But in this exchange and production economy, there are no relations of domination[2] of any kind; the exploitation can be accomplished through "invisible trade." It is possible to argue that there is exploitation without class in this economy,

---

[16] For a detailed presentation of this material, see Roemer (1982), pts. 1 and 2. For a summary, see Roemer (1982a).

[17] I am speaking of a pure form of Credit Market Capitalism; in actual credit markets, lenders often supervise debtors if sufficient collateral is not available, or if there would be problems in enforcing collection of collateral.

since all producers enjoy the same relation to the means of production: they work only on their own.[18] Indeed, this example may be taken as the archetype of exploitation, or unequal exchange, between countries where neither labor nor capital flows across borders. Differential initial endowments of countries will give rise to exploitation in trade, even when no relations of domination[2] through international labor migration or capital lending take place.[19]

The previous paragraphs claim to demonstrate that the existence of exploitation does not imply the existence of domination[2], and hence our putative interest in exploitation theory cannot be justified on grounds of a more basic interest in domination[2]. Here I follow Marx, in modeling capitalism as a system where there are no market frictions, but where goods exchange competitively at their market-determined prices. In particular, it seems appropriate, for this thought experiment, to assume all contracts are costlessly enforceable and can be perfectly delineated. For Marx wished to show the economic viability of capitalism in the absence of cheating: and that means contracts are well-defined and observed by all. Now the principal reason domination[2] exists is that the labor contract is not costlessly enforceable, nor can it be perfectly delineated. This point is usually put more graphically when Marxists speak of the problems of extracting the labor from the labor power. Indeed, the contemporary labor process literature addresses the methods capitalism (and perhaps socialism) has developed to solve this problem.[20] But for our thought experiment, we are entitled to assume the delivery of *labor* (not simply labor power) for the wage is as simple and enforceable a transaction as the delivery of an apple for a dime. In such a world, exploitation continues to exist, but domination[2] does not. And I claim Marxists would be almost as critical of such a perfect capitalism as they are of existing capitalism, replete as the real thing is with domination[2] due to the contract enforcement problem. Indeed, Marxists consider sharecroppers and borrowers to be *exploited* (unjustly so, that is), even when domination[2] is absent from those contracts. The Isomorphism Theorem I quoted was an attempt to develop this point formally, that in a world absenting deleterious domination[2] effects, the exploitation observed in labor markets would be indistinguishable from that observed in credit or sharecropping arrangements.[21]

A criticism of the Isomorphism Theorem can be made as follows. If one wishes to study the relationship between domination[2] and exploitation,

---

[18] For the details of this economy see Roemer (1982), chap. 1; for a simple example, see Roemer (1983).

[19] See Roemer (1983b).

[20] For example, see Braverman (1974) and Edwards (1979).

[21] Further discussion of some of these issues can be found in Roemer (1982b).

then the model of the Class Exploitation Correspondence Theorem and the Isomorphism Theorem is inappropriate, because it is there assumed that domination[2] is not an issue to the people involved. In reply to this point, I have worked out a revised model (which is available in detail from the author) where domination[2] effects exist. These are captured as follows: each agent has an initial endowment of means of production, which takes on a value as finance capital at given prices. He seeks to maximize a utility function of income and work performed. It matters to him whether the work is performed in his own shop, or under a boss. Thus, the utility function has three arguments: income, labor performed on one's own account, and wage labor performed for others. Subject to his capital constraint, determined by initial asset holdings and prices, each agent maximizes utility. The domination[2] postulate is that every agent would rather work on his own account than for a boss, and this is reflected in the utility function. At equilibrium, agents sort themselves into five classes:

> Class 1: those who only hire others
> Class 2: those who hire others and work on their own account
> Class 3: those who only work on their own account
> Class 4: those who work on their own account and sell wage labor
> Class 5: those who only sell wage labor.

I say an agent is *dominated* if he maximizes utility subject to constraint by placing himself in classes 4 or 5, and he is *dominating* if he optimizes by being in classes 1 or 2. The theorem, which can be called the Exploitation-Domination Correspondence, states that any dominated agent is exploited and any dominating agent is an exploiter. The converse, however, does not hold. In particular, agents in class position 3 will often be either exploited or exploiting, but they are neither dominated nor dominating.

It is therefore difficult to justify an interest in exploitation if our real concern is domination[2], for two reasons. First, domination[2] is directly observable (simply look at who hires whom) and exploitation is not. Hence, calculating whether an agent is exploited (a difficult calculation, necessitating all sorts of technological information to compute socially necessary labor times) would be a strangely circuitous route to concluding he is dominated[2]. Secondly, it is not true that an exploited agent is necessarily dominated or that an exploiter is necessarily dominating; the Exploitation-Domination Correspondence states the converse. Exploited (exploiting) agents who are not dominated (dominating) would have a confused ethical status if our judgment about them is made on the basis of exploitation, but our interest in exploitation is as a proxy for domination. The hard-working shopkeeper or sharecropper would have our ethical sympathy on grounds of exploitation but not domination[2]. This does not help us provide an independent reason for an interest in exploitation theory, of course, which is the task at hand. Thus exploitation is a poor statistic for domination[2] on several counts.

My conclusions concerning domination[2] are: (a) our interest in exploitation theory cannot be justified on grounds that it is indicative of or a proxy for domination[2], either logically or on pragmatic grounds; (b) although domination[2] is prevalent in existing capitalism, it is arguably a phenomenon of second order in a *Marxist* condemnation of capitalism, being associated with the imperfections in writing and enforcing contracts, while Marxist arguments should apply to a capitalism with frictionless contracts. In addition, although not argued here (as my concern is not with the evils of domination[2] but with the evils of exploitation), I think the analogy between domination[2] and slavery is ill-founded. It is arguable that the life of the small independent producer is not so marvelous compared to that of the factory worker, that the transition from poor peasant to urban proletarian is one made willingly, even gladly, and with reasonably good information, where the erstwhile independent producer is knowledgeable about the trade-offs. I say arguable, not obvious: but it is more than arguable that no population ever voluntarily committed itself to slavery willingly and gladly.

V.   The alienation theory

To discuss properly a possible justification of an interest in exploitation theory on grounds that it is indicative of different degrees of alienation, we must separate alienation from, on the one hand, domination, and on the other hand, differential ownership of the means of production, as those issues are discussed separately under (2) and (4). An interest in differential alienation must be defended *per se,* even in the absence of domination and differential ownership of the means of production. Perhaps the most graphic vision of exploitation is as the extraction of surplus labor from the worker: the extraction, that is, of more labor from him than he receives back as social labor in what he consumes or can purchase with his wages. His labor is alienated from him not because he performs it for another (under conditions of domination[2]) but because it is labor performed to produce goods for exchange, not for use. More precisely, the goods produced are traded to an anonymous final recipient on a market, and thus labor becomes alienated in a way it would not have been were there a social division of labor but the final disposition of goods was in one's "community." (See B. Traven's marvelous story "Assembly Line" for a discussion of alienation.)[22] Now if everyone started off with the same endowment of means of production and had the same skills and preferences, but all agents produced goods for a market, there would be alienation of labor in this sense, but not differential alienation, since it can be shown everyone would receive back as much social labor in goods as he alienated in production for the market. Exploitation can be said to exist in a market economy when some people alienate more labor than they receive from others, and some alienate less labor than they receive back. Why might alienation be a bad thing? Perhaps because one's time is the only really valuable asset one has, and production for the market is considered to be a waste of time. Perhaps because productive labor for oneself or one's community is what constitutes the good life, but the use of labor to earn revenues solely to survive, not to produce for others directly, is a prostitution of a deep aspect of the self. Thus alienation might be bad, and differential alienation might be unjust or *exploitative*. (There are certainly other forms of alienation in Marx, but this kind of differential alienation appears to be the only kind for which exploitation as the unequal exchange of labor is an indicator.)

Any ethical condemnation of differential alienation cannot be a welfarist one, in the sense of Amartya Sen,[23] based only on the preferences of individuals. For I will outline a situation where agents with different preferences start with equal endowments of resources and voluntarily enter into relations of differential alienation (i.e., exploitation) as the way to maximize their utilities. Consider two agents, Adam and Karl, who each start off with the same amount of corn, which is the only good in the

---

[22] Traven (1973). In the story "Assembly Line," a Mexican Indian has been offered a huge sum of money, more than he has ever dreamed of, to mass-produce little baskets for a New York department store, which he has formerly made only in small quantities for the local market. The New York buyer is astonished that the Indian is not interested in the proposal. The Indian explains: "'Yes, I know that jefecito, my little chief,' the Indian answered, entirely unconcerned. 'It must be the same price because I cannot make any other one. Besides, señor, there's still another thing which perhaps you don't know. You see, my good lordy and caballero, I've to make these canastitas my own way and with my song in them and with bits of my soul woven into them. If I were to make them in great numbers there would no longer be my soul in each, or my songs. Each would look like the other with no difference whatever and such a thing would slowly eat my heart. Each has to be another song which I hear in the morning when the sun rises and when the birds begin to chirp and the butterflies come and sit down on my baskets so that I may see a new beauty, because, you see, the butterflies like my baskets and the pretty colors in them, that's why they come and sit down, and I can make my canastitas after them. And now, señor jefecito, if you will kindly excuse me, I have wasted much time already, although it was a pleasure and a great honor to hear the talk of such a distinguished caballero like you. But I'm afraid I've to attend to my work now, for day after tomorrow is market day in town and I got to take my baskets there.'"

[23] See, for a definition of welfarism, Sen (1979b).

economy and can be used both as capital (seed corn) and as the consumption good. We have the same technological possibilities as in the model of Section II.

> Farm: 3 days labor produces 1 bushel corn
> Factory: 1 day labor plus 1 bushel seed corn produces 2 bushels corn

Adam and Karl each start with $\frac{1}{2}$ bushel of corn, and each will live and must consume for many weeks. (Recall, a week is the time period required in each case to bring corn to fruition, although the amount of labor expended during the week differs in the two processes.) Karl is highly averse to performing work in the present: he desires only to consume 1 bushel of corn per week, subject to the requirement that he not run down his seed stock. In the first week, he therefore works $\frac{1}{2}$ day in the Factory (fully utilizing his seed corn) and $1\frac{1}{2}$ days on the Farm, producing a total of $1\frac{1}{2}$ bushels, one of which he consumes at harvest time, leaving him with $\frac{1}{2}$ bushel to start with in week 2. Adam accumulates; he works $\frac{1}{2}$ day in the Factory, utilizing his seed, and $4\frac{1}{2}$ days on the Farm, producing $2\frac{1}{2}$ bushels gross. After consuming 1 bushel, he has $1\frac{1}{2}$ bushels left to start week 2. In week 2, Karl works up his own seed stock in $\frac{1}{2}$ day in the Factory producing 1 bushel; then, instead of going to the Farm, Karl borrows or rents Adam's $1\frac{1}{2}$ bushels of seed and works it up in the Factory. This takes Karl precisely $1\frac{1}{2}$ days, and he produces 3 bushels gross in the factory. Of the 3 bushels he keeps $\frac{1}{2}$ bushel, and returns $2\frac{1}{2}$ bushels to Adam (Adam's principal of $1\frac{1}{2}$ bushels plus interest of 1 bushel). Indeed, Karl is quite content with this arrangement, for he has worked for a total of 2 days and received $1\frac{1}{2}$ bushels, just as in week 1, when he had to use the inferior Farm technology. Adam, on the other hand, receives a profit of 1 bushel from Karl's labor, which he consumes, and is left again to begin week 3 with $1\frac{1}{2}$ bushels. He has not worked at all in week 2. This arrangement can continue forever, with Karl working 2 days each week and consuming 1 bushel, and Adam working 5 days during the first week, and zero days thereafter. Clearly there is exploitation in the sense of differential alienation in this story, in all weeks after the first, but its genesis is in the differential preferences Karl and Adam have for the consumption of corn and leisure over their lives. Thus exploitation cannot be blamed, in this story, on differential initial ownership of the means of production, nor can the situation be condemned on Paretian grounds, as no other arrangement would suit Karl and Adam more. They chose this path of consumption/leisure streams. Indeed during any week Karl could decide to work on the Farm and accumulate more seed corn, thus enabling him to cut his working hours in future weeks. (I am assuming he is *able* to do so; if he is not, then Karl is handicapped, and the ethical verdict is certainly more complicated.) But he does not.

Actually the above example does not quite rigorously make the point that differential alienation cannot be condemned on Paretian grounds: because if alienation is to be so condemned, then the agents themselves should distinguish between the performance of alienated and nonalienated labor in their utility functions. That is, each agent should prefer to perform nonalienated labor to alienated labor. If we now modify the story to include such a preference, then the above example fails, since Karl could have achieved the same outcome of 2 days labor and 1 bushel corn, each week, by continuing his autarkic program of working partly in the factory on his *own* seed corn, and then moving to the farm and working for his *own* consumption. Karl would perform no alienated labor (producing goods only for himself) and would hence be better off. Were this to occur, then Adam would have to work some in the Factory each period, since Karl refused to borrow seed capital from him. But this failure of the example can easily be fixed: simply note that Adam could work a little longer in the first week, producing a little more seed capital, and then in future weeks he could lend his seed to Karl at a sufficiently low interest rate that Karl would be compensated for his distaste in performing alienated labor by the savings in overall labor he achieves by borrowing from Adam. Thus both Adam and Karl can strictly benefit from cooperation, even if each has a distaste for performing alienated labor, so long as there is a trade-off between that distaste and the taste for leisure. Hence the claim is true: that even if alienation matters to people, an outcome of differential alienation cannot be condemned on Paretian or welfarist grounds, nor on grounds of inequality in the distribution of assets, since an example has been constructed where agents who start off with identical endowments choose to enter into relations of differential alienation. And if alienation, as I have defined it, seems unrealistic in a society of two people, then replicate the economy one millionfold, so there are a million each of Karls and Adams. Moreover, we can introduce many goods into the economy so that there is a real social division of labor, and some Adams make car fenders all day long and other Adams make pinheads all day long. But the same result can be constructed: starting from the same endowments, agents with different preferences for the various goods, leisure, and nonalienated labor, may well choose to enter into relations of differential alienation.

So if we are to conclude that differential alienation is *exploitative,* in the sense of ethically condemnable, that verdict cannot be arrived at on Paretian grounds. Indeed, the above example enables us to speak of "the impossibility of being a differential-alienation-condemning Paretian" in exactly the sense of "the impossibility of being a Paretian liberal."[24] For, as the last several paragraphs demonstrate, to avoid alienation Karl must produce only for himself (using both the Farm and the Factory), which will require Adam to work each week for himself. But in the example this is not a Pareto optimal allocation of labor. Only by engaging in differentially alienated labor can Karl and Adam take full advantage of the efficient Factory technology. Thus even the mild welfarist requirement of Pareto efficiency comes into conflict with exploitation-as-differential-alienation. There may still be grounds for calling such differential alienation *exploitative,* but it appears such grounds must be based on *rights,* not welfare outcomes as the agents see them.

We are led to ask, then, whether a person has a *right* not to perform more alienated labor than another person. We might be able to argue that one has a right not to be *forced* to perform more alienated labor than another: but that will lead straight into a discussion of differential ownership of the means of production, which is not the issue here.[25] For in our story Karl chooses to perform more alienated labor than Adam from a position of equality of resources and opportunity. Nobody forces him, unless we slide further down the slippery slope of defining the "resources" available to the person and argue that Karl was forced because he had no choice of the personal characteristics that gave rise to his *carpe diem* preferences. I cannot see a compelling argument for declaiming such a right, in part because I cannot see a compelling argument against the performance of alienated labor, let alone differential alienation. I think moral intuitions on this matter must take their cue from history. It is far from clear that people, in historical reality, have had an aversion to performing alienated labor. Indeed, many (including Marxists) argue that production for the market has been a liberating process for many populations, a process which they enter into willingly. (Recall, we are not concerned here with domination, of choosing to work for others, but only with alienation, of producing for a market.)

I think the argument for postulating that a person has a right not to perform more alienated labor than another person is extremely weak. Hence I cannot defend an interest in exploitation as a proxy for an interest in differentially alienated labor. The problem is that there is not necessarily anything condemnable with differentially alienated labor if it arises from differential preferences which we accept as well-formed and not like handicaps. To consider "myopic" preferences to be handicaps, we would have to argue that there is an upper bound on correct rates of

[24] On the impossibility of being a Paretian liberal, see, for instance, Sen (1979), chap. 6.
[25] For a discussion of why proletarians can be thought of as forced to alienate their labor, even in a world of voluntary wage contracts, see Cohen (1983a).

time discount, and people who discount time more highly are handicapped. While in some instances the case for such a handicap can be made (typically, when a high rate of time discount is a consequence of having been severely deprived of assets in the past), in the general instance, it cannot be. The last parenthetical aside cues the most important situation where we might view differential alienation, arrived at from differential preferences, as exploitative: when those preferences are in fact learned as a consequence of differential ownership of the means of production in the past. Suppose the rich learn to save, and the poor do not; having learned such rates of time preference from their past environments, formerly rich Adam may end up accumulating and exploiting formerly poor Karl, even when the new state starts them off with clean slates by redistributing the initial endowment to one of equality between them. But in this case our justification for thinking of differential alienation as exploitative is due to the rich background of Adam and the poor one of Karl; we are reduced to an argument for an interest in exploitation as an indicator of inequality in the ownership of assets, to which I soon turn.

The possibility remains that even though nondifferentially alienated outcomes cannot be defended on Paretian grounds, nor on grounds of rights, perhaps they can be defended for perfectionist reasons. I will not attempt here to defend my position against a perfectionist attack, except to say that my defense would amplify on the point of the two previous paragraphs. It seems that differential alienation of labor, from an initial position of equal opportunity and fair division of assets, can vastly increase the welfare and life quality of people, and so a perfectionist defense of nonalienation seems remote.

VI.   Differential ownership of productive assets

The fourth reason to be interested in exploitation is as an index of the inequality in ownership of productive assets. This approach is represented, for example, in the epigraph from Marx. The Marxist position that socialist revolution entails redistribution or nationalization of the means of production to eliminate exploitation traces to this conception of exploitation. (In contrast, the emphasis of exploitation as domination[2] gives rise to industrial democracy as the key aspect of socialist transformation.) In my recent book and in other articles I have claimed that this is the most compelling reason to be interested in exploitation, by showing in a series of models that the existence of exploitation is equivalent to inequality in distribution of initial assets, and that the rich exploit the poor. Hence exploitation theory can be justified if we accept a presumption that initial inequality in the wealth of agents is unjust, for exploitation (in these models) is essentially equivalent to initial inequality of assets. Nevertheless this may appear to weaken the argument for being interested in exploitation (defined as I have done throughout this article), for it is probably easier to observe inequality in ownership of assets than it is to calculate exploitation accounts. Surprisingly, however, if our ethical interest is really in initial inequality of ownership of assets, the importance of Marxian *class* theory is strengthened. For in the models I investigated, class membership is closely related to wealth: the "higher" one's class position, the wealthier one is in productive assets. In particular, any agent who optimizes by hiring others is wealthy and is an exploiter, and any agent who optimizes by selling labor power is relatively poor and is exploited. Now class relations are still easier to observe than wealth, and so the Class–Wealth Correspondence enables us to conclude a great deal about the initial distribution of productive assets by observing how people relate to the hiring and selling of labor power. Class position provides a convenient proxy for the fundamental inequality in which, I claim, we are interested; but exploitation drops out as an unnecessary detour.

Still, according to this description of the results, exploitation may be thought of as an *innocuous* appendix to our true ethical concerns: innocuous because although unnecessary, surplus value accounts correspond to underlying inequality in ownership of assets in the proper way. I now go further and claim that in the general case, exploitation theory leads to results which may conflict directly with the inequality-of-productive-assets theory. And therefore, finding no other reasons to be interested in exploitation accounts, I must say exploitation theory, in the general case, is misconceived. It does not provide a proper model or account of Marxian moral sentiments; the proper Marxian claim, I think, is for equality in the distribution of productive assets, not for the elimination of exploitation.

The "general case" in which exploitation accounts and inequality accounts diverge occurs when general preferences for agents are admitted. In particular, if preferences for income versus leisure differ across agents, the divergence can occur. Indeed, the two theories can diverge even for cases when preferences are identical for all agents, as I will show. In my book, I assumed preferences of all agents were the same, and of certain special forms: either all agents wanted to accumulate as much as possible, or they wanted just to subsist, two preference profiles that appear to be polar opposites. Indeed, there may be a strong case that the assumption of one of these profiles of preferences is not a bad one, historically, in which case exploitation theory might correspond empirically to Marxian ethical conceptions. But I am concerned here with the logical foundations of exploitation theory, and for that purpose general and abstract formulations with respect to admissible preference profiles are essential.

Before proceeding, it is important to correct a possible misimpression from an earlier article.[26] I argued there that a pure inequality-of-assets definition was better than the Marxian surplus value definition for characterizing exploitation; that claim is weaker than the claim here, for in that article I took the Marxian surplus value definition to mean "the extraction of surplus labor from one agent by another in a production relation." In the present paper, I am taking exploitation to be defined by "unequal exchange of labor," whether or not there is a production relation between the agents in which one "extracts" the labor of another. In the previous article, I did not argue against the "unequal exchange of labor" conception of exploitation, except to say that the inequality-of-property definition was a cleaner but equivalent characterization of the same phenomenon. I now claim that "unequal exchange of labor" is not characterized by the inequality of productive assets when we admit general preferences structures.

I shall show that if the preferences of agents do not satisfy a certain condition, then it can happen that the asset-rich are exploited by the asset-poor: the flow of surplus value goes the "wrong way." This can occur even when all agents have identical preference orderings for income and leisure – but what is critical is that the agents' preference for leisure must change rather substantially, and in a particular way, as their wealth changes. Once this example is demonstrated, one can no longer claim that exploitation is a significant index of inequality of initial assets which measures the flow from the asset-poor to the asset-rich.

I will first give a general explanation of why the correspondence between exploitation and wealth can fail. Then, a simple example will be given illustrating the phenomenon. Readers may skip directly to the example on page 89 without undue loss of comprehension.

A brief review of the Class Exploitation Correspondence Principle and the Class–Wealth Correspondence Principle is necessary. The model consists of many agents; agent i begins with a vector of impersonal assets ω^i that can be used in production, plus one unit of labor power. (I assume labor is homogeneous, as I have throughout this article. If labor is heterogeneous, then poking holes in exploitation theory is almost child's play. Homogeneity of labor at least gives the theory a fighting chance.) There is a common technology which all agents can use. Each agent has a utility function, over goods and leisure. Since we have shown that an interest in exploitation cannot be justified by an interest in domination or alienation, we need not put into the utility function any concerns with where or under whom the labor one expends is performed. *Assume all agents have identical preferences,* although they own different initial bundles ω^i.

---

[26] See Essay 2.

Facing a vector of commodity prices p, which I normalize by letting the wage be unity, agent i now has finance capital in amount $p\omega^i$. Given his capital constraint, he chooses how much labor to supply and how much income to earn in order to maximize his utility. An equilibrium price vector is of the usual sort, allowing all markets, including the market for labor, to clear. An agent typically has three sources of revenue in the model: wage income from selling some labor power, profit income from hiring others, and proprietary income, from working himself on his own finance capital. If we introduce a capital market, there will also be interest or rental income, but that does not change the story at all. An agent is exploited if his total revenues do not enable him to purchase goods embodying as much social labor as he chose to expend in production. Class position of agents has been discussed before, in Section IV above.

At the equilibrium prices, let us call the wealth of agent i: $W^i = p\omega^i$. Wealth is the valuation at equilibrium prices of his nonlabor assets, his finance capital. We can view the labor he decides to supply in production, by maximizing his utility, as a function, at equilibrium prices p, of this wealth. Call this labor supply function $L(W)$. If agents possessed different utility functions, then we would have to write different labor supply functions, $L^i(W)$, but by assumption, all agents have the same preferences. $L(W^i)$ can be thought of as a cross-sectional labor supply function, which tells how much labor any agent will supply at the equilibrium prices, if his wealth is W^i. Now the key lemma is this: membership in the five classes is monotonically related to the ratio $\gamma^i = W^i/L(W^i)$ and so is exploitation status.[27] That is, the larger is the ratio γ^i, the higher up the class ladder agent i is, and the more of an exploiter he is. (The class ladder is described in Section IV above.) When do class and exploitation status of agents give us a good proxy for the agent's initial wealth of nonlabor assets? Precisely when the index γ^i is monotonically related to wealth W^i. Thus exploitation and class can be indicators of our interest in wealth inequality precisely when $d\gamma/dW > 0$, that is, when the γ index increases with wealth. Taking the derivative:

$$\frac{d\gamma}{dW} > 0 \quad \text{if and only if} \quad \frac{dL}{dW} < \frac{L}{W} \quad \text{or} \quad \frac{dL}{L}\bigg/\frac{dW}{W} < 1.$$

This last condition is of a familiar type in economics: it says that the labor supplied by the agent is inelastic with respect to his wealth; that is, a 1 percent increase in the agent's wealth will cause him to increase his supply of labor by less than 1 percent. Summarizing:

---

[27] For a demonstration of this lemma, see Roemer (1982), p. 176.

Theorem: *Under identical preferences of agents, class and exploitation status accurately reflect inequality in distribution of finance capital (productive assets other than labor) if and only if the labor supplied by agents is inelastic with respect to their wealth at equilibrium prices. If preferences differ, then class and exploitation status accurately reflect wealth if and only if cross-sectionally labor is inelastically supplied as wealth increases.*

This elasticity condition is perhaps a reasonable condition on preferences.[28] In particular, we often think of agents supplying *less* labor as their wealth increases, in which case the above condition certainly holds. The condition allows agents to increase the labor they supply with increases in wealth, so long as they do not increase the labor supplied faster than their wealth increases. However, if we allow an "unrestricted domain" of preferences for goods and leisure (even if we constrain all agents to have the same preferences!), then the relation between exploitation and class, on the one hand, and wealth on the other, is lost. It will be possible to design cases where we have an agent Karl who hires labor (and does not sell it), who will be an exploiter by the Class Exploitation Correspondence Principle, and another agent Adam who sells labor and is exploited, *but* Adam is wealthier than Karl, *and* Karl and Adam have the *same preferences* over bundles of goods and leisure. This can only happen when the elasticity condition fails, and that provides the intuition which resolves the apparent paradox. With a wealth-elastic labor supply function, Adam, who is rich, wants to work terribly hard, while Karl, who is poor, hardly wants to work at all. Indeed Karl does not even want to work hard enough to utilize fully his paltry stock of productive assets, and so he hires Adam to work up the rest of his capital for him, which Adam is willing to do, even after he has worked all he can on his substantial stock of assets. Thus poor Karl hires and, by the Class Exploitation Correspondence Principle, exploits rich Adam.

Noneconomists might think of Karl and Adam in the above example as having different preference orderings, since one wants to supply a lot of labor and the other a little. But preference orderings are defined for

---

[28] In the two special cases I studied in Roemer (1982), the correspondence between exploitation and wealth followed because the elasticity condition held. For the subsistence model, the elasticity of labor supply with respect to wealth is negative and for the accumulation model it is zero. In the subsistence model, agents desire to minimize labor performed subject to consuming a certain subsistence bundle which is independent of wealth; in the accumulation model, they desire only to accumulate, and each works as much as is physically possible (an amount assumed to be the same for all). I believed, falsely, that since these two models posed behavior representing two extremes with respect to leisure preferences that the correspondence between exploitation and wealth would hold for any preferences uniform across agents.

an individual over all bundles of labor (or leisure) and goods he might consume, and so it is perfectly consistent for Karl and Adam to have the same preference orderings yet to supply labor differentially because of their different wealths. Saying they have the same preference orderings implies they have the same utility function and the same labor supply *function,* not that they supply the same amount of labor.

We have now to consider the case where differential preferences are admitted. Then, *a fortiori,* the index $\gamma^i = W^i / L^i(W^i)$ will in general not be monotonically correlated with wealth W^i. Now, $L^i(W)$ can vary with i. We cannot say the rich exploit the poor with any degree of rigor. We can only be assured that the rich exploit the poor when the elasticity condition holds cross-sectionally, that an increment in wealth implies a less than proportionate increment in labor supplied. Failing this relation, the poor can be exploiters of the rich.

Notice *cross-sectional* labor supply behavior which is wealth-elastic might be quite common if agents have different preferences for leisure and income. Indeed, it is possible for labor supply cross-sectionally to exhibit elasticity with respect to wealth, while each individual agent has a "well-behaved" wealth-inelastic labor supply schedule. Those who become wealthy (in one of the versions of the neoclassical paradigm) are those who have a low preference for leisure. Hence the individuals we observe as wealthy could have gotten that way by working long hours – although their own labor supply schedules might be inelastic as their wealth increases. We might then very well observe labor supply across the population increasing faster than wealth for some interval of wealths. For an individual's labor supply to be wealth-elastic, leisure must be an inferior good for him; but for the population labor supply to be cross-sectionally wealth-elastic, this is not the case.

For the sake of concreteness, here is the promised example illustrating the divergence between exploitation and inequality of assets. It does not matter, for this example, whether the different amounts of labor which Karl and Adam supply are a consequence of different preference orderings or the same preference orderings. All that matters is that given their different initial wealths, they optimize by supplying labor in the pattern indicated. I postulate the same Farm and Factory technologies as before:

> Farm: 3 days labor (and no capital) produces 1 bushel of corn
> Factory: 1 day labor plus 1 bushel seed corn produces 2 bushels corn

This time, however, Karl has an initial endowment of 1 corn and Adam of 3 corn. Denote a bundle of corn and labor as (C, L). Thus $(1, 1)$ represents the consumption of 1 corn and the provision of 1 day's labor. I assume, as before, that each agent is not willing to run down his initial stock of corn (because he might die at any time, and he wishes, at least, not to deprive his only child of the same endowment that his parent passed down to him). Suppose we know at least this about Adam's and Karl's preferences:

$$(\tfrac{2}{3}, 0) >_K (1, 1)$$

$$(3\tfrac{1}{3}, 4) >_A (3, 3)$$

(To translate, the first line says Karl would strictly prefer to consume $\frac{2}{3}$ bushel of corn and not to work at all than to work 1 day and consume 1 bushel.) Now note that Karl can achieve $(1, 1)$ by working up his 1 corn in the Factory in 1 day; he consumes 1 of the bushels produced, and starts week 2 with his initial 1 bushel. Likewise, Adam can achieve $(3, 3)$ by working up his 3 bushels in the Factory with 3 days' labor; he consumes 3 of the 6 bushels produced, and replaces his initial stock for week 2. But this solution is not Pareto optimal. For now suppose Karl lends his 1 bushel to Adam. Adam works up the total of 4 bushels in 4 days in the Factory, produces 8 bushels, and pays back Karl his original bushel plus $\frac{2}{3}$ bushel as interest for the loan. This leaves Adam with $3\frac{1}{3}$ bushels, after replacing his 3 bushels of initial stock. Thus Karl can consume $\frac{2}{3}$ bushel and work not at all, which he prefers to $(1, 1)$, and Adam consumes the bundle $(3\frac{1}{3}, 4)$ which he prefers to $(3, 3)$. We have a strict Pareto improvement. (The interest rate charged is the competitive one; for if Adam, instead of borrowing from Karl, worked on the Farm for an extra day he would make precisely $\frac{1}{3}$ bushel of corn.) This arrangement may continue forever: Karl never works and lives off the interest from Adam's labor. According to the unequal exchange definition of exploitation, there is no shadow of a doubt that Karl exploits Adam. However, Adam is richer than Karl. On what basis can we condemn this exploitation? Not on the basis of domination or alienation (we have decided), and surely not on the basis of differential ownership of the means of production, since the exploitation is going the "wrong way." Indeed, eliminating inequality in the ownership of the means of production should improve the lot of the exploited at the expense of the exploiters. (That is the property relations definition I formalized in Essay 2.) But in this case an equalization of the initial assets at 2 bushels of corn for each renders the exploiter (Karl) better off, and the exploited (Adam) worse off![29]

It should be remarked that the preferences postulated in this example for Karl and Adam are not perverse in the sense that they can be embedded

---

[29] Actually, even if there is a unique equilibrium there are some perverse cases in general equilibrium models when an agent can improve his final welfare by giving away some of his initial endowment. This is not such a case.

in a full preference relation which has convex indifference curves of the usual sort, in corn-leisure space. This is the case even when Karl and Adam possess the same (convex) preferences.

If we have reason for calling unjust the postulated inequality in the original distribution of seed-corn assets, then it is Karl who is suffering an injustice in the previous example, and not Adam; but according to exploitation theory, Karl exploits Adam. As I have said, I think the most consistent Marxian ethical position is against inequality in the initial distribution of productive assets; when exploitation accounts reflect the unequal distribution of productive assets in the proper way (that the rich exploit the poor), that is what makes exploitation theory attractive. But if that correlation can fail, as it has, then no foundation remains for a justification of exploitation theory.

It might still be maintained that two injustices are involved when productive assets are unjustly distributed: the injustice of that distribution of stocks, and the injustice of the flows arising from them.[30] Exploitation is a statement concerning the injustice of flows, but I have invoked it only as a proxy for the underlying injustice (more precisely, inequality) of stocks. There remains the necessity for some judgment of the injustice of flows emanating from an unjust distribution of stocks: my point is that flows of labor are an imperfect proxy for that. In the Karl–Adam example, I say that Adam is unjustly gaining from the flows between him and Karl, if the initial distribution of stocks is unjust against Karl, despite the formal exploitation of Adam by Karl. In cases where exploitation does render the correct judgment on the injustice of flows, then perhaps the degree or rate of exploitation is useful in assessing the degree of injustice in the flow. But in the general case counterexamples can be supplied against this claim as well – situations where A is exploited more than B but we would agree B is more unjustly treated. It is beyond my scope here to inquire into a robust measure of the injustice of flows emanating from an unjust stock.

Another point should be made with respect to the argument of this section. It might be argued that so long as exploitation comes about, then the initial distribution of assets was not "equal." An "equal" initial distribution might be defined as one which eliminates exploitation. First, such a position is circular with respect to any attempt to vindicate exploitation theory by claiming it helps to reveal an initial inequality of assets. Secondly, such a definition of equality of initial endowments is in fact a theory of outcome equality, not a theory of resource equality. We would still be left with the question: What is wrong with exploitation?

---

[30] I thank G. A. Cohen for pressing this point.

A fifth explanation of our interest in exploitation theory, which I have enumerated (4′) as I consider it to be convincing only when it paraphrases the inequality theory, might be called the expropriation theory. The expropriation theory is summarized, for example, by G. A. Cohen,[31] as follows:

(i) The laborer is the only person who creates the product, that which has value.
(ii) The capitalist receives some of the value of the product.
Therefore: (iii) The laborer receives less value than the value of what he creates, and
(iv) The capitalist receives some of the value of what the laborer creates.
Therefore: (v) The laborer is exploited by the capitalist.

The expropriation theory (which Cohen calls the Plain Marxian Argument) does not claim an injustice on grounds of alienation or domination, but on grounds of rightful ownership of what one has made. I think the argument is ethically defensible only when it coincides with the inequality-of-resources theory, that is, when the expropriation takes place because the laborer does not have access to the means of production he is entitled to. To see the unreasonableness of the expropriation theory in the general case, substitute "Karl" for "the capitalist" and "Adam" for "the laborer" in the above argument (i)–(v) where Karl and Adam are the *dramatis personae* of the last example. Statements (ii) through (iv) remain unobjectionable and perhaps statement (i) does as well; but statement (v) certainly does not follow as an *ethically* convincing statement (although *formal* exploitation exists). If we respect the ownership pattern of assets and the preferences of the agents (which, to repeat, can even be uniform preferences), I see no good reason to give exclusive ownership rights of a product to the person who has made the product. Only on grounds of alienation (which I have said is unconvincing) does it seem one's labor could confer special ownership rights over the product. Justly acquired initial resources, which the direct producer might borrow from another, must count as well in ascribing ownership of the final product. What power the expropriation theory appears to have comes from another assumption, not stated, that the capitalist starts out with a monopoly on the ownership of the means of production, unjustly acquired; it is the injustice of that monopoly which leads us to believe he has no just claim to the product of the laborer. As Cohen says, in his own criticism of the expropriation theory: "If it is morally all right that capitalists do and workers do not own the means of production, then capitalist profit is not the fruit of exploitation; and if the pre-contractual distributive position is morally wrong, then the case for exploitation is made."[32]

[31] Cohen (1979).
[32] Cohen (1983).

VII.   Mollifying the verdict

Many writers have shown the indefensibility of the labor theory of *value*, the claim that Marxian analysis gains special insight from deducing a relationship between embodied labor values and prices.[33] There is no theory of price formation, special to Marxism, with a rigorous foundation. With the demise of the labor theory of value, various writers in the Marxian tradition have shown that the theory of exploitation can be reconstructed on a foundation which does not utilize the labor theory of value.[34] (Marx's logic derived the theory of exploitation from the labor theory of price formation.) I have now argued there is no logically compelling reason to be interested in exploitation theory. This claim is not so destructive as might appear to the Marxian enterprise, however, for I think the reasons Marxists have been interested in exploitation theory are important and, to a large extent, distinguish Marxism from other kinds of social science: it is just that these reasons do not justify an interest in exploitation theory which is an unnecessary detour to the other concerns. First, within ethics, Marxism lays emphasis on the importance of equal access to the means of production. It regards with suspicion any large inequality in access to the means of production, while its foil in social science tends to justify such inequality on grounds of differential rates of time preference, skill, or even luck.[35] Having said that equality in the ownership of means of production is desirable as an initial condition, much is left to elaborate concerning inheritance, handicaps, and needs. Libertarian theorists view inheritance as a just means of acquiring resources;[36] Ronald Dworkin, in recent work on equality of resources, does not discuss inheritance;[37] Bruce Ackerman in recent work does attack that problem;[38] I imagine a Marxian theory of inheritance, when elaborated, will circumscribe inheritance rights quite sharply.[39] Secondly, Marxism calls attention to domination; domination is of interest on its own, even though it provides no reason to be interested in exploitation. Interest in domination has given rise to an important literature on the labor process and technical change under capitalism, which demonstrates how a specifically Marxian question, perhaps motivated by normative concerns, can give rise to new analysis of a positive type. Another example of positive analysis related to

---

[33] For a summary of the criticism of the labor theory of value see Elster (1985), chap. 3.
[34] See Cohen (1979), Roemer (1982), Morishima (1973).
[35] Robert Nozick (1974), for example, considers luck to be a just method for acquiring assets.
[36] Nozick (1974).
[37] Dworkin (1981a); see n. 9, p. 313.
[38] Ackerman (1980).
[39] For some very tentative indications, see Roemer (1983), pt. 4.

domination and exploitation is class theory. Class position is easily observable, and class may be an excellent indicator of alliances in struggles within capitalism, for reasons closer to domination than exploitation.[40] Thirdly, the concern with alienation is related to the interest Marxists have had in the emergence of market economies and the proletarianization of labor forces, both in the past and the present, an interest which again leads to the posing of questions which would not otherwise have been asked. Fourthly, the concern with accumulation has given Marxists a view of capitalism as guided by a pursuit of profits which in a deep sense is anarchic and collectively irrational, while the predominant opposing view (neoclassical economics) pictures capitalism as collectively rational, as the price system harnesses profit motives to serve the needs of people.[41] While Marxists have not developed a theory of crisis and disequilibrium which is as well-founded and intellectually convincing as neoclassical equilibrium theory, one suspects the Marxian questions will eventually lead to a rigorous theory of uneven development and crisis.

Unlike the labor theory of value, the reasons for a purported interest in exploitation theory have given rise to provocative social theory. There have, on the other hand, been costs to the adherence to exploitation theory, chiefly associated with what might be called the fetishism of labor. The costs are often associated with the inappropriate application of exploitation theory in cases where some underlying deeper phenomenon, which usually coincides with exploitation, ceases to coincide with it. For example, socialist countries have exhibited a reluctant history to use material incentives and decentralizing markets. To some extent, this may result from a confusion concerning the permissibility of "exploitation" when the initial distribution of ownership or control of the means of production is just. A second cost has been the equation claimed by some Marxists between socialism and industrial democracy, the belief that hierarchical forms of production are necessarily nonsocialist. A third example, associated with an overriding concern with alienation, views the final

[40] I have not considered in this paper a sixth possible reason to be interested in exploitation: as an explanation of class struggle, that the exploited struggle against the exploiters. I think that if the exploited struggle against the exploiters, that is because the former are dominated, are alienated, or suffer from an unfair allocation in the distribution of assets. The unequal exchange of labor cannot be the cause of class struggle: rather, that unequal exchange must be the symptom of what must cause class struggle. (People do not calculate surplus value accounts; in fact, one of the classical Marxian points is that the surplus value accounts are masked and veiled by the market, and so the exploited do not see the true nature of the unequal exchange from which they are suffering.) But I have shown, now, that exploitation is not a useful proxy for the various injustices which may, indeed, be at the root of class struggle. Hence my nondiscussion of exploitation as the cause of class struggle.
[41] It is this collective irrationality of capitalism which Elster (1985) sees as the main contribution of Marxian "dialectics."

social goal as a moneyless economy, perhaps with no detailed division of labor, in which, somehow, all of society becomes one community.[42] Strictly speaking, the last two examples do not impugn exploitation theory, but rather domination and alienation; but exploitation theory has formalized the concern with labor which reinforces this sort of misapplication.

It should be reiterated that the failure of exploitation to mirror properly the unequal distribution of the means of production is a logical one; as I noted, in what are perhaps the most important actual historical cases, preferences of agents are such that the unequal-exchange-of-labor theory coincides with the inequality-of-productive-assets theory, and so exploitation theory pronounces the "right" ethical verdict.[43]

Parallel to my view on the usefulness of exploitation theory as a proxy for inequality in the ownership of the means of production is George Stigler's observation concerning David Ricardo's use of the labor theory of value. Stigler writes:

I can find no basis for the belief that Ricardo had an *analytical* labor theory of value, for quantities of labor are *not* the only determinants of relative values. . . . On the other hand, there is no doubt that he held what may be called an *empirical* labor theory of value, that is, a theory that the relative quantities of labor required in production are the dominant determinants of relative values. Such an empirical proposition cannot be interpreted as an analytical theory. . . .

Stigler concludes with a statement which applies to my argument concerning exploitation:

The failure to distinguish between analytical and empirical propositions has been a source of much misunderstanding in economics. An analytical statement concerns functional relationships; an empirical statement takes account of the quantitative significance of the relationships.[44]

Unlike Stigler's Ricardo, I think the labor theory of value is not a useful empirical theory. While the errors in the labor theory of value are Ptolemaic, the defects in exploitation theory are Newtonian. As an empirical statement, surplus value accounts mirror inequality in ownership of the means of production pretty well, if it is true that cross-sectional wealth-elastic labor supply behavior is as empirically inconsequential as

[42] A fine discussion of the costs which dogmatic Marxism has imposed on developing socialist societies is in Nove (1983).

[43] A striking example which suggests that labor supply may be elastic with respect to wealth, and therefore that exploitation theory is even historically wrong, is presented by Pranab Bardhan (1982), p. 78. In India, as the wealth of middle-peasant families increases, poor relations come and join the family. Viewing this extended family as the unit, it appears that labor supply increases with wealth. It is not obvious that the family labor supply increases elastically with wealth, but Bardhan's example shows, at least, there is a range of wealths for which labor supply has positive elasticity.

[44] Stigler (1958), pp. 361, 366.

the precession in the perihelion of the orbit of Mercury. But for the sake of clarity and consistency, I think exploitation conceived of as the unequal exchange of labor should be replaced with exploitation conceived of as the distributional consequences of an unjust inequality in the distribution of productive assets and resources. Precisely when the asset distribution is unjust becomes the central question to which Marxian political philosophy should direct its attention.

What is exploitation?
Reply to Jeffrey Reiman

In a recent article, Jeffrey Reiman criticizes me for defanging Marx's concept of exploitation by replacing its classic definition with a "distributive" one.[1] Reiman writes that "a society is exploitative when its social structure is organized so that unpaid labor is systematically forced out of one class and put at the disposal of another" (3). I have written that a group[2] of people S is exploited by its complement S' in a society with private ownership of the means of production if S would benefit, and S' would suffer, by a redistribution of ownership in the means of production in which each owned his per capita share. Call this the property relations (PR) definition of exploitation.[3] A third definition of exploitation, the unequal exchange (UE) definition, states that an agent who expends in production more hours of labor than are embodied in the goods he can purchase with his revenues from production (which may come from wages, profits, or the sale of commodities) is exploited, while one who can purchase goods embodying more social labor than he expended in production is an exploiter.

In my book *A General Theory of Exploitation and Class,* I took the UE definition to be a generalization of Marx's. I showed that by using this definition, one could rigorously construct a theory of exploitation and class formation that captured many classic Marxist insights, and had the virtue of deriving as theorems what had been, classically, assumed as postulates. I located, however, certain cases in which the UE definition gave intuitively incorrect verdicts about who was exploited.[4] I argued that the PR definition was superior to the UE definition, in that it rendered the intuitively right verdict in these strange cases and agreed

---

[1] Reiman (1987). Page references to this article are given in parentheses.
[2] I say "group" instead of "class," not in order to further defang Marxism, but because, for me, class has a precise definition, and whether classes are exploited as such should be a theorem, not an assumption, of a definition of exploitation.
[3] I have used both a "withdrawal" criterion and the "redistributive" criterion proposed here, for the property relations definition of exploitation. For the former, see Roemer (1982), chap. 7; for the latter, see Roemer (1988), chap. 9. There are some defects in each approach, which I will not comment on here, as they are irrelevant to my disagreements with Reiman.
[4] See Essay 3.

with the UE definition whenever the UE definition seemed to work. I further claimed that the PR definition was superior in placing property relations at the center of exploitation, rather than unequal labor exchange, since the latter is a rather abstract idea (because socially embodied labor time is an abstract idea) whose moral associations come from the property relations that bring about the phenomenon. Reiman argues that I weakened the concept of exploitation by representing it as either UE or PR: both these definitions are "distributive," and gloss over the central fact of the forced extraction of unpaid labor, which is the heart of exploitation. The various hard cases I propose are hard, he claims, only because I am comparing two definitions of exploitation both of which are wrong.

There is difficulty in distinguishing among these definitions of exploitation because each of them suffices to diagnose exploitation in the standard case of capitalism with proletarians who own no means of production. I find Reiman's definition of exploitation inadequate, however, for several reasons. First, the notion of "unpaid labor" is undefined; I believe that identifying some labor as unpaid often requires a prior diagnosis of exploitation, and so Reiman's use of it in a definition of exploitation is circular. There are also problems with defining "forced," of course, but I will accept Reiman's intuitions on that here, as that is not the focus of my objections. Second, I think that being forced to provide unpaid labor (assuming that we agree what that means in some standard cases) is neither necessary nor sufficient for exploitation.

Consider example 1, which I have discussed elsewhere.[5] There are a number of agents each of whom possesses an endowment consisting of some labor and some produced commodities, which are inputs into the production of commodities. All agents have access to the same technology. There is no labor market or capital market. Each agent wants to consume the same "subsistence" bundle of commodities, subject to the constraint that he not deplete his initial endowment in value terms. Suppose that there is enough endowment in aggregate so that, were it divided equally among the people, each person could produce his subsistence needs in six hours. In the private ownership economy, prices established in a market for commodities allow agents to trade inputs, before production begins, and to trade outputs, after production has occurred. Each agent is a producer of commodities. He decides upon a production plan that minimizes the labor he must expend, subject to producing an output whose value, at the current prices, is sufficient to enable him to purchase his subsistence bundle. He is constrained by the value of his initial holdings: a producer

[5] Roemer (1982), pp. 33–43.

can choose only a production plan whose inputs he already has or can purchase by cashing in his initial holdings. A price vector p is an equilibrium price vector for this economy if, when each agent chooses his optimal production plan subject to p, the market for production inputs clears, and the market for trade in produced commodities after production clears: each agent ends up with his desired subsistence bundle. It can be proved that at an equilibrium, some agents (the ones whose initial endowments are small) work more than six hours, and others (the ones whose initial endowments are large) work less than six hours. Exploitation, in the unequal exchange sense, occurs *although there is no labor exchange of any kind;* the labor transfer occurs entirely through the trade of produced commodities. It is bizarre to speak, as Reiman apparently would, of unpaid labor in this example, when there is no institution for paying labor. Every agent is an independent producer who works only for himself. The only rationale for speaking of unpaid labor would be, circularly, if one already had concluded that the labor transfer that occurs is exploitative, and then designated the labor performed beyond labor embodied in the subsistence bundle as unpaid.

Marxists almost universally agree (in my experience) that there is exploitation in example 1, although there is neither a labor market nor a class structure. (A class structure comes into being when some agents work as independent producers, some agents hire others to work on their capital, and some agents sell labor power to those who hire.) The example is meant, of course, to point out that Marxian exploitation is a general phenomenon that can occur even without labor markets, if there is trade from an unequal initial distribution. While Reiman's definition fails in this case to diagnose exploitation, because of its reliance on the existence of unpaid labor, both the UE and the PR definitions work. If the endowments of produced commodities are redistributed so that each producer owns a per capita share, there will be no exploitation in the unequal exchange sense at equilibrium: each producer will work just the socially necessary labor time (six hours). Thus, PR and UE lead to the same verdict.

In example 1 the asset-poor[6] producers are "forced," by the distribution of property, to work more hours than are socially embodied in the

---

[6] Reiman takes it as "striking confirmation" of my having displaced class from center stage, and replaced it with distribution, that I define agents as "rich" and "poor" (26). I *define* agents by their initial endowments and preferences, and the class position they will occupy as a consequence of rational and constrained economic behavior. It may be an agent's class position that will determine his social behavior, and indeed the preferences of his children, but it is more revealing to deduce class position from prior causes than to take it as a defining characteristic of agents. (For a discussion of how it is consistent to take preferences as a defining characteristic of an agent and yet to argue that class membership forms preferences, see Roemer [1986a].)

subsistence bundle in order to produce commodities sufficient in value, at market prices, to exchange for their subsistence needs. But why is the forcing a bad thing, a cause for calling the outcome exploitative? I claim it is so only because, or if, we view the initial unequal distribution of ownership of inputs (the means of production in this case) as unjust. We require knowledge of the justice of property relations to pass judgment on whether the forcing is bad. To see this, consider example 2, an economy with two agents, Karl and Adam, who have different preferences regarding consumption over time.[7] Initially, each begins with the same amount of capital, which can also be consumed. There are two time periods. During the first period, and only during that period, it is possible for each agent to augment his capital stock. Karl prefers to work very little during the first period, when he is young; he is willing to trade future leisure for present leisure. Adam has the opposite preference; he prefers to take leisure during the second period, and is willing to work hard during the first in order to do so. Consequently, Adam works hard during period one and builds up a large capital stock. Karl consumes his capital stock in period one. In period two, Adam hires Karl to work on Adam's capital stock; using Adam's capital, Karl produces enough consumption goods for both of them. Now Karl *is* forced to work for Adam during the second period, for there is no other way for him to receive his consumption (for Adam will not just give it to him). There is exploitation according to the UE definition, because Karl works in period two for more hours than are embodied in the consumption goods he receives. According to Reiman's definition, there is exploitation (assuming that the "unpaid labor" is the labor embodied in Adam's consumption in period two). But, if Karl knew what the consequences of his leisure-taking in period one would be, and if his preferences were autonomously formed under conditions of equal opportunity, then I think we cannot call this outcome exploitative.[8] Adam and Karl are lucky that they are in a society together, where it is possible for both of them to achieve their preferred intertemporal streams of leisure and consumption by arranging the trade described. The PR definition of exploitation renders the correct verdict in this example: there is no exploitation because Karl and Adam each began with the same capital endowment. To make the example more dramatic, imagine that there are ten time periods, and in every one after the first, Karl is forced to work for Adam because only Adam has accumulated capital.

[7] See Roemer (1983).

[8] Surely, there are some deals that Adam and Karl might strike in which we might say that Adam had unfairly taken advantage of Karl's preference for leisure in youth. But any deal that allows Karl to not work during his youth will involve an "unequal exchange exploitation" of him by Adam in period two, and not all such deals are, in my opinion, exploitative.

I reach a verdict of no exploitation, as long as Karl chose willingly, and the initial distribution of capital was fair.

Thus, I claim that forcing is not sufficient for exploitation. Karl prefers taking a course of action in which he will later be forced to work for Adam to avoiding such a course of action. (Reiman could respond that, in fact, Karl is not forced to work for Adam in example 2, because he was free to choose a different course of action in the initial period. I think it is more natural to say, however, that Karl is forced to work for Adam in later periods, but that forcing is not a bad thing because of the justice of the initial distribution and the autonomous formation of preferences.) Neither, I think, is forcing necessary for exploitation. Consider example 3, in which Andrea is endowed with a big machine, Bob with a small one, and we are told that this inequality is unfair. Bob can produce his subsistence needs using his small machine, but Andrea offers to hire him to work her machine at a wage that permits him to earn his subsistence needs by expending less labor than he would require using his own machine, and at which her profits from his labor finance her subsistence as well. Thus Bob is not forced to work for Andrea, but Andrea lives off Bob's labor. I think that Bob is exploited in this case, even though there is no forcing, because the initial distribution of property rights was unfair. If rights were distributed so that Andrea and Bob each owned one-half of (the stock in) each machine, there would be no exploitation, regardless of their respective preferences for leisure and consumption (that is, regardless of who hires whom). The PR definition renders the correct verdict, and the UE definition happens to do so as well, while Reiman's definition does not.

A more delicate issue is the distinction between the PR and the UE definitions. In example 4, which Reiman reproduces (25), Maggie owns a big machine and Ron[9] a small one, and this distribution is unfair (the means of production should be equally distributed). Their preferences differ. Ron wants to take leisure, and is willing to consume just a small amount of the consumption good in order to do so. Maggie wants a lot of consumption good, and is willing to work very hard in order to maximize her consumption of it. Preferences have been autonomously formed. Maggie uses her own machine to capacity, but wants still more consumption, and so sells her labor power to Ron, who pays her a small wage to operate his machine, taking the profits therefrom for his consumption. Now there is an uenqual labor exchange (Maggie expends more hours of labor than are embodied in her consumption, and Ron expends fewer

---

[9] When I initially introduced the present example 4, in Essay 3 of this volume, the names of the characters were not Maggie and Ron. They have been so named here to distinguish them from the other dramatis personae.

than are embodied in his),[10] which implies, according to the UE definition, that Maggie is exploited. But I believe Maggie is not exploited, because the unequal exchange does not result from her lack of equal access to the means of production. In fact, she owns the big machine. The PR definition renders this verdict, while the UE definition does not. Reiman agrees that Maggie is not exploited, but says that is because she is not forced to work for Ron. I agree that she is not forced, but don't agree that explains why she is not exploited. (For in example 3, Bob was exploited by Andrea even though he was not forced to work for her.) What distinguishes the situations of Bob and Maggie is that, although both suffer from an unequal exchange, and neither is forced, the unequal exchange that Bob suffers is a consequence of his less-than-equal ownership of the means of production, while Maggie suffers from unequal exchange even though she is better endowed than she should be.

In the article in which I originally proposed example 4, I concluded that Ron was exploited, because he would benefit and Maggie would suffer from a redistribution of property ownership in which each owned one-half of society's capital stock. I am now less willing to conclude that, and more apt to believe that neither Ron nor Maggie is exploited in example 4. I therefore think that the PR definition is insufficient as a definition of exploitation, and would now prefer to say that an agent is exploited in the Marxist sense, or capitalistically exploited, *if and only if PR holds and the exploiter gains by virtue of the labor of the exploited* (that is, the exploiter would be worse off if the exploited ceased working).[11] In example 4, I think Ron suffers an injustice by virtue of the unequal ownership of the means of production, although he is not exploited by Maggie according to the amended definition because she does not gain by virtue of his labor.

[10] Because Ron does not work, but consumes some of Maggie's output.

[11] The suggestion to include the "labor" clause is Erik Wright's. I do not defend the idea that gaining by virtue of another's labor is morally worse than gaining through some other channel by virtue of another's unjustly having a small endowment; but the expending of effort is characteristically associated with exploitation, as opposed to other means by which unfair advantage might be taken of the poorly endowed. Imagine the case of two agents, one poorly endowed with several goods and one well endowed. They have different tastes, and they are able to trade with each other to achieve an equilibrium that strictly Pareto dominates the initial allocation. With an equal per capita redistribution of the original endowments, the erstwhile poor one would gain and the erstwhile rich one would lose in the final equilibrium. The labor clause saves me from calling the first equilibrium exploitative, because no labor is performed by the poor agent.

Instead of appending the labor clause, a slightly different tack would be to append the UE condition – that is, to say that a group is exploited if and only if both the PR and the UE characterizations hold. The upshot for the present example is the same; neither Ron nor Maggie is exploited. These two tacks are not equivalent, for note that, with the labor clause, the unemployed who receive some transfer payments are not exploited, but they are exploited under the PR + UE characterization of exploitation. I prefer appending the labor clause.

Reiman gets carried away with the forced aspect of the labor exchange between proletarians and capitalists when he writes that slavery is equivalent to "forced unpaid labor," and that therefore "any exploitative society is a form of slavery" (4). Calling capitalism a form of slavery is a bad mistake. My principal concern, however, is not that Reiman mischaracterizes the social relations of capitalism in history, but that getting the definition of exploitation right is important for the analysis of contemporary socialism. The most important economic innovations in socialist societies during the coming years will apparently be their experiments with markets and private accumulation. Class relations (that is, relations of selling and hiring of labor and borrowing and lending of capital among agents) will develop. Our views about whether these relations are instances of exploitation will depend upon which definition we adopt. Socialist planners have, I think, unfortunately shied away from using markets, because of an incorrect belief that class relations among private agents are necessarily the mark of exploitation.[12] I think these socialist theorists hold a conception of exploitation that is, essentially, Reiman's. In judging whether a relation is exploitative, this conception does not consider the moral status of the property relations that give rise to it. I maintain that our focus must be on the "initial" distribution of capital, what caused the class relations to emerge, and what opportunities exist for new generations and latecomers to the scene. Exploitation can occur without the buying and selling of labor power; and conversely, such buying and selling can occur, resulting in an unequal labor exchange, without exploitation.[13]

[12] They have also not used markets because the power of the bureaucracy is enhanced by its control of the allocation of resources. But I think theoretical views about exploitation have been important as well in giving market socialism a bad name among Marxists.

[13] I have not discussed in this reply all my differences with Reiman, in particular those concerning the labor theory of value. But I should remark that I accept his criticism of a paragraph I wrote that is unrelated to the present discussion (27–28).

Second thoughts on property relations and exploitation

Since my book *A General Theory of Exploitation and Class (GTEC)* was published in 1982, a number of good criticisms have been raised against the property-relations definition of capitalist exploitation that I put forth. In light of these remarks, I would like to amend my definition.

The definition of capitalist exploitation that I put forth was as follows. Let a society be divided into a coalition S and its complement S'. S is exploited and S' is exploiting if: (1) S would be better off if it withdrew with its per capita share of productive, alienable assets; (2) S' would be worse off if it withdrew with its per capita share of productive, alienable assets; and (3) S' would be worse off if S withdrew from society with its own assets. Call this the property-relations (PR) definition of exploitation. I favored the PR definition over the traditional approach, which focuses upon the relationship between capitalist and worker mediated by a labor market and consummated at the point of production, because the classical approach fails to locate the source of exploitation in the unequal and unfair distribution of the productive assets.

The criticisms that I will discuss take me to task chiefly on two points: that the PR definition fails to capture the relation of dominance or dependence between exploiter and exploited, and that it does not mention labor. I will be using the labor-exchange definition of exploitation that I used in *GTEC*; it will be helpful in this paper to have that definition at hand. Imagine an economy in which a coalition S and its complement produce some net product. The labor embodied in the net product is equal, by definition, to the total labor expended by S and its complement S'. S is said to be exploited if the share of the net product that it receives (i.e., comes to own) embodies less labor than its members expended in production. This is equivalent to saying that S' receives a share of the net product embodying more labor than its members expended. Call this the unequal-exchange (UE) definition of exploitation. In *GTEC* and a more recent article, I took the position that the PR definition was a

I am grateful to my critics, who have helped to clarify, for me at least, what exploitation really means. This work has been supported by a research grant from the National Science Foundation.

generalization of, and superior to, the UE definition.[1] I am now less convinced of PR's superiority to UE, a point I'll discuss near the end.

Jack Pitt (n.d.) points out that I intended the role of clause (3) of the PR definition to capture the relation of domination of the exploiters over the exploited, but that it fails to do so. (The definition works in diagnosing no exploitation in the following case, where there should not be any. There are two islands, rich and poor in resources, but inhabited by identically skilled populations. There is no trade between the islands. The inhabitants of Rich Island can subsist with 3 days' labor a week while the inhabitants of Poor must work 6 days. Clauses [1] and [2] suggest that Rich is exploiting Poor, but [3] blocks that wrong conclusion.) Consider the case of the invalid (S') who is supported by the rest of society (S). According to PR, it appears that society is exploited and the invalid an exploiter. This is not intuitively right, and so the definition of exploitation is inadequate.

I intended the PR definition of capitalist exploitation to work only in cases that can be described as arm's length economic transactions. Clearly, the clauses of the PR definition are not sufficient to guarantee this. Deciding what an arm's length transaction is may be, in some cases, delicate. I propose to require, in partial fulfillment of the requirement, that *there be no consumption externalities between the coalitions S and S'*, and that all agents be utility maximizers. Thus, the PR definition is not applicable in the invalid case, because the invalid's welfare enters the utility function of the rest of society. (If it didn't, society would ignore the invalid.) The consumption externality clause also works to prevent us from concluding that a child exploits its parents.

Jon Elster (1982, p. 368) proposes the next example, to show that the PR definition of exploitation fails to capture the right relationship between S and S'. His objection to the PR definition is that it characterizes exploitation counterfactually, while the kind of interaction between S and S' that is in fact necessary for exploitation cannot be captured by counterfactuals alone. Consider a society

composed of two groups, R and S, of equal size and with equal assets. They do not interact economically. R has a puritan religion that makes the members work long hours and produce much, but the religion only motivates them to work if they have before their eyes the lazy group S whom they smugly believe to be condemned to eternal suffering. Group S members work very short hours, because they wrongly think that the rigid, and to them abhorrent, life style of group R is due to the long working hours, not to the religion.

From the PR definition, one would conclude that S is exploited by R, because S is working less, and is the worse for it, than it would be were

[1] See Essay 3.

R absent, and R's members, apparently, would be worse off if they did not have the large level of consumption that they only enjoy by virtue of S's bad example.

Note that this case is dealt with by the consumption externality clause. The actions of the members of each coalition are an input into the utility functions of the other coalition's members. (R's members would not be so content, working as hard as they do, without observing S.)

Erik Wright maintains that for exploitation to occur it is necessary that the exploiters gain by virtue of the efforts, or labor, of the exploited.[2] Consider the case of two agents, Rich and Poor, who are initially endowed with 3 and 1 units of capital, respectively. This distribution is unfair: suppose that the fair distribution is egalitarian. Rich wants to consume prodigiously, while Poor only wants to subsist and write poetry (a good for which there is no market). Rich works up all his capital stock, but wants to consume even more than what is thereby produced, and and so Poor hires Rich to work up Poor's capital stock, paying Rich a wage and keeping enough of the product to enable him to subsist.[3] According to the PR definition of exploitation Rich is an exploiter and Poor is exploited. But this seems intuitively wrong because although Rich gains by virtue of being unfairly rich, he does not gain by virtue of the labor of Poor. I previously wrote that Rich did exploit Poor in this example, but I now do not think so. Therefore, I would substitute, for clause (3), the following: *S' gains by virtue of the labor of S.*

This example is a difficult one precisely because the UE definition and the PR definition give opposite verdicts. We feel that Poor may be taking unfair advantage of Rich's driving consumerism: but on the other hand, Rich had more than his fair share to begin with. (If Rich required his large consumption to survive, we might conclude otherwise, but in that case we might also say that the original distribution, reflecting differential needs, was not unfair.) According to the UE definition, Rich is exploited – he receives goods embodying less labor than he expended. Even with an equal division of the capital stock, this might be the case, due to the differences in preferences between Rich and Poor. Would we want to say, in that situation, that (formerly) Rich is exploited by (formerly) Poor? I postpone discussion of this point.

Jeffrey Reiman (1987) launches an attack against the PR definition in favor of a definition of exploitation as the provision of forced, unpaid labor. I have replied in detail to this attack elsewhere.[4] My main points are these. Deciding that certain labor is 'unpaid' presupposes a way of

[2] Personal correspondence, October 10, 1987.
[3] See Essay 3 for my original discussion of this example.
[4] See Essay 4.

deciding how much labor has been unfairly transferred. There are cases when there is unequal exchange of labor, but without a labor market – each producer works only for himself, and then trades commodities at prices that clear markets. The 'unequal exchange' consists in the fact that some agents end up with a consumption bundle embodying less labor than they expended, and others consume a bundle embodying more labor than they expended. There is no labor market, no institution for paying labor, and so speaking of unpaid labor is, so to speak, an anachronism. (What meaning is there to 'unpaid labor' before a labor market has come into existence?) But exploitation in the Marxian sense seems to occur. Second, although I agree that in the standard case of capitalism with a proletariat the workers are forced to sell their labor power, I do not think such forcing is sufficient or necessary for exploitation: not sufficient, because the kind of forcing that property relations induces is not exploitative unless the original distribution of property was unfair; not necessary, because economic actors can be exploited even when they have viable alternatives to the exploitative relationship.[5]

Shelly Kagan and Charles Taylor raise another issue.[6] What if the members of S, who own no alienable assets, are gaining by virtue of the skills of the members of S', who also own the alienable assets, so that if S were to withdraw with its per capita share of the assets, its members would be worse off than before? A proletariat kept in abject poverty and illiteracy would be an example. In my view, this is not a case of purely capitalist exploitation, for the exploited lack not only alienable means of production but skills as well. The problem here is not with the use of counterfactuals in the PR definition as such, but with the withdrawal criterion, which fails to isolate that part of the exploitation that is capitalist. An alternative would be to substitute for the PR definition the following: S *is exploited and S' exploiting if, with an egalitarian redistribution of the alienable assets in society, S would be better off and S' worse off.*[7] After the redistribution, S' and S continue to trade with each other, so that S' can still gain from the unskilled labor of S, and S can gain from the skills of S', but the members of S will be better off than they were under the

---

[5] Here is an example. Andrea has a big machine, and Bob a small one; I postulate this unequal distribution of the capital stock to be unjust. Bob could produce his subsistence needs on his small machine, but Andrea offers to hire him, to work her machine, at a wage that permits him to earn his subsistence needs, and by expending less labor than he would require were he to use his machine. Her profits from hiring Bob finance her consumption as well. Thus Bob is not forced to work for Andrea, but chooses to, and she lives off his labor. I consider Bob to be exploited; but this verdict depends upon the injustice of the initial distribution.

[6] With Kagan, personal correspondence, August 13, 1984; with Taylor, a conversation, some years ago.

[7] In Roemer (1988), I used this definition of exploitation, in part because of its simplicity.

prior distribution of the alienable assets. What S suffers in the new arrangement I have called, perhaps unadvisedly, socialist exploitation.[8]

There are other reasons to criticize the PR definition that have to do with economies of scale in production. If there are significant scale economies, then we will never conclude that an individual is exploited in a large society, for a single person would almost always be worse off if he withdrew with his per capita share of the assets. This problem is also taken care of by substituting the redistribution condition of the previous paragraph for the withdrawal criterion of the PR definition. When there are more than two groups with differentiated relationships to the means of production, the withdrawal criterion does not work well. Consider the case of the peasantry, the proletariat, and the capitalists. Let S be the peasantry, and suppose they trade with their complement, but do not work for them. We conclude that S' exploits and S is exploited. But perhaps this does not jibe with common sense, in the case when the proletariat is suffering just as much as the peasantry. In this case, the redistribution condition improves matters, for both the proletariat and the peasants gain by the redistribution of capital, while the capitalists lose.

The redistribution criterion, however, has its own problems. Some persons, whom we view as living a harmless life, may lose from a redistribution of society's capital stock by virtue of changes in relative prices that will follow. They were not taking unfair advantage of others, but would be called exploiters by the redistributive criterion. If the rate of interest falls with the redistribution of capital, were all those who held savings deposits before exploiters? These problems, however, are not necessarily due to the criterion for exploitation. They also indicate that in a society with complex economic interactions it is not easy to tell when one person is taking unfair advantage of another. Does a consumer of artichokes in New York take unfair advantage of a Mexican worker who harvests them in Salinas at starvation wages?

Our intuitions about exploitation work best when all economic actors are assumed to have the same preferences for bundles of work and consumption goods. In the models of *GTEC,* I assumed all agents had identical preferences; the reason for this was to focus on the distribution of productive assets as the essential difference between people. Suppose we allow people to have different preferences. Imagine an economy with three goods: corn, labor, and land. Labor applied to land produces corn. Agents have preferences (in general, different) over the bundles of corn and labor that they enjoy. Suppose that, because the arable land is relatively scarce,

---

[8] See Roemer (1982), ch. 8, and Essay 1.

there are decreasing returns to labor in the production of corn. Imagine that there is a firm that operates the farm: it hires labor to produce corn, and sells corn to the workers. How should the shares of ownership in the firm be distributed to the workers so that at the equilibrium there is no exploitation of any worker by another? (There are no bosses in this picture.) Alternatively, one might take the viewpoint that the firm should be publicly owned. But, for my purposes, this is just a semantic difference. If the firm is publicly owned, the question becomes, what allocation of labor and corn among the population will be free of exploitation? The first proposal might be to give each worker an equal share of the firm. (This is what the egalitarian distribution of productive assets recommends.) With different preferences, the ensuing equilibrium will involve some people consuming an amount of corn that embodies more labor than they expended, and others vice versa.[9] At the extreme, some agents may dislike work so much that they will not work at all in equilibrium, and will consume only the corn which they receive as their per capita share of the firm's profits. Surely, they live off the labor of others, although, trivially, they would not lose from a per capita redistribution of the productive assets. Do we think that they are exploiters? According to the property relations definition, they are not, but as I said, my intuitions are not firm in cases where preferences differ.

There is an alternative approach to defining exploitation when agents' preferences differ. In the corn economy just described, we could look for an allocation of labor and corn in which corn allotments are proportional to labor expended across the population. There are many such allocations, but it turns out there is an (essentially unique) allocation of this sort that is also Pareto optimal. Such an allocation always exists, regardless of the profile of preferences, so long as preferences are of the usual (quasi-concave) sort. Joaquim Silvestre and I propose this allocation as one that could be viewed as implementing public ownership of the farm technology.[10] In it, corn is distributed in proportion to labor expended, and one might say that this feature is the essential one for the absence of exploitation. This is the (unique) Pareto optimal allocation at which, according to the UE definition, there is no exploitation. If agents have identical preferences (and skills) and if each receives an equal share of the profits, then corn received will be proportional to labor expended in equilibrium; however, when preferences differ, these two criteria give rise to different allocations. It is noteworthy that the proportional allocation

---

[9] I now take up the issue, postponed above, of whether (formerly) Poor exploits (formerly) Rich.
[10] See Essay 13.

that I've discussed coincides with an equilibrium in the farm economy in which each agent receives a share of the firm's profits equal to *the share of his labor in total labor expended*. While the egalitarian distribution of the firm's profits might be justified by a view that each *citizen* should have an equal property right in the society's alienable productive assets, the proportional approach is recommended by a (perhaps Lockean?) view that one's property right in society's alienable assets is established by the amount of *labor* one performs. I can see no persuasive argument for adopting one of these characterizations of exploitation as the unique 'correct' one.[11]

In summary, I propose as *a* definition of exploitation, in a situation where neither S nor S' enjoy or suffer consumption externalities by virtue of the consumption or behavior of the other, that S is exploited and S' is exploiting if and only if:

(A)   the members of S would gain, and the members of S' would lose, by virtue of a redistribution of alienable assets so that each owned his per capita share, *or* the PR definition (clauses [1]–[2]); *and*

(B)   S' gains by virtue of the labor of S.

Neither of these two definitions, nor any one, will correctly diagnose exploitation precisely in the cases that we think it should. In particular, when labor is homogeneous across people, there may be good reason to define exploitation as a situation in which labor expended by agents is not proportional to the value of goods received.[12] As Robert Aumann has argued in another context, a good tool should not be discarded if it fails to do all jobs well.[13] The purpose of the property-relations approach is to provide an *economic* characterization of exploitation and to locate the source of exploitation in an unjust distribution of ownership of alienable assets, rather than in the nature of an institution that mediates the relation between exploited and exploiter, be it the labor market, the production line, or the price system. It is my firm intention to defend this view. What

[11] Marxists might object to the distribution of output in proportion to labor performed, because some workers are more able or skilled than others. In this paper, I am discussing only what in *GTEC* I called capitalist exploitation, the inequality that results from a person's lack of access to 'his fair share' of society's *alienable* means of production. The issue in question here is whether 'fair share' means an equal per capita share, or a share equal to the fraction of social labor that he performs.

[12] The proportional allocation discussed above can be defined and shown to exist in more complicated economies, where there are many produced goods and different kinds and skills of labor. See Roemer and Silvestre (1993).

[13] In non-cooperative game theory, there are some 26 proposals for the equilibrium concept. No concept performs well in all games, but for every game, there is a concept that performs well. The tool analogy is from Aumann (1985).

distribution of society's alienable assets is just, *if* we postulate that the distribution of inalienable productive assets (skills and talents) in persons is just, is a deep question, and the approaches that I have taken towards resolving it here are only first approximations that are intuitively plausible in simple cases.

Equality of resources

Introduction to Part II

The Marxian concept of exploitation, I maintain, is associated with a view of justice that holds that alienable productive resources should be equally distributed (or equally available) to all people. As such, Marx's theory of exploitation is a kind of equality-of-resource theory of justice. The specific way that Marx calculated whether a person was exploited, by comparing the labor embodied in the share of national income received with the share of labor performed – what I called the unequal exchange definition in Essay 4 – renders a different verdict than the property-relations (PR) definition of exploitation gives when preferences differ across people. I concluded that, in these cases, the property-relations definition was the superior one, from an ethical viewpoint, which led me to an interest in equality-of-resource theories of justice more generally.

The most important such theories were Rawls's theory (1971) of "maximinning" primary goods and Dworkin's theory (1981a) of "equality of resources." Dworkin's theory was both especially interesting to an economist and attractive: interesting because it proposed an actual economic mechanism for equalizing resources, and attractive because it attempted to limit the jurisdiction of the egalitarian policy to people's circumstances, while letting them remain responsible for aspects of their personal choices. (Dworkin wrote, as Essay 6 records, that the distribution of outcomes should be ambition-sensitive but not endowment-sensitive, where 'endowment' is identified with circumstances beyond one's control, and 'ambition' with self-directed choice.)

In "Equality of Talent" (Essay 6), I study the Dworkin insurance scheme and find it deficient as a mechanism for equalizing resources. Its major perversity is that, in certain cases, it renders the persons whom an equality-of-resource ethic wants to compensate *worse* off than they would have been without the insurance. Dworkin's response to this perversity has been to say that, in those cases where it occurs, he would not apply the insurance mechanism.[1] But this simply means that Dworkin has no mechanism to propose that is defined for all reasonable possible environments.

---

[1] At a conference in Halifax during the summer of 1984 and in private discussions.

Furthermore, the set of environments where the perversity occurs may well be large.

Essay 7 asks whether there is *any* mechanism that satisfies a number of axioms which, arguably, a resource-egalitarian allocation mechanism should satisfy – including an axiom which precludes the perversity that the insurance mechanism suffers from. On a reasonable domain of economic environments, it turns out there is a unique such mechanism: the one which distributes resources so as to equalize *welfares* in the population. But equality of welfare, Dworkin (1981) argued, does not hold persons responsible for their choices, their "ambitions," and is hence unacceptable as an egalitarian ethic. Put another way, the theorem says that any thoroughgoing conception of resource egalitarianism dissolves into welfare egalitarianism.

The argument that establishes this result is not particularly simple, and some comments on it would perhaps be enlightening. The conclusion of welfare egalitarianism follows from five axioms: Universal Domain, Pareto optimality, Symmetry, Resource Monotonicity, and Dimensional Consistency (CONRAD). (Refer to Essay 7, Section 3, Theorem 1.) All five axioms are necessary for the result – if any axiom is dropped, there is an infinite number of mechanisms satisfying the other four – so that it is not possible to say that one or two axioms are really responsible for the result. The axiom that precludes the perversity of Dworkin's insurance mechanism is Dimensional Consistency.

We can tell a story about what happens in part of the proof; here's the relevant part.[2] There is an economic environment ξ with two persons, A and B, with utility functions u and v and with a certain number, say five, goods to be distributed. We wish to compare the allocation of these five goods, under a mechanism satisfying the five axioms listed, to the allocation of the same five goods by the mechanism in another economic environment ξ' with two persons, A' and B', who have preferences u' and v', and who differ from A and B as follows: A' and B' derive more utility from any vector of goods than A and B, respectively. By invoking a theorem on the representation of concave utility functions (or concave preferences), one can assert that there is a certain environment ξ^* with one unit each of two more goods – call them the a good and the b good – with two characters A^* (female) and B^* (male) having preferences u^* and v^*, such that, if A^* (respectively, B^*) consumes one unit of the a good (respectively, the b good) then her (respectively, his) preferences over the first five goods look exactly like A''s (respectively B''s) preferences, and if she (respectively, he) consumes zero units of the a good (respectively,

2 For the proof of the theorem, see Roemer (1986).

the *b* good), then her (his) preferences look exactly like *A*'s preferences (respectively, *B*'s preferences). The Universal Domain axiom tells us that ξ^* is an acceptable environment for the mechanism to act upon, the Dimensional Consistency axiom tells us that the mechanism must allocate the five goods in ξ' exactly as they are allocated in ξ^*, and the Resource Monotonicity axiom tells us that, under the mechanism's operation, agents *A* and *B* in ξ must each end up with utility no higher than *A'* and *B'* do. Now the promised story that goes along with this is the following. We can view *A'* and *A** (and *B'* and *B**) as actually being the same person, where the *a* good (respectively, the *b* good) can be viewed as *A''*'s endorphins (respectively, *B''*'s endorphins) which were not explicitly shown in ξ' but are revealed in ξ^*. In ξ^*, the mechanism must treat these two goods as resources up for egalitarian distribution, since they are listed as goods, while in ξ', these goods express themselves merely implicitly as aspects of preferences. By exhibiting the environment ξ^*, we have shown that the difference in utility experienced by *A* and *A'* (respectively, *B* and *B'*) is reducible to a difference in their endorphin levels. Essentially what the above proof excerpt accomplishes is to reduce any difference in preferences between two people to a difference in some resource, perhaps an internal one, that they possess; then, by the mandate of resource equality, the mechanism must treat the difference between their preferences as a difference in endowments, and hence compensable at the bar of resource equality. It is therefore not surprising that the mechanism will not hold people responsible for the differences in their preferences. From this, it is perhaps not surprising that welfare egalitarianism is implied.

The story suggests that the theorem is not a challenge to Dworkin's effort to distinguish equality of resources from equality of welfare, because, as it relates, preference differences are reduced "merely" to resource differences, a reduction which goes against Dworkin's intended purpose, to distinguish qualitatively between preferences and resources. Although I will, soon, agree with the conclusion, the inference is too hasty. For the story is just that: it is a *comment* on a *proof* of a theorem. Any challenge to the theorem's salience in the egalitarian debate must challenge directly one or more of its axioms, for there may well be other proofs of the theorem that do not use the above argument. In broad strokes, what the theorem states is that if one precludes the perversity of Dworkin's insurance mechanism by requiring Dimensional Consistency, then there is no way to equalize resources except to equalize welfare.

Dimensional Consistency, however, *may* be too strong a way of precluding that perversity. I show that this is indeed the case in the Postscript to Essay 7; that is, there is a weaker axiom than CONRAD that precludes the perversity from occurring and that, in conjunction with the other four axioms, admits other possible allocation mechanisms than welfare equality. Nevertheless, I emphasize 'may' in this paragraph's first sentence, as Dimensional Consistency has other reasons to recommend it.

Richard Arneson (1989) and G. A. Cohen (1989) advanced the debate on egalitarianism by pointing out that the Dworkinian cut between preferences and resources was not the ethically salient one for egalitarian theory. An egalitarian should be concerned with opportunities, where opportunities should be equalized as far as possible across people, while leaving persons responsible for transforming their opportunities into outcomes. Thus, holding people responsible for their preferences but not resources, as Dworkin does, is not right, because preferences are in part determined by features of the environment over which a person has no control. In Essay 8, I distinguish between a person's circumstances and his will, where the consequences of differential circumstances are compensable at the bar of equality, while the consequences of the differential exercise of will are not. I propose how a society can distinguish between the effects on outcomes of circumstance and will, and a method for compensating people for the effects of the first but not the second. Some examples are presented that show how my way of drawing the line designating responsibility will produce a different, and I think fairer, policy than Dworkin's.

Equality of talent

1. Introduction

If one is an egalitarian, what should one want to equalize? Opportunities or outcomes? Resources or welfare? These positions are usually conceived to be very different. I argue in this paper that the distinction is misconceived: the only coherent conception of resource equality implies welfare equality, in an appropriately abstract description of the problem. In this section, I motivate the program which the rest of the paper carries out.

1.1. Welfarism versus resourcism

Although not popular among economists, nonwelfarist theories of distributive justice have become prevalent in political philosophy since 1970. "Welfarism," a term coined by Amartya Sen (1979b), is the position that the social choice function should have as its arguments the individual utilities of members of the society. The optimal income distribution, or most desired state of the world, is the one that maximizes the value of that function. The most classical of welfarist approaches is utilitarianism, which takes the welfare functional to be the sum of individual utilities, and therefore recommends that distribution of social resources which maximizes total utility. A second example, the egalitarian welfarist functional, recommends a distribution of resources which equalizes utilities of all individuals – or comes as close to it as possible. (The social welfare functional is, in this case, set equal to the minimum utility level in the population – maximizing it equalizes all utilities, absenting incentive problems of redistribution. The "maximin utility" solution is not to be confused with Rawls's proposal, on which more below.) Nonwelfarism, the position that social welfare or distributional justice is not only a function of individual utilities, derives from many criticisms, which will only be cursorily indicated here.

For discussion and comments which were very useful, I am grateful to G. A. Cohen, William Dickens, Ronald Dworkin, L. J. Helms, Louis Makowski, Peter Morton, Joaquim Silvestre, Hal Varian, and Martin Weitzman.

A first criticism of welfarism is that not all information relevant to equity considerations is summarized in utility. Sen (1977, 1979b) has discussed this extensively. In particular, utility information may ignore rights, and many take the position that certain rights trump or constrain the distributions which welfarism would recommend. Such problems arise when people have nosy or sadistic preferences – in general, when there are what might narrowly be called consumption externalities. This first criticism holds even if utility can be well-defined.

A second criticism of welfarism is that, even if utility is well-defined for individuals, it does not measure individual welfare, for a variety of reasons. Preferences may have been formed endogenously, by a process of cognitive dissonance, so that people learn to like what they are accustomed to or what is available to them (Elster, 1982a). Thus the slave may have adapted to like slavery; welfare judgments based on individual preferences are clearly impugned in such situations. Moreover, welfarism, at some level, is predicated on letting people choose for themselves; but people may not necessarily choose what they prefer (Tversky, 1981). "Revealed preference," which is really "choice," is not synonymous with "preference." This point is to be distinguished from the one that people may not prefer (and choose) what is good for them, which constitutes another branch of this second criticism of welfarism. (Preferences that are formed under nonautonomous conditions, or conditions of severely unequal opportunity, might nullify the appeal of a welfarist calculation.)

A third criticism of welfarism is that utility functions may not be well-defined. Welfare may be a vector of characteristics – success, pleasure, satisfaction, ethical feelings, and so on – and among the various vectors of welfare available to a person, comparisons may be impossible. A person may choose between two situations, but that "revealed preference" may in fact not reveal a preference so much as a choice made from consternation if the person finds the alternatives noncomparable owing to the vector nature of welfare. A less radical problem, but one which still prevents the definition of a real-valued utility function, is the nontransitivity of preferences, which may arise from the vector-valued nature of welfare. A person may be able to compare any two alternatives, but choices among pairs of three may be inconsistent. The problems of endogeneity of preferences and the vector-valued nature of welfare have given rise to terms like political preferences, personal preferences, moral preferences, and metapreferences (Sen, 1977; Harsanyi, 1977; Dworkin, 1981, 1981a).

These three criticisms pose problems which are in ascending order of difficulty for welfarism. In the first case, utility is measurable and reflects welfare, but does not fully capture what is relevant for equity considerations. In the second case, utility continues to be defined, but does not reflect welfare. In the third case, utility ceases to be well-defined. A fourth criticism of welfarism, which perhaps shares aspects of the first and second criticisms, is that people may have or cultivate expensive tastes in which case most welfarist functionals will assign them more of society's resources than they would have in the absence of those tastes (Dworkin, 1981). The issue to which welfarism is here insensitive is personal responsibility. People are, at least in part, responsible for their preferences, but a welfarist social choice function does not allow us to discriminate between people who require large bundles of goods to coddle their expensive tastes and people who require equally expensive bundles because of handicaps which make it difficult for them to produce welfare.

The above review makes no pretense at completeness. [For some recent essays on these subjects, see Sen and Williams (1982).] Its purpose is to motivate the current interest in what might be called resourcist theories of distributional justice. A resourcist mechanism uses information concerning the allocation of resources. All welfarist proposals are resourcist, but the converse is not true: resourcism is a wider category. A welfarist functional is resourcist since the utilities of agents are a function of the resources they and others get, but welfarism implies that resources can enter into the calculation *only* as they affect individual utilities, while in principle one might wish to allow for other possibilities. The natural appeal of nonwelfarist resourcist theories is that resources are the scarce things which are the object of distribution, so questions of distributional equity should be concerned directly with the pattern of resource allocation. Four examples follow of modern theories of distributional justice which are resourcist but not welfarist. Rawls (1971) proposes to equalize, so far as is possible, the bundle of *primary goods* available to each person. Precisely how to define this allocation is problematical, but Rawls's intent is to concentrate on resources of a certain kind, not on utility. (For the most part, economists have bowdlerized Rawls's theory of justice into one which allocates according to "maximin utility.") Sen (1980), in a paper entitled "Equality of What?," proposes to distribute resources in such a way as to equalize the *basic capabilities* of everyone; he distinguishes basic capabilities from both primary goods and from utility. Ronald Dworkin (1981, 1981a), in two papers entitled "What is Equality?," argues that the ethically relevant equality must be equality of *resources,* not equality of welfare. Although he does not claim that equality exhausts distributive justice, his position, more weakly, is that insofar as equality is a value, the appropriate equality is of resources, not of welfare or utility. Fourth, the Marxian theory of exploitation is argued by some (for example, see the first three essays in this volume) as associated with a call for equality of *alienable productive assets.* A person (or group) is exploited precisely because he/she (or it) does not own (in a capitalist economy) his/her per capita share of society's endowment of alienable productive assets.

Three of these four theories (with Sen's "basic capabilities" being the exception) call for *equality* of resources, of various kinds.[1] For Rawls, the jurisdiction of equality is limited to primary goods; for exploitation theory, the jurisdiction is alienable productive assets (which excludes, most importantly, skills and resources attached to the person); for Dworkin, resources seem to be defined most broadly, as they include not only alienable assets but also nontransferable ones of various kinds – talents, handicaps, and various inborn propensities which a person cannot be deemed responsible for having. When one includes inalienable traits such as talent in the jurisdiction of an equality-of-resource theory, the question arises how one might even appropriately define equality of resources, and it is largely with this question that the present paper is concerned.

It is not my purpose to argue for equality-of-resource ethics here, as opposed to other resourcist or welfarist ethics, or ethics in which rights are arguments of the justice functional. The purpose is apparently narrower: to ask, *if* one wishes to widen the definition of resources to include nontransferable ones of various kinds, what distributions of resources would constitute equality of resources? What definitions of resource equality capture the principles adherents of equality of resources require from their ethical intuitions? For example, the basic moral position behind equality-of-resource proposals is that those who have a poor endowment of resources should be compensated. Thus a mechanism for equalizing resources should improve the well-being (however measured) of those who, in the absence of resource equalization, would be on the bottom end of the resource ladder.

1.2.   The concept of a resource-equalizing mechanism

If one wishes to equalize resources, why not just divide all resources up equally among all people? Because some of the resources which concern us are nontransferable. "Talent" is the generic name for such resources. There are also, of course, some transferable resources, like money and food. We cannot physically and literally equalize all resources, and therefore a proposal to "equalize resources" requires specifying a mechanism which assigns the transferable resources in such a way as to compensate people appropriately for their bundles of nontransferable resources. If

---

[1] For Sen, resources are an input into the production of basic capabilities. His is an outcome equality theory, not a resource equality theory. It is not welfarist, since the outcome is not welfare but capability.

Bob has less talent than Andrea, resource equality probably will require he get more of some transferable goods. A *resource-equalizing mechanism* is a rule which associates, to any hypothetical economic environment or "world," a distribution of its transferable resources among the agents. Such a rule must satisfy various axioms. I will examine various candidates for an equality-of-resource mechanism, and exhibit the flaws they have (which is to say, the axioms they violate).

To examine the cogency of equality-of-resource mechanisms when inalienable or nontransferable resources are involved, it is appropriate to make a number of simplifying assumptions. This, I maintain, is justified, since I will conclude that even in the stylized cases I examine, our ethical intuitions are challenged. I will assume that preferences are well-defined, that people have well-defined utility functions. Utility measures welfare and well-being. There are no problems of liberty or freedom in this study which considerations of distributive justice would require us to consider. Essentially, my problem is to consider what constitutes an equal division of some kind of pie, or perhaps of many pies. Often, I assume everyone has the same utility function, or at least utility functions which are in a sense symmetric. It will be assumed that inalienable assets possessed by people are precisely known; there is no problem in getting the person to reveal what assets he possesses. This assumption is appropriate to the present context, as I wish to study equality theories independently of implementation problems. The purpose is to present a first-best ethical standard of egalitarianism.

For much of the paper, I will be commenting on the proposals of Ronald Dworkin (1981a), which constitute the most detailed proposal to date of an equality-of-resource theory. Unlike other critical discussions of equality-of-resource theories [for example, Narveson (1983) and other papers in the same number of that journal], I do not question *a priori* the attractiveness of egalitarianism, or even of equality of resources, but proceed by studying the consequences of implementing equality-of-resource mechanisms.

Dworkin (1981) poses the question with which this paper began: if one is an egalitarian, what should one want to equalize, welfare or resources? He presents a series of arguments against the ethical cogency of equalizing welfare, and concludes that resource equalization is the relevant egalitarianism. In Dworkin (1981a), an insurance mechanism is described for implementing resource equality. In Section 2, I describe the insurance mechanism and another mechanism, called equal division. In Section 3, I present some models of these mechanisms in a context of pure exchange. Section 4 introduces talent and production, and applies both of the mechanisms studied earlier to the problem of seeking an equal division of the resource "talent." Some results are presented which may challenge the appeal of equality-of-resource theories, as implemented, at least, by these two mechanisms. Section 5 presents a pure exchange model which I think captures the essential ethical problems associated with re-distribution of talent. (I claim that production is not the source of the ethical surprises of Section 4, but rather something else which can be modeled in a pure exchange context.) Section 6 carries out further comparisons of the two resource-equalizing mechanisms.

Section 7 presents the main result of the paper. I show that both the insurance mechanism and the equal-division mechanism can behave perversely: they can render worse off, in terms of welfare, the initially resource-poor agents who are supposed to benefit from the redistribution which a resource egalitarian seeks to implement. I claim, then, that neither mechanism is satisfactory as a resource-equalizing mechanism, if an acceptable resource-equalizing mechanism must, at least, improve the welfares of those who were poorly endowed with resources before the redistribution recommended by the mechanism was effected. Sections 8 and 9 discuss the essential philosophical problem which has been, thus far, only implicit: how can one distinguish between those aspects of a person which constitute his "preferences" from those which constitute his "resources"? This question is posed sharply by reporting a theorem which formalizes the intuition of the paper. There is no acceptable conception of resource egalitarianism that does not reduce to recommending equality of welfares. Thus the dichotomy between welfare egalitarianism and resource egalitarianism is misconceived at a level of abstraction appropriate for establishing a first-best ethical standard of egalitarianism.

2.   Two mechanisms for equalizing resources

If all resources are transferable, the natural mechanism for equalizing resources is to divide them up equally among the population. Saying all resources are transferable implies, in particular, that production is not at issue, for if it were, skills and labor would be relevant resources, and they are nontransferable. In a pure exchange economy, with transferable resources only, the equal-division endowment is not necessarily Pareto optimal, and so a natural step is to examine the allocation associated with a competitive equilibrium from an equal-division initial endowment. This allocation will have the property of being "envy free," in that no agent will prefer the bundle of another agent to his own, and, as well, the allocation will be Pareto optimal. Envy-free, efficient allocations have been called "fair" in the literature (see, for example, Foley, 1967; Varian, 1974; Thomson and Varian, 1985). Suppose, now, some of the resources are nontransferable. For example, people have different talents, and talent yields income. A similarly natural proposal is to divide up the property rights in all goods, transferable and nontransferable, so that each has an equal share in society's total resources. Thus in a society of n people, each would own, among other things, a $1/n$ share of the labor power of each person, valued at the wage rate that person earns at equilibrium. If I own some of your labor, I have a claim on you which you can pay off in money or corn, or in labor. We can investigate the equilibria of such an economy. This will be called the "equal-division" mechanism for equalizing resources. One might think, informally, of this mechanism as implementing "mutual slavery," but the connotation is misleading. Having a claim to the income from another person's labor does not extend to having complete rights over everything he does.

There are alternatives to taking the competitive equilibrium generated from equal division as the standard. One could, for example, consider various allocations in the core of the economy generated from equal division. For large economies, the core allocations are identical to the competitive equilibrium allocations. But there is another reason to favor the competitive equilibrium as a standard. Following Dworkin's discussion (1981a), the point of equality-of-resource theories is to give everyone an equal share of what is scarce in society, but then to insist that people pay the true social costs required to satisfy their preferences. Thus people are considered responsible for their preferences, as it were, but not responsible for their resource endowment. Society should indemnify people to the extent of guaranteeing each an equal endowment of resources but after that, the true social cost of one's demand for a good, which is measured by its value at market-clearing prices, should be borne by the person.

A second mechanism for equalizing resources, one proposed by Dworkin, is an insurance market. There is no problem in dividing up transferable resources equally. For nontransferable resources there are, first, a physical division problem (but not a problem in division of property, as I have just pointed out, at least in this world of perfect information), but second, an ethical problem. One might think it impinges on the person to assign property rights to others in his stock of labor and talent. As an alternative, Dworkin proposes that we ask: how much would a person have insured himself against the possibility of drawing a skill capable of earning only a low income, had he known the relevant probabilities? The amount of insurance he would have taken, had that been possible, can be calculated from knowledge of his preferences (toward risk, for example) and of the costs of insurance, reflected in the equilibrium premium. Those premiums are themselves equilibrium prices in the market for insurance, and hence are determined as a result of everyone's demand for insurance, and the total "supply of income," that is, the productive capacities of society. Dworkin argues that a reasonable way to implement equality of resources is to calculate the postinsurance income that would have come about, had people been able to insure themselves against a bad draw in the lottery for the nontransferable resources. Since such insurance was not in fact possible, society might tax people to realize a distribution of income which mimics what would have come about from the insurance mechanism.

Dworkin does not say society *should* tax people in that way, for to make that claim would require a veil-of-ignorance argument of the following sort. Behind the veil of ignorance, where people know their preferences but do not know the degree of talent they will draw in the birth lottery for talent, they agree mutually to insure themselves. Having made this agreement, the tax system is then justified. More weakly, Dworkin claims only that his insurance constitutes a *definition* of equality of resources, not an ethical mandate. [Since Dworkin is opposed to veil-of-ignorance approaches to distributive justice (see Dworkin, 1977, p. 157), he cannot consistently claim the ethical virtue of the mechanism.] Narveson (1983, p. 2) has criticized Dworkin, I think appropriately, for claiming he attempts only to define equality, not to justify it.

Whatever the ethical status of the postinsurance tax-mimic distribution, it is worth noting that the veil of ignorance adopted is a "thin" one, in which people know their preferences, but do not know their distribution of certain resources. Contrast this with the "thick" veil of ignorance in which one knows neither which preferences one will have, nor one's own resources (which is similar to the Rawlsian veil). I will make some observations about the difference in consequences of assuming veils of ignorance of different degrees of opacity.

Dworkin begins his discussion of equality of resources with the equal-division, envy-free equilibrium, where all resources are transferable. But when nontransferable resources are admitted, such as talent, Dworkin finds the insurance mechanism preferable to equal division, for he fears that equal division of property in labor among all people will lead to the "slavery of the talented." Suppose I am born with a socially valuable talent, but 99% of my labor supply is owned by the rest of society. To pay off my debt, which is high because my labor is so valuable, I will have to perform my highly valued skill, even if I should prefer to write, as Dworkin says, indifferent poetry. Hence follows the slavery of the talented. The insurance mechanism, Dworkin believes, will prevent this unpleasant consequence. People would not insure themselves to such a high level that if they "lose" the insurance gamble (that is, they draw the high skill), they would have to spend the great majority of their time working to pay off the premium. I will compare the equal-division mechanism to the insurance mechanism below, and will show that in general Dworkin's intuition is wrong. Indeed, a properly specified insurance mechanism can make the talented even worse off, *ex post,* than the equal division mechanism.

3.   Insurance markets for alienable resources

The prevailing model of insurance is the expected-utility model. Assume there are various possible states of the world, in each of which the agent will have different income or utility. He agrees to make payments to or to receive transfers from others, depending on which state of the world occurs, in such a way as to maximize his expected utility over the various states of the world. [The expected-utility model of behavior, and therefore in particular of insurance-taking behavior, has been challenged in recent years – with alternatives proposed such as prospect theory (Kahnemen and Tversky, 1979), regret theory (Loomes and Sugden, 1982), and theories where utility is assumed to be nonseparable across states of the world (Machina, 1983). But I shall retain the expected-utility model of insurance in this paper.] I will note below that Dworkin's conception of insurance is restrictive in a needless way, given the first-best nature of our inquiry.

3.1.   Identical preferences, single-good insurance

There is a population all of whom have the same preference for the single good corn. Assume a strictly concave von Neumann–Morgenstern utility function $u(C)$. There are, let us say, a million people, and n possible lots of corn. Fraction p_i of the population will be endowed with amount C_i of corn, for $i = 1, \ldots, n$. Thus, behind the thin veil of ignorance, where each knows his preference for corn is given by $u(C)$, but no one knows which lot he will draw, we imagine people decide on the optimal insurance policy. The probability of drawing lot C_i is p_i. An *insurance policy* is a vector of transfers T_i defining the transfer the agent will receive in state i; that is, if he draws endowment C_i, T_i is negative if he "loses" the insurance gamble and positive if he "wins." Thus T_i is the insurance payout net of the premium, in the usual parlance. The optimal insurance policy is a vector $(T_1, T_2, \ldots, T_n)$ which solves the program

$$\max \sum p_i u(C_i + T_i)$$

subject to $\sum p_i T_i \leq 0$.   (P3.1)

The constraint states that total payments do not exceed total receipts by the "insurance company"; it is the condition for feasibility of the insurance policy, or for non-negative profitability of the insurance company. The objective function chooses that feasible insurance plan which maximizes the expected utility of the agent; since all agents are identical in this model behind the thin veil of ignorance they will agree on the same insurance policy.

It is straightforward to calculate the solution to (P3.1). Marginal utilities must be equalized *ex post* for each "state of the world," and by concavity of $u(C)$, which implies

$$C_i + T_i = \text{const.} \quad \text{for all } i.$$

Hence $C_i + T_i = \sum p_i C_i$, and insurance takes the form of every agent agreeing to end up with precisely the average amount of corn.

Risk aversion generates this result. There is complete risk pooling with any concave utility function. The result is certainly pleasant for an equality-of-resource theory: everyone ends up with the same amount of the resource. However, the example is too simple to make interesting distinctions among alternative theories of distributive justice. For note that, as well as producing equality of the resource, this solution produces equality of utilities. And furthermore, it is the utilitarian solution. Maximizing $\sum p_i u(C)$ is equivalent to maximizing total utility in the population since p_i is the fraction of people with lot C_i in the draw.

Dworkin's notion of insurance is, however, far more restrictive. He suggests a constrained type of insurance policy in which people choose a *level* of corn $\bar{C}$ to which they want to insure. Thus the agent will pay a premium of some sort if he draws $C_i > \bar{C}$, and if he draws $C_i < \bar{C}$, he will receive $\bar{C} - C_i$ as a transfer. If we allow the premium to vary with income, then the rational insurer will solve program (P3.1) to arrive at $\bar{C} = \sum p_i C_i$, and Dworkin's restriction is no restriction. But if the premium is to be fixed across income, as Dworkin sometimes says, the solution will be suboptimal. In this kind of normative exercise we should study first-best solutions. The only reason for restrictions of the type Dworkin suggests would be implementability. I therefore define insurance behavior as expected-utility maximization from now on.

3.2.   *Different preferences, single-good insurance*

Suppose people have different preferences, but there is still only one good, corn, the distribution of which we wish to "equalize" through the insurance mechanism. For simplicity, assume there are two preference types in the population: those with von Neumann–Morgenstern utility function $u(C)$ and those with utility function $v(C)$. Assume the lots of corn $(C_1, \ldots, C_n)$ are as before, distributed with probability distribution

$(p_1, \ldots, p_n)$, and that the distribution is the same for each preference type. Then agents of type u solve the problem

$$\text{choose } (T_1, \ldots, T_n) \text{ to max} \sum p_i u(C_i + T_i)$$
$$\text{s.t. } \sum p_i T_i \leq 0, \tag{P3.1}$$

and agents of type v solve the insurance problem

$$\text{choose } (T_1', \ldots, T_n') \text{ to max} \sum p_i v(C_i + T_i')$$
$$\text{s.t. } \sum p_i T_i' \leq 0, \tag{P3.2}$$

One might think that additional insurance possibilities might exist if risks could be pooled across the two types. In fact this is not so here, since each group enjoys the same distribution of the resource, and there is only one resource. In Appendix A of the original version of this essay, several goods are introduced and the insurance problem becomes more complicated.

Both u and v are assumed to be strictly concave functions. Solving (P3.1) and (P3.2) yields

for all i, $C_i + T_i = \sum p_i C_i$,
for all i, $C_i + T_i' = \sum p_i C_i$.

Thus, *independent of preference type,* each agent ends up after insurance with exactly the average endowment of corn. The insurance mechanism produces precisely the same result as the equal-division mechanism would produce.

Note that the consequence of insurance is what can be called *sectional utilitarianism:* within each section of agents, a section being all agents of a given preference type, total utility is maximized. Total utility across the entire population, however, is not maximized by this kind of insurance.

To see this, let us proceed behind the thick veil of ignorance. Suppose it were decided that a person is not responsible for his preferences, as he is not for his resources, and we allow agents to insure themselves against drawing, in the birth lottery, a psychological makeup which does not give them much pleasure from life (corn). Perhaps $u(\cdot)$ is a depressive type and $v(\cdot)$ gets much more kick from corn. I here, for the first time, assume interpersonal comparability between $u(\cdot)$ and $v(\cdot)$. Suppose the population is composed one-half of u types and one-half of v types. The appropriate insurance problem behind the thick veil of ignorance is to choose an insurance policy $(T_i, \ldots, T_n, T_i', \ldots, T_n')$ to maximize

$$\tfrac{1}{2} \sum p_i u(C_i + T_i) + \tfrac{1}{2} \sum p_i v(C_i + T_i')$$
$$\text{s.t. } \sum p_i (T_i + T_i') \leq 0. \tag{P3.3}$$

That is, as far as a particular agent is concerned there are $2n$ states of the world: he can be born either a u type with corn endowment C_i, $i =$

$1, \ldots, n$, or a v type, with any one of the n corn endowments. Solving (P3.3) yields

$$\forall i, j \qquad v'(C_j + T_j') = v'(C_i + T_i') = u'(C_i + T_i) = u'(C_j + T_j). \qquad (3.4)$$

Marginal utilities are equalized both across endowments *and* across types. Now suppose that v, being the manic type, gets more marginal utility than u at any level of corn:

$$\forall C \qquad v'(C) > u'(C).$$

Then the first-order condition (3.4) requires more corn to be given to the v types in order to equalize marginal utilities across types. Hence, post-insurance, all u types will get the same amount of corn, all v types will get the same amount of corn, and the v types will get more corn than the u types.

From behind the thick veil of ignorance we derive inequality in the distribution of corn resources. In fact, from behind the thick veil of ignorance, the insurance proposal becomes utilitarianism. The distinction between an insurance approach where people are deemed responsible for their preferences (thin veil) and the insurance approach corresponding to the thick veil is the difference between utilitarianism and sectional utilitarianism. The thick veil approach is the argumentation used by Harsanyi (1977) to justify utilitarianism.

Thus, there is a thin line between insurance as an institution for realizing equality of resources and utilitarianism. This is perhaps surprising, given the antiwelfarist, *a fortiori* antiutilitarian sentiments of equality-of-resource proponents. This line will become even thinner in the sections below.

It is worthwhile to point out a little "paradox" which arises in considering veils of ignorance of different thicknesses. In solving the insurance problem with the thin veil [(P3.1) and (P3.2)], we noted that independent of type, *all* agents end up with the same consumption. One might hasten to conclude, therefore, that knowledge of one's type makes no difference to the problem, and therefore proceeding behind the thick veil, where one's type is unknown, will not alter the distribution of corn. I have just shown that this inference is false. Although consumption may be identical for all preference types (so long as all preference types are risk averse) if type is known, it is not independent of type if type is unknown and subject to insurance.

4.   Production and talent

In this section, a nontransferable resource is introduced. I construct the simplest model in which talent in productive labor is differentially distributed. Suppose corn is the only good which is produced and consumed, but people have different innate abilities to produce corn from labor. The *real wage s* of a person is the rate at which he can convert his leisure (labor) into corn. Thus s is a measure of one's talent. Suppose all agents have the same utility function $u(C, \ell)$ over corn and leisure. Everyone is born with zero units of corn and one unit of leisure, but people are born with different talents s. Clearly if there is no redistribution then the higher the s one is born with, the better off one is. I assume s is not an argument of the utility function: one gets no utility from performing "skilled" labor, from exercising a talent.

4.1. Insurance for talent

If we consider talent a resource, the distribution of which is morally arbitrary, then one might wish to compensate those who draw a low talent in the birth lottery. The insurance mechanism for equalizing talent would work as follows. Suppose the probability of drawing talent s in this population is $p(s)$. Before the lottery for talents is taken, the agent decides on an insurance policy $\{T(s); s = s_1, \ldots, s_r)\}$ which lists the transfer he will receive if he draws talent s, where there are r possible levels of talent s_1 through s_r. The insurance policy he chooses maximizes his expected utility. Now having received a transfer $T(s)$, after drawing talent s, the agent will decide upon the amount of labor to provide, and he earns s corn per unit labor expended. Let $e(s, T)$ be the amount of labor offered by an agent of talent s who receives a transfer T; e is his labor supply function. Then the insurance problem is

$$\text{choose } \{T(s) \mid s = s_1, \ldots, s_r\} \text{ to}$$
$$\max_s \sum p(s) u(T(s) + e(s, T(s))s, 1 - e(s, T(s)))$$
$$\text{s.t. } \sum p(s)T(s) \leq 0. \tag{P4.1}$$

The first argument in the utility function is the agent's total corn income and the second argument is his leisure. The constraint expresses the feasibility of this insurance policy for the population. In Appendix B of the original version of this essay, this program is solved and the following theorem is proved:

Theorem 1: *If $u(C, \ell)$ is separable in corn and leisure, then optimal insurance for talent implies*

1. *all agents end up with the same amount of corn, postinsurance;*
2. *the higher one's talent, the more one works;*
3. *the higher one's talent, the lower one's final utility, postinsurance.*

In trying to compensate those who draw a bad lot in the talent lottery, the insurance mechanism appears to overcompensate them: they end up better off in welfare than the more talented. This apparently perverse consequence of taxation of talent has been noted in other contexts (see, for example, Mirrlees, 1974, 1982).

Several things must be noted here. First, this insurance scheme can only work if talent is identifiable, for a self-interested agent will wish to conceal his true talent because final utility is monotone decreasing in talent. I have said earlier it is appropriate, for this paper, to assume full revelation of resource endowments.[2] Note, however, that the labor supplied by each agent is not coerced: it is his optimal labor supply, decided upon by him given his insurance tax (or transfer) and his real wage.

Second, note that the insurance mechanism is synonymous with utilitarianism in this model. Maximizing expected utility with a suitable transfer scheme is equivalent to maximizing total utility. This is the case because all agents have the same utility function. So although the identity between utilitarianism and equality of resources through insurance remains, the result no longer achieves equality of utility, as in Section 3.1. It is perhaps surprising that Dworkin's insurance proposal is closer, in this sense, to utilitarianism than to "equality of welfare," for I take it that Dworkin is more opposed to utilitarianism than to equality of welfare.

What should disturb a proponent of equality-of-resource ethics in this example? I do not think it is the "perversity" of the talented ending up worse off than the untalented: it is simply the consequence of unequal welfares. Where people's preferences are different there may be various reasons, explored by Dworkin, for rejecting equality of welfare. But if all agents have the *same* preferences, it seems any suitable equality-of-resource mechanism should bring about equality of welfare. In the talent problem, highly talented people are paying in welfare terms for their lucky draw in a resource, not for their particular preferences with regard to corn and leisure, which are identical with everyone else's.

There is a way to look at this problem which clarifies the result. In fact, every person's leisure is a different good. No one can consume anyone else's leisure. Hence the agents, from a formal viewpoint, have *different preferences:* for I have a taste only for corn and *my* leisure. A highly talented person is exactly like a person with an involuntary expensive taste: the only kind of leisure he likes to consume is expensive leisure, his own. His leisure is expensive because it has an alternative use which is highly valued by society. The utilitarian objective function of the insurance

---

[2] Dasgupta and Hammond (1980) calculate what optimal insurance looks like in a model similar to this one when talent is not revealed by the agent, so the insurance policy must be constrained by insisting that final utility be monotone nondecreasing in talent.

problem will require, for reasons of productive efficiency, that the talented work longer hours than the untalented, which thereby relegates the talented to lower welfare because of the equal corn consumption result.

Here is a final perspective on this result.[3] Suppose you know that over the course of a year you will have different skill levels on different days. Your preferences for leisure and corn remain constant, but with probability p_i your skill level on a given day will be s_i. Corn is perishable, and so you cannot stock corn to save up for consumption on those days when you have low skill. But you can contract with an insurance company, with whom others are similarly contracting, to supply you with corn on some days, in return for which you pay corn premiums on other days. Then you will choose precisely the pattern of transfers $\{T_i\}$ described in Theorem 1. Maximizing your total utility for the year requires you to consume the same amount of corn every day, but to work harder on your highly skilled days. I think this result does not bother our moral intuitions at all, because one person is pooling risks across his various states. It is altogether different, from an intuitive point of view, when after the die is cast, each person will be either of high or low skill for his whole life. One consequence of this difference is that in the story of skill variation across days of the year, each person ends up with the same total utility for the year, while in the veil-of-ignorance problem, some people end up with more utility than others, *ex post,* in their realized lives.

4.2.   *Differential utilities and differential talent*

Suppose there are different types of people, with different preferences over corn and leisure, each type enjoying the same distribution of talent. An insurance market for talent can be modeled as a contingent claims market. In fact, so long as there is only one transferable good, and the distribution of talent of agents is the same in each section of the population (defined as all those having the same preferences), there need be no transfers across sections. Hence the optimal insurance problem for this situation is simply a set of optimal insurance problems like that of Section 4.1, one for each section. Thus we have "sectional utilitarianism," and within each section, final utility is monotone decreasing in talent, after insurance, if utility is separable.

Hence, with different preferences, the insurance market for talent differs both from utilitarianism (because it produces only sectional utilitarianism) and from equality of welfare. But I submit that if proponents of equality of resources find the results of the insurance mechanism ethically

---

[3] I thank Duncan Foley for the example of this paragraph.

objectionable, they do so because of their antiutilitarianism. For as was pointed out, even within a section, different agents in fact have formally different preferences (because of the personalized nature of leisure), and the result of unequal utilities within a section is a consequence of the utilitarian mechanism of distributing resources to those best able to convert them into utility. Talented people are handicapped in a utilitarian world because the leisure they require as a consumption good has a high value to society in its alternative use.

4.3.   *Equal division of talents*

I investigate next the consequences of the equal-division mechanism in the world of differential talent. To simplify, suppose there are two people with high and low talents s_2 and s_1, respectively, where s_i is the real wage in corn per unit labor of person i. There are three goods: corn, 1's leisure, and 2's leisure. An equal-division mechanism gives each agent an equal property right in all three endowments. Suppose there is no corn initially (it must all be produced) and that each agent is endowed with one unit of leisure. The two of them have "identical" preferences $u(C, \ell)$ – not formally identical, because their preferences are for different kinds of leisure. Thus the value in corn of this society's total leisure endowment is $s_1 + s_2$, and each is given half of that in the equal-division world.

The competitive equilibrium problem is

$$1 \quad \text{chooses } C^1, \ell^1 \text{ to}$$
$$\max u(C^1, \ell^1)$$
$$\text{s.t. } C^1 + s_1 \ell^1 \le \tfrac{1}{2}s_1 + \tfrac{1}{2}s_2,$$
$$2 \quad \text{chooses } C^2, \ell^2 \text{ to}$$
$$\max u(C^2, \ell^2)$$
$$\text{s.t. } C^2 + s_2 \ell^2 \le \tfrac{1}{2}s_1 + \tfrac{1}{2}s_2$$

Markets clear:

$$C^1 + C^2 = s_1(1 - \ell^1) + s_2(1 - \ell^2).$$

Each person must purchase corn and his own leisure with his budget. Leisure not repurchased will be used to produce corn. The market clearing condition assures that the demand and supply of corn is equal (and the same will follow for leisure, by Walras's Law).

This is a rather simple equilibrium problem, since the equilibrium prices of leisure (s_1 and s_2) are known to be equal to the marginal productivities of their associated labors, and the price of corn is normalized at

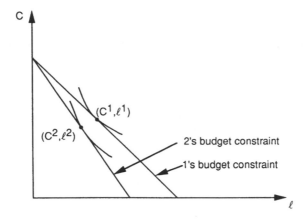

Figure 6.1

unity. Under standard assumptions on preferences, an equilibrium exists; simply add the two budget constraints, and note that they sum to the market clearing equation. Thus the pairs (C^1, ℓ^1) and (C^2, ℓ^2) which solve the utility maximizing problems above constitute an equilibrium allocation.

It can immediately be noted that the high-talent person 2 is worse off in welfare terms than low-talent 1, by examining the budget constraints. For 1 and 2 have the same income to spend, but 2 must buy corn and expensive leisure, while 1 buys corn and cheap leisure. (Recall, $s_2 > s_1$.) The result is illustrated in Figure 6.1. In general, as is clear from the figure, 1 and 2 will consume different amounts of corn as well as different amounts of leisure. It is not true that 1 must consume more corn than 2 but it is true that 1 always has higher utility than 2 at the equilibrium.

Hence, the "equal division of talents" mechanism differs from the insurance mechanism, as it did not in the case of transferable goods (see Appendix 1 of the original version of this essay). The qualitative result that the highly talented end up with lower utility than the talented (with identical preferences) remains, but the allocation of corn is in general not identical across people as it is with the insurance mechanism. With this divergence, the question can be posed: is one institution more ethically palatable than the other? I study this below.

Before proceeding, note that the equal-division mechanism can be used when agents have different preferences as well. Competitive equilibrium exists for ordinal noncomparable preferences. Hence this mechanism can be employed in a much more general setting than the simple example I have given.

5.   A pure exchange model of inalienable resources

At first glance, the problem of differential talents seems intrinsically more complicated than the problem of alienable resources because production is involved as well as exchange. But there is a pure exchange model which captures, I believe, the ethically relevant feature (for these concerns) of the differential talent problem, and has the advantage of being simpler to analyze. The essence of the talent problem is that the highly talented person has a taste for an expensive good – his own leisure. That good is expensive because it is scarce and useful to society, and hence commands a high price. Talent is a socially valuable good in production, but in its alternative use, as leisure, it has consumption value for only one person.

I construct a pure exchange model which captures this salient feature of talent. Imagine that there are two people and three consumption goods named C, G_1, and G_2 whose aggregate social endowments are in amounts $\bar{C}$, $\bar{G}_1$, and $\bar{G}_2$. Andrea has a taste for C and G_1 only and Bob has a taste for C and G_2 only, but their utility functions are otherwise "identical." Thus Andrea has utility function $u(C, G_1)$ and Bob $u(C, G_2)$. Suppose $\bar{G}_1 > \bar{G}_2$. Then G_2 is "scarce," and Bob has a preference for the scarce good. Think of C as corn, which they both can consume; G_1 plays the role of Andrea's leisure and G_2 of Bob's leisure. We can examine the insurance mechanism and the equal-division mechanism for "equalizing the resources" in the three goods. This is a model of exchange without production, but where agents have personalized consumption tastes. What is yet lacking is a way of making G_1 and G_2 socially valuable, not just valuable to Andrea or Bob, respectively. This can be accomplished by replicating the Andrea–Bob couplet one million times, so that there is an economy with two million people, one-half of whom are clones of Andrea, etc. Then G_1 and G_2 become valuable to society; there will be competition for acquiring G_1 among the Andreas, and competition for G_2 among the Bobs. We can speak of competitive prices as reflecting the social value of the various resources.

I next examine the consequences of the insurance mechanism and the equal-division mechanism in this model to verify the relevant identification of this model with the talent model of Section 4.

5.1.   The insurance mechanism

Behind the veil of ignorance before the agent knows his "talent," he does not know whether he will want to consume G_1 or G_2 – he does not know whether he will be an Andrea or a Bob. Insurance takes the form of agreeing on a way to distribute the "transferable" good C. It is clear that (whoever becomes) Andrea should get all the $\bar{G}_1$ and whoever is incarnated as Bob should get all the $\bar{G}_2$, since G_1 is wasted if any of it goes to Bob, and G_2 is wasted if any of it goes to Andrea. Hence the insurance problem is to decide upon an allocation (C_1, C_2) of $\bar{C}$ to Andrea and Bob to:

$$\max \tfrac{1}{2}[u(C_1, \bar{G}_1) + u(C_2, \bar{G}_2)]$$
$$\text{s.t. } C_1 + C_2 = \bar{C}. \tag{P5.1}$$

(I assume there is a 50% chance of becoming either an Andrea or a Bob.)

Assume now, as before, that utility function u is separable between C and G_1 or G_2. Then, since the solution of (P5.1) entails equal marginal utilities of corn for the two types, it implies

$$C_1 = C_2 = \tfrac{1}{2}\bar{C}.$$

Thus each of Andrea and Bob ends up with the same amount of corn, and each Bob (the "talented" one) has lower utility than each Andrea. This follows because $\bar{G}_2 < \bar{G}_1$, and so

$$u(\tfrac{1}{2}\bar{C}, \bar{G}_2) < u(\tfrac{1}{2}\bar{C}, \bar{G}_1).$$

We have the same qualitative result as in Section 4.1.

5.2. The equal-division mechanism

Assign property rights in the three goods equally,[4] so each of Andrea and Bob has an intial endowment of the goods $(\tfrac{1}{2}\bar{C}, \tfrac{1}{2}\bar{G}_1, \tfrac{1}{2}\bar{G}_2)$. Normalize prices by setting the price of corn C to unity. Then equilibrium prices $(1, p_1, p_2)$ solve this problem:

1. Let (C_1, X_1) be Andrea's demand for C and G_1. This demand solves

    $$\max u(C_1, X_1)$$
    $$\text{s.t. } C_1 + p_1 X_1 = \tfrac{1}{2}\bar{C} + \tfrac{1}{2}p_1\bar{G}_1 + \tfrac{1}{2}p_2 G_2. \tag{5.2.1}$$

2. Let (C_2, X_2) be Bob's demand for C and G_2. The demand solves

    $$\max u(C_2, X_2)$$
    $$\text{s.t. } C_2 + p_2 X_2 = \tfrac{1}{2}\bar{C} + \tfrac{1}{2}p_1\bar{G}_1 + \tfrac{1}{2}p_2 G_2. \tag{5.2.2}$$

3. Market clearing conditions:

    $$C_1 + C_2 = \bar{C},$$
    $$X_1 = \bar{G}_1,$$
    $$X_2 = \bar{G}_2.$$

---

[4] I now treat the economy as if there were only two people. It is well-known this captures the competitive equilibrium of the replicated economy.

Note that, of course, Andrea and Bob have the same income. In competitive equilibrium, since the utility functions are symmetric and G_2 is scarce relative to G_1, $p_2 > p_1$. Hence Andrea will have higher utility in equilibrium than Bob: the picture is exactly the same as Figure 6.1. Andrea and Bob have the "same tastes," and the same budget, but Andrea likes a cheap good and Bob a dear one. At equilibrium, Andrea, the "untalented one," is better off in utility than Bob.

There is an analogy between Bob, who has an expensive taste for a scarce consumption good in this model, and a skilled agent in the model of Section 3 who has an expensive taste for his own leisure. The analogy is not exact, however, since the skilled agent of Section 3 would be better off than the unskilled agent if left alone, while Bob would be worse off than Andrea if they were left alone (with, let us say, the same amount of corn). The simplicity that is purchased by working with a pure exchange model is worth the cost of the disanalogous aspects of these two models. The general points I make about the equal-division and insurance mechanisms by studying an Andrea–Bob model apply, as well, to models with production.

6.   Comparison of equal-division and insurance mechanisms for equality of talent

Ronald Dworkin discards the equal-division mechanism as ethically unpalatable, compared to the insurance mechanism, for equalizing talent, as he believes it will lead to "slavery of talented" (Dworkin, 1981a, pp. 311–12). He conceives of holding an auction in people's labor which is equivalent to the equal-division mechanism I have proposed, since each person in the auction would begin with equal wealth and would have to buy back his own leisure. In a large society, any person will owe 99% of the value of his potential labor to society with the equal-division mechanism, so a highly talented person will be forced to perform the service which produces his high wage to pay off his debt, even should he rather engage in less skilled activity ("writing indifferent poetry"). Hence the apparent "slavery of the talented."[5] In contrast, Dworkin believes that the insurance mechanism would not produce this unpleasant result. For he believes people would never insure themselves to guarantee ridiculously high levels of income. A ridiculously high level of income is one with this property: if one drew the talent enabling one to produce that income, one would "lose" the insurance gamble, not collect insurance, but would be forced to use the talent to pay the insurance premium, even if one

---

[5] As argued in Section 2, it is incorrect to call this slavery of the talented.

preferred to "write indifferent poetry." In such a case, the person again would be a "slave to his maximum earning power" (Dworkin, 1981a, p. 320).

Appealing as Dworkin's intuition might be, it is incorrect. In this section I show that the talented can end up *worse off* under a properly specified insurance mechanism than under the equal-division-of-labor method, which, as I have written, is the equivalent to Dworkin's labor auction. In this example, a person is more "enslaved" by the insurance agreement if he is born talented. I give an example of preferences under which the talented will be worse off under the insurance scheme than under equal division. Dworkin's objection to the labor auction, I claim, is based entirely on the low utility of the talented person under equal division, because of the labor he must perform to pay off his debt. But the insurance mechanism can be even worse in this regard. On these grounds, one cannot choose easily between the two mechanisms.

I will compare the consequences of operating the insurance mechanism and the equal-division mechanism when there are two agents with utility functions $u(C, G_i)$, where $i = 1, 2$. This is the Andrea–Bob problem of Section 5. Assume a utility function of the form

$$u(C, G_i) = \rho^3 (C^\rho + G_i^\rho), \qquad -\infty \le \rho \le 1; \tag{6.1}$$

$u(C, G_i)$ is a concave, monotone utility function and additively separable. Under the insurance mechanism, as in Section 5.1, it is easily calculated that Andrea gets all of $\bar{G}_1$ and Bob gets all of $\bar{G}_2$, and each agent gets $\frac{1}{2}\bar{C}$ of the first good, since u is additively separable.

Under the equal-division mechanism, Andrea and Bob likewise end up with the stocks of $\bar{G}_1$ and $\bar{G}_2$, respectively, but it is unclear how much corn (C) each agent gets. Depending on the value of ρ, Bob can end up under equal division getting more than one-half of the corn, exactly one-half of the corn, or less than one-half of the corn. Therefore the same is true for Andrea. But under insurance, as noted above, each agent always gets exactly one-half of the corn. Thus, for either agent, the insurance mechanism can lead to an outcome which is better than, the same as, or worse than the equal-division mechanism. In particular, if we think of Bob as the talented agent (as he has a preference for the scarce kind of "leisure"), he can end up even *worse off* under insurance than under the equal-division mechanism. If we considered him to be "enslaved by his talent" under equal division, *a fortiori* he is also enslaved by the insurance mechanism.

To be precise, the following theorem is proved in Appendix C of the original version of this essay:

Theorem 2: *Let there be three goods in amounts* $(\bar{C}, \bar{G}_1, \bar{G}_2)$ *with* $\bar{G}_1 >$ $\bar{G}_2$, *and two agents with preferences*

$$u(C, G_i) = \rho^3(C^\rho + G_i^\rho), \quad \text{for some } \rho \text{ in the region } -\infty \le \rho \le 1,$$

where agent i has a taste only for goods C and G_i. (Agent 2 can be viewed as "talented"; he has a taste for scarce "leisure.") *Then*

1. *if* $\rho < 0$, *the "talented" agent 2 ends up worse off in welfare under "equal-division" competitive equilibrium than under insurance;*
2. *if* $\rho = 0$, *the two institutions generate identical results;*
3. *if* $0 < \rho < 1$, *the "talented" agent ends up worse off under insurance than under equal division.*

To summarize: If Bob and Andrea have a certain kind of preferences (as indicated in Theorem 2), then Bob will owe even more to society under the insurance scheme than he will under the equal-division scheme. This is a model of pure exchange, but the same holds true in a model of production. With reasonable preferences, the agent who is born talented may owe more to society on account of the insurance he contracted for behind the veil of ignorance than he would owe if his talented labor were owned equally by all (and he owned, likewise, his share of everyone else's labor).

7.   The central paradox of equality of resources

Some surprises have emerged in studying the two mechanisms that have been proposed to implement equality of resources. The insurance mechanism implements "sectional utilitarianism"; the more similar are people in their tastes, the closer the postinsurance distribution is to the utilitarian distribution. This should surprise those who might have thought the insurance mechanism was a sharp alternative to utilitarianism. Second, when inalienable resources, in particular talents, become an object of redistribution, both mechanisms appear to overcompensate those whose bad luck we wished to repair. Third, the appeal of the insurance mechanism, with respect to its "enslavement of the talented," contrasted with the equal-division mechanism, is ambiguous. But none of these results are fatal to an equality-of-resource intuition. With regard to the utilitarian aspects of the insurance mechanism, one might argue that the commitment to equality of resources requires new interest in the utilitarian position; what remains discarded is equality of welfare. With regard to the second problem, one might say that since equality of welfare is of no import, or of second-order import, we should not be disturbed that "overcompensation" results. What is relevant is that society subsidizes those with unlucky draws in the natural lottery, not that those who are born lucky end up in the final account unfortunate relative to the ones born unlucky. Third, the ambiguous welfare treatment by the two mechanisms of the talented might require us to admit the possible usefulness of the equal-division mechanism, instead of impugning the only remaining interesting equality-of-resources mechanism, insurance.

In this section, I show that the two mechanisms suffer from a deeper problem. Both of them may render the people we wish to subsidize under an equality-of-resource ethic even worse off than they would have been without the subsidy, in terms of welfare. This is disturbing because, given we are admitting that people have preferences and a well-defined sense of welfare, one purpose of equalizing resources is to improve the *welfare* of those who have few resources, who have less than "their share" of resources, however we decide to define their share. With equality-of-welfare ethics, we redistribute resources in order to equalize welfare; with equality-of-resource ethics, we redistribute resources equally, not without *any* regard to welfare, but because we are motivated to improve, at least somewhat, the welfare of those who began with few resources. We wish to start people from a position of equal resource opportunities, not for the sake of some abstract symmetry, but because this will improve the *welfares* of those who otherwise would have been relatively lacking in resources. (It does not follow from this that we should *equalize* welfares and that is why an equality-of-welfare ethic differs from equality of resources, not because the latter ethic is unconcerned with welfare.) But even this ordinal admission, with respect to the improvement of welfare as a motivation for equality-of-resource ethics, suffices to flaw fatally the two "equality-of-resource" mechanisms studied in this paper. The insurance mechanism and the equal-division mechanism can damage those whom we wish to help. This damage, I submit, is a deep problem.

7.1.   The ethical inconsistency of the equal-division mechanism

Imagine Andrea and Bob, who have preferences for one good, corn (C). Andrea's utility function is $v(C)$ and Bob's utility function is $w(C)$. There is a social endowment $\bar{C}$ of corn. The equal-division mechanism divides the corn equally between them, and that is the end of the problem. Suppose that Andrea gets more pleasure from corn than Bob, that is,

for all C, $v(C) > w(C)$.

We now discover that the reason she gets more pleasure from corn than Bob is that there is a second good which we did not take account of, chemical endorphins, which Andrea and Bob are each consuming. In fact, Andrea and Bob have a utility function defined over corn and endorphins, and for this example, we may suppose it is the same utility function, that is,

$$v(C) = u(C, \bar{G}_1) \quad \text{and} \quad w(C) = u(C, \bar{G}_2), \qquad \bar{G}_1 > \bar{G}_2,$$

where $\bar{G}_i$ are their endorphin levels. The reason Andrea gets more pleasure from corn than Bob is that she is consuming, as well as the corn, more endorphins than he.

Now endorphins are just like a talent. They are an inborn characteristic which enables a person to process corn more efficiently into welfare. If our resource egalitarianism extends to talents, then we should recalculate the distribution of corn between Andrea and Bob, to take account of their differential endowment of the newly discovered "talent." How will the equal-division mechanism now distribute the three goods, corn, Andrea's endorphins, and Bob's endorphins? This is precisely the problem studied in Section 6, as the notation should make clear. Equal division is implemented by dividing the property rights equally between the two agents in corn, Andrea's endorphins and Bob's endorphins, and examining the associated competitive equilibrium. By Pareto optimality of that equilibrium, Bob will get back all of his endorphins, and Andrea will get back all of hers, but the corn will not, in general, be split evenly between them. In fact, as Theorem 2 says, it is entirely possible that Bob will end up with less than half the corn. In this case, *Bob would have been better off had we not extended the jurisdiction of resource egalitarianism to include endorphins, but simply divided the corn between them.* By trying to subsidize Bob with radical equal division, by which I mean equal division of all resources, including the personalized ones, he is rendered worse off than he would have been if we had not tried to compensate him for his bad luck.

It is not necessary that the goods be "endorphins," things the tastes for which are completely personalized, for this perversity to occur. Andrea could have some liking for G_2 and Bob some liking for G_1, and by continuity, the same perversity will occur. The equal-division mechanism displays an unpleasant inconsistency. As we extend the jurisdiction of resource equalization to a larger list of goods, in particular nontransferable ones, it can reallocate the previously distributed goods (corn) in a way which damages the person whom resource egalitarianism is putatively designed to compensate. I call this *inconsistency,* because the mechanism changes its recommended allocation based on the discovery of new goods, which were in fact there in the first place, but had not been explicitly mentioned.

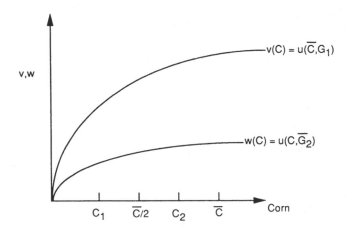

Figure 6.2. (C_1, C_2) distribution of total $\bar{C}$ equalizes $v'(C_2)$ and $w'(C_1)$

7.2. The ethical inconsistency of the insurance mechanism

We now apply the insurance mechanism to distribute corn between Andrea and Bob, who have utility functions $v(C)$ and $w(C)$. This problem was studied in Section 3.2. The agents will insure themselves so each ends up with one-half the corn.

Now suppose, as above, we discover endorphins, and view the problem as one allowing Bob and Andrea to insure themselves with respect to the distribution of corn and endorphins, where their utility functions are $u(C, G_1)$ and $u(C, G_2)$. This problem was also studied in Section 3.2. Now the corn will be distributed between them in such a way as to equalize their marginal utilities of corn. Suppose their utility functions are those depicted in Figure 6.2. Then the marginal-utility-equalizing distribution of corn awards more corn to Andrea than to Bob. That is, *Bob would have been better off had we not extended the insurance mechanism to try and compensate him for his unlucky draw of low endorphins in the birth lottery.* The insurance mechanism behaves *inconsistently,* as does the equal-division mechanism, in that it can, perversely, damage the agent whom resource egalitarianism is designed to help.

One might object: What kind of insurance is this that can penalize the person who ends up with the low "talent"? The answer is: expected-utility-maximizing insurance. Dworkin (1981a) does not propose this kind of insurance (which economists consider to be rational insurance), but rather a minimal floor insurance policy where a person insures himself not to maximize expected utility, but to guarantee some minimal income. Dworkin does not describe in a sufficiently precise manner how his catastrophe insurance is defined. Is there a way of defining an insurance mechanism which would implement equality of resources, not behave perversely and inconsistently as described above, and still preserve Dworkin's division between resource egalitarianism and welfare egalitarianism? The answer, explained in the next section, is no.

8.   Equality of resources implies equality of welfare

The strategy of this paper has been to examine in some detail two possible mechanisms for implementing a resource-egalitarian ethic. Both mechanisms have been shown to allocate goods, in certain cases, in ways which no resource egalitarian would support. Neither equal division nor optimal insurance implements a thoroughgoing resource egalitarianism, where among the set of resources we include "talents." This may suggest that we continue the search for a satisfactory resource-equalizing mechanism which respects the divide between resource equality and welfare equality.

Such a search would, however, be in vain. For I have proved that there is no mechanism which distributes transferable resources in a way which resource egalitarianism requires, except one: the mechanism that allocates resources to equalize welfare. Thus any prescription for a thoroughgoing resource egalitarianism becomes welfare egalitarianism. [This is proved in a sequel to the present paper (Roemer, 1986).] In particular, there is no way of altering the insurance mechanism to make it "ethically consistent" while still preserving a distinction between its actions and welfare egalitarianism.

The strategy for proving this theorem is similar to that used in social choice theory and bargaining theory. We wish to define a mechanism which can act on a relatively unrestricted domain of economic environments. Given any economic environment – a list of agents, the resources available, the utility functions of the agents, and the production function – the mechanism must assign an allocation of resources which is deemed to be "resource equalizing." We do not know precisely what this entails, but we can, at least, specify certain necessary conditions for what such equalizing means.

1.   The mechanism should, at least, distribute resources in a *Pareto optimal* fashion.
2.   It should be *resource monotonic:* as the amount of resources increases in any hypothetical world, the resource-equalizing dis-

tribution of goods should not change in such a way as to render any agent worse off than he was before.
3. The mechanism should be *symmetric:* if the world consists of two agents, between whom resources are to be distributed, and they have identical preferences and skills, then they should receive identical bundles of resources.
4. The mechanism should be *consistent.* Consistency is not easy to define in one sentence: it is the property described in Sections 7.1 and 7.2, which both optimal insurance and equal division lack.

Theorem 3: *Only one mechanism exists which is defined on a large domain of economic environments and satisfies these four properties, the mechanism which distributes resources in such a way as to equalize utility.*

This paper can be viewed as a preamble which might convince the reader of the plausibility of this theorem. (It was by working through the examples of this paper I conjectured the theorem.)

One of the objections Dworkin (1981) makes against welfare egalitarianism is that people have incommensurate conceptions of welfare, conceptions so different that it is meaningless to compare welfares of different people. In this paper, I have assumed welfare to be interpersonally comparable. For it seems to me that that assumption makes the contest between equality of welfare and equality of resources a sharp one. After all, if welfare is not interpersonally comparable, then equality of welfare can have no meaning, and hence equality of resources would appear to win the contest for meaningful egalitarianism by default. But this intuition, it turns out, is incorrect. Without interpersonally comparable utility, there is *no* mechanism which satisfies axioms one, two, and four above (Pareto optimality, resource monotonicity, and consistency). If welfare is interpersonally comparable, then no distinction between resource equality and welfare equality can be drawn; if welfare is interpersonally noncomparable, then the impossibility theorem states that resource egalitarianism is an incoherent notion.

9. Preferences versus resources: the slippery slope

The theorem I have reported does not solve this venerable philosophical debate, but it reduces the debate to one over the model and its axioms. The basic intuition which the theorem formalizes is the idea encountered in the discovery that the degrees of satisfaction Andrea and Bob derive from corn differ because they possess different endowments of a nontransferable resource, which I called endorphins. Suppose two people have different preferences over a list of n goods. There must be a reason.

Perhaps that reason takes the form of another good, or several other goods, which the two people are consuming in different amounts. Thus if you and I have different preferences, is it not because we have different levels of endorphins, different patterns of synaptic connections, exposures to different families (which is a kind of external resource), and so on? If we list a sufficient number of such "resources," some of which are internal to the person and some external, then you and I can be represented as having the same preferences – we differ "only" in our consumption of different vectors of resources. Some of these resources cannot, in fact, be transferred between us, but we have already accepted the postulate that resource egalitarianism requires compensation for those resources whose distribution is morally arbitrary, even if they are nontransferable.

The idea of reducing agents with different preferences to ones with the same *fundamental preferences* over an extended list of goods is not new; it has been discussed by Kolm (1972), Rawls (1982), and others. A recently proved theorem of R. E. Howe (for which see Roemer, 1986) demonstrates that such a mathematical reduction can always be performed. The consistency axiom I have discussed forces the resource-equalizing mechanism to take account of these "hidden resources" in deciding how to allocate the resources we see, and it can be shown that welfare egalitarianism is then the only admissible ethically consistent and resource monotonic allocation mechanism.

The reported theorem thus implements a reductionist, determinist program. It proceeds by reducing apparent differences in the preferences of agents to differences in their resource endowments. Thus what initially appears as a difference between people for which they must bear responsibility (i.e., preferences) becomes a difference for which they do not bear responsibility (i.e., resources). Where does one draw the line on this slippery slope, which separates those traits of a person which should properly be deemed part of his preferences, from those which are part of his resource endowment? If no line is drawn, then no coherent distinction exists between resource and welfare egalitarianism.

The difficulty can be illustrated (if such is required) by taking an example from Dworkin (1981a). He states that the equality-of-resource mechanism should be ambition-sensitive but not endowment-sensitive. A person is not entitled to the returns from a special endowment of resources he might possess, but he is entitled to returns from his ambition. But what is ambition? Is it the ability to work harder, or more persistently than the norm? That may be due to the possession of more adrenalin or endorphins than the normal person. Whatever ambition is, is there not some biological propensity which defines it, and should that propensity not be considered a resource? Or if differential ambition is due to differential external environments, surely that constitutes a difference in resources which resource egalitarianism should address. Dworkin also believes that the degree of risk a person wishes to bear is an aspect of his preferences, not his resources. But the same arguments can be given with respect to risk aversion as with respect to ambition. At what point do we decide the person bears responsibility?

10. Conclusion

Dworkin's resource egalitarianism is appealing because it is so thorough-going. He wishes to include as resources not just external goods, but talents. But this appeal is the source of the paradox. For if morally arbitrarily distributed traits and resources are grounds for compensation under a resource-egalitarian ethic, then different people cannot be made to bear the social costs of their "expensive" tastes. One has no choice but to equalize welfare; this is the message of Theorem 3.

There are, it seems to me, two ways out of this reduction. The first is to drop the assumption of first-best analysis, which both Dworkin and I have made. If it is assumed that information on preferences or on internal resources is not known to the planner, this places a severe constraint on what allocation mechanisms will be implementable in a decentralized manner. Incentive compatibility will drive a wedge between resource egalitarianism and welfare egalitarianism.[6] The second way, which is more in the spirit of this investigation, and meets the philosophical problem head-on, is to formulate criteria for differentiating those aspects of a person which constitute his resources from those which constitute his preferences. I suspect this resolution will be related to the first way: one reason we might treat an aspect of behavior as preference-, not resource-induced, is that we do not have the technology to measure the source of that behavior. But there is more to responsibility than measurement. This paper should focus debate on that question.

[6] Surely, great compromises must be made in implementing any policy of justice on account of revelation and incentive problems.

Egalitarianism, responsibility, and information

1. Outcome- versus resource-equalizing theories

Radical and liberal theories of egalitarianism are distinguished, in large part, by the differing degrees to which they hold people responsible for their own well-being. The most liberal or individualistic theory calls for equality of opportunity. Once such "starting gate equality," as Dworkin (1981a) calls it, is guaranteed, then any final outcome is justified, provided certain rules, such as voluntary trading, are observed. At the other pole, the most radical egalitarianism calls for equality of welfare (assuming that interpersonal welfare comparisons can be made, so that such equality makes sense). In between these two extremes are egalitarian proposals that equalize more than conventional opportunities, yet less than full welfare. Sen (1980) speaks of equality of basic capabilities as a goal; implementing that requires more than starting gate equality, because some will require more resources than others to attain the same capabilities. Meeting basic needs is another objective. Equality of needs fulfillment is perhaps less radical than equality of basic capabilities and more radical than equality of opportunity. Rawls (1971) takes equality of primary goods as a benchmark; he distinguishes primary goods from welfare, but includes among them goods that are more complicated than conventional resources and opportunities, all of which are supposed inputs into any conception of welfare. One could imagine proposing an egalitarianism that equalized some quite measurable outcome across populations, such as infant mortality. That would be an outcome-equalizing theory where the rate of infant mortality is a proxy, presumably, for some more complicated maximand, such as the degree of well-being of a population. A prominent opportunity-equalizing theory is that of Dworkin, who calls for equality of resources, and argues that equality of welfare is not a cogent egalitarianism. His conception of resources is comprehensive: It includes some aspects of people that are inalienable, their talents and propensities

I thank Thomas Scanlon and G. A. Cohen, from whom I have learned a great deal on these questions. The editors and referees of *Economics and Philosophy* made helpful suggestions. I am indebted to the National Science Foundation for supporting this research.

of various kinds. Dworkin's egalitarianism is more thorough than that which would be achieved by equalizing conventional resources only.

This survey is not exhaustive; the point I wish to illustrate is the varying degree of responsibility that these theories assign to individuals. Full equality of welfare holds a person responsible for nothing about himself: Any trait that detracts from his ability to process worldly resources into welfare is to be compensated for by the distribution that effects welfare equality. Equality of opportunity, conceived of in the usual sense, holds individuals responsible for a great deal – their own skills, including the ability to truck and barter, their rates of time preference, and their attitudes towards risk. Other theories take an intermediate stance concerning responsibility. Dworkin does not want to equalize welfare, but does want to compensate people for certain kinds of bad luck in the birth lottery, which assigns inalienable traits. He believes that people should be responsible for certain aspects of themselves, in particular, their conceptions of welfare. I do not claim that these theories hold people morally responsible (in varying degrees) for traits that they possess, just that individuals are effectively responsible for these traits, because society will not take account of them in its egalitarian calculus.

A.   *Economic environments*

I propose to think of outcome-equalizing theories, quite generally, in the following way. The world consists of some fixed bundle of resources, and of individuals who have ways of processing these resources into the outcome under consideration: Whether it is welfare, the fulfillment of basic needs, or the realization of capabilities. I summarize these personal technologies with a processing or outcome function $u^i(x)$, where x is a vector of resources, and u^i describes the effectiveness with which the ith individual processes resources into the outcome in question. In the infant mortality example, the "individual" i is a country, and u^i measures the infant survival rate in that country as a function of the resources its population consumes. If the outcome is welfare, then u^i is the ith person's utility function. An *economic environment* is a vector $\xi = \langle n, \bar{x}; u^1, u^2, ..., u^r \rangle$ where n is the number of resources in the environment (the dimension of the resource space), $\bar{x}$ is the aggregate endowment of resources (a vector in R^n), r is the number of agents, and u^i is the processing function of the ith agent. This representation is sufficiently abstract to allow for discussion of the theories outlined above, where the functions u^i take on different meanings, depending on what the outcome is.

In particular, this representation allows one to contrast an equality-of-resource approach with an equality-of-outcome approach. A first pass at resource egalitarianism would propose, in the environment ξ, to give each of the r agents the vector $\bar{x}/r$ of resources: equal split. But I claim below (in Section 2) that this is an unsatisfactory way of implementing equality of resources, at least if resources are taken to include some internal traits that people have, such as talents. Outcome egalitarianism would imply dividing the social endowment $\bar{x}$ in such a way that final outcomes are equal for all: give agent i vector $\bar{x}^i$ such that $\bar{x} = \sum \bar{x}^i$ and $u^1(\bar{x}^1) = u^2(\bar{x}^2) = \cdots = u^r(\bar{x}^r)$, if such an assignment is possible.

B.   *Allocation mechanisms*

How should resources be allocated in a given economic environment? For the sake of simplicity in exposition, from now on I assume that there are just two agents, and so the notation introduced above can be collapsed to $\xi = \langle n; \bar{x}; u, v \rangle$ where u and v are the outcome functions of the agents. Let the domain of possible economic environments be Σ. I choose Σ to consist of all environments ξ, where n is any positive integer, $\bar{x}$ is any nonnegative vector in R^n, and u and v are arbitrary continuous, weakly monotone increasing, concave real-valued functions of n variables, with $u(0) = v(0) = 0$. Monotonicity of the utility functions guarantees that the resources in question are goods (not bads); concavity guarantees that there is diminishing marginal productivity from each resource. Insisting on concavity is not necessary for the theory I will outline, but it imposes a reasonable economic restriction on the processing technologies. Thus, the domain of economic environments posited consists of sensible possible worlds. For simplicity, I have not represented the possibility of production in the model. The theory can be replicated if production is allowed.

An *allocation mechanism F* is a function, defined on Σ, which assigns to each economic environment ξ an allocation of the resources in that environment, that is:

$$F(\xi) = (\bar{x}^1, \bar{x}^2) = (F^1(\xi), F^2(\xi)),$$

where $F^i(\xi) = \bar{x}^i$ is the share of resource vector $\bar{x}$ assigned by F to person i. Specifying an allocation mechanism amounts to naming a rule for distributing resources in any environment. Moral beliefs about egalitarianism, or about distributive justice more generally, can be represented as requirements on the behavior of the allocation mechanism. We might view requirements on F's behavior as constraining an economic constitution, which should apply to any possible world.

C.   *Welfarism, outcomism, and resourcism*

A common position in social choice theory, at least until a decade ago, has been that a desirable allocation mechanism use information only on the possible outcomes. When the outcome is welfare, this position has been coined "welfarism" by Sen (1979a). Although formal social choice theory is different from the theory of allocation mechanisms on economic environments that I describe here, welfarism means the following in the present context. Let the outcome described by the functions u and v be utility. Then associated with any economic environment $\xi = \langle n; \bar{x}; u, v \rangle$ is a *utility possibilities set,* the set of possible welfare levels $(\bar{u}, \bar{v})$ that can be generated by dividing the resource vector $\bar{x}$ between the two agents in all possible ways. Let $A(\xi)$ be the utility possibilities set for the environment ξ. Suppose that there are two environments, ξ and ξ', that give rise to the same utility possibilities set. (These environments may even have different numbers of resources, and therefore surely different utility functions in them, but the sets of welfare pairs $(\bar{u}, \bar{v})$ they generate are identical.) Welfarism requires that an allocation mechanism assign the same welfare pair $(\bar{u}, \bar{v})$ in both environments.

Axiom of Welfarism: Let $\xi = \langle n; \bar{x}; u^1, v^1 \rangle$ and $\xi' = \langle m; \bar{y}; u^2, v^2 \rangle$ be two economic environments in Σ such that $A(\xi) = A(\xi')$. Then:

$$u^1(F^1(\xi)) = u^2(F^1(\xi')) \quad \text{and} \quad v^1(F^2(\xi)) = v^2(F^2(\xi')).$$

The Axiom of Welfarism is a strong restriction on the nature of the allocation mechanism. Suppose that ξ and ξ' generate the same set of possible outcomes (utility pairs). A welfarist mechanism must ignore the underlying resource and preference structures that differentiate these environments, as it assigns the same pair of utility levels in the two worlds. Utilitarianism is an example of a welfarist allocation mechanism. Indeed, any allocation mechanism that can be represented as maximizing a function of the utilities of the agents is welfarist.

Since we are allowing the processing functions to represent outcomes other than welfare, welfarism can, more generally, be thought of as a special case of *outcomism.* I will use the terminology of outcomism, recalling that welfarism is a special and important case. In particular, the Axiom of Welfarism becomes the Axiom of Outcomism.

Contrasted with outcomism is what might be called *resourcism,* the position that the economic structure (of resource availabilities and preferences) underlying the outcome possibilities set matters. A resourcist wants to pay attention to all the information given in the economic environment ξ. Consider, for example, an egalitarian who believes that splitting the aggregate resource endowment equally among the agents and then letting them trade to equilibrium is a good procedure. This is not a welfarist proposal. It is generically the case that if two economic environments give rise to the same utility possibilities set, then assigning the Equal Division Walrasian Equilibrium (ED-WE) allocation will not generate the same pair of utility levels in the two environments.

Although it is not clear whether the Rawlsian proposal can be represented in this model, it appears to be a resourcist and nonoutcomist proposal. Rawls wants to equalize (so far as incentive considerations permit) the distribution of primary goods, which are viewed as inputs into various kinds of outcomes (welfare, capability, etc.). This equalization cannot be implemented, given only the information of the utility or outcome profiles that are possible (that is, the specification of the relevant outcome possibilities set). This explains why the Rawlsian proposal differs from its common misinterpretation by economists, "maximin utility."

Indeed, any theory that assigns importance to property rights, or to rights over resources that individuals are deemed to have for reasons other than the outcome those resources will generate, must be a resourcist, nonoutcomist theory. For outcomism discards all the information about the resource structure, and limits its judgments to ones made with knowledge only of the outcomes that can be generated. Hence, resourcist, nonoutcomist positions comprise a major part of political philosophy. (For further criticisms of welfarism, see Sen (1979a); for elaboration on the informational poverty of welfarist theories, see Essay 9.)

D.   *Purpose of this paper*

It is difficult to say what resource egalitarianism consists in, if resources are taken to include inalienable traits, for how can one equally divide and distribute these important resources? The key to the approach that I describe is to change the question from "What is a resource egalitarian allocation?" to "What properties must an allocation mechanism have in order that it implement resource egalitarian allocations on a domain of possible worlds?" One can take a minimalist and somewhat agnostic approach to this problem by specifying certain necessary features that an allocation mechanism defined on the class of economic environments must have in order to qualify as resource egalitarian. In Sections 2 and 3, I propose several such necessary features, which appear formally as axioms on the behavior of the allocation mechanism.

The central theorem states: there is a unique allocation mechanism that satisfies several necessary conditions for resource egalitarianism; that mechanism divides the resources in such a way as to equalize *outcomes*. That is, a resource egalitarian who takes a comprehensive view with respect to resources is committed to outcome egalitarianism. In the language used earlier, if one endorses comprehensive resource egalitarianism, then one cannot preserve a realm of responsibility for people that permits differential outcomes. In the case of utility, the theorem is interpreted as saying that one cannot hold people responsible for their conceptions of welfare to the degree that left-liberal theory would like, if a sufficiently comprehensive view is taken with respect to what attributes of a person constitute resources.

A theorem like this does not settle the issue. It provides an occasion to examine the model in which it is proven in order to sharpen analysis of the underlying philosophical question. Sections 4 through 9 of the paper examine features of the model that I think are the main candidates for chinks in its armor. How is this unreasonable result smuggled in?

For exposition's sake, not all the details of the model are presented here, nor are the proofs of theorems. A rigorous presentation is available in Roemer (1986), which contains the proofs of the theorems discussed here, unless otherwise indicated. Some insights are lost by sacrificing mathematical detail; for example, assumptions that appear to be merely technical often hide indefensible positions about underlying issues. I have tried to report fully those aspects of the model that are germane to a critical evaluation, but such decisions are, of course, matters of judgment.

E.   *What does equality of resources consist in?*

Once an interpersonally comparable outcome is specified, it is clear what equality of outcome means in an economic environment, but, as Dworkin points out, it is much less clear what equality of resources might mean. For the following, suppose we are discussing welfare as the outcome. The first pass, proposed in Section 1.C, is to implement equality of resources in an environment ξ by equal division of the aggregate endowment $\bar{x}$. There are two immediate problems with this proposal. First, in general the equal division allocation is not Pareto optimal. If Pareto optimality is desirable, one might modify the equal division proposal into ED-WE. This is the allocation mechanism that assigns to the individuals that allocation which is the Walrasian or competitive equilibrium generated from equal initial endowments. The mechanism ED-WE is Pareto optimal, and seems to implement starting gate equality. It is the canonical envy-free mechanism (see, for example, Varian, 1975). Cohen (1986) characterizes this mechanism as the Steiner constitution, after Steiner (1977).

But ED-WE is not obviously an attractive implementation of resource egalitarianism, even when the outcome is welfare, if one takes the broader view proposed by Dworkin with respect to what characteristics of an environment constitute resources. In the description of an economic environment $\xi = \langle n; \bar{x}; u, v \rangle$ not all the things we might want to consider resources necessarily appear in the $\bar{x}$ vector. Perhaps some attributes of the agents which should be considered resources are reflected only in the processing functions.

To see this, consider the case of Andrea and Bob, who have processing functions u and v, respectively, for turning rice (x) into useful nutrition. The only resource listed is rice and it is the case that for all x, $u(x) > v(x)$. The most natural resource egalitarian proposal is to divide the rice equally between Andrea and Bob. This is, of course, the ED-WE in a one-good world. But then we learn that Andrea's superior rice-processing technology is due to her possession of an enzyme that Bob lacks. The enzyme is not a listed resource. Is it not reasonable, nevertheless, to treat the enzyme as a resource, which cannot be redistributed from Andrea to Bob, but of which account should be taken by a resource egalitarian in deciding how to allocate the rice?

If so, then ED-WE does not implement resource egalitarianism, for it only "equalizes" those resources that appear explicitly in the x vector. What if the enzymes of Bob and Andrea are explicitly listed as resources in the specification of the economic environment? Then ED-WE requires us to divide the property rights in enzymes so that each agent owns, as part of his initial endowment, one-half the enzymes of the other one and one-half of his "own" enzymes. This appears to foster an unattractive kind of dependence of each agent on the other one, the consequences of which will be elaborated in Section 2.

Thus the most obvious resource-equalizing mechanism may not be attractive to a resource egalitarian. What allocation mechanisms allocate the transferable resources in a way that compensates the agents appropriately, from a resource egalitarian viewpoint, for the endowments of inalienable resources they have?

2.   An example and an axiom

In this section, I propose one necessary condition for an allocation mechanism to implement an acceptable kind of resource egalitarianism. Continuing with the above example, it is discovered that Andrea has an amount $\bar{E}_A$ of the enzyme and Bob an amount $\bar{E}_B$. In fact, upon further investigation we can represent Andrea and Bob as each consuming two resources, rice and their enzyme, and their differential success at forestalling starvation, given the same amounts of rice, is the consequence of their differential enzyme consumption. Andrea and Bob can both be viewed as having the same nutrition function $w(x, E)$ over rice and the enzyme, and

$$u(x) = w(x, \bar{E}_A), \quad v(x) = w(x, \bar{E}_B), \quad \text{and} \quad \bar{E}_A > \bar{E}_B. \tag{1}$$

Because the greater enzyme consumption produces more nutrients for a given level of rice consumption (because the function w is monotone increasing in its arguments), the existence of the enzyme implies in the economic environment where only rice is explicitly listed as a resource that $u(x) > v(x)$.

To model the enzyme's inalienability, we must view Andrea's and Bob's enzymes as two different resources: Bob's enzyme is useless to Andrea, and conversely. (These enzymes are not like kidneys, which can, perhaps, be transmitted from one person to another; they are truly inalienable resources.) Letting E_A stand for Andrea's enzyme and E_B for Bob's enzyme, consider the extended outcome functions w_A and w_B defined by:

$$w_A(x, E_A, E_B) = w(x, E_A) \quad \text{and} \quad w_B(x, E_A, E_B) = w(x, E_B). \quad (2)$$

The functions w_A and w_B have been defined over rice and the two personalized enzymes; Andrea with nutrition function w_A gets benefits from consuming only rice (x) and her enzyme (E_A), while Bob with nutrition function w_B benefits from consuming only rice and his enzyme (E_B). The reader might naturally ask why Andrea's enzyme should be included as an argument of Bob's nutrition function, from which he derives no benefit; this is a technical trick whose purpose will become clear in a moment. Now consider the economic environment $\xi' = \langle 3; (\bar{x}, \bar{E}_A, \bar{E}_B); w_A, w_B \rangle$. This environment is similar to ξ; the difference between ξ and ξ' is that in the latter, the enzyme endowments of Andrea and Bob have been explicitly represented as resources. We may now ask of the resource egalitarian: How should the resources be allocated in ξ'?

It is quite clear that all of the enzyme that only Andrea can consume, $\bar{E}_A$, should be assigned to her and all of the enzyme that only Bob consumes, $\bar{E}_B$, should be assigned to him, for to deprive either person of the full consumption of a good that only he or she can use would be spiteful. (One can imagine that the resource allocator has a switch by which he can control the amount of an enzyme that a person consumes.) More formally, if Pareto optimality is one requirement of resource egalitarianism, then the allocation mechanism must assign all of the personalized enzymes to the right people. So Pareto optimality rules out spitefulness of a certain kind. (I am here borrowing the term "Pareto optimality" and using it in any outcome context, not simply the classical case where the outcome is utility.) It is to guarantee that the allocation mechanism gives all of $\bar{E}_B$ to Bob and all of $\bar{E}_A$ to Andrea that the trick of defining the two enzymes as different goods is introduced.

As I wrote, it is not obvious that in ξ' the rice should be divided equally between Andrea and Bob. Because the enzymes cannot effectively be equalized, due to their inalienability, resource egalitarian accounts should perhaps be squared by an unequal division of the rice. I will not suggest exactly how to resolve the rice allocation problem yet. My aim is to call into question the initial decision of the resource egalitarian, to divide the rice equally between Andrea and Bob, in the one-dimensional economic environment ξ. For if we decide that resource egalitarianism requires an unequal division of the rice in ξ', should it not require that same division of the rice in ξ? After all, ξ and ξ' are environments representing the same world, where resources have been uncovered in ξ' which were not visible in ξ. ξ is an incomplete description of the "actual" world, from the point of view of someone who wishes to include enzymes as resources within the jurisdiction of egalitarian compensation. This suggests that *however a resource egalitarian allocation mechanism F divides the rice in ξ', it should divide the rice in the same way in ξ.*

I call this necessary condition on resource egalitarianism Consistency of Resource Allocation Across Dimension (CONRAD). Formally, it is defined as follows:

CONRAD Axiom: Let $\xi' = \langle n + m; (\bar{x}, \bar{y}); u(x, y), v(x, y) \rangle$ be an economic environment where there are n dimensions of the x-goods and m dimensions of the y-goods. Suppose that each y-good is useful to, or liked by, only one person. Let $F(\xi') = ((\bar{x}^1, \bar{y}^1), (\bar{x}^2, \bar{y}^2))$. Consider the restricted outcome functions defined as follows:

$$u^*(x) = u(x, \bar{y}^1), \quad v^*(x) = v(x, \bar{y}^2)$$

and examine the n-dimensional environment

$$\xi = \langle n; \bar{x}; u^*(x), v^*(x) \rangle.$$

Then $F(\xi) = (\bar{x}^1, \bar{x}^2)$.

That is, in the environment ξ', the m y-goods are completely personalized in their use to the two people. By Pareto optimality, which I will assume below, the allocation mechanism must assign the various y-goods to Andrea and Bob in the obvious way, so that each gets all of the goods that only he or she derives benefit from. CONRAD then instructs us to examine the environment that is induced, once those personalized goods have been assigned, over just the x-goods; it requires that the allocation mechanism assign the x-goods in exactly the same manner in the smaller-dimension environment ξ as it assigned them in the larger-dimension environment ξ'. If, in the "big" environment ξ', proper account was taken, in distributing the x-goods, of the relative availabilities of the various personalized consumption goods (the enzymes), then CONRAD guarantees that in the dimensionally reduced environment ξ, proper account will be taken of personalized consumption goods, which there appear only implicitly in the processing functions of the agents. CONRAD is agnostic in not telling us exactly how to distribute the x-goods in ξ'; it merely requires *consistency* between the distribution of the x-goods in ξ and ξ'.

It is not immediately clear how F may allocate the resources in ξ, if F must satisfy CONRAD. We must consider all possible environments ξ' of which ξ is a reduced environment in the CONRAD sense. Say $\xi = \langle n; \bar{x}; u, v \rangle$. There may be many "CONRAD extensions" of ξ into dimensionally larger environments ξ' – environments with personalized consumption goods whose CONRAD restrictions are just ξ. CONRAD requires consistency between the allocation of $\bar{x}$ in ξ and the allocation of $\bar{x}$ in all those possible extensions ξ'.

Consider again the mechanism Equal Division Walrasian Equilibrium which assigns that allocation which is the Walrasian equilibrium from an initial equal division of all the resources between the agents. (One thinks of this allocation mechanism as a natural one when the context is utility and welfare, but it is well defined no matter what the outcome is called.) Consider the rice-enzyme environment

$$\xi' = \langle 3; (\bar{x}, \bar{E}_A, \bar{E}_B); w_A, w_B \rangle.$$

How would ED-WE divide the resources here? It would act as if property rights had been assigned, initially, of $(\bar{x}/2, \bar{E}_A/2, \bar{E}_B/2)$ to each of Andrea and Bob (that's the initial equal split). Of course, Andrea has no use for Bob's enzyme, nor does Bob have any use for Andrea's – except in trade. Thus, at Walrasian equilibrium, which is Pareto optimal, Bob will buy back all of "his" enzyme, which Andrea initially owns, and Andrea will buy back from Bob all of "her" enzyme, which he initially owns. No other final allocation of the enzymes would be Pareto optimal. But the "prices" of these two enzymes will not in general be the same in terms of rice. It may be the case that Bob has to sell some of his initial rice stock to buy back all of his enzyme (or it could be the other way around, that Andrea has to trade some of her rice to get back all of her enzyme). The point is that the allocation mechanism ED-WE will assign all of $\bar{E}_A$ to Andrea and all of $\bar{E}_B$ to Bob, since no other allocation of those goods would be Pareto optimal, but it will not in general divide the rice equally between them in the three-dimensional environment ξ'.

Now consider the original one-dimensional rice environment

$$\xi = \langle 1; \bar{x}; u, v \rangle.$$

Equal Division Walrasian Equilibrium, acting on ξ, simply splits the rice equally between Andrea and Bob. But the one-dimensional rice environment ξ is just the CONRAD-restriction of the three-dimensional rice-enzyme-enzyme environment ξ' that is induced by holding fixed the allocation of the two enzymes. We therefore conclude the ED-WE violates CONRAD, because it changes the allocation of rice it recommends when passing from ξ' to ξ. For the previous paragraph argued that in ξ', the rice is in general not equally split between Andrea and Bob under ED-WE.

One reason to reject ED-WE as a resource egalitarian mechanism is its violation of CONRAD. ED-WE does not take proper account of the personalized resources that may exist in an environment, but have not been explicitly recorded in its description. (As well, ED-WE violates the Resource Monotonicity axiom, to be introduced in Section 3.)

This discussion may lead the reader to believe that CONRAD is an unrealistically strong requirement to place on an allocation mechanism, in the sense that it may be difficult to find allocation mechanisms that satisfy CONRAD. This, however, is not the case. There are many allocation mechanisms that satisfy CONRAD. One may object to the claim that CONRAD is a necessary condition for resource egalitarianism, but one cannot object to it on the grounds that no mechanism satisfies it.

3.   Equality of resources: more axioms and a theorem

In this section I propose three other axioms which are arguably necessary conditions for the implementation of resource egalitarianism.

Pareto Optimality Axiom (PO): F should allocate the resources in any environment ξ in a "Pareto optimal" way. (The quotation marks appear because the outcome might not be utility.)

PO does not require much discussion. If it is possible to satisfy Pareto optimality, it would seem spiteful not to do so. Strictly speaking, one might say that Pareto optimality is not required for a mechanism to be resource equalizing, but if a mechanism that satisfies other necessary conditions for resource equality is also Pareto optimal, so much the better.

Symmetry Axiom (Sy): If $\xi = \langle n; \bar{x}; u, u \rangle$ then $F(\xi) = (\bar{x}/2, \bar{x}/2)$.

Symmetry says that if the two agents have the same processing function, then the resources should be divided equally between them. Whatever resource egalitarianism means, it should at least mean this. There is one perhaps contentious feature to be noted. This justification of the axiom is only plausible because outcomes have been postulated to be interpersonally comparable. If two people have the same utility function, for example, that means they get exactly the same degree of welfare from the same bundle of resources. If outcomes were interpersonally noncomparable, then I do not think the symmetry axiom would be justifiable. For in that case, the fact that two persons had the same outcome function would only represent their having the same ordinal outcome rankings over bundles of resources; it would not mean they had the same resource processing capability in an absolutely measurable sense.

Interpersonal comparability is easier to accept in some interpretations of the model than in others. If the outcome functions represent the rate of infant survival in different countries, comparability is clear; if they represent the degree of satisfaction that different people receive from consuming goods, comparability is a contentious assumption. For this reason, the model is easiest to accept when the functions measure some objectively comparable outcome across agents.

Resource Monotonicity Axiom (RMON): Let $\xi = \langle n; \bar{x}; u, v \rangle$ and let $\xi' = \langle n; \bar{\bar{x}}; u, v \rangle$ where $\bar{\bar{x}} \geq \bar{x}$. Then neither person's outcome level should be less under the action of F in ξ' than in ξ. That is:

$$u(F^1(\xi)) \leq u(F^1(\xi')) \quad \text{and} \quad v(F^2(\xi)) \leq v(F^2(\xi')).$$

Resource Monotonicity says that if the aggregate resource endowment increases from one environment to another, but nothing else about the environment changes, then the resources should be distributed in the more abundant environment in such a way that neither person ends up worse off, in outcome level, than he was in the environment in which resources were unambiguously scarcer. The motivation for RMON as an axiom is of the same minimalist sort: whatever equality of resources means, it should at least require RMON.

Finally, the Domain Axiom should be stated explicitly:

Domain Axiom (D^Σ): The allocation mechanism is defined on all economic environments $\xi = \langle n; \bar{x}; u, v \rangle$ where n is any positive integer, $\bar{x}$ is any nonnegative vector in R^n, u and v are any continuous, weakly monotone increasing, concave functions defined on R^n, with $u(0) = v(0) = 0$. The class of such economic environments is Σ.

As I wrote earlier, the assumptions on the processing functions imbue the model with some economic content. In this kind of axiomatic characterization of mechanisms, it is desirable to keep the domain as small as possible, for that disciplines the model to represent our intuitions more precisely. If, for example, one allowed nonmonotonic outcome functions, that would require discarding the interpretation of resources as "goods." It is a virtue of this theory that it is true on this relatively restricted domain of economic environments. This is to be contrasted, for example, with classical social choice theory which posits a domain with utility functions that are entirely arbitrary. The unrestricted domain assumption of social choice theory is that any ordering of the social states be admitted as a possible preference ordering for each agent. Here, the social states are distributions of a given resource vector, and only certain reasonable, "economically plausible" orderings are admissible according to the domain axiom.

The main result is:

Theorem 1: *There is a unique allocation mechanism F that satisfies the axioms D^Σ, PO, Sy, RMON, and CONRAD. $F(\xi)$ assigns that Pareto optimal resource allocation in ξ which equalizes the outcome levels of the agents.*

The interpretation is that if a resource equalizing mechanism must satisfy at least the necessary conditions summarized by the axioms, then it can only do one thing: equalize outcomes. Hence, if resource egalitarianism entails the five axioms, then no distinction between equality of resources and equality of outcomes can be sustained.

Consider what the theorem says in the case where agents are countries, and each outcome function registers the rate of infant survival as a function of the resources a country consumes. The planner is directed to allocate an aggregate resource endowment to countries, restricted only by the axioms. An allocation of those resources is not acceptable if it would be possible to choose another allocation that increases the rate of infant survival in some countries without lowering it in others (PO). If the vector of aggregate resources becomes more abundant, then the planner must recommend an allocation that does not increase the rate of infant mortality in any country, compared with what it was when resources were scarce (RMON). If it so happens that all countries are identical with respect to their ability to use resources to reduce infant mortality, then resources should be evenly divided among them (Sy). Finally, suppose that in our description of the countries and the resources, certain nontransferable resources are listed, such as the climates, water supplies, and geographical locations of the countries. Listed as well are transferable resources, such as food and medicine. The planner decides upon an allocation of the transferable resources, taking account of the climates and geographical locations of the countries, which influence what their rates of infant mortality will be. Then he must allocate the transferable resources in exactly the same way, were he to face a description of the world in which climate and geographical location were not explicitly specified, but affected the rates of infant mortality of the countries nonetheless through their infant survival functions (CONRAD). If the planner respects these rules, and he is required to propose an allocation rule that will work for all possible worlds (Domain Axiom), then he has no option but to distribute resources in that way which equalizes the rates of infant mortality in all countries.

Perhaps one point should be made, to avoid some confusion about the possibility of equalizing outcomes. The usual utility possibilities set for an economic environment is the one depicted in Figure 7.1A – a strictly

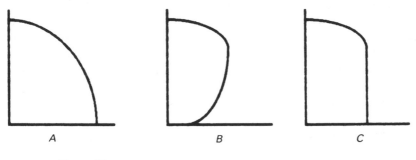

Figure 7.1

comprehensive, convex set. Utility sets like the one in Figure 7.1B, which are familiar from Rawlsian discussions, do not occur in this model. In Figure 7.1B, the interpretation must be that the first agent has a failure of incentive if he is taxed too much, and both agents become worse off. In the model here, the utility (or outcome) possibilities frontier consists of points that are either Pareto optimal or at worst "weakly Pareto optimal." Thus the utility set of Figure 7.1B would in fact appear as depicted in Figure 7.1C, with a vertical line segment dropped from the point at which the first agent's incentive fails. Strictly speaking, since there is no production in the model I have outlined, this incentive problem does not appear. But if production were incorporated, as it can be, then utility possibilities sets like Figure 7.1C can occur. In that case, the Pareto Optimality Axiom must be replaced with the Weak Pareto Optimality Axiom and then Theorem 1 states that the unique mechanism which obeys the stated axioms plus a continuity axiom is the outcome-equalizing mechanism. But considerations of incentives are not a concern of this article, and I will not pursue this issue further.

4. Criticisms

Theorem 1 performs a reduction that is disagreeable. There should be a distinction between equality of resources and equality of outcome. I will examine several aspects of the model, which comprise what seem to me to be the most compelling criticisms against it.

A.   Nameless goods

In the economic environments I have described, the resources have no names. Thus the same "economic information" depicted in the vector $\langle n; \bar{x}; u, v \rangle$ describes many different worlds, each with n goods, but in which the identities of the goods differ among worlds. In one world the goods may be shelter and food, and u and v are functions that describe how the agents transform these resources into welfare; in another, the goods might be beer and champagne, while the agents in that world have the same pleasure or inebriation functions, u and v, over these resources. The resource egalitarianism that many advocate would require us to distinguish between the treatment of these two worlds, depending upon the names of the goods in them, but such differential treatment is ruled out by the domain axiom of this model.

B.   The Domain Axiom

I wrote above that the domain of economic environments is smaller than the usual unrestricted domain of social choice theory. Monotonicity and concavity of the processing functions ensure that the domain consists of objects in which outcome is related to resources in a nonperverse and classic way. On the other hand, it might be too much to assume that any concave, monotone function should be admitted as a possible processing function, for some interpretations. This criticism is related to the namelessness of goods.

C.   CONRAD and hidden goods

As discussed in Section 3, CONRAD is a strong axiom. In Section 6, I describe what CONRAD commits us to, with respect to goods, like enzymes, that are perhaps hidden inside people.

D.   Resource Monotonicity

Resource Monotonicity is a powerful axiom which perhaps commits us to more than our intuitions warrant. In Section 7, I discuss how this axiom can be weakened, still preserving the outcome-egalitarian conclusion of Theorem 1.

E.   Interpersonal comparability

It is an assumption of the model that the outcome levels measured by the processing functions in an economic environment are interpersonally comparable. One way out of Theorem 1 is to remove this assumption. Without interpersonal comparability, the symmetry axiom has no inherent appeal as a resource egalitarian axiom; and so one might ask what allocation mechanisms satisfy all the axioms except Sy, plus an axiom enforcing the noncomparability of outcomes of agents in an environment. Indeed, Dworkin (1981) has argued that one reason to be a resource egalitarian as opposed to a welfare egalitarian is that people have such different conceptions of welfare as to be interpersonally noncomparable. In Section 8, a theorem is reported showing that if a resource egalitarian is committed to making no interpersonal welfare (outcome) comparisons, then there is *no* mechanism that satisfies the axioms. Given the rest of the structure of this model, interpersonal comparability of outcome is required to have any general conception of resource equality.

F.   Full information

It is assumed in this model that the outcome functions (and the resource availabilities) are known to whatever agency is implementing the allocation mechanism *F*. Suppose, to the contrary, that there is incomplete or asymmetric information: only the individual knows his processing function, and the agency must propose a mechanism for dividing the resources that will be compatible with the privacy of individual information. In Section 9, I propose that our ethical conception of responsibility depends upon the incompleteness of information.

5.   Naming goods

A.   The Anonymity of Goods

There are two issues of namelessness in the model of economic environments: neither the goods are named, nor is a name given to the kind of outcome measured by the outcome functions (whether it is utility, fulfillment of needs, or the degree of achievement of basic capabilities). The namelessness of outcome may be an important issue for resource allocation, for it is reasonable to think that the kind of outcome involved makes a moral difference. This is illustrated, for example, in an article by Yaari and Bar-Hillel (1984), who asked a survey population to decide upon the appropriate division of resources in a number of hypothetical cases. In particular, the respondents' opinions about what division of resources was fair depended quite strongly on whether the problem was phrased in terms of fulfilling needs or desires. That is to say, opinions about fair division of a resource bundle in two "worlds" differed when their descriptions as economic environments were identical, but the names given to what the processing functions measured in the two worlds were not the same.

Indeed, one can criticize the model of economic environments because only one kind of outcome is represented, the kind measured by the functions u and v. Since there are many kinds of outcome, perhaps each should be represented with its own function in a fuller description of an environment. (As I noted, Dworkin points out that one of the problems for welfare egalitarianism is that the kinds of welfare that are of concern to people may differ: one cares about pleasure, the other about living a worthwhile life.) I propose, instead, to interpret the model more narrowly, as follows. Imagine that we have decided upon the outcome that is of concern for the analysis at hand, and let u and v be the processing functions for the two agents representing that kind of outcome. Then the axioms reflect resource egalitarian requirements, given that we are concerned about this particular kind of outcome. The model applies to analyzing resource egalitarianism once some particular kind of outcome has been decided upon as the relevant one. If the kinds of outcome for different people are not the same then the axioms are less convincing. What, for example, would justify the Symmetry Axiom if the processing function u, for Bob, measures his happiness and the same function u, for Andrea, measures her healthiness?

To discuss the namelessness of resources in the model, some additional formal structure is useful. Economic environments can be viewed as equivalence classes of informationally denser objects, descriptive of possible worlds, called environments with named goods. To describe environments with named goods, we begin with an infinite list of named goods, called Ω, which might include goods named beer, champagne, rice, Bob's enzymes, Andrea's enzymes, and so on. An *environment with named goods* is a vector $e = \langle N, n; \bar{x}; u, v \rangle$ where $N \subset \Omega$ is a finite list of n goods, $\bar{x}$ is the aggregate endowment of those goods, and u and v are the outcome functions of the agents over those goods. Let the class of all such environments with named goods be Δ.

Let $e' = \langle N', n; \bar{x}; u, v \rangle$ be another environment with named goods in which the "economic information" is the same as in e but the list of goods N' differs from N. The theory of allocation mechanisms defined on the class of economic environments Σ, as outlined in Section 3, can be redone as a theory of resource allocation mechanisms acting on Δ, with one additional axiom: that the mechanism F, now defined on Δ, should allocate the resources in the same way between the agents in the two environments e and e' when those two environments with named goods differ, as above, only in the names of their goods. This is an Anonymity of Goods Axiom, for it says the allocation mechanism looks just at "economic information" and ignores the names of the particular goods. Formally:

Anonymity of Goods Axiom (AnonG): Let $e = \langle N, n; \bar{x}; u, v \rangle$ and $e' = \langle N', n; \bar{x}, u, v \rangle$ be two economic environments with named goods in Δ. Let F be an allocation mechanism defined on the space of environments with named goods. Then $F(e) = F(e')$.

AnonG is palatable if we think that all relevant information about goods is summarized in the processing functions, whose outcome has been named, and the endowment vector. This might not hold if, for example, the agents in e have views about certain rights that people in e have with respect to some of the goods in N, which do not apply if the goods are in N'. These views are not represented in the processing functions. For instance, N might contain certain internal goods, like personalized enzymes, while N' might contain only goods in the external world, and people's opinions about proper egalitarian compensation might differ in these two cases, even if all the economic information is the same.

The anonymity of goods can be defended as follows. Once the type of outcome that is our concern has been named, then the names of resources that generate it should not count further. Resources are, by presumption, instrumental only insofar as they produce outcomes, and this is captured by the processing functions. Distinguishing among goods in an allocation decision on the basis of their names, once the outcome has been named, would be gratuitous.

The position against AnonG is bolstered by our opinions about our own world, in which the names of goods appear to matter in our ethical judgments.[1] But it is not so clear they should, given the hypothesis that the type of outcome that the processing functions measure is named and fixed for all environments in Δ. The laboratory results of Yaari and Bar-Hillel depended upon changing the names of the outcomes across economic environments, not changing the names of goods while holding the notion of outcome fixed. Once we agree that we are studying the realization of basic capabilities, let us say, should it matter whether the resources are apples and oranges or shelter and education? If our opinions do change as the names of goods change (but the name of the outcome remains fixed), that may be due to cognitive errors on our part, to framing. Appealing to our beliefs about our own world is not a foolproof test.

I am undecided about the moral appeal of the anonymity of goods in the present context. It is worth giving a more concrete example of what such anonymity commits one to, because it is such an important, but until now, implicit assumption. Consider again the rice-enzyme environment $\xi = \langle 3; (\bar{x}, \bar{E}_A, \bar{E}_B); w_A, w_B \rangle$ where $\bar{x}$ is the amount of rice and $\bar{E}_A$

---

[1] This point was communicated to me by T. Scanlon.

and $\bar{E}_B$ are the enzyme endowments of Andrea and Bob, and $\bar{E}_A > \bar{E}_B$. The same economic description could apply to an environment in which the second and third goods are not enzymes, but scotch and gin. Andrea likes only rice and scotch, Bob likes only rice and gin, and there is more scotch in the world than gin. The rice-scotch-gin economic environment is also described exactly by ξ. (One point of the example is that goods whose use in consumption is completely personalized need not be internal goods.) In the second world, all the scotch goes to Andrea and all the gin to Bob, by Pareto optimality, just as in the first world Andrea and Bob were each assigned all of their own enzymes by the mechanism. And because of the anonymity of goods, the allocation of rice under the mechanism F must be the same in these two worlds.

Is it correct that resource egalitarianism should take no account of whether goods are internal or external? Perhaps so, in the radical kind of resource egalitarianism under discussion, where all resources, independent of their physical location, are within the jurisdiction of social compensation. Once a conception of welfare or outcome has been identified, then anonymity claims the only relevant attribute of a resource is the manner in which it enters into the production of benefit for the people in that world. Even relative to a single kind of outcome, this is a weaker statement than an endorsement of welfarism, or outcomism, which requires that two economic environments that give rise to the same set of outcome possibilities should not be distinguished with respect to the final outcome levels assigned.

Being undecided about the appeal of the Anonymity of Goods Axiom, I proceed on two fronts. One, now concluded, has been to defend anonymity.

B.   Dropping the Anonymity of Goods Axiom

The second front is to study resource egalitarian mechanisms defined on Δ where the Anonymity of Goods is not imposed. It will turn out it is possible to recover the main theorem while working on the domain Δ, and without the Anonymity of Goods Axiom, but at a cost.

The axioms necessary for a mechanism to be resource egalitarian, when defined on the class Δ, can be written as follows. These axioms are, with one exception, each weaker than their counterparts in Section 3, since no longer are all environments in Δ lumped together, whose economic descriptions are the same.

  N1.   (Domain D^Δ) F is a function assigning an allocation to each e in Δ.

  N2.   (PO) F assigns a Pareto optimal allocation for each e in Δ.

N3. (Symmetry) If $e = \langle N, n; \bar{x}, u, u \rangle$ then $F(e) = (\bar{x}/2, \bar{x}/2)$.

N4. (Resource Monotonicity - RMON*). Let $e = \langle N, n; \bar{x}, u, v \rangle$ and $e' = \langle N, n; \bar{\bar{x}}; u, v \rangle$ be two economic environments with named goods, identical except that $\bar{\bar{x}} \geq \bar{x}$. Then $F(e')$ weakly Pareto dominates $F(e)$.

N5. (Consistency - CONRAD*) Let $e = \langle N \cup M, n+m; (\bar{x}, \bar{y}); u, v \rangle$ be an economic environment with $(n+m)$ named goods comprising the union of two disjoint sets N and M, where M consists of personalized consumption goods, and let $F(e) = ((\bar{x}^1, \bar{y}^1), (\bar{x}^2, \bar{y}^2))$. Consider the n-dimensional environment in Δ defined by $e^* = \langle N, n; \bar{x}; u^*, v^* \rangle$ where $u^*(x) = u(x, \bar{y}^1)$ and $v^*(x) = v(x, \bar{y}^2)$. Then $F(e^*) = (\bar{x}^1, \bar{x}^2)$.

Theorem 2: *Exactly one allocation mechanism F satisfies axioms N1–N5; F chooses a Pareto optimal allocation for each environment in Δ which equalizes the outcome levels of the agents.*

Note the sense in which axioms N4 and N5 are weaker than their counterparts in Section 3. Axiom RMON says that if the processing functions of the agents in two environments are the same, but the resources in one environment are more abundant than in the other, then the allocation mechanism must make everyone better off in the more abundant environment – even if the resources in the two environments have different names. But Axiom RMON* only requires that benefits be (weakly) increasing for all agents when, in addition, the resources in the two environments have the same identities. It is therefore a weaker axiom than RMON. Similarly, CONRAD* only requires consistency between the resource allocation in the $(m+n)$-dimensional environment and the induced n-dimensional environment when the two environments are specified as having the same n-goods in common, from the set N. CONRAD, however, requires consistency even when no assurance is given that the two environments share the same set of n-goods. Thus, RMON* and CONRAD* capture more faithfully the resourcist intuitions that I used to motivate RMON and CONRAD.

It would seem that Theorem 2 patches up a chink in the model's armor, for it shows that the result of outcome egalitarianism is preserved when the allocation mechanisms act on the domain of objects Δ, and the Anonymity of Goods Axiom is not imposed. But that is not quite the case: for the ability to name goods has been purchased at the expense of a domain axiom that is less palatable than the Domain Axiom of the model Σ.

C. The Domain Axioms

The domain Σ of Theorem 1 consists of all economic environments, all objects $\xi = \langle n; \bar{x}; u, v \rangle$. The domain Δ of Theorem 2 consists of all objects

$e = \langle N; n; \bar{x}; u, v \rangle$ where N is any subset of size n of the universal set of named goods Ω, and the other economic information $\bar{x}$, u, and v is arbitrarily specified from the relevant families of objects. The crucial point is that while it may be palatable to accept a domain Σ, it is much less so to accept the domain Δ. The Domain Axiom D^Σ states that for any positive number n, and any vector $\bar{x}$ and functions u and v, there is *some* set N, of n resources, with respect to which $\langle n; \bar{x}; u, v \rangle$ represents a possible world. But the Domain Axiom D^Δ requires that for any n and *any* set, N, of named goods of size n, and for any vector $\bar{x}$ and functions u and v, there is a possible world represented by $\langle n; N; \bar{x}; u, v \rangle$. The force of naming goods is due, in large part, to our belief that certain goods enter into the outcome functions of all people in fairly restricted ways, for a fixed kind of outcome. Is it reasonable to suppose that there is a possible world in which the trade-offs between caviar and shelter can be specified in an arbitrary way? This is what the Domain Axiom of Theorem 2 requires. If there are some constraints on human biology and nature, then for any kind of outcome, the domain of possible processing functions that can be associated with a particular set of named goods N will not be the universal class of concave, monotonic functions. To make the axiom N1 palatable, we have to relax these human nature constraints: but that seems equivalent to sterilizing the identification of goods of the meaning it has. Naming goods is meaningful just because the way specific goods enter into the production of any outcome is restricted by human nature.

I have argued that AnonG is more acceptable than might first appear, because I am interpreting the type of outcome which the processing functions measure as fixed and named. If anonymity is unacceptable, we have learned more precisely why the names of goods are important, by seeing which axioms strain credibility when goods are named. It is our belief in the restriction on possible worlds by virtue of human nature, once goods are named, which can vitiate Theorem 2.

6.   CONRAD and hidden goods

I motivated CONRAD in Section 2 with the story of Andrea's and Bob's enzymes. CONRAD was presented as a necessary condition for assuring that an allocation mechanism charged with compensating people for their endowments of personalized nontransferable resources carries out its mandate. There is another motivation for CONRAD that derives from considering the limited information available to the planning agency, which implements the resource allocation. The planner is assigned the task of allocating a certain set of resources among agents. Some resources, in particular personalized goods of various kinds, are not in this set; indeed, the planner does not even know what these resources are, or, *a fortiori*, who has how much of each. Surely, the planner should allocate the transferable goods in such a way that, were he to gain further information about the personalized goods that were not in the original set, the decision about the allocation of the resources that has been made would not have to be altered. CONRAD assures this. Thus CONRAD enables the planning agency to economize on information. If the allocation mechanism satisfies CONRAD, the allocating agency can distribute its incomplete set of resources, knowing that the full allocation that will be realized is the one that would be chosen with fuller information about the nontransferable resources. It does not matter how many nontransferable resources there are, in what amounts they exist, nor what their identities are.[2]

This motivation for CONRAD derives from our ignorance of what personalized consumption resources may exist in the world in which our allocation mechanism must act. Scanlon (1986), however, believes that the resource egalitarian rationale I offered for adopting CONRAD depends on claims about what goods are *actually* hidden in the world under consideration. I will paraphrase his argument using the named goods axiom CONRAD*, because the adoption of named goods responds to part of Scanlon's criticism. Consider two environments referred to by CONRAD*, $e = \langle N \cup M; n+m; (\bar{x}, \bar{y}); u, v \rangle$ and $e^* = \langle N; n; \bar{x}; u^*, v^* \rangle$, the CONRAD*-restriction of e. Scanlon writes that the Andrea and Bob story provides no reason to enforce consistency between the mechanism's action in distributing the goods $\bar{x}$ in e^* and its distribution of the goods $\bar{x}$ in e, unless we know that the goods in the set M (the enzymes) are *actually hidden goods* in the environment e^*. Although in the construction carried out to define e^*, that environment materializes as a restriction of an environment e with more goods, the allocation mechanism is directed by CONRAD* to allocate the goods $\bar{x}$ in a certain way in e^*, even if e^* were to have no relationship to e, with respect to the goods M. Once e^* is defined, it exists as an environment unto itself, with no necessary relation to e in the terms of goods that may or may not be "actually" hidden in the world described by e^*.

It is possible to formalize this criticism, with the introduction of more notation, which will specify for a given environment which goods in it are "actually hidden" and which are "visible." Consider a class of "named environments with hidden goods," called Γ, whose generic member is $f = \langle n, N; h, H; (\bar{x}; \bar{z}^1; \bar{z}^2); u, v \rangle$. The interpretation is that the set of goods N comprises the visible goods explicitly listed for allocation, and there are

---

[2] I am grateful to David Donaldson for this interpretation of CONRAD.

n of them with aggregate endowment $\bar{x}$; the set of goods H is the set of actual, hidden goods, there are h of them, and they are being consumed by the two agents in amounts $\bar{z}^1$ and $\bar{z}^2$ respectively; and the processing functions u and v are defined only over the set of visible goods, N. Thus, the environment we see in Δ if the hidden goods are ignored in f is $e = \langle n; N; \bar{x}; u, v \rangle$. We can now define a version of CONRAD*, which pays attention to which goods are hidden, as follows:

*CONRAD** (CONRAD* with actually hidden goods):* In Γ, consider the environment $f = \langle N \cup M; n+m; 0, \emptyset; (\bar{x}, \bar{y}); u, v \rangle$ where the goods $N \cup M$ are visible and there are no hidden goods ($\emptyset$ is the empty set). Suppose the goods in M are personalized in their use for the agents in f, and let $F(f) = ((\bar{x}^1, \bar{y}^1), (\bar{x}^2, \bar{y}^2))$ be the allocation. Consider the environment f^* in Γ defined by $f^* = \langle n, N; m, M; (\bar{x}; \bar{y}^1, \bar{y}^2); u^*, v^* \rangle$, where the hidden goods are now M, their allocation to the agents is $(\bar{y}^1, \bar{y}^2)$ and the visible utility functions are $u^*(x) = u(x; \bar{y}^1)$ and $v^*(x) = v(x; \bar{y}^2)$. Then $F(f^*) = (\bar{x}^1, \bar{x}^2)$.

CONRAD** enforces consistency of the distribution of the visible goods $\bar{x}$ in the environment f^* with the distribution of those goods in f only when we are told that the smaller-dimensional environment f^* is one in which the goods in M, which appeared explicitly in f, are actually hidden in f^*. What is the relationship of CONRAD** to CONRAD*? It is, of course, weaker than CONRAD*. We can view CONRAD* as following from CONRAD** with the addition of another axiom, which implements an "independence of hidden goods." The Independence of Hidden Goods Axiom, which I shall not write down, stipulates that two environments in Γ should be treated in the same manner if their lists of visible goods are the same, and their visible processing functions are the same, even if their lists of hidden goods differ or even if there are no hidden goods in one of the environments. That is, of course, precisely the contentious point with Scanlon. It is the "independence of hidden goods" that I used to motivate CONRAD as an information-economizing condition above.

If CONRAD* is replaced with CONRAD** in Theorem 2, the new theorem can be preserved by including the Independence of Hidden Goods as an axiom. This is just a formalization of Scanlon's criticism, not an answer to it. The criticism is that our beliefs, about whether compensation should be made to people because of the hidden attributes that contribute to determining their welfare, depend on what the hidden goods are. If the attributes are enzymes over which the agents have no control, perhaps they should be compensated; if the attributes are degrees of effort, or religious views, perhaps they should not be. To the extent that opponents of welfare egalitarianism base their argument on the identities of hidden goods, the Independence of Hidden Goods Axiom is an important chink in the model's armor.

7. Resource Monotonicity

The original Resource Monotonicity Axiom (RMON) can be criticized as outcomist, because it ignores the names of goods. That objection is countered by the amendment to RMON*, which weakens the axiom and pays appropriate attention to named goods. Here, I address some other issues with respect to RMON and RMON*. I will refer to RMON, but the comments apply to either axiom.

RMON appears to be a reasonable requirement, but it is perhaps more powerful than our intuitions about resource egalitarianism warrant. For RMON compares a given economic environment to a continuum of other environments, ones which differ from each other in the size of their resource endowment. Our intuitions are based, I think, on making a finite number of comparisons – usually, comparing one world to some other benchmark world, some proposed counterfactual. Because our intuitions are poor when it comes to uncountable infinities, it is possible that RMON is not justified by the intuitions which recommend it.

This objection can be countered, as RMON can be replaced by another axiom that just compares a given world to one other benchmark world.[3] This axiom is mindful of Sen's (1973) weak equity axiom, and so it will be called:

Weak Equity Axiom (WE): Let $\xi = \langle n, \bar{x}, u, v \rangle$ be in Σ with $u(x) \geq v(x)$ for all x. Consider the benchmark environment $\xi^* = \langle n, \bar{x}, v, v \rangle$. Then the second agent in ξ should not get a lower outcome level under F's action then he does in ξ^*.

The Weak Equity Axiom says that an agent who is "handicapped" in his ability to process resources into outcome, compared to another, should not suffer due to his being in a world with the more "talented" agent. If we postulate Symmetry, then in ξ^* the agents split the endowment. Thus, Weak Equity with Symmetry says that the "handicapped" agent in ξ should get at least the outcome level that he derives from one-half of the aggregate resource bundle.

---

[3] There is another detour possible around resource monotonicity. Suppose the domain of economic environments is taken to be all environments $\langle n; \bar{x}; u, v \rangle$ where u and v are restricted only to being monotonic, but not necessarily concave, functions. Call this domain Λ. On Λ, outcome egalitarianism is characterized by the axioms Sy, PO, and CONRAD. No monotonicity axiom of any kind is required! This surprising result shows the sensitivity of this class of theorems to the domain assumption. (The proof is available from the author.)

Consider the following axiom, which strengthens the symmetry axiom:

Axiom of Limited Self-ownership (LSO): Let $\xi = \langle n, \bar{x}, u, v \rangle$ with $u(x) \geq v(x)$ for all x. Then $u(F^1(\xi)) \geq v(F^2(\xi))$.

LSO says that in a world with a "talented" and a "handicapped" agent, the talented agent should end up with at least as high a level of benefit as the handicapped one. The name of the axiom derives from the fact that the mechanism does not penalize the talented agent by virtue of his possession of a talent for processing resources. Note that LSO implies the Symmetry Axiom.

If RMON is replaced by Weak Equity and Symmetry is replaced by LSO, then the outcome-egalitarian conclusion remains true:

Theorem 3: *Let an allocation mechanism satisfy D^{Σ}, PO, LSO, WE, and CONRAD. Then F is outcome egalitarian on all environments.*

Weak Equity is more palatable than RMON in not committing us to a continuum of comparisons. I do not view the replacement of Symmetry by LSO as imposing a significant cost.

8.   Interpersonal comparability

Interpersonal comparability of outcome has been assumed thus far; it is that comparability which motivates the Symmetry Axiom, and LSO just above. Dworkin objects to welfare egalitarianism as an ethic, because among other reasons, he believes people have incommensurable conceptions of the good. If utility is noncomparable, then welfare egalitarianism is meaningless, and any cogent egalitarianism, he says, must be resource egalitarianism. The interpretation of the model I have insisted upon is one in which the kind of welfare measured by the processing functions is the same for all agents, and so Dworkin's incommensurability argument does not apply. As I noted, this narrows the scope of the model, but it makes the assumption of interpersonal comparability easier to accept.

What happens if the outcome measured by the processing functions is postulated to be noncomparable? The Symmetry Axiom can be dropped and replaced with an axiom of "cardinal noncomparability," which requires the allocation mechanism to view the processing functions as being unique only up to linear transformations.

Axiom of Cardinal Noncomparability (CNC): Let $\xi = \langle n, \bar{x}, u, v \rangle$ be an environment in Σ and let $\xi^* = \langle n, \bar{x}, \alpha u, \beta v \rangle$ be another environment in Σ where α and β are arbitrary positive constants. Then $F(\xi) = F(\xi^*)$.

Axiom CNC says that the allocation chosen by the mechanism is invariant when the outcome scales are transformed by arbitrary (and different) changes of units, for each individual.

Theorem 4: *Let an allocation mechanism satisfy D^Σ, PO, CNC, RMON, and CONRAD. Then F is dictatorial: for all environments, it assigns all the resources that both agents like to the first (or the second) agent.*

Of course, the dictatorial mechanisms are not egalitarian. We can justifiably eliminate them by insisting, for egalitarian reasons, that there should be at least one environment in Σ for which the mechanism assigns some universally liked resources to both agents. In this case, Theorem 4 immediately implies an impossibility theorem: there is no allocation mechanism that satisfies the axioms.

The interpretation of Theorem 4 is that unless interpersonal comparability of outcome is assumed, there is no coherent conception of resource equality. In terms of Dworkin's contention about incommensurability, this theorem argues that the assumption of noncomparability rules out both welfare and resource egalitarian ethics as meaningful.

9. Full information

In the model of this paper, the planner has a great deal of information: he knows the processing functions of the agents, and the resource bundle to be distributed. (He may not know the "hidden resources" that exist, but he does know the processing functions, which incorporate those resources.) The question of responsibility, with which I began, is related to the incompleteness of information concerning internal traits and processing functions. For some interpretations, this is less an issue than for others: the infant survival functions may be objectively computable, while utility functions may not be. I will suggest that the incompleteness of information concerning welfare functions, in particular, carves out a realm for personal responsibility, and thereby drives a wedge between welfare and resource egalitarianism.

I propose four reasons why we may deem a person to be responsible for an action he has done or a trait he has; two of these are intimately related to the incomplete information we have about people's internal states, a third may be related, while the fourth one derives its cogency from an anti-egalitarian premise. (1) Free will: A person is responsible for an action he has taken or a trait that he has acquired because he could have reasonably been expected to have behaved differently. (2) Incentive compatibility and moral hazard: We hold a person responsible because we cannot measure or verify what caused him to do what he did. (3) Value of choice: We allow a sphere of personal responsibility because there is value in letting people make choices for themselves. (4) Social cost: We declare a realm of personal responsibility because it is too costly for society to compensate people fully.

I think reasons (2) and (3) are founded on the incomplete information we have about people, while (1) may be. The incentive compatibility argument is most clearly so founded. We declare the murderer responsible if he cannot demonstrate to us that he was temporarily insane. To allow him simply to declare his insanity, without offering proof, would expose society to a possible moral hazard, an incentive for all murderers to escape responsibility by declaring their (unverifiable) insanity. Private information held by an actor motivates an assignment of personal responsibility by society to him.

The free will argument for responsibility also involves the lack of information, in some of its variants. We can make room for free will in the model by supposing that the processing function measures the *potential* welfare (outcome) level an agent could achieve with full application of his effort and faculties. In fact, a person with processing function $u(x)$ may expend some less-than-full degree of effort, in which case he achieves less than $u(x)$ as an outcome level, with consumption of resources x. Then the theorems state that the axioms imply equality of potential welfare, not equality of actual welfare, where the difference is due to the variable efforts expended by the agents exercising their will.[4] If one is an incompatibilist, and if the variation in effort could be accounted for by a variation in an enzyme or a neurotransmitter over which the agents have no control, that chemical could be included as a resource, and effort would not be an act of free will.[5] To say an instance of effort is an act of free will implies, under incompatibilism, that in the causal tree preceding the act, there is a cause that is not reducible to material, physiological responses. If there is, in fact, no further physical reduction of this non-material cause, then the description of the act's cause is complete. But a "soft" free will belief attributes an act to free will if we lack the information to specify physically some node in the act's causal tree. In this case, the link between free will responsibility and incomplete information is clear. For a compatibilist, on the other hand, it is possible that the causal tree be completely physically specified, yet the act be one of free will. In this case, there is no dependence of free will responsibility on incomplete information; but see Van Inwagen (1983) for arguments against compatibilism.

The "value of choice" argument for reserving a realm of personal responsibility is due to Scanlon (1988), who in turn attributes it in part to Hart. Even given a belief in the "Causal Thesis," Scanlon argues there is

---

[4] I owe this argument to G. A. Cohen.
[5] An incompatibilist believes determinism and free will are incompatible. Thus, if effort were physically determined, it could not be an instance of free will. See Van Inwagen (1983) for an excellent discussion of the various positions on determinism and free will.

value in letting people choose, and a concomitant assignment of responsibility for the consequences of choice; he decomposes that value into three constituent values. There is (1) a predictive or instrumental value in letting people choose, as they will presumably choose what they prefer, and others might not be able to do that for them; (2) a demonstrative value in choice, as when I show my wife the quality of my feelings for her by the very act of choosing an anniversary gift for her; and (3) a symbolic value in personal choice, as when my choice from a menu of exotic Chinese dishes exhibits my competence to others. I think these three values of choice all derive from the incomplete information that is available to us. If I knew everything about you, there would be no predictive or instrumental value in letting you choose: your welfare could as well be fulfilled by my choosing for you, insofar as your getting your preferred option is concerned. If my feelings were transparent, there would be no demonstrative value in the act of my spending time and exercising judgment for my wife's present; she would know the quality of my feelings with certainty, and any such act would be either redundant or a futile attempt at dissemblance. Finally, if you knew everything about me, there would be no symbolic value in my choosing, for the choice only has such value to me if there is some doubt in your mind about my competence.[6]

The social cost argument maintains that people should be responsible for some aspects of themselves because it would require too much sacrifice on the part of others fully to compensate them for their handicaps or traits. Although there may be value to this position, it begs the question for the present discussion: for my purpose is to understand the demarcation of the sphere of personal responsibility in order to conclude what degree of social compensation is appropriate. The social cost argument concludes, conversely, that society has limited liability with respect to compensating me by virtue of some already conceived standard concerning how much sacrifice from others can be demanded. Personal responsibility is assigned because excessive social costs would otherwise be incurred. The preconceived standard is one which constrains egalitarianism by some independently arrived at notion of reasonable sacrifice.

[6] There remains the question of whether there is a value in choice for the sake of autonomy, which cannot be reduced to the three values discussed by Scanlon. It is hard to think clearly about whether autonomy would have value in a world with perfect information. It seems the "autonomy" value of choice has to do with the value I get from acting and participating in the determination of my own life: but would such a value exist if I knew everything about myself, and there were no uncertainty with regard to the outcomes of the various plans I might choose? The autonomy value of choice seems closely linked to the existence of these uncertainties: it is the value I get from testing and finding my limits, and charting a successful course through unknown seas. The problems posed by this question are deep: I relegate it to a footnote not because it is easily settled, but to acknowledge it.

10.   Conclusion

I have argued that, with respect to the naming of resources and types of outcome, it is the latter which are important. Once the type of outcome is identified and fixed, then there is an argument for postulating the anonymity of goods, based on our feelings that the necessity to differentiate, for distributive purposes, among the treatment of goods of different types has to do with our inference that those different goods are important as inputs into outcomes of different types. If, however, our views about the outcome, say welfare, depend on what goods bring it about, then the anonymity of goods is not defensible.

It can be questioned whether the domain of economic environments that is posited is too large: even without naming goods, should it be the case that for any type of welfare (say, infant survival) a possible world exists with arbitrarily specified processing functions, with respect to some set of inputs? Probably not. There are certain "technological" constraints, coming from human biology and culture, which limit the domain to a smaller one than is postulated for the theorems. Thus, even if the anonymity of goods is defensible, the Domain Axiom is a chink in the model's armor, related to whatever inflexibility is characteristic of human nature.

CONRAD can be weakened to include naming goods, and to include a specification of the goods which are actually hidden in a given environment. If this is done, then an Independence of Hidden Goods Axiom must be postulated, which requires the allocation mechanism to treat an environment independently of which goods (if any) are actually hidden in it. I provided a defense of this axiom, on grounds of informational simplicity. The independence of hidden goods assures the planner that the allocation he settles on is the right one, regardless of which goods are later revealed to be hidden in the environment. This is a pragmatic, not an ethical, defense of the axiom. The axiom can still be challenged, as by Scanlon, for not allowing us to distinguish among different internal causes of the same outcome functions, which may in turn imply different views about responsibility and compensation.

I argued that resource monotonicity is a strong axiom, but showed it could be replaced with a Weak Equity Axiom, which only requires comparing a given economic environment to one benchmark environment.

I find the most compelling criticism of the model to be its full information specification. I think our assignment of responsibility is in large part linked to the incomplete information that we have about how people actually process resources into outcomes. Yet this incompleteness is not represented in the model. More than any explicit axiom, this appears to me to be the key to the evaporation of responsibility in the melding of resource and outcome egalitarianism.

The criticisms provided of the Anonymity of Goods, the Independence of Hidden Goods, the Domain Axioms, and the full information assumption are, if taken on board, sufficient to prevent the melding of resource and welfare egalitarianism. The investigation of the theorems presented here focuses the contest of resource versus welfare egalitarianism on these issues, which may not have been the clear issues before. In any case, more careful evaluation of the criticisms is possible, once they are stated in a formal and precise way.

Postscript (1992)

CONRAD was motivated as an axiom that prevents a particular perversity, described in Section 2 of the above essay, that "in passing from the environment in which only rice was recognized as a resource to [one] where rice and endorphins are recognized, resource egalitarianism should not make Bob worse off, as he is the one with the smaller amount of the newly discovered resource." Here, I replace CONRAD with a new axiom that also prevents this perversity, but that, in conjunction with the other axioms D^{Σ}, PO, Sy, and RMON, does not characterize equality of welfare.

The new axiom is:

Perversity Prevention Axiom (PP): Let $u, v \colon \mathfrak{R}_+^{n+2} \to \mathfrak{R}$, for any $n > 0$, be concave utility functions such that:

(1) for all $x \in \mathfrak{R}_+^n$ and for all $y \in \mathfrak{R}_+$, $u(x, y, 0) = v(x, 0, y)$, and
(2) $\forall z \in \mathfrak{R}_+$, $u(x, 0, z) = u(x, 0, 0) = v(x, 0, 0) = v(x, z, 0)$.

Let $\xi = \langle n+2, (\bar{x}, \bar{A}, \bar{B}), u, v \rangle$, where $\bar{A} \geq \bar{B}$, and $\xi^* = \langle n, \bar{x}, u^*, v^* \rangle$, where for all x, $u^*(x) \equiv u(x, \bar{A}, 0)$ and $v^*(x) \equiv v(x, 0, \bar{B})$. Then:

$$v(F^2(\xi)) \geq v^*(F^2(\xi^*)).$$

According to constraint (1) of the axiom, the $(n+1)^{\text{st}}$ good does exactly for the u-agent what the $(n+2)^{\text{nd}}$ good does for the v-agent: we can think of the $(n+1)^{\text{st}}$ good as being u's endorphins and the $(n+2)^{\text{nd}}$ good as v's endorphins. Constraint (2) says that u's endorphins are useless for the second agent and v's endorphins are useless for the first agent. In the environment ξ, endorphins are recognized as resources, while in environment ξ^* they enter implicitly only as they affect welfare through the utility functions. The axiom states that the second agent, who is endorphin-

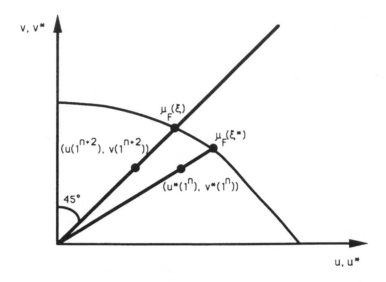

Figure 7.2

poor, should fare no worse when endorphins are recognized as resources (in ξ) than she does when they are not (in ξ^*).

I now specify an allocation mechanism that satisfies D^Σ, PO, Sy, PP, and RMON, but differs from welfare egalitarianism. Let 1^n denote the vector in $\mathfrak{R}^n$ all of whose components are equal to one. Given any environment $\xi = \langle n, \bar{x}, u, v \rangle$, consider the point in utility space $P = (u(1^n), v(1^n))$. Let $(\bar{u}, \bar{v})$ be the point on the utility frontier of $A(\xi)$ intersected by the ray from the origin through P. Define $F(\xi)$ as the allocation in ξ generating $(\bar{u}, \bar{v})$.

It is easy to see that F satisfies D^Σ, PO, Sy, and RMON. I show that it satisfies axiom PP. Let ξ and ξ^* be environments as specified in PP. First, note that $A(\xi^*) = A(\xi)$. Second, note that $u(1^{n+2}) = v(1^{n+2})$, so that in ξ, F chooses the Pareto optimal resource allocation generating equal utilities. But in ξ^* we have:

$$u^*(1^n) = u(1^n, \bar{A}, 0) = v(1^n, 0, \bar{A}) \geq v(1^n, 0, \bar{B}) = v^*(1^n)$$

and so the point $(u^*(1^n), v^*(1^n))$ lies below the 45° degree line in $A(\xi^*)$ (see Figure 7.2). Hence it follows that F awards less utility to the second agent in ξ^* than it does in ξ, verifying that PP holds. But F does not equalize welfare on the domain D^Σ; so we have an allocation mechanism that satisfies the desiderata for resource egalitarianism which is not equality-of-welfare.

A pragmatic theory of responsibility for the egalitarian planner

I. Equality and responsibility

What should an egalitarian seek to equalize? Welfare is, of course, an obvious candidate, and each contributor to the recent discussion has taken it as the foil for his own proposal. To review briefly: John Rawls proposes "primary goods"; Ronald Dworkin proposes "resources," a resource being defined in a comprehensive way to include various talents and handicaps;[1] Amartya Sen proposes "capabilities to function";[2] in two recent articles, Richard Arneson has proposed "opportunity for welfare" as the appropriate equalisandum;[3] G. A. Cohen has recently proposed "access to advantage."[4] All of these proposals attempt to equalize opportunities, rather than outcomes: for Rawls and Dworkin, primary goods and resources, respectively, are the wherewithal with which people carry out projects that lead to outcomes that have value to them; for Sen, the capabilities to function in various ways are the prerequisites for what individuals make of themselves; and Cohen's "access" is similar to Arneson's straightforward "opportunity."

If the first issue of contention in modern egalitarian theory is what the equalisandum should be, the second is the distinction between a person's actions that are caused by circumstances beyond his control and those for which he is personally responsible. This issue, among the five authors named, is most actively addressed by Dworkin, Arneson, and Cohen. The general form of the egalitarian ethic that emerges from these three writers is that *society should indemnify people against poor outcomes that are the consequences of causes that are beyond their control, but not*

I have benefited from penetrating questions posed by those who attended the Ethics and Economics Summer School at the University of Siena in July 1991 and a philosophy seminar at Brown University in November 1991. This article has been much simplified and improved as a result of challenges and suggestions from Richard Arneson, G. A. Cohen, and the Editors of *Philosophy & Public Affairs,* to whom I am deeply indebted.

[1] Dworkin (1981, 1981a).
[2] Sen (1985a).
[3] Arneson (1989, 1990).
[4] Cohen (1989). See also Cohen (1990).

against outcomes that are the consequences of causes that are within their control, and therefore for which they are personally responsible. Dworkin, for example, says that the distribution of resources should be ambition-sensitive, but not endowment-sensitive, endowments being the "circumstances" a person has no control over, and ambitions being formed and carried out by virtue of a person's will.[5]

I agree that the correct egalitarian ethic is the one emphasized in the last paragraph. My task in this article is to articulate that ethic in a concrete form, so that it could, in principle, be applied in actual social situations by an egalitarian planner. In so doing, I take no stand on the question of what the proper equalisandum is: I only attempt to determine when opportunities for X have been equalized in a population, where X can be any outcome (for example, welfare, expected welfare, advantage, self-realization, and so on).

Before proceeding to my constructive task, it is perhaps worthwhile briefly to distinguish the senses in which Dworkin, Arneson, and Cohen define the realm of personal responsibility. Dworkin takes "preferences" to be matters for which the person is responsible, whether or not they were brought about by factors within her control, as long as she identifies with them, and "resources" to be matters for which she is not responsible. Sometimes Dworkin also refers to "ambitions" and "endowments" as representing, respectively, these two categories. Equality of welfare is undesirable as a goal because it fails to hold people responsible for their preferences or ambitions. Equality of resources equalizes only what people are not responsible for and is the ethically appropriate policy. How to implement equality of resources is a significant part of Dworkin's discussion, and has itself stirred up some controversy.[6]

Arneson makes two principal points. First, he claims that Dworkin's cut between resources and preferences is not the conceptually correct one for capturing the salient issue of responsibility: that cut should be between "opportunity" and "outcome." What a person is *not* responsible for are her opportunities; she *is* responsible for transforming opportunities into outcomes. In particular, a person may not be entirely responsible for her preferences. Second, the appropriate outcome the opportunities for which should be equalized is welfare. Arneson defines "equality of opportunity for welfare" as follows:

We construct a decision tree that gives an individual's possible complete life-histories. We then add up the preference satisfaction expectation for each possible

---

[5] Not all writers would agree with the emphasized ethic. Scanlon (1988) argues that people should be held responsible for some actions even if determinism – what he calls the Causal Thesis – is true.

[6] See, for example, Roemer (1986) and Essay 7 of this volume.

life-history. In doing this we take into account the preferences that people have regarding being confronted with the particular range of options given at each decision point. Equal opportunity for welfare obtains among persons when all of them face equivalent decision trees – the expected value of each person's best (= most prudent) choice of options, second-best, . . . n^{th} best is the same. The opportunities persons encounter are ranked by the prospects of welfare they afford.[7]

In particular, what need not be equalized for Arneson are the welfares (or, if there is uncertainty, the expected welfares) resulting from the paths of their decision trees that people actually choose, for the person is viewed as responsible for making the choice.

Cohen contrasts "access to advantage" to Arneson's opportunity for welfare. He writes:

Equality of opportunity for welfare is a better reading of egalitarianism than equality of welfare itself is, but it is not as good as what currently strikes me as the right reading of egalitarianism, namely, that its purpose is to eliminate *involuntary disadvantage,* by which I (stipulatively) mean disadvantage for which the sufferer cannot be held responsible, since it does not appropriately reflect choices that he has made or is making or would make.[8]

Cohen prefers the term "access" to "opportunity," as he thinks the former includes personal capacities in a way that "opportunity" precludes. The main distinction for my purposes is this: equality of access to advantage is intended to give all people an equal shot at advantage by compensating those who otherwise would have a poor shot owing to matters over which they have no (or little) control. This contrasts with Arneson's proposal, to design taxes and transfers that would equalize welfare (or advantage) were each to choose the option that is *most prudent* (or second-best, or third-best, . . .) for him. The distinction between Cohen and Arneson is important if it is not within a person's control to choose the option that would be most prudent for him, or, less extremely, if it would require exceptional willpower for him to do so. Thus, Cohen would say that equalizing the expected welfare of the various paths on the decision trees of two people (following Arneson) equalizes their *opportunities* for welfare, but not their *access* to welfare, and it is access to welfare that is ethically relevant.

My own proposal is that *equality of opportunity for X holds when the values of X for all those who exercised a comparable degree of responsibility are equal, regardless of their circumstances.* Two people are said to have the same circumstances if they share a set of socioeconomic and genetic characteristics, where the choice of that set *by society* reflects society's view of those factors that affect a person's choices and over which

[7] Arneson (1989), pp. 85–86.
[8] Cohen (1989), p. 916.

he has no control. The modifier "by society" is emphasized because what I describe is an algorithm by which any society, with its particular views concerning the extent to which persons can overcome their circumstances by acts of will, can implement an egalitarianism of opportunity consonant with those views. In this sense, my proposal is political and not metaphysical.

The tricky part is to decide when two people in different circumstances have exercised a "comparable degree of responsibility"; articulating this concept will take up most of the remainder of the article. In particular, the quoted phrase in the last sentence does not mean the *same* degree of responsibility, because two people, by virtue of their very different circumstances, may have exercised very different degrees of responsibility – although, when we take their circumstances into account, we may decide that the degrees of responsibility that they have exercised are "comparable." Rather than trying to define the concept in question quite generally, I will proceed with some examples.

II.   Lung cancer and responsibility

Suppose we try to apply these ideas to decide the amount that society should pay of a person's medical expenses for treatment of lung cancer contracted from smoking, given the information available to smokers about the disease. Variations in the number of years people smoke are attributable to circumstances (beyond their control) and to choices for which they are responsible. Society must first decide what circumstances seem to be important in determining a person's smoking behavior: we might decide these are a person's *occupation,* her *ethnicity* and *gender,* whether her *parents* smoked, and her *income* level. For the purposes at hand, we would consider these five characteristics of a person to be factors beyond her control.[9] The next step is to divide the relevant population into *types,* with each type consisting of the subset of the population having approximately the same values for all five characteristics.

Within each type, there will be a range of smoking behavior. The median number of years smoked (for people age sixty, say) will vary across type. I will say that two sixty-year-olds, each of whom has smoked the median number of years for his type, have exercised a *comparable degree of responsibility* with respect to smoking behavior.

[9] One might question whether her occupation is beyond her control. For the purpose of analyzing smoking behavior, we might say it is, while we might say it is not for the purpose of explaining her income level, because a person arguably should not be held accountable for not considering the effect of her occupational choice on her smoking behavior, while she might well be held accountable for not considering the effect of that choice on her income.

Here is the motivation. Within a type, the variation in smoking behavior is taken, by society, to reflect the different degrees of responsibility its members have exercised. For, by definition, society has already accounted for, in the definition of type, all the circumstances affecting smoking behavior that it considers to be beyond a person's control. Now let us compare two people of different types, both of whom are at the median of their respective type-distributions for years of smoking. Although it might not make sense to say that they have exercised the *same* degree of responsibility, we can say that the two have exercised comparable degrees of responsibility, taking into account what others in their types have done. According to the egalitarian ethic announced in Section I, these two people should be equally indemnified by society for the harm they have suffered. Thus, suppose one lung cancer victim is a sixty-year old, white, female college professor whose parents stopped smoking when she was seven; she smoked the median number of years for her type, which, let us say, is eight years. A second lung cancer victim, also aged sixty, is a black, male steelworker whose parents were both chain-smokers. He also happens to be the median smoker for his type, and has smoked for twenty-five years. My egalitarian ethic says that both should receive the same degree of social indemnity: if all the medical expenses of the professor are covered by society, then the same should be the case for the steelworker. (Perhaps providing such complete medical subsidies to the median smokers across types would result in more smoking at the median, and less health as a result. If so, then the policy of complete medical subsidy is not optimal. As I will elaborate in the next two sections, the optimal pattern of medical subsidy is one that maximizes the expected lung health of the median smoker of the "worse-off" type, given the total budget that society is willing to allocate to lung cancer.)

Let us compare my proposal to Dworkin's. Dworkin would ask what amount of insurance the steelworker and the professor would have taken out behind a veil of ignorance, where each knew his or her preferences and the probability of getting lung cancer as a function of number of years smoked (and other variables, if relevant). It is key, however, that Dworkin's souls use their own preferences in making this decision. Of course, if the insurance system is efficient, it will charge more to a subscriber who contracts lung cancer after having smoked for twenty-five years than to one who contracts it after having smoked for eight years. One might well imagine that the professor would take out full insurance behind the veil of ignorance, and the steelworker would not, even if both had the same amount of wealth (one of Dworkin's conditions behind the veil). Thus, Dworkin would not have society pay the same fraction of medical expenses for the steelworker and the professor.

It is not hard to extend this principle to people who are not "median" smokers. The median number of years smoked by people of a given type is the number such that exactly 50 percent of people of that type have smoked that number of years or fewer. Now replace 50 percent by any percent, say p percent. I will say that two people, of different types, have exercised a comparable degree of responsibility if each is at the pth percentile of his type-distribution, for some p.

III.   Education and income

I shall next discuss a much more important problem. The income a person earns is closely correlated to the amount of education she receives. Conservatives hold that, as long as public schools are available to all children, all have equal opportunity to become educated, and hence no tampering with the outcome (differential income) can be ethically justified. In this section I will study the issue of equal educational opportunity, using the ideas I have put forth about responsibility.

To discuss a person's responsibility for becoming educated, it is useful to distinguish among preferences, beliefs, and the rational pursuit of interests. The population is partitioned into *types,* a type being characterized by a vector of socioeconomic and personal characteristics. Society has decided, let us say, that the five traits of parental income, parental education, ethnicity, performance on certain intelligence tests, and health status capture the causes of a person's behavior relevant to educational attainment that are beyond his control. All persons who have approximately the same values for these five characteristics constitute one type. The values for these components constitute a person's *circumstances.*

The pertinent *preferences* are ones individuals have over years of education and amount of future income. A simple example is the preference ordering represented by the utility function $u(y, x) = -y^2/s + x$, where y is years of education (or level of diploma), x is amount of future income, and s is a parameter representing the psychic costs of education.[10] In this example, as is conventional in economic theory, education is viewed as costly for the person to attain, and income in a later period is the reward for the effort exerted. I shall assume, for the sake of simplicity, that the costs of education are borne by the state. The pertinent *beliefs* are the person's view of what the returns to education actually are, the statistical distribution of income that she can expect for every given level of education she might attain. Given the person's preferences and beliefs, there is an optimal level of education for her – one that maximizes her expected utility. (The expectation is taken because the income she will receive is

---

[10] One can think of s as measuring talent. The higher the value of s, the less arduous it is for a person to attain a given education level.

only stochastically related to the amount of education she attains.) But not everyone will necessarily implement the solution to this optimization problem: if a person does so, she is said to "rationally pursue her interest." A person might fail to rationally pursue her interest, owing, for instance, to weakness of will.

An important possibility is that a person's beliefs may be wrong. That is to say, there is a distribution of income for all those of a given type who attain a given level of education, but a person may have incorrect beliefs about what that distribution is. Some people are pessimists – that is, they underestimate the true returns to education – and others are optimists. To rationally pursue her interest, a person need not have correct beliefs: she need only solve her optimization problem correctly and implement that solution, given her beliefs.

Assume, for the moment, that within each type, all persons choose the same level of education. (I do not mean that people of different types choose the same level of education.) According to my proposal, we would say that all persons have exercised a comparable degree of responsibility. Suppose the goal of this society is to equalize the opportunity for expected welfare, where welfare is measured by the person's utility function, given above. The policy implication following from the general principle is that income taxation should equalize expected welfare for all, or, more generally, should maximize the minimum of those expected welfares.

Now suppose that not all persons classified as of a given type choose the same level of education. Consider a person who attains some level of education different from the median level for persons of that type (either higher or lower). The theory's explanation is that either that person has preferences or beliefs that differ from those of the median person of his type, or one of those people did not optimize given his preferences and beliefs. Society treats the difference between the behavior of these two people as due to the different degrees of responsibility they exercised, regardless of the reason, for all relevant differences in their circumstances were factored out when the two individuals were assigned to the same type. Thus, it may be the case that a person's preferences or beliefs themselves reflect the degree of responsibility a person has exercised. One person of the type may have done more research than the other about the returns to education, and this clearly would count as having exercised more responsibility. The key point is that, once society has specified the components of type, by definition any variation within type must be due to personal responsibility. By specifying the *dimension* and *fineness* of the type grid differently, different societies clearly will consider different types and amounts of behavior to be due to personal responsibility.[11]

[11] The dimension of type is the number of components that constitute it; the fineness is determined by how close the type vectors must be to be considered of the same type.

Some standard and important characteristics of preferences that may be in large part environmentally determined, such as attitudes toward risk and rates of time preference, are easily covered by the model.[12] For example, the von Neumann–Morgenstern utility function $u(y, x) = -y^2/s + (x - \frac{1}{2}x^2)/(1+r)$ represents preferences of persons who are risk-averse in income lotteries and who discount future income at rate r. Let us note, for example, how class background and talent appear in the model. Variables that measure these characteristics should, in my view, be included in the definition of type; they affect a person's preferences and beliefs and are beyond her control. For example, high talent shows up as a high value of s in the utility function – it is less costly for talented people than for untalented people to attain a given level of education. High talent may also be reflected in a favorable distribution of income. Let $F^t(y)$ be the true distribution of income for those of type t who attain education level y. Consider two types, t^1 and t^2, for which the mean of $F^{t^1}(y)$ is greater than the mean of $F^{t^2}(y)$: for any given amount of education, t^1 can expect a higher income than t^2 can expect. This could reflect the greater talent of t^1. A privileged class background may show up either as a high value of s or as having true or optimistic beliefs about the returns to education. (Thus, even if education is fully subsidized, it is less costly for a rich person than a poor person to become educated, for the opportunity cost of being in school is lower; and the rich person may view many high-flying jobs as attainable to him with a given amount of education that a poor person may not believe attainable with that amount of education.)

Discrimination can be handled within the model. If a black child suffers damage to her self-esteem because of racist treatment or as a result of poor performance on standardized tests that are calibrated for white, middle-class students, this might be represented as a low value of s in her utility function. Consider the case of a black student who has the same talent and receives the same amount of education as a white student, but nevertheless suffers from discrimination in employment. This is modeled by stipulating that the actual distribution of income for the black person has a lower mean than the distribution of income for a white person with the same level of education.

In the work of Rawls, Dworkin, Arneson, and Cohen, a central example that clinches the case against equality of welfare as the ethically correct

---

[12] The rate of time preference expresses an individual's degree of "impatience." If one individual requires a higher rate of interest to induce him to save money than another, the first is said to have a higher rate of time preference, or time discount. If an individual invests little in his future, it may be the consequence of having a high rate of time preference.

kind of egalitarianism is the required treatment of a person with voluntarily cultivated expensive tastes. Under welfare egalitarianism, such a person must receive a larger-than-normal bundle of scarce resources, which appears to render him a kind of exploiter of others with more frugal tastes. In the model I have presented, a person who has a high rate of time discount (r) or who views education as very costly (low value of s) has expensive tastes, for he will choose a low level of education (*ceteris paribus*), will consequently have low expected future income, and will have a low expected welfare.

To take a classic example, consider the person who derives satisfaction from a drink only if it is a pre-phylloxera claret.[13] Such a person requires more money to derive the same satisfaction that a beer lover derives from her brew. Here is how Dworkin, Arneson, and I would differ in the treatment of such a person. Dworkin would not compensate the one who could derive satisfaction only from pre-phylloxera claret if she *identifies* with those tastes. Arneson would not compensate her if it had been *prudent* for her to learn to like beer: presumably, if she knew that she would not have the income to purchase the ancient claret, and if she had the opportunity to develop frugal tastes, then it would have been prudent for her to do so. I propose that the decision whether to compensate her depends on how the median person of her type behaved. Let us say that her type is "child of impoverished aristocrats." If the "median preferences" of persons of that type are for pre-phylloxera claret, then she is entitled to compensation to increase her level of welfare to what the person of frugal tastes, who exercised a median degree of responsibility in other circumstances, can experience with his resources.

IV.   A formal model of the education problem

We may think of the social planner as being charged with choosing a tax policy to implement the degree of opportunity egalitarianism that society desires. In this section, I describe how the planner might do this in the case described in Section III. As we will see, there is no satisfactory way of equalizing opportunity for all. Essentially, doing so would require optimizing an infinite number of objectives at once, which is impossible. One must therefore be satisfied with a second-best approach. Readers with little taste for mathematics may take this point on faith and skip to Section V.

---

[13] Being at the University of California at Davis, the home of a distinguished enology and viticulture department, I once had the pleasure of teaching a course on distributive justice in a classroom the walls of which displayed pictures showing how vines attacked by phylloxera could be identified with infrared photography.

Assume that the population has been partitioned into T types, where the members of type t make up the set Ω^t. Let H be the probability distribution of types (that is, for any subset S of the set of types, $H(S)$ is the fraction of the population whose type is in S). There are two relevant time periods. I shall assume that education is acquired at date 0; the person takes into account, *inter alia,* the income that he expects to earn at date 1 for any given level of education y. His beliefs on this matter may be incorrect; that is, they may not coincide with the actual distribution of incomes attained by type t persons who receive education y. I assume that the planner knows the correct distribution of income for any type t at any acquired level of education; call it $F^t(y)$. Let the maximum possible education level be $\bar{y}$, and let the interval of possible education levels be $\bar{Y} = [0, \bar{y}]$. Let $\bar{X}$ be the set of possible incomes. Formally, for any y and t, $F^t(y)$ is a probability measure on $\bar{X}$; that is, for any set $X \subset \bar{X}$, $F^t(y)(X)$ is the fraction of persons of type t who, when acquiring education level y, earn incomes in X.[14]

A *tax policy* is a function $\tau(y, x, t)$ that specifies the amount of tax to be paid by a person of type t who acquires education y and ends up earning income x. τ can be negative, which means that the person receives a transfer. It is assumed that the planner can choose a tax policy from a certain class $\mathfrak{I}$ of policies. For instance, the planner may not be able to differentiate taxation with respect to type or education level attained, in which case the tax policies would be of the form $\tau(x)$, which is a special case of the above. There may be a number of political and incentive considerations that determine the class $\mathfrak{I}$. We need not concern ourselves further with these.

I shall not worry about the econometric problem of estimating the response of members of the population to different tax policies. In any practical implementation scheme, one could not be so cavalier. I shall simply assume that, for each tax policy τ, the planner knows what the distribution of education levels attained in each type will be.[15] Formally, there is a probability measure $J(\tau, t)$ for each t and τ on the set $\bar{Y}$; for any subset $Y \subset \bar{Y}$, $J(\tau, t)(Y)$ is the fraction of Ω^t who will attain education levels in Y if tax policy τ is enacted. Since the planner also knows the distributions $F^t(y)$, he can then calculate the expected distribution of education and income levels for the entire population corresponding to any policy τ.

[14] For some t and some y, $F^t(y)$ may not be defined, if no person of type t ever achieves education level y.

[15] In practice, this assumption is not as heroic as it may appear, because the planner will be limited to a fairly small class of tax policies for political reasons, and will have econometric evidence of the relevant supply-and-demand elasticities with respect to parameters of those policies.

The final tool the planner needs is a social welfare function that enables her to compare the expected welfares of any two members of the population. Welfare, in our problem, depends on education level achieved, the consequent expected income, and perhaps the person's type; thus, it can be written as a function $\Phi(y, \tau, t)$, because the planner, knowing y and t, can compute expected pretax income, knowing τ, can calculate expected post-tax income, and hence can calculate expected welfare. The welfare that Φ measures is interpersonally comparable: that is, "$\Phi(y, \tau, t) > \Phi(y', \tau' t')$" means that a person of type t who acquires education y under tax policy τ has higher expected welfare than a person of type t' who acquires education y' at tax policy τ'. It is not important, for my purposes, whether the notion of welfare used by the planner takes into account the preferences of the individuals of type t or whether it is an objective or perfectionist measure. Indeed, Φ might rank education level–income pairs differently than the individual. While an individual may view education chiefly as a cost, to be borne for the sake of future income, the planner (that is, society) may view education as contributing to a public good, such as a citizenry capable of democratic participation or self-governance. The resolution of these issues is oblique to my concerns here: the point I wish to make is that the model is sufficiently supple to allow any resolution of them.

It should be stressed that the present formulation does not even presume that individuals choose their education levels, when facing a tax policy, by maximizing some utility function. The process by which they choose their education levels is a black box, as far as the model is concerned: the planner need only know the observed responses to tax policies, which are specified by the distributions $J(\tau, t)$. Perhaps some people of type t maximize utility and implement the solution to their programs; perhaps others maximize but then do not implement, owing to weakness of will; perhaps others never really face the issue of choosing an education level, but simply follow the path of least resistance.

Society has included in the specification of type all causes influencing a person's behavior deemed to be beyond his control. Thus, the differences in education levels achieved by the members of a given type are, by definition, within the sphere of personal responsibility. The tax policy that the planner implements will endeavor to equalize, as far as possible, the expected welfares of all those who exercised a comparable degree of responsibility across the population, but to allow differences in expected welfare within types to reflect the different degrees of responsibility exercised.

It is time to defend, in a somewhat deeper way than I have so far, the view that two persons at the same percentile of their type-distributions of years of education attained have exerted a comparable degree of responsibility. The claim can be based on the assumption that the level of education achieved within a type is a *strictly monotonic* function of the degree of responsibility exercised.[16] For each type, there is some distribution of degrees of responsibility exercised that we cannot observe. It is natural to say that if two people, of different types, are at the same percentile of their distributions of responsibility exercised, they have exercised a comparable degree of responsibility. The problem is to deduce degree of responsibility exercised from observed educational levels.

Holding constant the type (t) and the tax policy (τ), we have assumed that there is an unobserved variable, responsibility (ω), which is distributed in some way among members of the type, say according to a distribution $D(\tau, t)$. We have assumed that the education level attained, y, is a strictly increasing function of responsibility within each type: $y = f(\omega)$, where f is strictly monotonic. (The function f is the unobservable "reduced form" that collapses the process of preference and belief formation and expresses achieved education level directly as a function of degree of responsibility exercised.) We have assumed that the achieved education levels for type t persons at tax scheme τ are distributed according to the measure $J(\tau, t)$. Thus $J(\tau, t)(\{y \le \hat{y}\})$ is the fraction of the type t population that achieves education level less than or equal to $\hat{y}$. By the monotonicity assumption, $\hat{y}$ corresponds to some unique value of responsibility, say $\hat{\omega}$, in the type t population, and

$$D(\tau, t)(\{\omega \le \hat{\omega}\}) = J(\tau, t)(\{y \le \hat{y}\}), \qquad (1)$$

which just says that the persons who exercised responsibility less than or equal to $\hat{\omega}$ are precisely the persons who achieved education levels less than or equal to $\hat{y}$. Now designate $\hat{y}$ as the median of the J distribution. Then $J(\tau, t)(\{y \le \hat{y}\}) = \frac{1}{2}$, which, by equation 1, implies that $D(\tau, t)(\{\omega \le \hat{\omega}\}) = \frac{1}{2}$, which means that $\hat{\omega}$ is the median of the D distribution. This proves that the median of observed education levels is achieved by persons whose exercise of responsibility is at the median of the distribution of degrees of responsibility exercised.

---

[16] This assumption need not be true. It may be that some people, after researching the returns to education, decide not to educate themselves as much as others of their type who naively believe that the returns to education are much greater than they actually are. If this is the case, then monotonicity fails, and the tax proposal I recommend below is not so attractive. What we need, more generally than monotonicity, is a way of imputing a person's percentile ranking in the responsibility distribution for his type from some observed behavior. If monotonicity holds, the percentile ranking in the responsibility distribution is the same as in the distribution of observed behavior (years of education achieved, or years of smoking). Even without monotonicity, however, we may be able to perform the required imputation.

Let $y(\rho, \tau, t)$ be the education level at the ρth percentile of the distribution of education levels attained by persons of type t facing tax policy τ. (Thus, $y(\frac{1}{2}, \tau, t)$ is the median education level of such persons.) Formally, we can define $y(\rho, \tau, t)$ by the equation

$$\int_0^{y(\rho, \tau, t)} dJ(\tau, t) = \rho.$$

To achieve equality of opportunity for expected welfare, we would like to find a tax policy that, for any ρ, equalizes the expected welfares of all types – and if there are many such policies, we would like to choose among them one that maximizes some function of expected welfare. Unfortunately, there is in general no such policy. Nor is there an obvious "maximin" alternative to equalization, since we are facing an infinite number of things to equalize, for the degree of responsibility exercised, ρ, takes on a continuum of values. Alternatively stated, we cannot maximin the expected welfare for those at the fiftieth percentile of the responsibility distribution and simultaneously maximin the expected welfare for those at the fortieth percentile, the thirtieth percentile, and so on. We are forced to consider some second-best approach.

The approach I favor is as follows. The planner chooses that tax policy which maximizes a weighted average of minimum welfares across types of persons of the same degree of responsibility, where the weight attached to the welfare of those at a given degree of responsibility is the population frequency of persons of that degree. Let h_t be the fraction of type t persons in the population, and let $j(y; \tau, t)$ be the density function of $J(\tau, t)$. Let $\varphi^i(\rho, \tau) = \Phi(y(\rho, \tau, i), \tau, i)$; in words, $\varphi^i(\rho, \tau)$ is the welfare of the person of type i, at tax rate τ, who is at the ρth percentile of her type's distribution of responsibility. Then the planner would choose τ to:

$$\underset{\tau \in \Im}{\text{Sup}} \int_0^{\bar{y}} \sum_{t=1}^{T} h_t\, j(y(\rho, \tau, t); \tau, t) \underset{t'}{\text{Min}}\, \varphi^{t'}(\rho, \tau)\, dy(\rho, \tau, t)$$

This can be simplified to:

$$\underset{\tau}{\text{Sup}} \int_0^1 \underset{t}{\text{Min}}\, \varphi^t(\rho, \tau)\, d\rho.$$

The interpretation of the last expression is as follows. The planner fixes a candidate tax policy τ; now she averages, over all degrees of responsibility ρ, the welfare of the worst-off type at that degree of responsibility. The planner then looks for the τ that makes this number as large as possible. This seems to me to be the salient way of balancing the interests of those at every degree of responsibility in the planner's objective function.

An objection has been raised to the social policy that would be chosen by the policymaker who takes the approach I am advocating. The policy would, according to this objection, simply transfer income to those with pessimistic beliefs or high rates of time preference, rather than provide them with incentives to further their education. But this belief is, in general, mistaken. If the policymaker is able to determine the number of years of education attained, and is not otherwise prevented from making the tax policy a function of it, then the optimal policy will generally involve elements of both education subsidy and income transfer. An education subsidy takes the form of assuring the person that, should a high level of education be attained, a certain (high) level of expected future income will be guaranteed. This will induce persons with pessimistic beliefs, for instance, to educate themselves more than they otherwise would have. Recall that monetary costs of education do not enter directly into this model; income appears only in the second period. This is just a modeling choice: I could reformulate the model to include a *belief* element of what the monetary costs of education are and a specification of *true* monetary costs; social policy would then involve direct financial education subsidies of the usual sort.[17] For purposes of exposition, however, it is simpler to include beliefs as a factor in only one time period. I have chosen to let them enter into the calculation only of the returns to education.

Those who raise the above objection are concerned that the policy recommended by program (2) would not induce people to educate themselves "as much as they should." First, it should be understood that the beliefs and preferences that people have in the model are those that they have after all has been said and done to explain to them the true costs of and returns to education. Thus it is pointless to say that more money should be spent to change their beliefs, rather than to subsidize them: society has already allocated what resources it deems appropriate to changing beliefs. Second, I am not concerned here with the incentive effects on the next generation of children, whose intellectual formation and behavior may be influenced by what they know about the government's past taxation policy. Concerns of that sort would require at least a three-period model, and, of course, the analysis would become more complex: it would, in

---

[17] I have not been able to find studies of people's beliefs about the returns to education, but I have found studies of people's beliefs concerning the costs of education. David Post (1990) reports that in a predominantly Chicano high school in Los Angeles, students overestimated the costs of attending a junior college and a state college by factors of 15 and 4, respectively. It has been reported that members of Congress think the most urgently needed addition to the Higher Education Act is a program that would inform younger students about the college admissions process, costs, and the availability of loans and grants. ("Congress Seeks 'Early Intervention' Effort to Spur Children to Prepare for College," *Chronicle of Higher Education,* 3 July 1991, p. A15.)

particular, have to include a judgment of how to weight the opportunities for welfare of the two generations in the policymaker's social welfare function. Third, we should not be concerned to educate the population as much as possible. The social welfare function Φ incorporates our views of how education influences welfare or advantage. In particular, some people with overly optimistic beliefs may educate themselves too much without government intervention; the optimal policy would induce them to choose less education than they would have otherwise chosen by threatening to tax severely the high incomes these optimists falsely think they would receive with high levels of education.

V. Further examples and objections

Although I have discussed several problems of distributive justice, it is natural to ask how my proposal would extend to other situations.

1. Consider the case of Nazi SS members. Would my proposal render them not responsible for their behavior? First, one must recognize that there is a concern that might lead to punishing such persons that is beyond the scope of this article: an exemplary one. It may be important to create examples to influence the behavior of people in the future. Aside from this concern, the answer to the question is, it all depends on what society chooses to include as dimensions of type. My conjecture is that even if one included as dimensions such things as "whether one was beaten by one's father when young," "whether one's parents were virulently anti-Semitic," and so on, one would still find that the behavior of SS members was deviant from the median behavior of their type. The median German was probably one who minded his own business, did not join the SS, and did not confront the regime. I do not consider such people responsible for what happened to the Jews, even if they knew about it.[18] But if (what I would consider) a reasonable list of exogenous factors were perfectly correlated with SS membership, then I would not consider that behavior punishable except for exemplary reasons. This, of course, does not mean that a society should not announce penalties for such behavior, for such an announcement itself becomes a factor in a person's circumstances and, hence, intellectual formation.

[18] Here I am asserting something new that the reader may either accept or not: that the German who exercised the median degree of responsibility concerning his collaboration with the regime was not responsible for what the regime did. For example, suppose the behavior we are examining is whether Germans illegally sheltered Jews. If not sheltering them constituted median behavior for a type, while sheltering them constituted median behavior for another type, then I would not consider the shelterer to be more morally admirable than the nonshelterer. One still might want to commend the former's behavior, for exemplary reasons.

2. Should South African white children, who have grown up with privileges in large part due to the exploitation of blacks and who therefore have more expensive tastes, be assured of more income than black children in a post-apartheid regime, since they cannot be held responsible for these tastes?[19] Again, one must first ascertain that exemplary concerns are not at issue. I admit that I find grating the prospect of adopting a social policy the effects of which would be to render the white children materially better off than black children just because the whites might suffer mental anguish if they were only materially just as well off as blacks. Note that even if the optimal social policy in this situation would render whites materially better off than blacks, it would in all likelihood involve more subsidies to blacks than to whites in order to induce blacks to choose higher levels of education than they would have otherwise chosen.

Another response to this challenge is to argue that this is a case in which Cohen's "advantage" is saliently different from welfare. The social policy that equalizes the access to welfare of black and white children may still leave blacks relatively disadvantaged. Depending on our definition of advantage, it may be possible to tilt the material distribution more in favor of blacks (than it would be under equality of access to welfare) to equalize access to advantage.

3. Scanlon has argued that there are various reasons to hold an individual responsible for his choices, even if determinism, or what he calls the Causal Thesis, is true.[20] These reasons have mainly to do with the fact that an individual's choices signal to others the kind of person he is, which imparts value to him. I agree that for some kinds of choices what Scanlon says is correct.[21] Thus, I do not intend the egalitarian theory I have outlined to be applicable to all kinds of inequality among people. I have deliberately chosen the case of education and its relation to income as one that falls clearly within the domain of problems to which the theory is applicable.

Similarly, Dworkin argues that society should not be obliged to subsidize the person who adopts excessively ambitious goals (for example, the conservationist who requires a huge share of resources to save the snail darter). To make the case hard for me, Dworkin might further specify that all those with a particular social and cultural background adopt these conservationist projects.

---

[19] Approximately this question was posed by Bernard Williams.

[20] See note 5 above.

[21] It might be argued, to take an example of Scanlon's, that society should not indemnify a person for the sufferings he endures owing to a choice of religion, even if his religious choice was determined by his circumstances.

Again, I must reply that my proposal is not intended for application to all possible distributional questions. My complaint is that the positions of Dworkin and Scanlon on responsibility for preferences and choice purport to be universally applicable, while in fact they are plausible for only a fraction of the distributional problems that a society must face. For many concrete distributional issues, I think their proposals would undersubsidize people with truncated opportunities – the lung cancer example being a case in point with respect to Dworkin.

I would characterize the class of cases for which my proposal is applicable as follows. A person can perform an action to various degrees, and the less he performs the action, the more at risk he is for a harm.[22] Furthermore, the action is performed at some personal cost. Society must decide how much to compensate those persons who suffer the harm. In one case I have studied, the action is "to stop smoking," and the harm is lung cancer, or, more precisely, the costs of treating it. In the other, the action is "becoming educated" and the harm is a low future income level.

4. I think that my proposal is consonant with Sen's theory of distributing resources so as to equalize everyone's capacities to function in various ways. The critical point is that Sen would equalize *capacities* to function, not actual degrees of functioning. The degree to which a person makes use of his capacities, to actually function in various ways, is up to him, and I do not think that Sen intends to insure people against low levels of functioning (and the consequent low welfare levels), which are a person's own responsibility, in the sense that the discussion of type has made clear.

VI. Conclusion

Behind the egalitarian principle emphasized in Section I lies, I think, the view that there is a core of human nature common to all. Except for their (social and genetic) circumstances, all people would have, in particular, the same *capacity* to exercise equal degrees of responsibility for their actions. People will, however, exercise different degrees of responsibility, for two reasons: first, their circumstances may cause them to, in a way that is beyond their control, and second, some will simply try harder than others. The principle in question says that persons' fortunes can legitimately diverge, from an ethical viewpoint, only to the extent that those persons are differentially ambitious on their own hook.

---

[22] I have discussed the "monotonicity condition" in note 16. If the monotonicity condition fails, the theory may still be applicable to the problem at hand: what one requires is an observable aspect of the behavior of persons within a type that provides us with an ordinal ranking of the degrees of responsibility they have exercised.

The question that must be answered for social policy is: How can one determine when people in different circumstances have exercised a comparable degree of responsibility? I have proposed an answer to that question, based on the assumption that the degree of responsibility exercised is deducible from some observable component of behavior on which distributional transfers can be based. When that degree is monotonically related to the value of an observable action, we have a simple, special case.

Finally, each particular society will choose the extent to which it treats deviation from median behavior as due to circumstance or to personal responsibility by choosing the list of traits that define type and the number of types it admits (the dimension and fineness of the type grid). Because its choice of these parameters cannot but be influenced by the physiological, psychological, and social theories of man that it has, the present proposal would implement different degrees of opportunity egalitarianism in different societies.

Bargaining theory and justice

Introduction to Part III

At first thought, it might seem that one should study questions of distributive justice by thinking about different ways one might allocate resources in a given, fixed world. But in Essay 6 another idea was proposed: to study the set of possible allocation mechanisms on a large domain of possible worlds, and to formalize one's views concerning justice as axioms on the behavior of such allocation mechanisms. Essay 7 implemented this methodological approach, and characterized the welfare egalitarian resource allocation mechanism with a set of five axioms.

This approach – of studying the class of allocation rules on a large domain of possible worlds – began in economics in the early 1950s with axiomatic bargaining theory, as developed by Nash (1950), and social choice theory, as developed by Arrow (1951). More recently, Thomson and Lensberg (1989) have applied these techniques to the study of egalitarianism. As developed by these authors, these theories assume an axiom of *welfarism,* namely, that the only information that is relevant about a possible world is the set of utility possibilities that it generates for its inhabitants. Sen (1979b) coined the term 'welfarism' and argued that it is an unacceptable postulate in ethics. The essays in this part argue a different point from Sen's: that welfarism is a methodologically unacceptable premise in studying distributive justice because it forecloses the possibility of modeling property rights, which are of the essence in many discussions of distribution. These points were raised in Essay 7, and an alternative was proposed, a theory modeling the desiderata of resource egalitarianism as axioms on the class of resource allocation mechanisms, where welfarism was not assumed *a priori.* When I speak of the mismarriage of bargaining theory and distributive justice in Essay 9, I am using 'bargaining theory' in the precise sense of welfarist axiomatic bargaining theory, as developed by Nash and his followers up to the present day.

The generalization of bargaining theory, so defined, is the axiomatic study of allocation mechanisms on *economic environments,* objects where goods and property rights can be precisely represented. Essays 9, 10, and 12 (as well as Essay 7) are case studies in this approach. The substantive question of political philosophy addressed in Essay 10 is one inspired by

199

G. A. Cohen: Can one challenge the inegalitarian conclusion reached by the libertarian theory of Robert Nozick without challenging its postulate of self-ownership? Both Rawls and Dworkin deny self-ownership to reach their rather egalitarian conclusions. Cohen asks whether, admitting self-ownership, an egalitarian conclusion can nevertheless be reached by postulating that the external world is publicly owned, rather than initially unowned, as Nozick and Locke assume. This essay proposes a different way of modeling private ownership of self in conjunction with public ownership of the external world, and examines what allocation mechanisms satisfy this complex of property rights.

Essay 11 is methodological and not substantively political. It takes as a case study the main theorem of Essay 7, and asks what happens as one tries to prove it with different informational assumptions about the possible worlds in which the theory takes place. Axiomatic bargaining theory represents only the utility possibilities in possible worlds. "Mismarriage" argues that this informational environment is too thin to represent our intuitions about property rights, and moves to a thicker informational description of possible worlds, where resources and utility functions are specified. But one might wish to admit an even thicker description, one in which the goods have *names* which signify the kind of welfare they bring about – some goods (like milk and bread) signal that a need is being fulfilled, while some (like diamonds and paintings) signal that aesthetic pleasure is the issue. (The naming of goods was raised in Essay 7.) The conclusion of Essay 11 is that precise axiomatic characterization theorems of allocation mechanisms can be preserved as we move to theories with thicker description of possible worlds, but only at the cost of assuming increasingly powerful and ethically unappealing domain axioms. If we wish to work with the thickness of description that seems right for questions of distributive justice, and also to assume palatable domain axioms, then there will be no nice characterization results: that is, there will be large classes of allocation mechanisms that satisfy our sets of axioms in such theories. This conclusion is perhaps a disappointment, but I think that it is the correct one: the problem of real distributive justice is sufficiently complex, given the complexity of the real world, that there is no single correct way of implementing it. We must give up the elegance of simple and precise characterizations, associated with axiomatic allocation mechanism theory, if we are to be honest about the problem of distributive justice.

Essay 12 contains a substantive result, a characterization of the "leximin" allocation rule on economic environments. But I include it primarily for another reason: it is the only essay in this book which asks whether actual organizations, mandated to solve a problem in distributive justice, seem to follow the prescriptions of axiomatic mechanism theory. I argue that the ideals of the World Health Organization (WHO), charged with distributing its resources in a just way among countries, are embodied in a set of substantive axioms, which, together with a universal domain axiom, characterize the leximin allocation rule. But WHO does not allocate its resources among countries according to the leximin rule. My explanation is that the domain axiom is completely unrealistic as a normative restriction on an organization, which only faces a very small number of actual distributive problems over a period of years. (Roughly, it faces one problem each time it formulates its annual budget.) In fact, WHO can satisfy all the substantive axioms and assign nonleximin allocations, because of the small domain of problems it actually faces.

Thus, Essays 11 and 12 both locate the Achilles' heel of axiomatic mechanism theory, insofar as developing a theory of distributional justice is concerned, in the domain axiom.

The mismarriage of bargaining theory
and distributive justice

1.   Distributive justice and bargaining theory

Bargaining theory studies the division of utility between or among agents who, if agreement is not reached, each receive a utility designated by a threat point. For example, if there are two agents, then a bargaining problem is specified by a pair $\{S, d\}$ where S is usually taken to be a convex, comprehensive[1] set in the plane (representing possible utility pairs for agents) and d is a point in S specifying the utilities each gets in the absence of agreement. A *bargaining mechanism* is a function F which assigns to each bargaining problem $\{S, d\}$ a point s in S, the agreement point under that mechanism:

$$F(\{S, d\}) = s.$$

The axiomatic approach to bargaining proceeds by specifying a set of axioms which acceptable mechanisms must obey and characterizes the class of acceptable mechanisms. For a comprehensive review of the area, see Roth (1979); a more recent survey is provided by Kalai (1985).

Various writers have argued that bargaining theory provides the appropriate formal apparatus for studying distributive justice. A classical example of this approach is Braithwaite (1955). More recently, Yaari and Bar-Hillel (1984) have applied various solution concepts of bargaining theory in an empirical study of respondents' attitudes toward problems of

I have benefited from the comments of many people on matters discussed in this paper. I acknowledge especially Roger Howe, Aanund Hylland, Louis Makowski, and William Thomsom. I gratefully acknowledge, as well, support from the National Science Foundation grant SES-8509695.
[1] A comprehensive utility possibilities set is one which models the idea that utility is freely disposable. Thus, if a point x is in a comprehensive set S, and $y \leq x$, then y is in S. All points to the southwest of a given point in S lie in S. Comprehensiveness is not an innocuous assumption. In particular, it rules out the typical problems which arise due to incentives, when a skilled person withholds his labor due to a high tax, thus decreasing the utility of both agents below what it otherwise could have been. The utility possibilities set for a 'Rawlsian' problem is typically not comprehensive. Problems of incentives and asymmetric information are ignored in this article; this is reflected, in part, in the comprehensiveness assumption.

distributive justice. Brock (1979) advocates a particular solution concept from bargaining theory (the Nash solution) as implementing the 'just' division. Perhaps the most sustained advocacy for the application of bargaining theory to distributive justice is that of Gauthier (1985), who argues that justice should be viewed as a bargaining problem and that a particular mechanism (the Kalai-Smorodinsky [1975] solution) is the most accurate conception of what bargaining is.[2] In a recent paper, Binmore (1984) applies new developments in game theory to bargaining theory and supports the Rawlsian maximin criterion as the outcome of a bargaining game.[3] These authors all advocate the application of bargaining theory, as formally described above, to problems of distributive justice. In addition, other writers advocate a contractarian approach to justice (e.g., Harsanyi [1977], Rawls [1971], Howe and Roemer [1981], and Scanlon [1982]), without endorsing the formal apparatus of bargaining theory. While contractarianism could be considered to be related to bargaining, I shall not be concerned with that approach as my interest is in the application of the formal apparatus of bargaining theory to distributive justice.

I will argue in this paper against the application of bargaining theory to problems of distributive justice on grounds that the domain which bargaining theory takes – objects of the form $\{S, d\}$ – is informationally too impoverished to capture the important issues in distributive justice. Bargaining theory admits information only with respect to utilities of the agents once the threat point has been determined, while distributive justice is concerned with issues of rights, needs, and preferences as well. Note that *preferences,* which are not specified in the set S, and utility *numbers,* as specified in the set S, are very different objects. Being told only what the utility possibility set is differs from being told what agents' preferences are over allocations or alternatives of various kinds. The class of mechanisms which can be defined on the informationally impoverished domain of bargaining theory is very 'thin' since the objects in that domain have little structure. By defining a domain of 'economic environments,' which can include information on resources, preferences, needs, skills, and so on, the class of possible allocation mechanisms becomes much richer because the objects on which the mechanisms act are ones containing complex information. Bargaining theory, I will claim, is too simple an apparatus for studying distributive justice.

[2] Actually Gauthier, in "Bargaining and Justice," advocates a solution which is a slight variant of the Kalai-Smorodinsky solution. For two-person bargaining games, the two solution concepts coincide.

[3] Binmore introduces into the bargaining problem the additional issue that the time elapsed in reaching a bargaining solution is costly to the agents. He also gives a new axiomatic foundation for the Nash solution, using axioms which take into account the costliness of bargaining.

It is important to mention the fallacy of one apparently appealing argument against the application of bargaining theory distributive justice. Some might say that bargaining theory is 'welfarist' in the sense that it admits only utility information; Sen (1979b) and others have argued, persuasively in my opinion, against welfarism as an adequate approach to distributive justice. But bargaining theory, contrary to appearances, is not welfarist. For the threat point of a bargaining game, although described as a pair of utilities, can (and, indeed, one might say, must) be specified from knowledge of the underlying rights, needs, and so on. Thus, specification of the bargaining game *may* take account of underlying rights and justice-relevant attributes described in some richer environment. What utilities the agents receive, failing a bargain, might be defined in many different ways, each corresponding to a different conception of their rights. Hence, my criticism of bargaining theory as a tool for studying distributive justice will not be that it is welfarist. (Nevertheless, one might say the application of bargaining theory to distributive justice is almost welfarist in that nonutility information is dispensed with very early on, as soon as the threat point has been determined.)

As well as make my negative argument, I will propose a new technique for studying problems of distributive justice: mechanism theory performed on a domain of economic environments instead of on environments of the form $\{S, d\}$. Several examples will be given of how to formulate problems of distributive justice using this tool, and the relation of the approach to a bargaining-theory approach will be discussed. I think the weakness of the bargaining-theory approach to justice can only be fully appreciated after seeing this alternative method.

It is important to distinguish what can be called the positive and normative applications of bargaining theory to distributive justice. The *positive* approach argues that justice should be viewed as a bargaining problem; that being determined, it tries to discover the best characterization of rational bargaining. This approach is associated, for instance, with Gauthier and Binmore. In this approach, the axioms on the bargaining mechanism are probed only for their accuracy in capturing how people rationally bargain. But many writers, at various times, fall into what I would call the *normative* approach, which views the bargaining axioms as capturing, directly, our moral intuitions.

I will give several examples of how writers in the area present normative justifications for axioms intended to describe positive bargaining. There are several variants of a 'monotonicity' axiom in bargaining theory. One version says: consider two bargaining problems $\{S, d\}$ and $\{T, d\}$ where $S \subset T$. Then neither agent should receive a lower utility at the solution in T than he does in S. It is appealing to justify this axiom on ethical grounds (if the size of the pie increases, neither should suffer in utility terms), although that would be inappropriate in bargaining theory. The question must be, Is there a reason for *bargaining* solutions to be so characterized? (Kalai and Samet [1985] give proper bargaining foundations, based on considerations of incentive compatibility, for certain monotonicity axioms, although not for the particular axiom I have mentioned.) A second example of a normatively motivated axiom in bargaining theory comes from the recent work of Thomson and Lensberg (1989), who have studied an axiom called 'population monotonicity.' Suppose we have a solution to a bargaining problem $\{S, d\}$ with two people, and there is an associated problem $\{T, d'\}$, with three people, having the property that the slice of T in the coordinate plane in which the utility of the first two agents is specified is the set S. That is, in the three-person problem, three agents share the same pie, so to speak, that is available in the original two-person problem. The axiom says: neither of the first two people should get more utility in the solution to the problem $\{T, d'\}$ than they got in the solution of $\{S, d\}$. Thomson and Lensberg's justification of this axiom is on ethical, not positive, grounds – that it models solidarity. When the third person appears on the scene, bringing 'no additional resources,' both of the first two people must chip in to give him some utility in the new three-person problem. This may be an appropriate motivation for that axiom in a theory of justice, but not for bargaining theory. It would be pleasant to show that rational bargaining has this property, but it should not be an axiom of bargaining.

I do not evaluate in this article whether the theory of rational bargaining has, as its proper informational domain, the space of objects which just admit utility information, $\{S, d\}$. I will not discuss what constitutes the correct theory of bargaining. My argument is against those who claim the same formal apparatus properly models problems of distributive justice. Against those who take the normative approach, my argument is fairly straightforward: I must only exhibit the loss of relevant information for justice considerations which occurs in the bargaining theory environment. I will argue against the positive application of bargaining theory to distributive justice in the third section below. Others have discussed the informational poverty of bargaining theory as a model of the bargaining process.[4]

In the interest of concreteness, I proceed by presenting in the next section an example of a problem in distributive justice and the approach I find natural to take in studying the problem. This approach involves studying mechanisms on a class of economic environments. In the third

---

[4] See Roth (1983), Roth and Schoumaker (1983).

section, I return to my criticism of the bargaining-theory approach to distributive justice by indicating how bargaining theory might approach the same problem.

2.   Private and public domains: conflicting claims

Consider the problem of Able and Infirm, who jointly own all the land in the world, and who each own themselves. The land is used to produce corn, which they each need or want to consume. There is a known technology for producing corn; Able is skilled in producing corn, and Infirm is less skilled or unable to produce corn. How much corn should be produced, who should produce it, and how should it be divided between them if we are to respect two principles: (1) the two agents' self-ownership of skill and labor and (2) their joint ownership of the land? Assume, for the moment, the extreme case that Infirm cannot work at all. Since they jointly own the world, Able cannot use any land to produce corn until he and Infirm have agreed upon that use, which presumably will only occur (assuming Infirm can enforce his joint property right in the land) after Infirm has assured for himself some of the corn which Able produces. On the one hand, is this an incursion against Able's self-ownership? On the other hand, if Able turns over none of the corn produced to Infirm, does that not violate Infirm's joint ownership of the land?

I call this the Cohen problem after G. A. Cohen, who poses it (although not in quite this form) in two recent papers.[5] The Cohen problem is a fundamental one in the debate on the legitimacy of capitalist inequality. Suppose the world is populated by people who, we deem, should have equal opportunities insofar as the resources in the external world permit but unequal opportunities insofar as their 'personal' assets, such as skills, make available. (Such equality of opportunity should hold, at least, before agents have mixed their labor with external resources in such a way as may entitle them to appropriate external resources as their own assets.) Various conceptions of such equal opportunities in respect to external assets can be put forward. Nozick (1974) puts forth one such conception: that a person has the right to appropriate any amount of the external asset (land) so long as others are made no worse off by such appropriation. Other versions of the Lockean proviso can be expressed. Cohen suggests that the appropriate counterfactual to private ownership of the land might not be Nozickian no-ownership, but joint ownership. Thus, no one could use the land, if it is jointly owned, unless the owners agree to that use by whatever procedure is taken to define agreement. How

---

[5] Cohen (1985, 1986).

much inequality in final welfares of the agents is permissible if we adhere to these two principles? Will self-ownership of skill effectively nullify any appropriation by Infirm of the corn Able produces, or will joint ownership of the land trump Able's right to the lion's share? Are there, even, any distributions of corn and labor between the agents which will respect the claims which follow from these apparently competing domains of rights? Of course, one might not agree that justice requires the delineation of the private and public domains as I have outlined them; but if one does, what allocations of corn and labor between the agents will be acceptable?

A bargaining-theory approach would take as initial data the preferences of the two agents for bundles of corn and leisure, the technology, the skill levels of the agents, and the amount of land. From this, the utility possibilities set S would be calculated. Deciding what the threat point should be, however, is a major problem for which bargaining theory has no standard solution. This problem is extraneous to bargaining theory as such. Even should a threat point be decided upon, I think bargaining theory cannot properly use the given information on joint and private rights, as will become evident below.

To capture fully the relevant information, I propose another approach, which begins by defining an *economic environment,* a vector

$$\xi = \{\bar{W}; u(C, l); f(W, L); s^1, s^2\},$$

where $\bar{W}$ is the amount of land in the world, $u(C, l)$ is a utility function representing the (common) preferences for bundles of corn and leisure of the two agents, $f(W, L)$ is a production function which specifies the amount of corn which can be produced from bundles (W, L) of land and labor, and s^i is the skill level of agent i. It is also given that each agent is in possession of one unit of leisure, which can be converted into labor at will. Assume there are constant returns to scale in production, so that if agent 1 expends L^1 units of labor and agent 2 expends L^2 units of labor on W acres of land, then total production of corn is $f(W, s^1 L^1 + s^2 L^2)$. That is, skill level is defined as the labor in efficiency units which an agent is capable of performing per unit of time. The economic environment defined above is a simple one: for instance, it assumes both agents have the same preferences, that only leisure, and not skill level, is an argument of the utility function, and that skill is defined in a simple way.

Let $\Omega(\xi)$ be the set of feasible allocations of corn and leisure available to the two agents in environment ξ. A *mechanism* is a mapping which associates to an economic environment a feasible allocation:

$$F(\xi) \in \Omega(\xi).$$

By specifying various axioms on F's behavior, one can restrict its action to conform to requirements which respect the two agents' joint ownership of the land and their private ownership of skill. The problem is: we do not have any well-defined conception of what joint ownership means, and so the axioms can only express necessary conditions for joint ownership, whatever it means. Similarly, it is not entirely clear what private ownership of skill means when another asset which must be used in conjunction with skill is jointly owned. The advantage of the axiomatic approach, once again, is that it commits one only to necessary properties of private ownership, not to a complete characterization of what that ownership must entail. Not knowing precisely what these rights entail makes it problematical to define the threat point in a bargaining game between Able and Infirm. With the present axiomatic approach, we need not fully resolve these hazy issues; perhaps they will be resolved to some extent for us, in spite of this agnosticism.

In the following, let ξ and ξ' be two economic environments where

$$\xi = \{\bar{W}; f; u; s^1, s^2\} \quad \text{and} \quad \xi' = \{\bar{W}'; f'; u'; s'^1, s'^2\}.$$

Let $F^i(\xi)$ be the allocation of corn and leisure to agent i which the mechanism assigns in the environment ξ. Thus $u(F^i(\xi))$ is the utility of agent i under F's action in the environment ξ. It is convenient to name one particular mechanism, called E, which implements welfare egalitarianism. $E(\xi)$ is that allocation of corn and leisure assigned to the two agents which is Pareto optimal and equalizes their utilities.

I propose that any mechanism F which respects private ownership of self and joint ownership of the external world should satisfy the following axioms.

C1:   Unrestricted domain. F is defined on a domain of environments ξ where u can be any (concave) utility function, f any (constant or decreasing returns to scale) production function which is increasing in both of its arguments, and W, s^1 and s^2 can be any nonnegative numbers.

C2:   Pareto optimality. $F(\xi)$ is a Pareto optimal allocation in $\Omega(\xi)$.

C3:   Land monotonicity. Let ξ' and ξ differ only in that $\bar{W}' > \bar{W}$. Then for $i = 1, 2$: $u(F^i(\xi')) \geq u(F^i(\xi))$.

C4:   Technological monotonicity. Let ξ' and ξ differ only in that the production function f' dominates f. (For all (W, L), $f'(W, L) \geq f(W, L)$. Then for $i = 1, 2$: $u(F^i(\xi')) \geq u(F^i(\xi))$.

C5:   Self-ownership of skill. In ξ, suppose $s^i \geq s^j$. Then $u(F^i(\xi)) \geq u(F^j(\xi))$.

The next axiom is perhaps most controversial.

C6:   Protection of Infirm. Let $s^1 \geq s^2$. Then:

$$u(F^2(\{\bar{W}; f; u; s^1, s^2\})) \geq u(F^2(\{\bar{W}; f; u; s^2, s^2\})).$$

Call a mechanism F which satisfies these axioms[6] *acceptable*.

Axiom C1 says that the mechanism can be seen as a constitution which prescribes an allocation for 'any' economic environment. Axiom C2 is clearly desirable and requires no motivation. Axioms C3 and C4 are the necessary conditions for joint ownership of the land and the technology. Whatever joint ownership means, they say, it requires at least that an increase in the amount of the jointly owned resource (or jointly owned technology) should not harm either agent. Since land and technology are 'goods' and not 'bads,' if we jointly own them, an increase in their availability should not be to the detriment of either of us. Axiom C5 is necessary for self-ownership of skill. Able will always be at least as well off as Infirm. This is the only axiom which requires interpersonally comparable utility to be sensible. For note that C5 implies *symmetry:* if the two agents are equally skilled, then they are assigned an allocation, under F, which equalizes their utility. (On the subclass of environments where $s^1 = s^2$, any acceptable F must coincide with the egalitarian mechanism E.) Such symmetry is defensible only if the utility which the function u measures is interpersonally comparable and in fact is 'level comparable.' Axiom C6 is designed to protect Infirm from invasion of his rights to welfare on account of the other agent's ability. The environment which appears on the left-hand side of the inequality in axiom C6 is the given environment upon which F's action is here being restricted. Axiom C6 says that Infirm should not be worse off, in the given environment, than he would have been in an environment where Able were as unskilled as he. That is, *Infirm should not suffer on account of Able's ability*. I do not have a compelling justification for axiom C6 from the two fundamental principles, although perhaps it can be justified on those grounds. I think, in any case, the axiom is appealing, as it assures that Infirm does not suffer a negative externality from the fact that the other's skill is more than his own.

The somewhat remarkable theorem is that only one mechanism satisfies the six axioms, C1–C6: the welfare egalitarian mechanism E. If a mechanism is acceptable, it must, for each economic environment admitted by the domain assumption, assign that allocation of corn and labor to the two agents which is Pareto optimal and equalizes their utility levels.[7] If

[6] The axioms contain some redundancy, which I have left in to give the flavor of this approach. In fact, C4 implies C3 because an increase in the amount of land can, alternatively, be viewed as a 'land-augmenting' technical change.

[7] For a proof of the theorem, see Moulin and Roemer (1989).

the axioms represent necessary conditions for a mechanism to implement public ownership of the land and technology (i.e., the external world) and private ownership of skill, then the rights of public ownership effectively trump rights of self-ownership in the sense that no outcome equality is, in the end, acceptable.

One can challenge whether these axioms indeed represent the agents' rights that they purport to represent; there is some discussion of that issue in the paper referred to in the previous footnote. The interpretation of the theorem is that even a relatively conservative socialist program, which requires joint ownership of the external resources but respects (at least a priori) some rights of agents to benefit from their skills, achieves the radical outcome of welfare equality. My purpose here is not to defend or criticize the particular axioms I have proposed or to evaluate the theorem. It is, rather, to illustrate the method and to contrast it with the approach which bargaining theory might take to the same problem.

Before doing so, it is worth remarking that the mechanism 'equal division–competitive equilibrium' (ED-CE) is not acceptable; it cannot be, by the theorem stated, since ED-CE does not, in general, assign equal utilities to the agents, and only the welfare-egalitarian mechanism satisfies all the axioms. Equal division–competitive equilibrium assigns that allocation which would have been achieved by dividing the land and ownership rights in the technology equally between the two agents and letting them trade to Walrasian equilibrium. Equal division–competitive equilibrium has been viewed, by various writers, as a good implementation of fair division (see, e.g., Varian [1974] and Thomson and Varian [1985] for a review of the literature on 'envy-free' allocations, which are closely associated with the ED-CE mechanism). Equal distribution–competitive equilibrium might appear to implement an appropriate conception of joint ownership of land and private-ownership skill; but it is easily shown that ED-CE violates axioms C3 and C4. Hence ED-CE cannot implement *this* conception of joint ownership.

3.   The informational poverty of bargaining theory

How might one try to capture axioms C1–C6 of the Cohen problem, limiting oneself to the domain, which bargaining theory admits, of utility possibilities sets and threat points? One cannot. For an economic environment ξ contains much more information than a utility possibilities set S, and the axioms of the Cohen problem restrict the action of mechanisms on economic environments, while bargaining theory restricts the action of mechanisms on utility possibilities sets. Still, one might propose something like the following as the bargaining theory analog to the formalization of the Cohen problem. We wish to characterize a mechanism F which maps bargaining pairs $\{S, d\}$ into a point of S and respects the private and joint property domains of agents as outlined in the previous section.

B1: Unrestricted domain. F acts on a domain $\{S, d\}$ where the S is any strictly convex, comprehensive set which contains a strictly positive utility pair (or n-tuple, if we do the problem in R^n).

B2: F is individually rational. F assigns a utility allocation in the non-negative orthant, when the point d is chosen as origin.

B3: $F(S)$ is Pareto optimal in S.

B4: If S is symmetric (with d chosen as origin), then $F^1(S) = F^2(S)$.

B5: Monotonicity. If $S \subset T$ then $F^i(S) \le F^i(T)$, for $i = 1, 2$.

As I said, there is no exact translation of the axioms C1–C6 into a bargaining-theory environment (that, indeed, is the point of this paper), but the above represents a canonical attempt at translation. Axiom C5 is translated as axiom B4. Axioms C3, C4, and C6 are all implied by axiom B5. These three axioms are highly restricted versions of 'utility monotonicity' B5, and it is hard to think of a weaker bargaining axiom than B5 which would imply them. Each of C3, C4, and C6 says that if the underlying economic environment changes *in a certain way* so as to increase the set of utility possibilities, then neither agent's utility falls. B5 is not capable of referring to economic environments since they do not exist for it; but if there were underlying economic environments to which B5 were implicitly referring, it would require that *no matter what changes* in the environment give rise to the increasing utility possibilities, neither agent's utility should fall.

I have not discussed how to define the threat point for the Cohen problem in the bargaining-theory context. In the treatment of the second section, such discussion was unnecessary. That issue is, for now, tangential to my purpose, which is to observe the following:

Theorem: *There is a unique F which satisfies axioms B1–B5: equal utility split from the threat point. F assigns that Pareto optimal point in S at which utilities are equalized, taking d as the origin.*[8]

To illustrate the simplicity of this approach (which I do for a reason), I give a proof. First:

Lemma: *If F satisfies axioms B1, B2, B3, and B5, then F must be a* monotone-path *solution. That is, given any threat point d, there exists a*

[8] The bargaining theory version of this theorem is essentially equivalent to Kalai (1977).

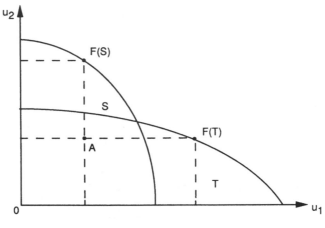

Figure 9.1

monotone path which characterizes the acceptable solutions for all problems $\{S, d\}$.

(A monotone-path solution is constructed by drawing some monotone nondecreasing path, in utility space, from the threat point d as origin; the solution is the intersection of that path with the Pareto frontier of S.)

Proof of lemma: I do the proof for two dimensions. It generalizes to n dimensions. Suppose there is an F satisfying the listed axioms which is not a monotone-path solution. Then there must be two utility sets with the same threat point, called S and T in Figure 9.1 such that $F(S)$ lies to the northwest of $F(T)$. Neither S nor T contains the other; for if $S \subset T$, for example, then by axiom B5, $F(T)$ would lie to the northeast of $F(S)$. Consider the utility set $S \cap T$, which is in the domain by B1. By monotonicity, $F(S \cap T)$ lies to the southwest of both $F(S)$ and $F(T)$ since $S \cap T$ is a subset of both S and T. Hence $F(S \cap T)$ must lie in the rectangle whose diagonal is OA. But this contradicts the Pareto optimality of $F(S \cap T)$ in the set $S \cap T$. (To make this "proof" into a proof requires using the comprehensiveness and strict convexity of the sets S and T and also axiom B2.)

Proof of theorem: Any acceptable F must be a monotone-path solution. But we know for symmetric sets by B4 that the solution lies along the 45° ray from d as origin. Hence the 45° ray is the only acceptable monotone path. Hence, any acceptable solution is equal utility split from d.

Q.E.D.

This theorem might appear to be appealing from the point of view of distributive justice, if we could resolve the threat-point issue. But I claim it is not, even if we could settle on the determination of the threat point, for two reasons: (1) the axioms are too strong, and (2) the class of acceptable mechanisms is too thin. Why, for instance, is B5 too strong? Thinking back to economic environments, there are all kinds of ways an environment ξ could change into an environment ξ' so that their associated utility possibilities sets are nested: $S \subset T$. There might, for example, be a change in the utility function from ξ to ξ', combined with some nondominating change in the production function. I have no moral intuition regarding how a justice-implementing mechanism should change its assignment as a consequence of such a change in the economic environment; but axiom B5 commits the mechanism to a monotonic change in utilities, as long as the first utility set is contained in the second one. Axioms C3, C4, and C6, in contrast, commit the mechanism to a monotonic change in the utility vector only when the economic environment changes in ways which our 'bill of rights' refers to specifically. The same criticism can be leveled against the symmetry axiom B4. Imagine an economic environment where agents have different preferences, different skills, and so forth, but it happens that the utility set S is symmetric (about the threat point). Axiom B4 commits the mechanism to an equal utility split. But surely this is too strong a moral commitment. Axiom C5, in contrast, commits us only to a clear (and weak) notion of self-ownership, which implies, in particular, that when agents are identical with respect to all the economic information, they are equally treated.

These criticisms amount to a point which is well known in the social-choice theory context (see, e.g., Sen) that axioms of the type B1–B5 are *welfarist* in that they treat two environments as identical if they have the same utility possibilities sets. In contrast, the setup of the Cohen problem in the second section is what can be called *resourcist* in that it allows information not just on final utilities but on the resources and preferences which enter into forming utility. All welfarist theories are resourcist since welfare is derived from resources and preferences, but not conversely. Many contemporary theories of justice are resourcist but not welfarist in that they take account of information concerning resources which is not summarized in the utility possibilities set. Rawls's theory is resourcist and not welfarist in the attention it pays to primary goods, independent of their utility-generating capacity, and Dworkin's interest in equality of resources is, similarly, a resourcist nonwelfarist one. Sen's interest in basic capabilities is of the same nature, and Barry's (1979) emphasis on equal division of time in the Braithwaite problem is a special case of a resourcist, nonwelfarist approach. The Marxian theory of exploitation is, I think, best viewed as a resourcist nonwelfarist theory, in which agents are viewed as exploited because of their lack of access to certain kinds of resources, alienable means of production. In general, any theory which emphasizes equality of opportunities will require information available in economic environments but not available in utility possibility sets. For opportunities are stated in terms of initial resources of some kind – whether they be primary goods, capability-fulfilling goods, alienable means of production, talents, or time. Economic environments are required even to open discussion on these problems.

The second criticism I enumerated two paragraphs ago is that the class of mechanisms acting on the domain of objects $\{S, d\}$ is too thin. There is so little structure on objects $\{S, d\}$ that one is severely limited in describing the action of mechanisms on them. For instance, it is impossible to define the mechanism ED-CE given only the information $\{S, d\}$. To be precise, it is easy to write down two economic environments ξ and ξ' which give rise to the same utility possibilities set S, but in which ED-CE carried out in ξ and ξ' will lead to allocations associated with different points in S. Thus even if we view all utility sets S as coming from economic environments, we cannot construct a function which implements the equal division mechanism given only the information in S. Many conceptions of how to implement distributive justice in economic environments simply cannot be discussed given only utility information.

The combination of these two criticisms makes the proof of the above theorem simple. The axioms are too strong, and the space of mechanisms is too thin, so it is too easy to eliminate most of the feasible mechanisms. Doing mechanism theory on a space of economic environments is delicate since the appropriate axioms are weaker and the class of feasible mechanisms is richer.

It is easy to fall into the error of justifying axioms made in a bargaining-theory framework by illicit reference to underlying resources which do not exist in that framework. For instance, Thomson (1983) justifies his 'population monotonicity' axiom, which I described in the first section, by asking the reader to imagine the following experiment. Recall his framework is bargaining theory. There is a population with some resources, making available some utility, summarized in the set S, and then a newcomer arrives on the scene, bringing with him no additional resources. The same resources must now generate utility for more people. Population monotonicity requires that no one from the original population end up better off in the second situation than in the first; everyone in the original group chips in to subsidize the impoverished newcomer. But such a motivation cannot be allowed because Thomson's environment is not economic; it includes no specification of resources and utility functions.

Consequently, Thomson's axiom is much stronger than the above thought experiment suggests. It will implement not only the kind of solidarity described in that story but far more, just as the monotonicity axiom B5 does far more than implement the kinds of resource-generated monotonicity which axioms C3, C4, and C6 describe. 'Population monotonicity' commits us to 'welfare solidarity' in situations where no resource-based intuition justifies it. One can justify the axiom from a normative point of view only if one is an unabashed welfarist. I think hardly anyone has intuitions which are that welfarist; rather, those who find axioms like population monotonicity attractive are applying their real moral intuitions, which are resource based, to situations where they are inappropriate.[9]

In the first section, I said my purpose is to criticize the application of bargaining theory to distributive justice because of its informational impoverishment, and this applies to the *normative* use of bargaining theory. But there remains what I called the positive application of bargaining theory to distributive justice, which claims nonnormative justification of axioms and argues simply for justice as bargaining; this approach is represented by Gauthier and Binmore. Others have criticized this approach for reasons which appear to be quite orthogonal to what I have been discussing, namely, the irrelevance of bargaining power for considerations of justice (see Barry for this argument and a summary of other pertinent literature). I will limit myself to a criticism of the positive approach in the spirit of this paper. As I said, it is too facile to characterize the positive approach as welfarist because nonutility information is admitted in determining the threat point of the bargaining game whose outcome is called just. If rights are important, they must be fully incorporated into the threat point. I do not think all the rights-relevant information can be summarized in the threat point. As I have shown, once the threat point is determined, then the class of definable mechanisms on the space $\{S, d\}$ immediately shrinks to a thin one. Thus, much maneuverability which we might want for the implementation of justice is immediately lost once the threat point is determined. I think this puts an unsupportably heavy informational burden on the threat point. To be precise: given any procedure for deciding upon the threat point from underlying economic information, I think it would be possible to construct two economic environments leading to the same object $\{S, d\}$ but which our ethical intuitions would treat differently. I do not present this argument as a proof against the positive use of bargaining theory in distributive justice but as a conjecture (of which I am quite confident). It may, indeed, turn out to be

---

[9] These criticisms of Thomson's work should not be misconstrued. Thomson is an extremely careful worker. That even he could be guilty of this methodological peccadillo demonstrates the pervasiveness of this kind of error.

equivalent to the criticisms which Barry and others have made, in this sense. Is it possible, for any given economic environment, to define a threat point which appropriately sterilizes the ethically unacceptable bargaining advantages that some players have over others? If so, then Barry's criticism would be neutralized. But my claim is that there is not sufficient informational density in objects of the form $\{S, d\}$ to do that. Hence one *must* use axioms which have normative content; and, having admitted that, I have shown that such axioms must be defined on a domain of economic environments, not utility possibilities sets.

The recent empirical paper of Yaari and Bar-Hillel provides evidence for the misuse of bargaining theory in distributive justice. The authors propose various stylized problems of fair division to a group of 150 respondents, who are instructed to choose the fair allocation in each case. The framing of the problems differs. In some cases, the issue is to divide foods which contain nutrients, which the two agents in the problem process differentially. In some cases, it is a question of dividing luxury goods between agents who have different tastes. In some cases, goods must be divided between people who have different (and perhaps erroneous) beliefs about the true size of the total endowment available, or about what they want or what is good for them. Classes of problems are cleverly constructed so that, although they involve different environments – in the sense that the 'utility functions' describe needs, tastes, or beliefs about different kinds of goods – the bargaining objects $\{S, d\}$ associated with all problems in one class are the same. The respondents choose very different allocations as 'fair' for different problems which are 'bargaining equivalent.' Thus, they are using information which is not summarized in the object $\{S, d\}$. One could say that the respondents are unjustifiably imposing their 'value judgments' on the little societies in these stories. One could say they are being tricked by the framing of the problems in the sense that Kahneman and Tversky (1982) discuss. But I think it is more natural to say that bargaining theory cannot capture the information relevant for considerations of justice.

4.   Conclusion

Bargaining theory is context free. All that matters is the utility possibilities set and the threat point, specified in terms of utilities. I claim this is an inappropriate apparatus with which to study problems of distributive justice. Many contemporary theories of distributive justice are resourcist, not welfarist, and require explicit language with which resources and preferences can be discussed, a language which bargaining theory lacks. It is impossible to make any statements regarding property rights in the bargaining-theory model since property does not exist in the domain of environments which bargaining theory posits. This is what I have called the informational poverty of bargaining theory. I propose to replace bargaining theory with the study of allocation mechanisms defined on a domain of economic environments for the purpose of studying questions of distributive justice and political philosophy.

There is information important for ethical considerations which I have not modeled. The Yaari–Bar-Hillel paper shows that people treat ethical problems differently depending on whether the issue at hand is one of needs or tastes or beliefs. One can say, people consider not only the amounts of the goods and the utility functions, but the *names* of the goods and the *name* of what the utility function measures. Notice that information on these names does not exist in the economic environments I have specified. We might define an *ethical environment* as a list of names of goods, names of what the 'utility' functions measure, amounts of the goods, and specifications of the utility functions. Then two different ethical environments could give rise to the same economic environment. For example, a particular economic environment $\xi = \{3; (\bar{x}^1, \bar{x}^2, \bar{x}^3); u, v\}$ refers to a situation with three goods in amounts specified by the $\bar{x}^i$, and two people with utility functions given by u and v. ξ could come from two ethical environments; in the first, the goods might be scotch, champagne, and beer, and u and v represent tastes for alcohol; in the second, the goods might be milk, education, and shelter, and u and v represent the effectiveness with which the two people process those goods into the probability of realizing (or even forming) a life plan. We might wish to render different judgments on the just way to distribute the goods in these different ethical environments, but given the domain of economic environments, we cannot do so: for the economic environments do not specify names of goods, and these two ethical environments are, by hypothesis, represented by one economic environment. Just as the welfarist is not willing to impose his 'value judgment' to distinguish between two different economic situations which give rise to the same utility configuration, so the resourcist (according to my definition) is not willing (or able) to distinguish between ethical environments which give rise to the same economic environment.

The domain assumption of the model I describe in this article eliminates the names of goods. The only information that is recognized in an economic environment is 'economic' information: endowments, utility functions, production functions, but not names of goods. Economic environments represent a significant advance in making available ethically relevant information which is not in utility possibilities sets. Furthermore, they are still mathematically tractable, while ethical environments (where names are included) may not be. There is a cost, that is, to including more information in the domain of objects to be studied: it becomes harder to state any general rules about how considerations of justice should treat those objects. One moves from theory to thick description. I suggest that mechanism theory be carried out on economic environments before one attempts to model ethical environments. I have discussed more thoroughly elsewhere the hierarchy of domains which can be postulated – from the bargaining-theory domain of utility sets, to economic environments, to ethical environments.[10]

It is finally necessary to mention the issues of asymmetric information and incentive compatibility which I have ignored in this paper. I think the main compromises a theory of justice will have to make are on account of these issues. My concern here has not been with institutions which will implement the just allocation, in which case incentive problems would have to be considered, but simply with what allocation is desirable. This is first-best normative analysis. Before one begins to compromise, it would be nice to know what the goal would be, if everyone knew everything.

---

[10] For a more detailed discussion, see Roemer (1988) and Essay 11.

A challenge to Neo-Lockeanism

I.   Neo-Lockean inequality

The Neo-Lockean justification of the highly unequal distribution of income in capitalist societies is based upon two key premises: that people are the rightful owners of their labor and talents, and that the external world was, in the state of nature, unowned, and therefore up for grabs by people, who could rightfully appropriate parts of it subject to a 'Lockean proviso.' The argument is presented by Nozick (1974). Counter-proposals to Nozick's, for the most part, have either denied the premise that people should morally be viewed as the owners of their talents, or have challenged Nozick's Lockean proviso.

Rawls, and to a more limited extent Ronald Dworkin, deny self-ownership. As Rawls writes: '. . . the difference principle represents, in effect, an agreement to regard the distribution of natural talents as a common asset . . . The naturally advantaged are not to gain merely because they are more gifted, but only to cover the costs of training and education and for using their endowments in ways that help the less fortunate as well. No one deserves his greater natural capacity nor merits a more favorable starting place in society.[1]' Behind the Rawlsian veil of ignorance, those who deliberate about justice are deprived of knowledge about characteristics whose distribution is morally arbitrary. In Dworkin's proposal for resource egalitarianism, agents calculate the insurance policy they would hypothetically ask for, were they denied knowledge of what talents they will draw in the birth lottery. Compensation for unequal talents is, according to Dworkin, properly made by taxing and transferring income according to the way it would have been distributed as a consequence of such insurance. Dworkin's veil of ignorance is thin, because agents in the appropriate posture for deliberating about income distribution know

I am indebted to G. A. Cohen. I thank my co-authors H. Moulin and J. Silvestre for permission to include some material from my joint papers with them, and Ignacio Ortuño for research assistance. This research was supported by a grant from the National Science Foundation (U.S.).
[1] Rawls (1971), pp. 101–2.

their preferences and attitudes toward risk, but not their talents. For both Rawls and Dworkin, the self-ownership premise is challenged by constructing a veil of ignorance in which people are deprived of knowledge of certain personal characteristics, knowledge of which would bias their opinions, from a moral viewpoint.

Nozick's Lockean proviso can be challenged in several ways. While Locke declared that a person could annex part of the external world as his own as long as he left 'enough and as good in common' for others, Nozick weakens the proviso, in declaring that appropriation of a thing is justified as long as no person is *left worse off* by the appropriation than he would have been, had the thing remained in common use. Thus Nozick shifts the constraint against acquisition from one stated in physical terms, to one stated in terms of final welfare. This may seem harmless, but it is not. Suppose, for example, that there is a small amount of good pasture land, and Adam, who is one of many in a population of shepherds, appropriates the land and designs a schedule for grazing that increases its productivity enough so that everyone is better off under the new allocation of time between shepherding and leisure than he was when the land was in common use, even after paying rent to Adam. Adam can design such a schedule because, by restricting grazing, he resolves the 'tragedy of the commons' that was occurring when the pasture remained in common use (see Proposition 1, below). The appropriation is justifiable by Nozick's version of Locke's proviso. But suppose one of the many others could have organized the same grazing schedule on the pasture, and would have done so for a small fee (less than Adam's rent) from the others. Everyone (except Adam) could then have been even better off than under Adam's appropriation. If, indeed, Adam had left as much and as good pasture in common for others, then the many others could still have effected this improvement in their welfare, but because the land is indeed scarce, they cannot. Thus Locke's actual proviso is more difficult to satisfy than Nozick's.[2] I do not, however, claim that this Nozickian revision of Locke is an undesirable one. The welfare criterion is perhaps more sensible than the more restrictive one phrased in terms of physical resource availability.

Recently, G. A. Cohen (1986) and James Grunebaum (1987, pp. 173–4) have challenged the libertarian proposal by questioning the second premise of Nozick's argument, that in the state of nature the external world is properly viewed as unowned. There is another alternative: that it is properly viewed as *publicly* owned. (Public ownership is not the same as common ownership, as I will clarify below.) Why should not the land be held in trusteeship, as it were, for future generations by the living

---

[2] An essentially similar example is provided in Cohen (1986).

generation, and therefore not up for grabs? Cohen's and Grunebaum's suggestion points out the implicit individualism of the libertarian argument. Just because no individual should be viewed as owning a natural resource in the state of nature does not mean that groups should not be viewed as owning it.

Suppose we view the appropriate property rights in the state of nature as these: each person owns his talents, and the external world is publicly owned. What distribution of income is justifiable? It is clear that if the pasture land in the above example were publicly owned, Adam might well not be awarded the franchise to 'develop' it, given the better alternative for the public that is postulated to exist. If we could show that these property rights imply considerably more egalitarianism than exists in capitalist society, there would be an argument for equality of condition that would not depend upon denying self-ownership. While I am in sympathy with Rawls's challenge to self-ownership, it is important to know how far we can move toward a more egalitarian income distribution without challenging it.

In what follows, I present an economic model that proposes how to calculate the distribution of income and welfare that would be realized in a society where the external world is publicly owned and people own their own labor. This necessitates an economic characterization of public ownership. I will conclude that the distribution of income (or welfare) is much more egalitarian than what exists in a capitalist economy, and so the libertarian argument that supports the vast inequalities of capitalist society can be successfully challenged without tampering with the postulate of self-ownership.

II.   Common versus public ownership

Imagine that the world has one useful good, fish, which people catch by fishing on the one resource, a lake. The production function for fish is $f(L) = Y$, where Y is the amount of fish that will be caught if L days of labor are expended in fishing. Perhaps people have different degrees of skill at fishing. If Andrea has a skill level of s^1 and Bob a skill level of s^2, then in L^2 days Bob catches $f(s^2 L^2)$ fish and in L^1 days Andrea catches $f(s^1 L^1)$ fish, if each fishes alone on the lake. If they fish together on the lake, they produce a catch of $f(s^1 L^1 + s^2 L^2)$. The numbers s^i can be viewed as factors which convert raw labor, expended by various agents, into efficiency units of labor. (For instance, we can interpret the situation where $s^1 = 2$ and $s^2 = 1$ as one in which Andrea fishes twice as much area of the lake in unit time as does Bob.)

I define *common ownership* of the lake as the right of each to free access to the lake, that is, each can fish as much as he wishes, however much others are fishing. I take common ownership of the lake by Andrea and Bob to be a situation in which there is no coordination of their fishing: each calculates his optimal fishing schedule, assuming he can make no agreements with the other. Suppose the production function exhibits decreasing returns to labor (in efficiency units). This will be the case if the lake is small relative to the number of people fishing, or more precisely, if the number of fish is small. Then each fisherman inflicts a negative externality on the others. Each will catch more fish per day if no one else is on the lake. This follows because, with decreasing returns, the more other people fish, the less productive is an hour of my labor on the lake.

To calculate the final allocation of labor and fish in a lake economy with common ownership, we must introduce the notion of a Nash equilibrium. Suppose Andrea and Bob have utility functions $u^1(Y^1, L^1)$ and $u^2(Y^2, L^2)$ for fish and labor, where utility is increasing in fish (Y) and decreasing in labor (L). Suppose that when both Bob and Andrea fish on the lake together, they each catch a number of fish which is proportional to the (efficiency) units of labor which they expend. (Of course, it is still true that each would catch more were the other not there, per day.) An *equilibrium under common ownership* (more precisely, a Nash equilibrium) is an allocation of fish and labor $((Y^1, L^1), (Y^2, L^2))$ with the property that each person's choice of labor to be supplied is optimal for him, given the labor choice of the other. That is, if Andrea plans to fish for L^1 days, Bob's utility maximizing choice[3] will be to expend L^2 days fishing, in which case the division of fish between them will be (Y^1, Y^2); and if Bob plans to fish L^2 days, Andrea's utility maximizing strategy is to fish for L^1 days, in which case the division of fish between them will be (Y^1, Y^2).

The 'tragedy of the commons' is a nickname for the following proposition.

Proposition 1a: *If f is strictly concave (exhibits decreasing returns to scale) then an equilibrium under common ownership is not Pareto optimal.*

The intuition behind Proposition 1 is as follows. When Andrea decides how much to fish, taking as given that Bob will fish for L^2 hours, she is not forced to take into account the negative effect that her fishing will

---

[3] Bob calculates his optimal labor supply as follows. Given that Andrea fishes L^1 hours, Bob can calculate the total catch of fish on the lake, for any amount of labor L he expends. The fish, he knows, will be distributed in proportion to the efficiency units of labor they each expend. Thus any labor choice L for him, given Andrea's L^1, implies a fish catch Y for him. He can therefore choose L to maximize his utility, $u(L, Y)$.

have on Bob's productivity. She optimizes by maximizing the difference between her private benefit and private cost. There is a social cost that she does not take into account from her fishing, due to the decreasing returns inherent in the technology. The lack of coordination in their individual optimizing strategies results in an allocation which is socially inefficient. It is commonly said that the lake is overfished in this case, because the welfare of both agents could be increased by a plan in which each fished less.

Suppose that f is a convex function (exhibits increasing returns to scale). Then each fisherman bestows a positive externality on others by his fishing. (We might imagine that the flies fishermen use attract fish out of the grottos, and so the more lines in the water, the more fish to catch.) Then free access to the lake results in its being underfished, because each fisherman does not take account, in his calculus, of the social benefit he creates by his fishing.

Proposition 1b: *If f is strictly convex (exhibits increasing returns to scale in efficiency units of labor), then an equilibrium under common ownership is not Pareto optimal.*

If f exhibits constant returns to scale (i.e., for some $\alpha > 0$, for all L, $f(L) = \alpha L$) then under common ownership, each fishes as much as she chooses and consumes the catch. No one inflicts any production externality on another, because $f(s^1 L^1 + s^2 L^2 + \cdots + s^n L^n) = \sum f(s^i L^i)$. Free access, in this case generates a Pareto optimal allocation of fish and labor. Hence, whatever public ownership of the lake would mean, it could not possibly produce an allocation which is better for anybody without harming someone else, compared to the allocation achieved under common ownership.

What allocation should *public ownership* of the lake recommend, when the labor of the fisherman is privately owned? In the case where f exhibits constant returns to scale, the allocation achieved under common ownership of the lake seems also to be the clear implementation of its being publicly owned, in conjunction with private ownership of labor: for each has free access to the publicly owned asset, each decides how much labor to expend and how much fish to consume, and the allocation is Pareto optimal. But when f does not exhibit constant returns, the common ownership equilibrium is not in general Pareto optimal, and we should hope that, whatever public ownership consists in, it will generate a Pareto optimal allocation. I view public ownership of the lake, as yet undefined, as a system that co-ordinates the fishing of all, in contrast to the anarchy of common ownership.

III.   An axiomatic approach to public ownership

In Section II, I showed that it is not clear what distribution of output and labor should be recommended under public ownership, if the production function involving the asset does not exhibit constant returns to scale. In this section I propose a possible answer to the question posed in the last paragraph. The approach will be to ask what allocation mechanisms, defined on a class of possible worlds, respect in all cases the private and public property rights of the population.

1. Economic environments: Let us represent a possible world, or an *economic environment,* as a vector $\xi = \langle f; s^1, s^2, ..., s^n; u^1, u^2, ..., u^n \rangle$, where $f(L) = Y$ is a production function describing the production of a single output (fish) from a single input (efficiency units of labor), by use of a publicly owned asset or technology (the lake). There are n agents, and the ith one is endowed with s^i units of labor in efficiency units. Alternatively, it is perhaps more intuitive to think of the ith agent as owning 1 unit of labor power, which he can use with skill level s^i. Agent i has a utility function, defined over fish and labor, $u^i(Y^i, L^i)$. The notation for an economic environment is sometimes abbreviated as $\xi = \langle f; s; u \rangle$, where $s = (s^1, s^2, ..., s^n)$ and $u = (u^1, u^2, ..., u^n)$.

Let the class of all such economic environments – where f can be any production function which is continuous and increasing in labor, s^i are any non-negative real numbers, and u^i are any continuous functions of fish and labor which are increasing in fish and decreasing in labor – be called Σ. My task is to propose a conception of public ownership of the technology that is cogent on the domain of possible worlds Σ.

2. Allocation mechanisms: An *allocation mechanism defined on* Σ is a function F that assigns to any economic environment ξ in Σ a feasible allocation of labor and fish. A feasible allocation is a vector $((Y^1, L^1), ..., (Y^n, L^n))$ – a fish–labor plan for each fisherman – which can be achieved in ξ, that is, such that:

$$L^i \leq 1, \quad f(s^1 L^1 + \cdots + s^n L^n) = \sum Y^i.$$

There are an infinite number of allocation mechanisms, because an allocation mechanism is just a function defined on the domain Σ mapping into R^{2n} (where R is the real numbers). For instance, one allocation mechanism assigns to each economic environment the Nash equilibrium that would be achieved by common ownership.[4] Another allocation mechanism

---

[4] There may be several Nash equilibria, and so this function might not be single-valued, and would therefore not quite qualify as an allocation mechanism as here defined. This is a detail that is unimportant for my purposes here.

might mimic market behavior with private ownership of the technology. The mechanism 'equal division competitive equilibrium' assigns to each environment ξ the competitive equilibrium associated with initial endowments in which each agent owns a $1/n$ share in the profits or losses of the firm, and his own labor.[5]

3. Axioms for public ownership: To study the concept of public ownership, I shift the focus from a single economy ('What does public ownership mean in this particular economic environment?') to allocation mechanisms. What restrictions should be placed on the behavior of an allocation mechanism for it to be a candidate for implementing public ownership of the technology and private ownership of labor? Each such restriction is phrased, formally, as an axiom on the behavior of such a mechanism. Each axiom is to be viewed only as a necessary condition on a public-ownership implementing allocation mechanism.

Axiom D (Domain): The allocation mechanism which implements the required property rights must be single-valued, and defined on the domain Σ.

This axiom requires our conception of public ownership to be sufficiently general that it can give a solution to the query for any possible world. The assumption of single-valuedness is a restriction which can be relaxed, at some loss of sharpness of the results below, but not at a loss of the general flavor of the results.

Axiom PO (Pareto optimality): The allocation mechanism should assign, for each environment ξ in Σ, a Pareto optimal allocation of labor and fish.

Whatever public ownership means, in these economies, it should at least require an efficient allocation of resources. Thus public ownership must resolve the inefficiency that results from the anarchy of common ownership, when the technology does not exhibit constant returns to scale in labor.

Axiom FALE (Free Access on Linear Economics): If $\xi = \langle f; s; u \rangle$ and f is a linear function $[f(L) = \alpha L$ for some $\alpha > 0$, for all $L]$ the allocation mechanism F assigns the allocation achieved under free access, where each agent chooses her optimal bundle (Y^i, L^i).

This axiom is motivated by the discussion of Section II. Whatever public ownership of the technology in conjunction with private ownership of

---

[5] Again, this allocation mechanism is not always single-valued.

labor consists in, it should at least require that the free access solution be implemented when there are no production externalities.

The next axiom is a new idea. If a technology or an asset is publicly owned, and if that technology or asset improves in an unambiguous fashion, or becomes more abundant, then no one of the public should end up worse off in terms of welfare than he was before the improvement. Formally:

Axiom TM (Technological Monotonicity): Let $\xi^1 = \langle f; s; u \rangle$ and $\xi^2 = \langle g; s; u \rangle$ be two economic environments in Σ, and for all L, $f(L) \geq g(L)$. Then $u(F(\xi^1)) \geq u(F(\xi^2))$, where $u(F(\xi))$ is the allocation of utility achieved by the allocation which F chooses in the environment ξ.

TM says that if the technology is unambiguously more productive in ξ^1 than in ξ^2, but characteristics (skills and preferences) of the agents remain the same, then the public-ownership-implementing allocation mechanism must be such as to render each person at least as well off in ξ^1 as in ξ^2. If there are more fish in the lake in year 1 than in year 2, but skills and preferences are unchanged, then all fishermen must have welfare at least as high in year 1 as in year 2, under public ownership of the lake. This axiom is proposed as one formal implementation of a concept of public ownership that requires all to benefit from the use of a publicly owned asset (in this case, for all to benefit from the improvement in a publicly owned asset).

I have taken a minimalist approach to suggesting what public ownership consists in: I do not know what public ownership precisely requires, but I suggest that it requires at least the four properties listed. The allocation mechanism F for which we are searching can be viewed as an economic constitution that can serve to implement the public and private property rights we wish to preserve, in any reasonable possible world. Each axiom can be viewed as representing the rights of the agents. Pareto optimality represents one right for each agent: against a proposed allocation, each can call for another allocation which makes him better off, so long as no others are harmed. This yields Pareto optimality. When no agent inflicts or bestows any externality in production against any other, each has the right to use the technology as he pleases (FALE). This is a formalization, if one wishes, of Locke's proviso, but where the right is one of use, not of ownership: each has the right to *use* a publicly owned asset so long as enough and as good is left for others. (Indeed, we could just as well allow agents to appropriate as their own the part of the lake they use in a constant-returns world, for there is plenty of lake for everyone.) Finally, technological monotonicity represents the right of each agent to gain by virtue of an improvement in the publicly owned asset, and the concomitant duty of each agent to share in the loss if the publicly owned asset should deteriorate in productivity.

Given this bill of rights for an economic constitution, what economic constitutions remain acceptable? The perhaps surprising fact is that there is only one acceptable allocation mechanism satisfying these axioms.

Theorem 1: *There is a unique allocation mechanism satisfying D, PO, FALE and TM. F is the linear equivalent allocation mechanism.*[6]

The allocation assigned in the economic environment $\xi = \langle f; s; u \rangle$ by the 'linear equivalent mechanism' can be described as follows. Consider the linear economies ξ_α, in which the agents have the same characteristics as those in our given economic environment ξ, but in which the technology exhibits constant returns to scale: $\xi_\alpha = \langle f_\alpha; s; u \rangle$ and $f_\alpha(L) = \alpha L$, for some positive number α. Let α be very small, and look at the allocation $F(\xi_\alpha)$, which is defined by the FALE axiom as the free access allocation. If α is small enough, the utility pair the agents get at $F(\xi_\alpha)$, which I have called $u(F(\xi_\alpha))$, lies strictly inside the utility possibilities set for ξ. The *utility possibilities set* for ξ is the set of pairs of utility numbers that can be achieved by agents of ξ, under all possible feasible allocations in ξ. Now increase α. For α sufficiently large, the technology f_α becomes more productive than f, and the point $u(F(\xi_\alpha))$ lies outside the utility possibilities set for ξ. For some unique value of α, $u(F(\xi_\alpha))$ lies on the Pareto frontier of ξ's utility possibility set. The linear equivalent mechanism chooses, in ξ, that feasible allocation that induces this point on the Pareto frontier. See Figure 10.1, where $A(\xi)$ is the utility possibilities set for ξ, and the curve OB traces out the utilities achieved by the agents in the linear economies ξ_α as α increases.

The allocation mechanism so defined is called 'linear equivalent (LE)' because it chooses, for each environment ξ, a Pareto optimal allocation for ξ which is Pareto indifferent (i.e., utility equivalent) to the allocation that would be chosen under free access in some linear economy with agents of the same skill and preference characteristics. There is a unique such linear economy, and a unique such utility allocation. The LE mechanism is attractive as an implementation of the desired property rights because, first, it satisfies the axioms that I argued any such implementation should satisfy and, perhaps more directly, because it does, in a sense, the closest thing possible to what free access in the linear economies accomplishes. It chooses a Pareto optimal allocation which cannot be distinguished, in terms of utility, from the allocation that the same agents would choose were they in a linear economy, which is in some

---

[6] The proof of Theorem 1 is in Roemer and Silvestre (1987).

utility of agent 2

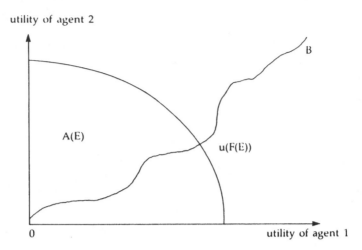

Figure 10.1. Schematic representation of the linear equivalent allocation mechanism

sense technologically equivalent to the given economy. The LE mechanism can therefore be viewed as extending to all economies the plausible interpretation of public ownership that I gave for the one case where these property rights have a clear meaning: in the linear economies.

IV.   How much inequality is there with public ownership?

It is quite clear that the allocation that the LE mechanism assigns is far more egalitarian than the one we have in modern capitalist economies. Under the LE mechanism, the welfare people end up with is precisely the welfare that they would end up with, given their preferences and skill levels, in some economy whose technology is linear, and roughly equivalent to the actual technology. Suppose, for the moment, that in Canada there were only one consumption good (fish), produced with a labor input, using a technology in which the capital stock (lakes, fisheries, etc.) were privately owned and distributed roughly as capital is distributed today among Canadians (and others). Suppose, further, that the technology was linear in labor, $F(L) = \alpha L$, where α is the output/labor ratio of the actual Canadian economy. Those who own the capital stock hire others to fish at the competitive wage. The fish wage will be considerably less than α per unit of efficiency labor (or αs^i per unit of labor agent i), for part of the product of labor must return to the owners of capital as profit. The income distribution that results will be roughly the present Canadian income distribution. Now suppose that the fisheries, etc., are national-ized. The production function remains just as before, but now each per-son chooses to fish just as much as she wants to, has free access to the technology, and earns a return of α fish per unit of efficiency labor (or αs^i per unit of labor). The resulting income (and welfare) distribution is the one assigned by the LE mechanism; there will be differential returns to differential skill but what before was distributed as profits to capital now is spread out among all those who work.

V.   The poverty of the bargaining theory approach

It is becoming popular to cast arguments about distributive justice in terms of the model of classical bargaining theory, where agents are viewed as bargaining over a pie of *utility,* represented by a utility possibility set, as illustrated in Figure 10.1. Gauthier (1986), for example, concludes that the just allocation is the one associated with a particular solution to the bar-gaining problem known as the Kalai-Smorodinsky bargaining solution.[7] Formally, classical bargaining theory is the study of utility-allocating mech-anisms, with a domain consisting of the set of all possible utility sets. The distinction between a domain of utility sets and a domain of economic environments may seem pedantic, but it is far from that. One need only note that given only information contained in the utility possibility set, there is no language to say anything about property rights. Labor, fish, preferences, and skills cannot be discussed if one works only in utility space, for these things have been sterilized out of the model! One can talk only about different possible distributions of utility. These distribu-tions are themselves the primitive concepts of the model, not being deriv-able from some allocation of economic goods.

   In particular, *none of the allocation mechanisms discussed in this article exist in the classical bargaining theory model,* because there is no language in that model to discuss the features that characterize these mechanisms. There are no linear economies or non-linear ones in the bargaining theory domain, for there are no *economies:* only sets of possible utility allo-cations. One cannot discuss equal division of resources, because there are no resources. One cannot discuss free access because there are no economies with respect to which access might be defined. This is what it means to work on a domain where no conception of property rights can be formulated.

   Therefore, when Gauthier and others attempt to evaluate proposals for distributive justice by working on the domain of classical bargaining

---

[7] After Kalai and Smorodinsky (1975).

theory, they commit themselves before the project starts to not using any conception of property rights. (To be precise, this is not exactly the case, for Gauthier defines the threat point of the game, whose solution provides the just allocation, as the utility allocation associated with some appropriate distribution of property, in some economy, before the bargaining starts. Once the game has been formulated in utility terms, however, the critique of the previous two paragraphs applies. Gauthier discards the information about property too early on.)

Modeling distributive justice as a classical bargaining problem, that is to say, is an appropriate stance for only a welfarist to take. A *welfarist* believes that social decision problems need consider only the utility consequences of actions; no reference need ever be made to non-utility descriptions of the situation (such as one in which resources and rights to them are mentioned). In particular, rights of any kind are instrumental only insofar as they have certain desired welfare consequences. A welfarist commits himself *ex ante* to ruling out the kinds of economically based schemes I have discussed. The apparent ability of a welfarist approach to make specific and unique recommendations from simple axioms results from its having eliminated, by its domain assumption, all the proposals that make essential use of economic information. There are, so to speak, not many options for the social planner to consider after this sterilization of resource information.

VI.   Conclusion

Nozick argues that apparently self-evident property rights in the state of nature imply, with an apparently attractive proviso restricting appropriation of private property, highly unequal distributions of income. By formalizing Cohen's and Grunebaum's proposal to challenge Nozick's implicit assumption that the land and lakes are unowned in the state of nature, I have shown that only a much more egalitarian income distribution can be justified – while still respecting the private ownership of labor that libertarians cherish. And, as a lagniappe, we observe that those who study distributive justice with the classical bargaining theory model simplify the problem unacceptably by ruling out, *ex ante,* any proposal for implementing a distribution that makes essential reference to property rights.

Informational complexity in axiomatic models: benefits and costs

1.   Levels of information

Consider the problem of how to divide n different commodities among r players whose preferences are given by concave, monotonic, continuous utility functions $u^i: R_+^n \to R$. The first modeling option is how abstract a setting to choose for stating the problem. Axiomatic bargaining theory (ABT) (see Nash, 1950; Roth, 1979; Thomson, 1991) chooses to study the problem in utility space. Let $\bar{x} \in R_+^n$ be the vector of commodity endowments available for distribution. The utility possibilities set is

$$S = \{(\bar{u}^1, \bar{u}^2, \ldots, \bar{u}^r) \in R^r \mid \exists x^1, x^2, \ldots, x^r \in R_+^n, \sum x^i \le \bar{x}, u^i(x^i) = \bar{u}^i\}.$$

ABT studies the distribution problem by taking as primitive information just the set S, which is presumed to summarize the relevant information.

But the objection can be raised that too much important information has been discarded by the ABT approach. If we are studying the distribution of commodities, then we should study *economic environments,* objects $\xi = \langle n, \bar{x}, u^1, \ldots, u^r \rangle$. This includes more information than is available in S, and so the theory will probably be more intricate.

Yet another objection can be raised. It might be relevant to know what the *identities* of the commodities are that are being distributed. We may wish to allocate certain goods (say, those fulfilling needs) differently from how we allocate those fulfilling desires, although this distinction may not be retrievable from the utility functions. (That is to say, the utility functions may not summarize all information relevant for distribution.) Hence, the appropriate level of abstraction may be to postulate *economic environments with named goods,* objects $\sigma = \langle n, N, \bar{x}, u^1, \ldots, u^r \rangle$, where Γ is a countable list of goods with names, and $N \subset \Gamma$ is a subset of cardinality n. Developing the theory of resource allocation on a domain of such objects will be still more complex.

In this essay, I will trace the development of one theorem at these three levels of abstraction. My purpose is not to study this particular

231

theorem in its various forms – that has been done elsewhere[1]– it is methodological. As we move to domains containing more information, there is a benefit and a cost. The benefit is being able to represent intuitions more exactly. The cost is more subtle: preserving theorems requires adopting ever stronger domain axioms. I will argue that what we gain in precision we lose in credibility. Thus I treat the family of theorems discussed as an example with which to make an "economic" point about the choice of a level of abstraction. I conclude with some comments about the limitations of axiomatic modeling.

2.   Notation

A.   Spaces

Let S be a strictly comprehensive, closed convex subset (*scccx*) of R_+^r; let $\Lambda = \{S \mid S \, scccx \, \text{in} \, R_+^r\}$. Sets S are to be thought of as utility possibilities sets for r players. Let $\xi = \langle n, \bar{x}, u^1, \ldots, u^r \rangle$ be an economic environment where n is a positive integer, $\bar{x} \in R_+^n$, $u^i \in U^{(n)}$ where $U^{(n)}$ is the set of continuous, monotonic, concave, real functions on R_+^n for which $u^i(0) = 0$. Σ is the class of all economic environments; $\Sigma^{(n)}$ is the subclass of all economic environments of dimension n. (We fix throughout the number of players at r.) The utility possibilities set from an economic environment ξ is $A^1(\xi)$, as defined in Section 1.

Let Γ be a countable list of goods. Then a vector $\sigma = \langle n, N, \bar{x}, u^1, \ldots, u^r \rangle$ is an *economic environment with named goods,* where $\xi = \langle n, \bar{x}, u^1, \ldots, u^r \rangle$ is any environment in Σ and $N \subset \Gamma$ with $|N| = n$. The set of all economic environments with named goods is Δ.

B.   Mappings

Let $\varphi: \Lambda \to R_+^r$ such that $\varphi(S) \in S$. φ is a *bargaining solution* on Λ. Let $F_n: \Sigma^{(n)} \to R_+^{nr}$, such that $F_n(\xi) \in A^1(\xi)$. Then F_n is a *resource allocation mechanism* on $\Sigma^{(n)}$. We define a resource allocation mechanism on Σ as

$$F: \Sigma \to \bigcup_{n=1}^{\infty} R_+^{nr},$$

where on each subdomain $\Sigma^{(n)}$, the induced projection F_n is a resource allocation mechanism.[2]

---

[1] In Roemer (1986), the theorem on economic environments is proved. In Essay 7 of this volume, the theorem on economic environments with named goods is discussed, but not proved.

[2] I have defined $F(\xi)$ to be single-valued. Actually, it suffices that $u(F(\xi))$ be single-valued in utility space. F can be a correspondence that is "essentially single-valued," in this sense.

For a resource allocation mechanism F, define $F(\xi) = (F^1(\xi), ..., F^r(\xi))$. Thus $F^i(\xi)$ is the allocation of resources to player i by F.

For a resource allocation mechanism F and an economic environment $\xi = \langle n, \bar{x}, u^1, ..., u^r \rangle$, define $u \circ F: \Sigma \to R^r_+$ as $u(F(\xi)) = (u^1(F^1(\xi)), ..., u^r(F^r(\xi)))$. Thus $u \circ F$ is the mapping induced by F into utility space.

An allocation mechanism of named goods, f, associates to each $\sigma \in \Delta$ a feasible allocation of the goods in σ. This can be viewed as a mapping $f: \Delta \to R^\infty_+$ where R^∞_+ is the set of nonnegative vectors with a countable number of components and at most a finite number of nonzero components. We adopt the convention that the allocation of good j (called G_j) to player k is given by the $r(k-1)+j$ component of the vector $f(\sigma)$, for $\sigma \in \Delta$.

The mapping $A^1: \Sigma \to \Lambda$ associates to each $\xi \in \Sigma$ its utility possibilities set $A^1(\xi)$, as defined above.

The mapping $A^2: \Delta \to \Sigma$ is defined by

$$A^2(\langle n, N, \bar{x}, u^1, ..., u^r \rangle) = \langle n, \bar{x}, u^1, ..., u^r \rangle.$$

It associates to each environment with named goods the economic environment in Σ which is gotten by deleting the names of the goods.

Let φ_E be the *egalitarian bargaining solution* that associates to each $S \in \Lambda$ the Pareto optimal point with equal coordinates (this point exists by strict comprehensivity of S). Let E be the *egalitarian resource allocation mechanism* that associates to each $\xi \in \Sigma$ an allocation that generates equal utilities; that is, $u(E(\xi)) = \varphi_E(A^1(\xi))$. The *egalitarian allocation mechanism for named goods* is the allocation rule f_E on Δ that distributes the goods in that Pareto optimal way that equalizes utility. That is, $f_E(\sigma) = E(A^2(\sigma)) = \varphi_E(A^1(A^2(\sigma)))$. (There is some abuse of notation since f_E and E do not have the same range, but the meaning should be clear.)

3. One theorem, three models

A. The domain Λ

Our starting point is a theorem of ABT due to Kalai (1977). We work on the domain Λ, and seek to characterize the bargaining solution φ_E.

Domain axiom (D^Λ): φ is a bargaining solution (i.e., defined on Λ).

Efficiency axiom (PO^Λ): $\varphi(S)$ is Pareto optimal in S.

Monotonicity axiom (MON^Λ): If $S, T \in \Lambda$, $T \supset S$ then $\varphi(T) \geq \varphi(S)$.

Symmetry axiom (S^Λ): If $S \in \Lambda$, S symmetric then $\varphi(S) = \varphi_E(S)$.

Theorem 1 (Kalai): $D^\Lambda \cap PO^\Lambda \cap MON^\Lambda \cap S^\Lambda = \{\varphi_E\}$.

(A proof of Theorem 1 is presented in Essay 9.)

Remark: The class of bargaining solutions satisfying an axiom is labeled by the acronym of the axiom. Thus Theorem 1 is read: the class of bargaining solutions satisfying D^Λ, PO^Λ, MON^Λ, and S^Λ is the class consisting of the egalitarian bargaining solution.

Theorem 1 appears to settle a normative approach to distribution quite nicely. Suppose, in the actual world, our distribution problem is fully described by an environment with named goods; we have beer, champagne, shelter, food, and so on, to distribute among players with certain utility functions. We decide that the ethically relevant information is just the utility possibilities set. We look for distribution rules which satisfy some normatively motivated axioms. The distribution rule (in this model, a bargaining solution) should be efficient, monotonic, and symmetric. This determines a unique rule. Thus if the axioms are normatively appealing and the domain chosen is appropriate we are finished.

Note that the domain axiom requires that our rule be defined on Λ. This is a reasonable requirement only if we think that the actual problems we may be called upon to solve can induce as their utility possibilities sets, any $S \in \Lambda$. If some sets S would never represent a problem we might face, then the domain axiom is unnecessarily restricting the class of mechanisms that would be satisfactory for us.

B.   The domain Σ

Suppose it is objected that too much relevant information has been discarded in choosing the domain Λ. We should, the objector says, work on the domain Σ where the amounts of the resources and the utility functions are represented. There are two reasons to do so. First there are many reasonable resource allocation mechanisms that can be defined on Σ but which have no counterpart on Λ. Consider, for example, the mechanism "equal division Walrasian equilibrium (EDW)" that assigns to $\xi \in \Sigma$ the Walrasian equilibria from initial equal division of the resource vector $\bar{x}$ among the r players.[3] This may be an allocation rule with some attraction, one which should not be eliminated *ab initio,* but it cannot be defined on Λ, as there are no resources in the S objects to divide. Formally, the EDW mechanism has no counterpart on Λ because one can find $\xi^1, \xi^2 \in \Sigma$ such that $A^1(\xi^1) = A^1(\xi^2)$ but $u(\text{EDW}(\xi^1)) \neq u(\text{EDW}(\xi^2))$.

---

[3] EDW is not "essentially single-valued" (see note 2), but it can be made so, e.g., by choosing that equilibrium that is best for player 1, or by some other such rule.

Second, the objector argues that the axioms MON and S are too coarse to reflect our normative intuitions. MON probably seems attractive to those who believe that if the *resources* increase in a problem *ceteris paribus,* then no player should end up worse off under the distribution rule. Formally, we can state this as an axiom on Σ:

Resource monotonicity axiom (RMON$^\Sigma$): $\xi^1, \xi^2 \in \Sigma$,

$$\xi^1 = \langle n, \bar{x}^1, u^1, \ldots, u^r \rangle, \ \xi^2 = \langle n, \bar{x}^2, u^1, \ldots, u^r \rangle, \ \bar{x}^1 \geq \bar{x}^2$$
$$\Rightarrow u(F(\xi^1)) \geq u(F(\xi^2)).$$

But RMON is weaker than MON, in this way. Given $S, T \in \Lambda$, $S \subset T$, there may be economic environments ξ^1, ξ^2 with $S = A^1(\xi^1)$, $T = A^1(\xi^2)$, but there is no clear relationship between ξ^1 and ξ^2. Perhaps $\dim \xi^1 = 7$ and $\dim \xi^2 = 23$, and their utility functions, *a fortiori,* are unrelated. Nevertheless, MON commits us to assuring that $\varphi(T) \geq \varphi(S)$, but RMON would say no such thing with respect to the behavior of a resource allocation mechanism F on ξ^1 and ξ^2. Thus, when the domain is informationally too thin, axioms about allocation mechanisms commit us to more than our economically based intuitions warrant.

The same comment applies to the symmetry axiom. The motivation for symmetry is probably economic symmetry:

Economic symmetry axiom (Sy$^\Sigma$): $\xi \in \Sigma$, $\xi = \langle n, \bar{x}, u, \ldots, u \rangle \Rightarrow F(\xi) = (\bar{x}/r, \ldots, \bar{x}/r)$.

But Sy$^\Sigma$ is a much weaker axiom than S$^\Lambda$. In the same way, axiom S$^\Lambda$ commits us to far too much.

The objector suggests that we try to reconstruct Theorem 1 on the domain Σ, with the weakened axioms RMON$^\Sigma$ and Sy$^\Sigma$.

Question Q1: *Is $D^\Sigma \cap PO^\Sigma \cap RMON^\Sigma \cap Sy^\Sigma = \{E\}$?*

The answer is no. Counterexample: choose the reference vector $(1, \ldots, 1) = 1^n \in R^n$. We construct a resource allocation mechanism satisfying the four axioms that is not E. For $\xi \in \Sigma^{(n)}$ let $F(\xi)$ be an allocation which generates the point on the Pareto surface intersected by the ray through $u(1^n) = (u^1(1^n), \ldots, u^r(1^n))$. It is easy to verify that f satisfies the four axioms, but $F \neq E$. There is clearly a large class of allocation mechanisms satisfying these axioms.

We can, however, reconstruct Theorem 1 on Σ with some more work. Consider the unweakened monotonicity axiom MON but defined on Σ instead of Λ:

MON$^\Sigma$: $\xi^1, \xi^2 \in \Sigma$, $A^1(\xi^1) \supset A^1(\xi^2) \Rightarrow u(F(\xi^1)) \geq u(F(\xi^2))$.

We can prove:

Theorem 2a: $D^{\Sigma} \cap PO^{\Sigma} \cap MON^{\Sigma} \cap Sy^{\Sigma} = \{E\}$.

However, MON^{Σ} is unpalatable, as discussed above, for the same reason that MON^{Λ} is. Note that MON^{Σ} implies the axiom of welfarism:

Welfarism axiom (W^{Σ}): $\xi^1, \xi^2 \in \Sigma$, $A^1(\xi^1) = A^1(\xi^2) \Rightarrow u(F(\xi^1)) = u(F(\xi^2))$.

The axiom is so named because it directs the mechanism, defined on Σ, to ignore all information except that which is represented in the utility possibilities sets of the economic environments. If W^{Σ} is assumed, then our analysis, though formally conducted on Σ, might just as well be conducted on Λ, since any $F \in W^{\Sigma}$ treats all environments in Σ giving rise to the same $S \in \Lambda$ in the same way, so far as the distribution of utility is concerned. It should not be surprising, therefore, that:

Theorem 2b: $D^{\Sigma} \cap PO^{\Sigma} \cap W^{\Sigma} \cap RMON^{\Sigma} \cap Sy^{\Sigma} = \{E\}$.

Theorem 2b, however, is objectionable if Theorem 1 is; for W^{Σ} requires the allocation mechanism to discard all economic information not represented in the utility possibilities set.

There is a way of replacing W^{Σ} with a much weaker axiom that does not discard economic information.

Consistency of resource allocation across dimension axiom ($CONRAD^{\Sigma}$): $\xi \in \Sigma^{(n+m)}$, $\xi = \langle n+m, (\bar{x}, \bar{y}), u^1, \ldots, u^r \rangle$, $F(\xi) = ((\bar{x}^1, \bar{y}^1), \ldots, (\bar{x}^1, \bar{y}^1))$, $u^{i^*}(x) \equiv u^i(x, \bar{y}^i)$, $\xi^* \equiv \langle n, \bar{x}, u^{1^*}, \ldots, u^{n^*} \rangle$, $A^1(\xi) = A^1(\xi^*) \Rightarrow F(\xi^*) = (\bar{x}^1, \ldots, \bar{x}^n)$.

CONRAD requires a kind of consistency between pairs of economic environments that are related to each other in a certain intimate way. The axiom is given a normative motivation in Essay 7 of this volume and a positive one in Roemer (1988).

Note that $W^{\Sigma} \subset CONRAD^{\Sigma}$. To see this, recall that W^{Σ} says that if two economic environments generate the same utility possibilities sets, then the agents should be assigned the same utility vectors in both environments. $CONRAD^{\Sigma}$ says if two economic environments ξ and ξ^* in Σ have a certain intimate relationship to each other, *and* have the same utility possibilities sets, then the players should be assigned allocations that yield the same utility allocations in ξ and ξ^*. $CONRAD^{\Sigma}$ is, indeed, much weaker than W^{Σ}. We have:

Theorem 2: $S^{\Sigma} \cap PO^{\Sigma} \cap CONRAD^{\Sigma} \cap RMON^{\Sigma} \cap Sy^{\Sigma} = \{E\}$.

(For the proof, see Roemer, 1986.)

The *substantive* axioms (i.e., all except the domain axiom) in Theorem 2 are each weaker than their counterparts in Theorem 1. This statement is not yet quite precise because the domains of the two sets of axioms are different. This minor problem will be attended to in Section 4.

Note the cost of reconstructing the idea of Theorem 1 on the domain Σ: the domain axiom D^Σ is stronger than D^Λ, in the sense that we require a resource allocation mechanism defined on Σ to answer many more questions than a bargaining solution defined on Λ must answer. This can be illustrated formally as follows. According to a theorem of Billera and Bixby (1973), the mapping A^1 is onto. Let $\Sigma_0 = (A^1)^{-1}(\Lambda)$ be a minimal inverse image of A^1 (i.e., $A^1 \colon \Sigma_0 \to \Lambda$ is onto and there is no proper sub-class of Σ_0 for which this is true). Billera and Bixby show that Σ_0 can always be chosen so that it contains no economic environment with dimension higher than $r(r-1)$. It is then easy to show that:

Theorem 1a: $D^{\Sigma_0} \cap PO^{\Sigma_0} \cap MON^{\Sigma_0} \cap S^{\Sigma_0} = \{E\}$ *where symmetry is defined as:* $S^{\Sigma_0} \colon \xi \in \Sigma_0, A^1(\xi)$ *a symmetric set* $\Rightarrow u(F(\xi)) = \varphi_E(A^1(\xi))$.

(The proof of Theorem 1a uses an observation of Billera and Bixby to reduce the problem to Theorem 1.)

Theorem 2, however, essentially requires the full domain Σ. (By 'essentially', I mean that Theorem 2 is false on any subdomain of Σ in which the dimension of the economic environments is bounded.) So the weakening of the substantive axioms, in passing from Theorem 1 to Theorem 2, comes at the expense of requiring a stronger domain axiom. Theorem 2 is compelling only if its domain axiom is, which states that the allocation mechanism should be able to deal with any economic environment, of any finite dimension – even dimensions greater than the number of molecules in the universe.

C.   The domain Δ

An objection is raised. The identities of the goods might matter. Goods which satisfy biological needs should, perhaps, be distributed different-ly from goods which satisfy aesthetic tastes. The objector proposes that we reconstruct the theory as one of allocation mechanisms on environments with named goods, on the domain Δ, where there is a language for distinguishing among kinds of goods. He or she notes that the axioms $CONRAD^\Sigma$ and $RMON^\Sigma$ are too coarse to capture our normative intuitions, which do, in fact, take account of the names of goods. Thus $RMON^\Sigma$, written as an axiom on Δ, becomes:

$RMON^{\Delta}$: $\sigma^1, \sigma^2 \in \Delta$,

$$\sigma^1 = \langle n, N^1, \bar{x}^1, u^1, \ldots, u^r \rangle, e^2 = \langle n, N^2, \bar{x}^2, u^1, \ldots, u^r \rangle, \bar{x}^1 \geq \bar{x}^2$$
$$\Rightarrow u(f(\sigma^1)) \geq u(f(\sigma^2)).$$

But note that the goods in σ^1 and σ^2 are not necessarily the same ($N^1 \neq N^2$). If we think distribution should be sensitive to the *kinds* of goods at issue, why should the distribution of goods in σ^2 be related to the distribution of goods in σ^1 in any clear way? Thus $RMON^{\Sigma}$, viewed as an axiom on Δ, is too coarse, just as MON, viewed as an axiom on Σ was. The same argument[4] can be made against $CONRAD^{\Delta}$.

We note that the following reconstruction of Theorem 2 on the domain Δ holds. The mapping $A^2: \Delta \to \Sigma$ is onto. Let $\Delta_0 \subset \Delta$ be a minimal inverse image of A^2 (write $\Delta_0 = (A^2)^{-1}(\Sigma)$).

Theorem 3a: $D^{\Delta_0} \cap PO^{\Delta_0} \cap CONRAD^{\Delta_0} \cap RMON^{\Delta_0} \cap Sy^{\Delta_0} = \{f_E\}$.

Proof: Let f be an allocation mechanism for environments with named goods, satisfying the stated axioms on Δ_0. $f(\sigma)$ for $\sigma \in \Delta_0$ is a vector in R_+^{∞}, with zeroes in all but nr components. For $x = f(\sigma)$, let $\psi(x)$ be the projection onto R_+^{nr} in which only the components of x associated with the goods in the environment σ occur. Note that $\psi \circ f \circ (A^2)^{-1} = F$ is a resource allocation mechanism defined on Σ. It is easy to check that F inherits on Σ the axioms that f satisfies on Δ_0; hence, by Theorem 2, $F = E$. Therefore $f = \psi^{-1} \circ E \circ A^2 = f_E$, completing the proof.

Theorem 3a is the analog to Theorem 1a. We wish to reconstruct Theorem 2 as a theorem on the domain Δ with substantive axioms appropriately weakened to reflect our normative intuitions on Δ. Thus:

$RMON^{*\Delta}$: $\sigma^1, \sigma^2 \in \Delta$, $\sigma^1 = \langle n, N, \bar{x}^1, u^1, \ldots, u^r \rangle$, $\sigma^2 = \langle n, N, \bar{x}^2, u^1, \ldots, u^r \rangle$, $\bar{x}^1 \geq \bar{x}^2 \Rightarrow u(f(\sigma^1)) \geq u(f(\sigma^2))$.

This axiom weakens $RMON^{\Delta}$ because it only requires monotonicity when the goods in the two environments are indeed the same.

$CONRAD^{*\Delta}$: $\sigma = \langle n+m, N \cup M, (\bar{x}, \bar{y}), u^1, \ldots, u^r \rangle$, $f(\sigma) = ((\bar{x}^1, \bar{y}^1), \ldots,$ $(\bar{x}^r, \bar{y}^r))$, $u^{i*}(x) \equiv u^i(x, \bar{y}^i)$, $\sigma^* = \langle n, N, \bar{x}, u^{1*}, \ldots, u^{r*} \rangle$, $A^1(A^2(\sigma)) =$ $A^1(A^2(\sigma^*)) \Rightarrow f(\sigma^*) = (\bar{x}^1, \ldots, \bar{x}^r)$.

$CONRAD^{*\Delta}$ only forces a comparison of the mechanism's behavior on σ and the dimensionally smaller σ^* when both environments have the same set N of x-goods. In $CONRAD^{\Delta}$, which I did not write down, no such restriction is imposed.

Analogous to the question Q1, we may ask:

---

[4] These arguments do not, however, apply to Sy or PO.

Question Q2: *Is* $D^{\Delta_0} \cap PO^{\Delta_0} \cap CONRAD^{*\Delta_0} \cap RMON^{*\Delta_0} \cap Sy^{\Delta_0} = \{f_E\}$?

The answer is again no. A counterexample follows. Choose Δ_0 in Δ as follows. $\Delta = \bigcup_{i=1}^{\infty} \Delta^i$ where Δ^i consists of all environments of dimension n. Label the goods in $\Gamma - \{G_1, G_2, \ldots\}$. Choose Δ_0^1 to be all one-dimensional environments with the good G_1. Choose $\Delta_0^2 \subset \Delta^2$ to be all two-dimensional environments with goods (G_2, G_3). For $n = 3$, choose $\Delta_0^3 \subset \Delta^3$ to be all three-dimensional environments with goods G_4, G_5, G_6. Define $\Delta_0 = \bigcup \Delta_0^i$. Note that no two environments in Δ_0 of different dimension have any goods in common. Let f be the allocation rule on Δ_0 which associates to each $\sigma \in \Delta_0$ an allocation generating the utility point in which the ray through $u(1^n)$ intersects the Pareto frontier. $f \in D^{\Delta_0} \cap PO^{\Delta_0} \cap RMON^{*\Delta_0} \cap Sy^{\Delta_0}$ and $f \in CONRAD^{*\Delta_0}$ vacuously, for $CONRAD^{*\Delta_0}$ is no restriction on the subdomain Δ_0 (because environments of different dimension have no goods in common). But $f \neq f_E$.

We have, however:

Theorem 3: $D^{\Delta} \cap PO^{\Delta} \cap CONRAD^{*\Delta} \cap RMON^{*\Delta} \cap Sy^{\Delta} = \{f_E\}$.

Theorem 3 reconstructs Theorem 2 on Δ, with substantive axioms which are weaker than those on Σ. But the domain axiom D^{Δ} is stronger than D^{Σ}.

4. Codifying the theorems on a single domain

It is now instructive to rewrite these results on a common domain. We work on the full domain Δ. We define three successively stronger monotonicity axioms on Δ. For the following, let $\sigma^1 = \langle n, N^1, \bar{x}^1, u^1, \ldots, u^r \rangle$ and $\sigma^2 = \langle m, M, \bar{x}^2, v^1, \ldots, v^r \rangle$.

RMON*: $\sigma^1, \sigma^2 \in \Delta$ as above.

$$m = n, N = M, u^i = v^i, \bar{x}^1 \geq \bar{x}^2 \Rightarrow u(f(\sigma^1)) \geq u(f(\sigma^2)).$$

RMON: $\sigma^1, \sigma^2 \in \Delta$ as above.

$$m = n, u^i = v^i, \bar{x}^1 \geq \bar{x}^2 \Rightarrow u(f(\sigma^1)) \geq u(f(\sigma^2)).$$

MON: $\sigma^1, \sigma^2 \in \Delta$ as above.

$$A^1(A^2(\sigma^1)) \subset A^1(A^2(\sigma^2)) \Rightarrow u(f(\sigma^1)) \geq u(f(\sigma^2)).$$

Note that MON $\subset$ RMON $\subset$ RMON*, but not conversely.

Similarly, we can define CONRAD*, CONRAD, and W as three axioms on the domain Δ, and W $\subset$ CONRAD $\subset$ CONRAD*.

Similarly, we can define two versions of symmetry on Δ, Sy, and Sy*, and Sy $\subset$ Sy*.

Theorems 1, 2, and 3 can be written:

Theorem 1*: $D^\Delta \cap PO \cap W \cap MON \cap S = \{f_E\}$.

Theorem 2*: $D^\Delta \cap PO \cap CONRAD \cap RMON \cap Sy = \{f_E\}$.

Theorem 3*: $D^\Delta \cap PO \cap CONRAD^* \cap RMON^* \cap Sy^* = \{f_E\}$.

Here, all axioms are defined on the domain Δ, so the superscript $^\Delta$ is not needed. The virtue of writing the three theorems this way is that it is clearly seen that 3* is a stronger result than 2*, which is stronger than 1*, since their axioms are nested. What is obscured by writing them this way is the fact that each theorem requires a stronger domain axiom than the previous one. As we have noted, Theorem 1* can in fact be viewed as a theorem on the domain Σ_0, while Theorem 2* can be viewed as a theorem on $\Sigma \supset \Sigma_0$ or $\Delta_0 \subset \Delta$. Thus it requires a stronger domain axiom than Theorem 1* and a weaker one than Theorem 3*.

5.   How palatable are strong domain axioms?

Suppose we take Δ as our domain for a baseline. If we endorse welfarism, then it is sufficient to work on the domain Λ. Theorem 1, on Λ, says that we need only admit the existence of a fairly small class of possible problems in Δ to characterize a distribution rule, given welfarism. We need to choose a subclass $\Delta^\Lambda \subset \Delta$, the images of whose members under $A^1 \circ A^2$ generate Λ (i.e., such that $A^1 \circ A^2 \colon \Delta^\Lambda \to \Lambda$ is an onto map). In particular, Δ^Λ need contain no environment with more than $r(r-1)$ goods (by Billera-Bixby).

If, not being welfarists, we think that economic information is important, but that the names of goods do not matter because the utility functions tell us everything salient about the goods, we work on Σ. From the baseline domain, we need to postulate a class of possible worlds Δ^Σ which is much larger than Δ^Λ; in particular, to retrieve Theorem 2, Δ^Σ must contain economic environments of arbitrarily high dimension. Precisely, Δ^Σ must satisfy:

$$(\forall \xi \in \Sigma)(\exists \sigma \in \Delta^\Sigma)(A^2(\sigma) = \xi) \tag{1}$$

Now, suppose we believe that the names of goods are important independently of how goods enter into the production of utility. Then we need to work on the full domain Δ. The severity of the assumption D^Δ can be seen as follows. The domain Δ satisfies:

$$(\forall \xi \in \Sigma)(\forall N \subset \Gamma, |N| = n)(\exists \sigma \in \Delta)(\sigma = (\xi, N) \equiv \langle n, N, \bar{x}, u^1, \ldots, u^r \rangle) \tag{2}$$

The characterization of Δ^Σ in (1) says that for every vector of economic information (ξ), there is *some* list of goods with respect to which that economic information defines a possible world. But the characterization of Δ in (2) says that for every vector of economic information, and for *all* lists of goods of the right length, there must be a possible world. But this sterilizes the naming of goods of much of the meaning it has! One reason we believe naming goods may be important is that we believe there are limitations in the ways that certain goods can enter into people's preferences. No rational person in the world as we know it will ever be willing to trade all of his food for fine paintings. But trade-offs like this must be represented in elements of Δ. Δ contains possible worlds, that is, which make no sense to us.

6.   Conclusion

Our ethical views are formed by experiences in the real world as we know it, thick with description as it is. To capture properly these views therefore requires postulating a domain of possible worlds where our ethics should apply, articulated with the appropriate degree of information. A welfarist, who believes that property rights, or rights more generally, goods, and the identities of goods, are only instrumental insofar as they induce a certain class of utility possibilities sets will be satisfied to posit a universe of possible worlds like Δ^Λ. Similarly, a resourcist, who believes that economic information is important, but thinks that names of goods are important only insofar as they indicate the way in which the goods produce welfare, is satisfied to work on Δ^Σ.

If one believes that the identities of goods are important, then for the axioms faithfully to represent our ethical or normative views requires postulating a domain of possible worlds of, say, the complexity of Δ. But the domain Δ is not one on which we can expect to have complete ethical views. How should food and paintings be distributed among a community of r people, $r-1$ of whom are willing to trade off all their food against paintings, and the rth one of whom loves food and detests paintings? The obvious solution grates against our senses. But how can we judge this question, since there are no such worlds in human experience? This would require Martian ethics.

For axiomatic theory to be credible as a normative tool, we must work on domains in which the information is sufficiently dense that we can represent our intuitions properly, but which are also sufficiently delimited to exclude crazy worlds. The lesson of this essay is that we will get no clean characterizations of policy from a small set of ethical principles on such domains, for example, domains smaller than Δ, but where the axioms take account of the names of goods. Many allocation rules will satisfy our normative axioms on such small, informationally dense domains.

In other words, the mathematics is telling us that there are no simple solutions to properly posed problems of distributional ethics.

Distributing health: the allocation of resources by an international agency

1.   The problem

An agency of the United Nations has at its disposal an endowment of resources that it will distribute to various countries, with the aim of lowering their rates of infant mortality. The rate of infant survival, abbreviated RIS (one minus the rate of infant mortality), is taken to be an important indicator of the general level of physical well-being of a population, for a high rate is only achieved by good nutrition for women of child-bearing age, clean water supplies, and programmes providing ante-natal care to women. If infant mortality is low, the factors responsible have an impact upon others (than infants and mothers) in the population generally. The level of a population's physical well-being is, of course, an essential ingredient of its quality of life.

When the UN agency looks at the various countries, the data that are most important to it are the rates of infant survival in each country, and the 'technology' that the country will use to convert the resources it is granted into a higher RIS. Technology must be broadly interpreted. One country may be particularly efficient at using such resources because it already has a well-organized network of rural clinics in place. Another country might make less effective use of resources granted, not because it has a less adequate distribution system for bringing the resources to the population, but because the regime in power channels too large a fraction of the resources, from the agency's point of view, to the urban middle class, who constitute a small fraction of the population. The agency is powerless to affect this kind of political decision, in part because it is an international and not a supranational agency.

The technology for increasing the RIS, from the agency's viewpoint, is a function $u(\mathbf{x})$, where $\mathbf{x}$ is the vector of resources per capita that the agency grants to the country, and $u(\mathbf{x})$ is the consequent RIS achieved.

I am indebted to the following officers at the World Health Organization, Geneva, for their assistance: Dr. J. Cohen, Mr. A. Creese, Dr. T. Fülöp, Dr. J. Keja, Dr. F. Partow, Mr. C. G. Sandstrom, and Dr. E. Tarimo. Research was funded by the World Institute for Development Economics Research (WIDER) and the US National Science Foundation.

Thus $u(\mathbf{0})$ is the RIS before UN intervention. I take $u(\mathbf{x})$ to have the usual features of a production function: it is non-decreasing in each component of $\mathbf{x}$, it is continuous and concave. If, for example, a country siphons off, and uses for another purpose, some of the resources that it is allocated to increase its RIS, then '$\mathbf{x}$' in $u(\mathbf{x})$ stands for the vector of resources per capita allocated by the agency, not the vector of resources actually used effectively by the country. The UN has no control of the siphoning: this is what it means to say that u is the technology from the UN's viewpoint.

A first attempt at formulating the resource allocation problem that the agency faces is to represent the relevant information by an ordered set $\tilde{E} = \langle M, n, \Omega, (u^1, N^1), (u^2, N^2), ..., (u^r, N^r) \rangle$, where M is the budget of the agency, n is the number of resources the agency decides are relevant, Ω is the set of all n-dimensional vectors of resources that the agency can purchase, at going prices, with budget M, u^i is the technology the ith country uses, from the agency's viewpoint, to increase its RIS, and N^i is the population of country i. Each u^i is a function of the n resources, and it expresses the country's RIS as a function of the resources per capita allocated to it by the agency. There are r countries, the ith one of which has a pre-intervention RIS of $u^i(\mathbf{0})$.

Other information may, however, be relevant to the allocation decision. Perhaps the agency will take into consideration the various endowments of the countries, which affect their RIS, although they are not specifically represented in E: their climates, their population densities, the degree of organization of their health services. These things appear in E only implicitly, as they affect the technologies u^i. Perhaps the agency should make use of its knowledge of this information directly. For example, suppose two countries have the same technologies $u(\mathbf{x})$ (in particular, they have the same pre-intervention RIS, $u(\mathbf{0})$), and the same population size. In the first country, there is a good water supply, a favourable climate, and a corrupt government, which siphons resources away from their intended use. In the second, there is an unfavourable climate and dirty water, but a conscientious bureaucracy, which uses the resources allocated effectively. The upshot is that the two countries have the same effective technology u. Should the UN allocate the same bundle of resources to both countries? If not, then one believes it should make use of this other information.

The ancillary information, for a country i, can be represented by a set Φ^i, which summarizes all kinds of political, social, geographical, and cultural information about a country, which may be relevant to decisions involving resource allocation for the purpose of raising the RIS. Ancillary information is taken to include only facts that are known to the agency. (One such fact might be that, for a certain country, the agency knows that it has very little ancillary information.) A more complete representation of the problem the agency faces is

$$E = \langle M, n, \Omega, (u^1, N^1, \Phi^1), (u^2, N^2, \Phi^2), \ldots, (u^r, N^r, \Phi^r) \rangle.$$

I have argued that the information summarized in E should suffice for the agency to decide how resources should be allocated among countries to achieve its goal. How might the agency proceed? Given the problem E, what distribution of resources $(x^1, x^2, \ldots, x^r)$ of some feasible resource bundle $\bar{x} \in \Omega$ should the agency choose, where x^i is the vector of resources allocated to country i, $\sum x^i = \bar{x}$, and $\bar{x} \in \Omega$?

2. Necessary conditions for resource allocation

What the agency must discuss is the *budget allocation rule,* which will associate with every reasonable problem E that the agency might face, an allocation of resources that the agency should implement. The rule, F, thus far unknown, can be viewed as a function that maps possible problems E into feasible allocations for those problems: using the above notation, $F(E) = (x^1, x^2, \ldots, x^r)$. In fact, we can dispense with the information on the agency's budget, and consider problems of the type $\xi = \langle n, \Omega, (u^1, N^1, \Phi^1), \ldots, (u^r, N^r, \Phi^r) \rangle$. The feasible set upon which the agency concentrates is the set Ω of possible resource bundles that it can purchase with its budget. The budget is only needed to determine the set Ω. From now on, it is only necessary to consider problems of the form ξ.

I will propose that the agency proceed by discussing general principles that should or must apply to any resource allocation rule that it might adopt. This is a piecemeal approach, less ambitious than trying to come up with a complete allocation rule all at once. Deciding upon these principles can considerably narrow down the class of acceptable rules. I will consider five general principles, and particular axioms that follow from these principles. The perhaps surprising conclusion is that, having adopted restrictions on the class of acceptable allocation rules that are required by the five principles, the problem of choosing an allocation rule will have been completely solved.

Let $F(\xi) = (x^1, \ldots, x^r)$ specify the allocation rule; define $F^i(\xi) = x^i$. Thus $u^i(F^i(\xi)/N^i) = u^i(x^i/N^i)$ is the RIS in country i after it receives and puts into use the resources it has been allocated.[1] The notation $u(F(\xi)/N)$ is the r-vector whose i^{th} component is $u^i(F^i(\xi)/N^i)$.

1. *Efficiency.* The allocation of resources should be efficient in the sense of *Pareto optimality* (PO). That is, no other allocation of any vector of

---

[1] It is more realistic to think of $u^i(x^i/N^i)$ as the RIS that the agency *expects* to attain after the country uses the resources x^i.

resources in Ω can raise the RIS of some countries above what it is at $F(\xi)$ without lowering the RIS of some other country. This will be called axiom PO. Pareto optimality is probably not a contentious principle, in the context of a resource allocation problem.

2. *Fairness.* Suppose that two problems ξ^1 and ξ^2 differ only in that, in the first, the agency faces a feasible set of resources Ω^1 which includes the set of resources Ω^2, available in the second. The principle of *monotonicity* (MON) states that every country in the first problem should end up, after the allocation, with at least as high an RIS as in the second. Formally, let $\xi^1 = \langle n, \Omega^1, (u^1, N^1, \Phi^1), \ldots, (u^r, N^r, \Phi^r) \rangle$ and $\xi^2 = \langle n, \Omega^2, (u^1, N^1, \Phi^1), \ldots, (u^r, N^r, \Phi^r) \rangle$ be possible worlds with $\Omega^1 \supset \Omega^2$. Then

$$u(F(\xi^1)/N) \geq u(F(\xi^2)/N).$$

In particular, MON implies that if the budget increases, but nothing else changes, then each country should end up at least as well off (in terms of its RIS).

Monotonicity certainly does not summarize all aspects of fairness that may be of import, but it is arguably a necessary condition of a fair allocation rule. Note that MON is a weaker principle than one that would require each country to receive more of every resource as the agency's resource bundle increases. It says that no country should suffer in terms of its RIS as resources become collectively more abundant. It also requires that if the agency's budget is reduced, each country should (weakly) share in the decrease of aggregate RIS that must ensue.

MON is not a principle that is patently required for ethical reasons. For instance, if the agency were only concerned with increasing the world's aggregate RIS, taken as the population-weighted sum of the countries' individual rates, then it should not adopt MON as a principle. Population-weighted utilitarianism, the allocation rule that allocates resources in that way which maximizes the weighted sum of the countries' rates of infant survival, violates MON.[2] MON is adopted only if the agency views its charge as reducing the rate of infant mortality in *each* country, not simply the rate of infant mortality internationally. This kind of principle might be adopted, for instance, if all countries contributed to the budget of the UN. If the allocation rule violated MON, some country could have reason to reduce its allocation to the UN, in order to increase thereby its effective allocation from the agency.

A second principle of fairness is *symmetry* (S): if all the countries happen to be identical, with respect to both their technologies for processing

---

[2] That is, there are problems ξ having the property that, should resources increase, the international RIS (i.e. the population-weighted average of the country RISs) is increased by transferring some resources from a low RIS country to a high RIS country.

resources and their sets of ancillary information, then the resources should be distributed in proportion to their populations. Formally, if

$$\xi = \langle n, \Omega, (u, N^1, \Phi), (u, N^2, \Phi), \dots, (u, N^r, \Phi) \rangle,$$

then $F^i(\xi) = (N^i/N)\bar{x}$, for some $\bar{x} \in \Omega$, for all i.

3. *Neutrality.* For a problem $\xi = \langle n, \Omega, (u^1, N^1, \Phi^1), \dots, (u^r, N^r, \Phi^r) \rangle$, the distribution of resources should depend only on the technological information $u^1, \dots, u^r$, the populations N^i, and the resource availabilities Ω. I call this the *irrelevance of ancillary information* (IAI); it is formally stated as follows. Let ξ be as above, and let $\xi^* = \langle n, \Omega, (u^1, N^1, \Phi^{*1}), \dots, (u^r, N^r, \Phi^{*r}) \rangle$ be another problem with technologies, populations, and resource data exactly as in ξ, but in which the vectors of ancillary information (may) differ. Then $F(\xi) = F(\xi^*)$: resource allocation should be the same for the two problems.

IAI may be a contentious principle, as can be seen from the examples given in Section 1. The reason behind it may be motivated by noting that the agency is directed by the General Assembly[3] of the UN to distribute its endowment in a neutral fashion, that is, without regard to the internal politics and culture of the countries. Its task is one of engineering – given the present state of resource-processing technologies as summarized in the u^i, to allocate resources in a fair manner in order to reduce infant mortality.

Because the independence of ancillary information is assumed throughout, we may delete the symbols Φ^i and from now on represent a problem as $\xi = \langle n, \Omega, (u^1, N^1), \dots, (u^r, N^r) \rangle$.

4. *Consistency.* There are many versions of consistency conditions in resource allocation problems. Generally, consistency means that if two problems are related in a certain natural way, then their solutions should be related in a similarly natural way. I consider two consistency axioms.

Suppose the agency faces a problem in which there are $n + m$ resources to distribute:

$$\xi = \langle n+m, \Omega, (u^1, N^1), \dots, (u^r, N^r) \rangle.$$

The technologies are defined as functions of all the resources, $u(\mathbf{x}, \mathbf{y})$, where $\mathbf{x}$ represents the first n resources per capita and $\mathbf{y}$ the last m resources per capita. Under the allocation rule F, the distribution of resources is $F(\xi) = ((\mathbf{x}^1, \mathbf{y}^1), \dots, (\mathbf{x}^r, \mathbf{y}^r))$, where $(\mathbf{x}^i, \mathbf{y}^i)$ is the allocation to country i. Suppose the y-resources are distributed first, as planned: $(\mathbf{y}^1, \mathbf{y}^2, \dots, \mathbf{y}^r)$. The agency can now be viewed as facing, temporarily, a new problem, as the countries are 'consuming' the y-resources. The technologies of the countries with the y-resources fixed are now

---

[3] If the World Health Organization (WHO) is the agency, then the question is decided by its own general assembly. WHO operates as an independent affiliate of the UN.

$$u^{*1}(\mathbf{x}) = u^{*1}(\mathbf{x}, \mathbf{y}^1/N^1), \dots, u^{*r}(\mathbf{x}) = u^r(\mathbf{x}, \mathbf{y}^r/N^r),$$

and there are n $\mathbf{x}$-resources left to distribute. The new problem is

$$\xi^* = \langle n, \Omega^*, (u^{*1}, N^1), \dots, (u^{*r}, N^r) \rangle,$$

where Ω^* describes the possible allocations of the $\mathbf{x}$-resources (it is the projection of Ω on to the n-dimensional subspace of $\mathbf{x}$-resources at the point $(\mathbf{y}^1, \mathbf{y}^2, \dots, \mathbf{y}^r)$). The principle of *consistent resource allocation across dimension* (CONRAD) states that the solution to ξ^* must be $(\mathbf{x}^1, \dots, \mathbf{x}^r)$: that is, F must allocate the $\mathbf{x}$-resources in ξ^* just as it allocated them in ξ.

Formally, CONRAD says that, for any problem ξ as described above, if $F(\xi) = ((\mathbf{x}^1, \mathbf{y}^1), (\mathbf{x}^2, \mathbf{y}^2), \dots, (\mathbf{x}^r, \mathbf{y}^r))$, and if ξ^* is defined as above with respect to $(\mathbf{y}^1, \dots, \mathbf{y}^r)$, then $F(\xi^*) = (\mathbf{x}^1, \dots, \mathbf{x}^r)$. If this principle of consistency holds, then, having decided upon the allocation of all the resources, the agency can distribute resources to countries as they become available, and it will never be faced with a need to revise its plan.[4]

The second consistency axiom is called the *deletion of irrelevant countries* (DIC). Suppose there is a problem $\xi = \langle n, \Omega, (u^1, N^1), \dots, (u^r, N^r) \rangle$, and $F^1(\xi) = 0$: the first country is allocated no resources. Consider the same problem, but without the first country: $\xi^* = \langle n, \Omega, (u^2, N^2), \dots, (u^r, N^r) \rangle$. Then $F^i(\xi^*) = F^i(\xi)$, for $i = 2, \dots, r$. That is, if a country that is allocated nothing withdraws from the problem, the allocation of resources to the other countries should not change.[5]

5. *Scope.* The agency must adopt an allocation rule that will be applicable for a variety of problems it may encounter. It may, over the course of years, face many different budgets, many different prices that change the resource availabilities, and variations in the number of resources, their identities as well as their quantities. It can be expected that the technologies of the countries will change, and their rates of infant survival too. The *domain* (D) axiom states that the resource allocation rule the agency adopts should be capable of application to any possible problem ξ specified by arbitrary choice of n, for any convex set Ω in R^n_+, for any concave, monotonic, continuous functions $u^1, u^2, \dots, u^r$ defined on R^n, and any distribution $N^1, \dots, N^r$ of populations. The agency must also be able to solve problems for all r, such that $2 \le r \le \bar{r}$, for some integer $\bar{r}$.

---

[4] Indeed, the dimension of time is fabricated for this example, and may make CONRAD a less appealing axiom than it actually is. The axiom states that if the agency faces two problems that are related to each other in the manner of ξ and ξ^*, then it must allocate the $\mathbf{x}$-goods in the same way in both problems – there is no presumption that the agency faces ξ^* after it faces ξ. It should also be pointed out that the version of CONRAD stated here is stronger than what is actually required below for Theorem 1. CONRAD need only apply when the $\mathbf{y}$-goods have a special property: that they are completely country-specific in their use, that is, that each $\mathbf{y}$-good is useful to only one country. For further discussion of CONRAD, see Essay 7.

[5] This axiom is a very weak version of an axiom called stability in bargaining theory, introduced by Lensberg (1987).

Formally, let Δ be the domain of possible worlds on which the allocation rule is defined. Then for all $\{n, \Omega, (u^1, N^1), ..., (u^r, N^r)\}$ as specified, there exist $\Phi^1, \Phi^2, ..., \Phi^r$ such that $\xi \in \Delta$, where $\xi = \langle n, \Omega, (u^1, N^1, \Phi^1), ..., (u^r, N^r, \Phi^r) \rangle$.[6] This is a large class of possible worlds, but it consists of technologically reasonable ones. Some realism is imposed by requiring that the technologies be concave, monotonic functions of $\mathbf{x}$.

I should emphasize that the principles discussed in this section are not ethically mandatory, but rather ones that a sensible agency may impose upon itself. The monotonicity axiom, for example, may be justified on purely pragmatic grounds: if all countries contribute to the budget, it may not be politically feasible, in a democratic organization of countries, to reduce the allocation to some countries when the budget increases.

3.   Acceptable allocation rules

A resource allocation rule F is a function mapping any element ξ in the domain Δ into a feasible allocation. It is remarkable that the seven axioms discussed above suffice to determine a *unique resource allocation mechanism* on one domain $\tilde{\Delta}$, a sub-domain of problems of Δ defined precisely in the appendix of Roemer (1989).

Theorem 1: *Let a resource allocation rule, F, be defined on $\tilde{\Delta}$, and satisfy axioms PO, MON, S, IAI, CONRAD, DIC, and D. Then F must choose, for every problem ξ in $\tilde{\Delta}$, the distribution of resources that realizes the lexicographic egalitarian distribution of the rates of infant survival; that is, F is the leximin allocation rule.*[7]

Resources are allocated in the following way under the leximin rule. First, resources are allocated to the country with the lowest RIS until its RIS is raised to the RIS of the second lowest country. Then resources are used to raise the RISs of these two countries, until they become equal to the RIS of the third lowest country, etc. More generally, no resources are devoted to raising the RIS of a country until all countries with lower RISs have been raised either to its level, or, if that is impossible, as high as they can be.

In a sense, the axioms S, MON, CONRAD, and DIC appear to be weak restrictions on the behavior of the allocation mechanism, because they are all concerned with situations that hardly ever occur. How often must the agency deal with a problem in which all the countries are identical, as postulated by S? How often must it deal with a pair of problems that are identical in their technological descriptions, except that there are more

---

[6] The domain is more precisely defined in the unpublished appendix (available from the author) in which the theorem is proved, where the admissible technologies are discussed.

[7] The proof is available in the appendix of Roemer (1989).

resources in one problem than in the other (MON)? (One might take the problems in consecutive years to be of this form, if the budget has increased, but, to be precise, this is not exactly the case, because the technology functions change at least slightly from year to year.) And how much of a restriction is DIC, since it hardly ever occurs that the agency faces a problem in which some country will be allocated no resources? Similarly, CONRAD refers to only a very small class of pairs of problems, which bear a certain intimate relation to each other.

It would appear that the axioms can be seen as either quite weak, in the sense of the above paragraph, or as quite reasonable, or both. The domain axiom (D) is, however, strong, for it requires the agency to have a solution to problems that will never come up. The theorem claims to answer definitively the policy problem of the international agency. In the remainder of the paper, I discuss how salient this model and theorem are to the practice of one international agency.

4.   The World Health Organization (WHO)

WHO is an international organization with 166 member countries, which is affiliated to the United Nations, although it is a juridically separate organization. Its own World Health Assembly, which meets annually, is the supreme decision-making body. The budget of WHO comes from two sources, the first of which is the assessment of member countries. The United States, for example, is committed to supplying 25 per cent of the biennial budget of the organization.[8] The planned income from member assessments in 1986–7 was $543 million. Secondly, WHO relies on 'extra-budgetary sources', contributions from private philanthropic organizations in various countries, and other national governmental sources, which contribute money to specific programmes. These sources for the same budget period are estimated at $520 million. Thus, WHO operates on a biennial budget of approximately $1 billion.

WHO has a sequence of plans nested in time, which guide its operations. The World Health Assembly adopted a long-term strategy in 1981 for the 'attainment of health for all by the year 2000'.[9] The measures of health are defined with various degrees of precision by the organization. The most aggregate measures consist of twelve indicators, each defined as the number of countries in WHO that have achieved a certain degree of success with respect to a particular health indicator. For example, one such indicator is the number of countries in which at least 90 per cent of new-born infants have a birth weight of at least 2,500 grams. Others are:

[8] At the time of writing (1988), the Reagan administration is delinquent with its payments.
[9] The twenty-year strategy is summarized in World Health Organization (1981a).

the number of countries in which the infant mortality rate is below 50 per 1,000 live births; in which life expectancy is over sixty years; in which the adult literacy rate for men and women exceeds 70 per cent; in which the GNP per capita exceeds $500; in which safe water is available within fifteen minutes' walking distance; in which there is complete immunization against diphtheria, tetanus, whooping cough, measles, polio, and tuberculosis; and so on.[10] The next level of planning consists of a six-year plan. Finally, there are the biennial plans, which are specifically budgeted in the biennial budgets.

It is, therefore, a great oversimplification to model the problem of WHO as seeking to improve one indicator, such as the rate of infant mortality. Indeed, there are some fifty-four programmes in WHO, administered under twenty divisions of the organization.[11] There is no attempt to form a single objective function to aggregate the many indicators, which measure success, into one welfare measure.

As well as the programme or function dimension, there is an area dimension along which the operations and budget of WHO are disaggregated. The world is divided into six regions (Africa, the Americas, South-east Asia, Europe, the Eastern Mediterranean, and the Western Pacific), as well as a Global and Interregional category, which handles interregional programmes. Each region has a regional director (RD), appointed by the executive board in consultation with a regional committee. For each country, there is a WHO representative (WR), who represents the concerns of headquarters. Very briefly, the budget is negotiated as follows. First, only the regular budget – the budget from country assessments – is officially negotiated and allocated in this process. The secretariat proposes a division of the budget among the six regions and a global and interregional category. As will be seen below, this division is highly constrained by history. When the regular budget is virtually constant in real terms, as it has been during the 1980s, there is not much room for altering the division of the budget among regions from year to year. The regional allocation is followed by discussions between the regional committees of WHO and the governments in each region concerning the allocation

---

[10] These indicators may seem to be quite precise, but they are in fact quite broad. An example of a more precise health indicator, taken from a list of over a hundred such, is: the percentage of children in a country whose upper-arm circumference is no less than the value corresponding to the fifth percentile of the frequency distribution for well-nourished children. This physical measurement is apparently a sensitive indicator of malnutrition.

[11] There are divisions of environmental health, epidemiology, health education, communicable diseases, vector biology and control, mental health, health manpower development, non-communicable diseases, and so on. There are programmes in malaria control, parasitic diseases, immunization, diarrhoeal disease control, biomedical information, and so on.

of the regional budget among countries and among programmes. Each region compiles a regional budget. Officially, the regions have control of these decisions. Countries must request specific programmes. The important point is that, from an accounting point of view, the interregional division of the budget takes place first, in a centralized way, and the interprogramme division is secondary and decentralized to the regional level.

In terms of our model, it is clear that the relevant units are not countries, but regions of the world: this is the level of disaggregation that is relevant for budget decision-making at WHO headquarters.

WHO has had surprisingly little discussion of the general principles that should guide budget allocation.[12] There is, however, a clearly enunciated principle of monotonicity: 'the Director-General has sought to effect necessary reallocations by means of selective application of increases in available resources, without reducing the current level of allocation to any one region' (World Health Organization, 1979). In the same document, the question is raised whether it is possible objectively to quantify health needs, and, if so, whether or to what extent the allocation of WHO resources between regions should be guided by these factors. 'The definition of need is itself a subjective process, and it is not at all clear that criteria applicable to one population apply with equal force to all populations. The answer of the modern public health planner to the problem of allocation of resources would be to set up a mathematical model, using as objective, quantitative criteria as possible, but agreement on the parameters of such a model would be hard to reach.' It is admitted, however, that 'in view of the complexity of the matter and the great number of largely unquantifiable factors involved, it has been a matter of "feeling one's way" over the years in arriving at the allocations of WHO resources between regions' (p. 7).

In Table 12.1, the regular budget allocation among regions is presented for each biennial budget, beginning in 1978–9, calculated both in current prices and deflated prices, this last to make a real comparison with the previous biennial budget possible. It is important to note that only the regular budget is subject to this careful process, and the regularities that I discuss are observed only with respect to it. Note that the last period in which the regular budget increased in real terms was 1982–3. In the budgets of that and previous periods, there is monotonicity with respect to regions. The only deviation from monotonicity is in the treatment of the global and interregional budget, from 1978–9 to 1980–81, when this allocation fell from \$153 million to \$142 million in real terms. This fall was

---

[12] Officers of WHO whom I interviewed knew of only one document in which these principles were discussed, summarizing a meeting of the executive board held in 1979. The statements that follow are taken from that document.

Table 12.1. *WHO regular budget allocations by region by year*

	Africa	Americas	SE Asia	Europe	E. Med.	W. Pacific	Global and Interregional	Total
1988–9 (p = 86)[a]	98.9	57.9	68.8	33.6[b]	62.2	50.8	170.5	542.7
1986–7 (p = 86)	98.9	57.9	68.9	32.2[b]	62.2	50.8	172.4	543.3
1986–7 (p = 84)	90.1[b]	51.3	62.9	35.3	55.1	47.1	178.3	520.1
1984–5 (p = 84)	94.3[b]	50.8	61.3	35.2	53.8	46.1	178.5	520.1
1984–5 (p = 82)	82.9[b]	40.4	53.1[b]	32.6[b]	47.5[b]	38.3	172.6	467.4
1982–3 (p = 82)	81.3	44.0	52.9	32.3	45.6	39.1	172.8	468.9
1982–3 (p = 80)	70.7	37.6	46.8	24.0	41.1	34.4	182.3	436.9
1980–1 (p = 80)	68.1	37.5	45.0	23.8	39.7	33.0	180.2	427.3
1980–1 (p = 78)	61.3	31.7	40.3	21.2	35.3	29.8	141.9[b,c]	361.5
1978–9 (p = 78)	55.4	30.3	36.2	20.2	32.4	26.6	153.2[b]	354.3

[a] (p = 86) means in 1986 prices.   [b] Violation of monotonicity.   [c] Decreasing allocation to the secretariat, due to 1978 WHO resolution.
Source: Compiled from *Proposed Programme Budgets* (WHO, Geneva). Biennial budgets 1980–1 to 1988–9.

the consequence of a World Health Assembly decision in 1978 to cut back on the operations at headquarters, and to direct a larger fraction of resources to country programmes.

Beginning in 1984–5, the budget stagnated in real terms. In that period, when the real regular budget fell by $1.5 million, there were indeed violations of monotonicity. All regions should suffer a cutback, according to the monotonicity axiom, when the total budget is cut back;[13] but only the Western Pacific and the Americas region suffered, with the brunt being borne by the Americas. Upon further investigation, I was told that the apparent *large* fall in the Americas budget is due to an accounting procedure.[14] Nevertheless, some real fall must have been absorbed by the Americas region, since the total budget fell. The fall in the African real budget in 1986–7 is due to the same accounting practice. The only other violation of monotonicity occurs in 1988–9, when the European region is budgeted for a real increase, while other regions either experience no change or a slight decrease in their budgets, due to a small fall in the total real budget. But this turns out to be due to a reclassification of some global and interregional programmes to the European region.

Thus, the only clear violation of the monotonicity principle in these years is in the 1984–5 budget. Why does WHO seem to follow budget monotonicity in such strict fashion? From discussions with planners in the organization, it appears that this process is politically rather than ethically motivated. It would be difficult to cut the budget of any region, in an organization in which each region has political representation, and in which all regions contribute to the budget.

Although the motivation for budget monotonicity seems to be pragmatic, it is perhaps not coincidental that in many documents WHO expresses an egalitarian philosophy with regard to its project. 'At present, health resources are not shared equally by all the people: significant gaps still exist in many countries and health is the privilege of the few. Indicators should reflect progress toward correcting this imbalance and closing the gap between those who "have health" and those who do not' (World

---

[13] In fact, MON states that the RIS of no country should rise when the budget falls; throughout this discussion, however, I am taking the *budget allocation* to a region as the magnitude whose monotonicity is relevant. It is, of course, possible that the budget allocation to a region fall, while its RIS rises.

[14] Each region is asked to estimate the mark-up on its previous biennial allocation which is required due to changes in exchange rates alone. For the 1984–5 period, the Americas estimated a bigger mark-up than the secretariat was willing to grant. It would grant the mark-up only on the condition that the real budget allocation to the region would be proportionately reduced. Hence, the *nominal* allocation to the Americas was the same as it would have been with a slight increase in its real budget, had it not overestimated the mark-up, from the secretariat's point of view.

Health Organization, 1981: 12). To be sure, this statement refers to in-equality within a country, but the same egalitarian sentiment is expressed to apply across countries. As we have seen, monotonicity is closely linked with an egalitarian outcome, so the practice of monotonicity, if not ethically motivated, is serendipitous.

While monotonicity is observed at the regional level, it does not hold at the country level. There are many violations at the country level of disaggregation, which are mainly due to the lumpiness of programmes. When an immunization programme ends, for example, the allocation to the country may fall in the next period. These indivisibilities are not seen at the regional level, because there are, on average, twenty-eight countries per region.

How does the WHO budget allocation process conform to the other axioms? It is impossible to test for Pareto optimality, because we lack precise formulations of the functions which characterize the 'technologies' for the various countries. (Indeed, calculating such functions is not simply an engineering problem; it also involves deciding upon a social welfare function that appropriately aggregates the many different measures of health achievement.) It also seems impossible to test the symmetry axiom and the deletion of irrelevant countries axiom, because the situations described in the hypotheses of these axioms do not occur in practice. But it seems unconventional to claim that the planners would follow these axioms if the occasion arose.

With regard to the irrelevance of ancillary information, there is some evidence. Among the most important of considerations for planning a programme in a country is the 'probability of achieving successful and useful results, . . . a reasonable assurance from the government that the programme will be continued' (World Health Organization, 1979: 11). Whether a country will, with reasonable assurance, continue a programme is a characteristic not summarized in the technological information that describes it – although the function $u(\mathbf{x})$ does summarize how effectively the country uses resources. This must therefore count as a violation of IAI, although not, perhaps, an important one. I do not know how often this criterion comes into play in deciding upon the allocation of resources among countries, or how well correlated the 'reasonable assurance' trait is with the effectiveness of the technology u.

An apparent violation of IAI by WHO is that the Assembly voted, in 1947, to apply sanctions to South Africa, preventing it from voting in the World Health Assembly and from receiving assistance from WHO. This is tantamount *de facto* to excluding South Africa from membership in WHO; there is, however, no provision for explicit exclusion in the WHO constitution. Here is a case where a country is refused assistance because of aspects of its society that are not clearly reflected in its technology – that is, because of ancillary information. It is noteworthy that this is, in fact, no violation of IAI, because South Africa does not enter the specification of the budget allocation problem.[15] *Among its effective members,* WHO claims to make budget decisions using only the 'technological' and resource information about a country.

The allocation process conforms to the model in the respect that services and resources, not grants, are distributed to countries. Whether, however, resource allocation satisfies the consistency axiom (CONRAD) is difficult to judge – again, because it is difficult to imagine situations in which the axiom might actually act as a constraint on behaviour. Suppose the agency decides to allocate resources to regions in a certain way, given a problem with ten resources. Someone asks: if the agency faced a problem where the first five resources had already been allocated as the agency had decided they should be in the ten-resource problem, should it reconsider how the remaining resources are to be allocated? If the answer is 'no', then resource allocation is consistent in the sense that CONRAD requires.[16] I do not claim that CONRAD must be observed. It is certainly not a requirement of 'rational' budget planning, although planning will be 'inconsistent' without it.[17]

Let us suppose that there is some technology function for each region that, although unknown to the secretariat, is being maximized subject to the resources made available to the region. That is to say, although the planners are not able to articulate the functions $u^i(\mathbf{x})$, it is as if the problems they face are described in the form $\xi = \langle n, \Omega, (u^1, N^1), \ldots, (u^r, N^r) \rangle$. I have argued that it is reasonable to suppose that the axioms PO, S, MON, DIC, CONRAD, and IAI are being followed. Yet it is clear that the allocation rule is not the lexicographic egalitarian rule: even when there is a small increase in the total real budget, the resources allocated to all the areas are increased, while according to leximin, all the resources

---

[15] I thank Joshua Cohen of the Massachusetts Institute of Technology for this point.

[16] Recall the caveat that the CONRAD axiom does not actually have a time dimension. This is for heuristic purposes only.

[17] An example of an allocation rule that does not obey CONRAD is 'equal division Walrasian equilibrium'. Divide the available resources among countries as they would be allocated according to the Walrasian equilibrium from equal initial endowments of the resources, where countries are assumed to take their technologies as utility functions. While it would be difficult to claim this allocation mechanism is irrational, it is inconsistent. Suppose, for example, we begin with a problem with two resources, and we compute the equal division Walrasian equilibrium allocation. We now fix the first resource as it has been allocated, and ask, in the new one-resource problem, how will the equal division Walrasian equilibrium mechanism allocate the remaining resource? In general, the allocation will not be the same as in the original two-resource problem.

should be assigned to the region with the worst health status – this is perhaps Africa – until its health indicators are brought up to the level of the next worst region, perhaps South-east Asia. We can say this without knowledge of the particular technologies.

What may account for this apparent contradiction of the theorem is the domain axiom, which states that the allocation mechanism must be defined for 'all' possible problems. The WHO planners only have to produce an allocation every two years. In the period of a generation, they will face only twelve 'problems'. It is not difficult to allocate budgets, for twelve problems, which obey the six 'substantive' axioms listed above, but fail to conform to the leximin allocation rule. What we *can* say is that it is impossible to extend the budget rule that WHO has been using to the class of all possible problems it might face, while not violating some of the six substantive axioms. But this objection may seem pedantic, for the probability is almost zero that the organization will ever be forced into a violation of an axiom in any finite number of years. Discussion of this point is pursued in Section 5.3.

5.   Further evaluation

Three questions will be discussed: (1) the tension between egalitarianism and utilitarianism in WHO; (2) the appropriateness of the specification of the technologies in the model; (3) the domain assumption of the model.

5.1.   *Egalitarianism versus utilitarianism*

A prominent competitor of the leximin allocation rule is the population-weighted utilitarian rule, which distributes resources among countries in that way that maximizes the population-weighted sum of the regional (or country) rates of infant survival. Indeed, it can be verified that the utilitarian rule satisfies all the axioms of Theorem 1, except MON, and because of this our concentration on the observance of MON in the above discussion was not entirely innocent.[18] Note that population-weighted utilitarianism would, when faced with an allocation decision between two countries of the same population, assign the larger fraction of resources to the country whose health status would gain the most. In particular, it is well known that utilitarianism is insensitive to the initial statuses, $u^i(0)$; it takes into account only the rates at which the health indicators would improve under resource allocation.

---

[18] The population-weighted symmetry axiom S is satisfied by population-weighted utilitarianism. If unweighted utilitarianism were the rule, the appropriate symmetry axiom would have to be unweighted symmetry, which is blind to the population of countries. This is an indefensible axiom.

While in modern ethical theory utilitarianism, as applied to the allocation of goods among persons, is the subject of much criticism,[19] in the present context of health status among nations it is arguably quite an attractive alternative to leximin. To maximize the population-weighted sum of the country rates of infant survival is equivalent to *maximizing the total number of infant lives saved internationally.*[20] The difference between utilitarianism applied to persons and countries is this. Utilitarianism among persons treats each individual as a vessel for utility, but pays no attention to the boundaries, or rights, of the individual; utilitarianism with regard to countries treats each country as a vessel for health, but pays no particular attention to national boundaries, or the rights of countries. What in the first case violates conceptions that some of us hold about individual rights – about the ethically relevant boundaries between individuals – in the second ignores what some of us consider to be ethically irrelevant national boundaries.

The tension between population-weighted utilitarianism and lexicographic egalitarianism is observable in WHO. The stated goal of allocating resources to countries in which they will be most effectively used is utilitarian; the stated concern with egalitarianism suggests the leximin rule. In evaluating the achievement of various of the health indicators, stated in terms of the number of *countries* which have achieved certain levels, there is often a companion statement referring to the fraction of the world *population* that has achieved health: 'It will be seen that 98 countries, representing 62 per cent of the world population, have achieved a life expectancy of 60 years or more. . . . On the other hand, more than a quarter of [the countries], representing 29 per cent of the world population, still have rates [of infant mortality] above the level of 100 per 1000 live births' (World Health Organization, 1987: 70, 73).

The indicators that WHO has adopted, phrased in terms of the number of countries that have achieved specific levels of health status, are neither population-weighted utilitarian nor leximin. It will count more to lower the rates of infant mortality of several small countries over the threshold of 50 infant deaths per 1000 births than to lower the infant mortality rate of India from 100 to 80, although the second could save vastly more lives. By the same token, these indicators are not faithful to implementing leximin either. According to that objective, perhaps all the resources in the infant mortality programme should go to Sierra Leone, whose rate of infant mortality is the highest in the world.

---

[19] For example, see the essays in Sen and Williams (1982).

[20] Actually, this is only strictly true if the intervention of WHO does not affect the total number of births. If, for example, education about and distribution of contraceptives is one programme for reducing the rate of infant mortality, this will not necessarily be the case.

To maximize the number of countries whose rate of infant mortality is less than 50 per 1000, which is WHO's success indicator, one should proceed as follows. For each country i, calculate the cost, C_i, of bringing its RIS up to 950 per 1,000. Arrange the countries in order of these costs, so that C_1 is the lowest cost. Let M be the budget and let j be the largest integer such that $\sum_{i=1}^{j} C_j \leq M$. Then the budget should be spent entirely on countries 1 through j, to bring their rates of infant survival up to 950 per 1,000. This procedure, in particular, would usually mean not giving any resources to the worst off countries, so it is antithetical to leximin. On the other hand, it will tend to discriminate against large countries, because, other things being equal, they will require more resources to raise them up to the required rate – so it is quite antithetical to population-weighted utilitarianism. It is closest to an 'unweighted country utilitarianism', in the following sense. Define a new welfare indicator for each country, v^i. Let $v^i(\mathbf{x}) = 1$ if, with resources $\mathbf{x}$, country i has a rate of infant mortality of 50 or less, and $v^i(\mathbf{x}) = 0$ otherwise. Then maximizing the number of countries whose rates of infant mortality are 50 or less is equivalent to distributing resources to maximize $\sum v^i(\mathbf{x}^i)$. I will therefore call the policy that follows from this procedure 'modified unweighted country utilitarianism'.

I asked planners at WHO to what extent the secretariat was guided by trying to maximize the 'numbers of countries' indicators, and was told that these were rules of thumb, but were not observed when their maximization clearly involved ignoring the severe problems of large countries. I was told that the indices were 'indicators', not 'objectives'. Still, in a large and complex organization, where workers at the lower levels may take seriously the precise indicators of performance set by higher authorities, it may be the case that such indicators guide policy more literally than is intended.

There have been some examples in the recent history of WHO where resource allocation has been guided by unmodified unweighted country utilitarianism, but these examples seem to be isolated cases. Several years ago, it was decided to allocate a larger than usual amount of resources to certain countries – one was Sri Lanka – which were judged to be capable of showing fast and dramatic results. This move was a political one, whose intent was to demonstrate the potential impact of WHO programmes. Apparently, the policy was quickly discontinued.[21]

It is probably impossible to attain the WHO objective of Health for All by the Year 2000, by its own definitions of what constitutes health. Indeed, the slogan is put forth as a 'strategy'. That the organization follows in some cases a modified unweighted country utilitarian objective, sometimes a country egalitarian one, and sometimes a population-weighted

---

[21] I learned of this episode from Dr. Joshua Cohen of WHO.

utilitarian one is in part due to political considerations (in the World Health Assembly, each of 166 countries has one vote), and in part due to having no clearly enunciated second-best policy. The most general policy statements from the Director General tend to propose objectives which are impossible (such as health for all); their flavour, however, is decidedly egalitarian across people. For example: '*All* people in *all* countries should have a level of health that will permit them to lead a socially and economically productive life . . . It [the policy] does mean that there will be an even distribution among the population of whatever resources for health are available' (World Health Organization, 1981*a*: 31–2). If one tries to implement this policy by concentrating on the worst-off country first, one gets leximin; if one tries to maximize the number of people who approach the goal, one gets population-weighted utilitarianism. If one tries to set a particularly simple indicator, which can be measured with some precision, and which can be easily communicated to and understood by politicians, potential donors, and the public at large, one has a modified, unweighted country utilitarian policy.

5.2.   *Specification of the technologies in the model*

WHO distinguishes itself from the United Nations International Children's Emergency Fund (UNICEF) in that UNICEF provides materials and WHO provides technical assistance. (According to the organization, it 'engages in technical cooperation with its Member states'.) WHO intends to build up countries' technical expertise and health infrastructure, rather than to supply them with materials. In an immunization campaign, for example, WHO is concerned with building up local clinics and educating health personnel so that immunizations will take place every year. UNICEF supplies the vaccines. Although the WHO allocation is just a tiny fraction of the health budget for each country, its importance is understated by this figure, because of the organizational nature of the service that it provides.

This suggests that the model I have studied may be misspecified. It may be more accurate to model the WHO problem as the allocation of resources to *change* most effectively the technologies that the countries possess. Let U be the class of all possible technologies. We can represent the technology of technical change by a mapping $T: U \times R_+ \to U$, where R_+ is the set of positive real numbers, interpreted as follows: $T(u, y) = v$ means that expending y dollars can transform technology u into technology v. Suppose that 'conventional' resources, such as vaccines, are available in amount $\mathbf{x}$. Then the provision of 'technical assistance' in amount y by WHO has the effect of changing the RIS from $u(\mathbf{x})$ to $T(u, y)(\mathbf{x}) =$

$v(\mathbf{x})$. If we fix u, as it is fixed in a country, and recall that the set of available resources is Ω, then $T(u, y)(\mathbf{x})$ can be viewed as a mapping t_u from $\Omega \times R_+$ into R_+: $T(u, y)(\mathbf{x}) = t_u(\mathbf{x}, y)$. It may be appropriate to assume that t_u is *convex* and increasing in y and concave and increasing in $\mathbf{x}$.[22] The convexity in y follows from the fact that investment in the development of infrastructure may be best viewed as one of increasing returns to scale. The better the infrastructure is, the less costly it is to improve the 'technology' for transforming resources into a rate of infant survival. The function t_u is concave in $\mathbf{x}$, for with fixed y, t_u is just a normal 'technology'.

Suppose that the conventional resources to which a country has access are given – from the viewpoint of WHO. The conventional resource distribution among countries is $(\mathbf{x}^1, \mathbf{x}^2, \dots, \mathbf{x}^r)$. WHO has budget M. The technical change transformation T is given, and the technologies $u^1, u^2, \dots, u^r$ are given. Define, for any positive scalar y, $T(u^i, y)(\mathbf{x}^i) \equiv w^i(y)$. By our assumptions, w^i is a convex, increasing function of y. WHO's problem would then be summarized as $\epsilon = \langle M, (w^1, N^1), \dots, (w^r, N^r) \rangle$: that is, how to distribute a budget M as $M = \sum y^i$ among the countries. Instead of the resource allocation problem with concave functions studied in Sections 1–3, we face a budget allocation problem with convex functions.

The analysis of problems of the type ϵ will not be carried out here. Is the criticism against the concave model, in regard to the specification of the WHO problem, apt? I am not sure. The technical assistance that WHO provides to a country takes the form of supporting specific programmes. Within a programme, the technology may be properly characterized as one of decreasing returns to scale (concave). If we take the case of the rate of infant survival, for example, it is surely the case that at some level the functions u^i become concave: for a doubling of resources will not forever bring a doubling of the RIS.

5.3. *The domain assumption*

Even if the other axioms are followed by WHO in its resource allocation procedure, the domain axiom is not compelling, in the sense that the organization need only worry about efficiency, fairness, consistency, and so on, for a very small number of problems. Theorem 1 tells us that it is impossible to extend the resource allocation decisions that WHO has made over the past decade to a procedure which would be defined for every possible problem in the domain Δ, without violating at least one of the six substantive axioms. But is this not a foolish consistency to ask for?

---

[22] By increasing in y, I mean that if $T(u, y) = v$ and $T(u, y') = v'$, for $y' > y$, then for all $\mathbf{x}$, $v'(\mathbf{x}) \geq v(\mathbf{x})$.

The theory of resource allocation that I have presented depends, as does much of social choice theory and bargaining theory more generally, on the requirement that the allocation rule be defined for a large domain of possible problems. This axiom, in many circumstances, is justified not by the claim that, in the application at hand, all possible problems in the domain will eventually be encountered, but rather by the fact that one *does not know beforehand* which problems will be encountered, and so the allocation rule must be specified for all problems. But in WHO, and doubtless in most organizations, the allocation rule is not written down; the agency has the freedom to choose the allocation *after the problem has been specified*. With a history of a finite number of solved problems, it is almost always the case that when a new problem is introduced, the agency will have a great deal of latitude in proposing a solution for it, while not violating the substantive axioms that embody the agency's principles of resource allocation, within the set of problems that comprises recent history.

It is this difference in procedure, I think, that renders the formal theory of allocation mechanisms largely irrelevant for the study of practical policy. The domain axiom of the theory is most easily justified by the requirement – an unstated axiom – that the choice of mechanism must precede the specification of problems that are to be solved. In the real world, organizations have the freedom to specify the allocation after the problems are encountered. The use of mechanism theory to describe what resource-allocating agencies do must therefore be severely circumscribed.

My ambivalent thoughts are best phrased as a pair of questions: If WHO decides that it either should (e.g. consistency) or must (e.g. monotonicity) follow the substantive axioms, then, knowing that it will only encounter a small number of 'problems', should it nevertheless follow a leximin policy? (Alternatively, an axiomatic characterization of population-weighted utilitarianism could be derived, and a similar question posed.) Or should the planners feel that they are following the spirit of the general principles, even if the leximin rule is not followed, knowing that they can in all likelihood avoid any overt axiom violation for the foreseeable future? As a normative tool, at least, I think the axiomatic analysis is useful. Planners can perhaps gain insight about contrasting policies by understanding the axioms (such as monotonicity) that distinguish between them.

Public ownership and socialism

Introduction to Part IV

Essays 9 and 10 addressed the question: How should goods, and consequently welfare, be allocated when some productive assets are privately owned (labor) and some are publicly owned (technology)? Essay 13 begins by arguing that the economic theory of public ownership is poorly developed in contrast to the theory of private ownership, which, as summarized in general equilibrium theory, is perhaps the crowning achievement of the last two centuries of economic thought. Ideally, one would like to have a *positive* theory of public ownership, that is, a theory describing how resources will *actually* be allocated in an economy where some assets are publicly owned. But it would also be valuable to have a *normative* theory of public ownership, one which describes what sets of allocations in an economy seem consistent with the rights summarized in the specified pattern of ownership, when some assets are publicly owned and others are privately owned. The normative approach was taken in the essays in Part III mentioned above.

In Essay 13, which reports my joint work with Joaquim Silvestre, an economic environment consisting of a finite number of agents is postulated, where there is one technology (fishing on a lake) that produces one output (fish) from inputs of labor. Fishers have preferences over fish consumed and labor expended. It is postulated that the fishers *privately* own their labor, but the lake is *publicly* owned. What resource allocation mechanism respects these property rights? It is argued that, if there are constant returns to labor expended in fishing, then there is one natural solution to the problem: let each fisher spend as much time as she wishes fishing, and each keeps her catch. But when fishing on the lake is characterized by decreasing returns to labor, this "free access" solution is no longer desirable, as it leads to a Pareto inefficient outcome (the so-called tragedy of the commons). The essay proposes four resource allocation rules in this situation, each of which leads to a Pareto optimal solution, and each of which generalizes in a different way the free access solution from the case where returns to scale are constant. It can be argued that each of these rules is a normatively appealing way to allocate resources that respects the public and private property rights of the fishers.

Essays 14 and 15 argue that a variety of market socialism offers the best hope for egalitarian improvements in income distribution in our world at this time. While Essay 13 pursues a question of high theory, Essay 14 asks how, in actual economies, one might try to achieve a more equal income distribution than capitalism brings about without a large sacrifice in efficiency. It is argued that markets are required to achieve any degree of efficiency in complex economies, but that using markets does not preclude a distribution of profit income that is considerably more egalitarian than one finds in capitalist economies. The present generation of market-socialist models pays careful attention to the criticisms of market socialism made by Friedrich Hayek and Janos Kornai, among others.[1] As well, blueprints for market socialism now borrow techniques that capitalist economies have used to overcome the principal–agent problems which, arguably, were the cause of the economic failure of the centrally planned economies.

[1] For a discussion of the history of the idea of market socialism, see Roemer (1994).

On public ownership

1.   Introduction

From the vantage point of a late twentieth-century economist, a moment's reflection is required to recall that the concept of private ownership, for most of the last 2,000 years, has been primarily a *political* concept, defined by specifying the rights that individuals possess with respect to a thing. A person who privately owns a thing has, according to Roman law, the right to "use and abuse" it, and others are forbidden from using the thing. Over the millennia and across space, these rights have been modified to regulate the uses to which a person might put his property, because of negative or positive externalities to which some uses expose other persons.

The crystallization of economics as a science is well measured by the degree to which this political conception of private ownership was seen to imply certain economic behavior, and to imply that resource allocation in a society in which all resources were privately owned was more or less well determined. Suppose in medieval times we had asked a philosopher to describe the trajectory of resource allocation in an economy beginning from some initial position. Of course, it would be anachronistic to pose our question in the language of preferences, technology, and competition. Nor would the ideal type of a private ownership economy have been a useful model for the economic relations of the time. Assuming that we could communicate, the scholastic would probably have answered that "it all depends." The outcome of trade depends, he would mean, on how people exercise their various rights of ownership, which I conjecture would have been viewed as not intrinsically amenable to precise analysis. Developing the right language to discuss this question – that is, the concepts of preference, technology, self-interest, and endowment – was an intellectual accomplishment yet to come. For that language staked out a program whose claim was that these particular aspects of the human and social condition should be singled out from its potentially infinitely complicated description as the essential determinants of economic activity.

267

The answer is at hand when it becomes possible to ask our question as follows: Given a society in which all assets are privately owned, and in which preferences, technology, and endowments are specified as such and such, and in which there are many economic agents each of whom is very small, and in which preferences and technology are convex, and so on, what resource allocation will emerge? The language, indeed, summarizes the research program that specifies a proposal for what "it all depends" on.

Others are certainly more competent than I to speak about the history of the idea that the economic outcome in a society characterized by private ownership is more or less well determined. Schumpeter credits the jurist Grotius (1583–1645) with making a significant contribution in arguing that the validity of political and legal principles was natural, in the sense of being based on a general human nature, rather than contingent, in the sense of depending on the particular conditions of individual countries.[1] Hans Brems (1986) names Richard Cantillon, a French mercantilist, with first posing the economic problem as one of price and income determination in a system where the determining concepts include, as well as technology, the preferences of agents. Cantillon wrote his *Essai sur la nature du commerce en général* in 1730. Adam Smith further codified "the analytical proposition that free interaction of individuals produces not chaos but an orderly pattern that is locally determined."[2] Carl Menger was probably the first to locate a driving force, that resources flow to their most highly valued use: this formulation went further in separating the question of resource allocation from the vagaries of the exercise by various individuals of their political rights of private ownership.[3] (Of course, 'most highly valued use' presupposes the concept of utility.) The next great steps were taken by Walras, and then by von Neumann, Wald, Arrow, Debreu, and McKenzie.

The history of the "economicization" of the political concept of private property is not over. In fact, some (the Austrian school) view Walras as derailing Menger's insight that resources, in an economy of private ownership, flow to their most highly valued use. Walras rendered economic agents more impotent than they actually are, with his assumption

---

[1] Schumpeter (1954), p. 118.

[2] Schumpeter's characterization (1954), p. 185.

[3] See Menger (1954, originally 1871), p. 131. "If a good can be used for the satisfaction of several different kinds of needs, and if, with respect to each kind of need, successive single acts of satisfaction each have diminishing importance according to the degree of completeness with which the need in question has already been satisfied, economizing men will first employ the quantities of the good that are available to them to secure those acts of satisfaction, without regard to the kind of need, which have the highest importance for them."

of price-taking individuals. If individuals pursue self-interest, they will not be so passive, but each will squeeze all that he or she can out of the rest of society. This concept of the aggressively entrepreneurial individual has a parallel development, through Hayek and von Mises, to its contemporary crystallization in the work of Ostroy (1980). Makowski and Ostroy (1987) show that only for rare economic situations is there a final resource allocation that is consistent with the mutual exercise of self-interest by all parties. This conclusion brings with it an agnosticism concerning our ability to characterize economically the outcome of a political process. Abba Lerner's phrase, that economics earns its royal status in the social sciences by considering only solved political problems, is an apt characterization of the Walrasian program. But it is less apt as a description of the "Austrian" program, and the program of contemporary game theory, in which it seems clear that the right language has yet to emerge. Our battery of concepts – preference, rationality, self-interest – seems insufficient to solve the noncooperative bargaining problem. I think today an economist must say, when asked about the outcome of bargaining, with specified initial conditions, "it all depends." The language that will resolve this uncertainty will perhaps use words like 'norms', 'focal point', 'perception'.

With respect to the concept of public ownership, we are intellectually located, by analogy with private ownership, somewhere in the eighteenth century. If I describe an economy by specifying the preferences of the individual agents, the technology, the private endowments of individuals, and the public endowments of the community, and ask you what the outcome of economic activity will be, you would probably say "it all depends." Public ownership of a thing is, like private ownership, politically defined, by saying that the community has the right to use the thing as it decides. But we have no adequate theory to answer the question of what it will decide. For the individual in a private economy, the language of preference, rationality, and self-interest sufficed to provide an answer to the question how an individual decides to use his private property (at least in the well-behaved, classical atomistic economy). But these same concepts seem insufficient to solve the question of how a community of agents will decide to use its publicly owned property. We even have some reasons for agnosticism with respect to ever answering that question (the impossibility theorems of social choice theory); some would therefore say that public ownership is an inherently political concept, by which they mean that no basic principles of human behavior will ever crystallize to provide a general answer. This position is similar to the one criticized by Grotius in the seventeenth century, which is not to say that it is wrong.

There is a literature describing the behavior of publicly owned firms in capitalist economies, and, of course, of such firms in socialist economies.

The formal theory to date mainly concerns itself with the theory of pricing of the outputs of public firms.[4] In addition, there is the theory of public goods, which is not coextensive with the theory of public ownership, but has some intersection with it, as public goods may often be provided by publicly owned enterprises.[5]

My preface on private enterprise indicates, however, that I am here concerned with how an economy in which ownership rights are specified as private and public should allocate resources, a topic that is not expressly considered in this literature. J. Silvestre and I have worked on this question, and I will describe some of that work here. Readers who wish to pursue the topic further should consult Silvestre (in press a, in press b).

Before proceeding, I wish to say why I think this effort is important. It should be of interest to any economist to understand resource allocation in an economy with private and public property, simply because most economies are of this form. I have in mind, however, three specific applications that can attend such a theory.

First, there is the issue of decentralization of economic activity in socialist economies. The public ownership of the means of production has been viewed by many as coextensive with central planning and allocation by the state, an error that gives credence to the popular view that socialism is a dead letter because of the failures of central planning. Suppose there were a theory of resource allocation in a mixed economy. Formally, one would propose a resource allocation mechanism, similar to the Walrasian mechanism in a private economy, which would associate to each possible mixed economy an allocation of resources. This mechanism would embody the economic consequences in terms of resource allocation of the exercise of the public and private property rights in the economy in question. We could then ask, using the theory of implementation of allocation mechanisms,[6] Does there exist a way of decentralizing or "implementing" the allocation mechanism in question? Indeed, if the first seventy years of socialism can be characterized as the period of central allocation, the next seventy years will, I think, be called the period of decentralization.

Second, although we are currently in a period in which some public assets are being privatized in many capitalist economies, it is probably correct

---

[4] See D. Bös (1986) for a summary. I should emphasize that I am concerned not with the theory of provision of public goods, but with the theory of public enterprise, whether the goods produced are public or private.

[5] Here, perhaps the signal names in the formalization of a proposal for resource allocation are Lindahl (1919) and Foley (1970).

[6] I refer here to the theories of implementation of social choice rules in dominant strategies, in Nash equilibrium, and in Bayesian Nash equilibrium. For a summary, see the papers in Hurwicz et al. (1985).

to say that the twentieth century has been characterized as a time when certain important productive activities in capitalist economies have come under the aegis of public ownership. With a theory of public ownership, we could simulate the consequences of nationalizing various assets. Just as it is important to know what income distribution will attend a change in the tax laws, so it would be important to know the effect of the nationalization of the steel and automobile industries.

Third, there are certain thought experiments that are important in our normative evaluation of capitalism and socialism that cannot be carried out without a well-defined procedure for calculating the resource allocation in a mixed public economy. The most serious attempt in contemporary political philosophy to justify capitalist property relations is put forth in the work of Robert Nozick (1974), who begins with the premise that, in the original position that is appropriate for thinking about distributional justice, persons should be taken as privately owning their own labor, while no one owns the resources of the external world. He proceeds to provide rules under which the private appropriation of external resources by persons is legitimate, and in this way finally justifies a society in which the entire external world is legitimately owned by individuals, perhaps in very unequal amounts. Recently, political philosophers G. A. Cohen (1986) and James Grunebaum (1987) have challenged Nozick by arguing against the defensibility of the premise that the external world should be taken as initially unowned. Why, after all, should one not suppose that the external world, which is owned by no one individually in its pristine state, is owned by everyone?[7] Cohen asks, What would be the income distribution if, initially, the external world were jointly or publicly owned by all persons, who individually own their own labor power? With an economic conception of resource allocation in a mixed public and private economy, one could answer this question. How much would differential skills and talents, which come with privately owned labor, influence income distribution if the external world's resources were publicly owned?

2.   A simple model of a mixed economy[8]

I will illustrate various conceptions of resource allocation in a mixed economy by using a three-good model. Fish are produced from individuals working on a publicly owned lake, utilizing their privately owned

---

[7] A further discussion of the approaches of political philosophers on this issue is in Moulin and Roemer (1989), which also pursues an economic approach to resource allocation in a mixed economy that is not further described in the present essay.

[8] This section, except for 2C, summarizes Roemer and Silvestre (1987); 2C summarizes material in Roemer (1987).

labor. We represent such an economic environment as $\xi = \langle u^1, u^2, ..., u^n;$ $\omega^1, ..., \omega^n; f \rangle$, where $u^i(L, Y)$ is a utility function representing the preferences of the ith fisher for labor and fish, ω^i is the fisher's endowment of the private good (labor), and $f(L) = Y$ is the production function that describes the conversion of labor into fish on the lake. Thus, the publicly owned lake does not explicitly appear in the representation ξ; its proxy is the production function f, which is taken to be known by all. A *feasible allocation* for ξ is a vector $((L^1, Y^1), ..., (L^n, Y^n))$, where $L^i \leq \omega^i$, $f(L) \geq Y$, $L := \sum L^i$, and $Y := \sum Y^i$. What feasible allocations of fish and labor are consistent with private ownership by the fishers of their labor and their public ownership of the lake, or here, the technology?

A.   *Common ownership*

Before proposing an answer, it is useful to distinguish between what public ownership of the technology might entail, and what is entailed by its *common ownership*. I define common ownership to be the situation where every individual has the right of free access to the resource in question. Clearly, this differs from private ownership; what I mean to underscore is that it differs from public ownership as well. We have an accepted conception of the economic consequences of common ownership: it is the resource allocation associated with the Nash equilibrium(-a) of the game in which each agent optimally decides upon his or her labor contribution on the commons given the amounts of labor the others are contributing. Formally, the feasible allocation $\zeta = ((\hat{L}^1, \hat{Y}^1), ..., (\hat{L}^n, \hat{Y}^n))$ is a *common ownership allocation* if for each i, the following hold:

(C1) $\hat{L}^i / \hat{Y}^i = \hat{L}^j / \hat{Y}^j$ for all $i, j = 1, n$, and $f(\sum L) = \sum Y$.

(C2)   For each i, and for all $\tilde{L}^i$, $u^i(\hat{L}^i, \hat{Y}^i) \geq u^i(\tilde{L}^i, \tilde{Y}^i)$, where $\tilde{Y}^i = (\tilde{L}^i / \tilde{L}) f(\tilde{L})$ where $\tilde{L} = \tilde{L}^i + \sum_{j \neq i} \hat{L}^j$.

(C1) asserts that, in a common ownership allocation, the fish are distributed in proportion to labor expended on the lake. This is due not to any ethical principle, but to the fact that each fisher is equally skilled and equally lucky, and hence the distribution of fish is proportional to time spent on the lake. (C2) says that the best strategy for fisher i, given the labor contributions of others, is $(\hat{L}^i, \hat{Y}^i)$.

It is well known that if preferences are quasi-concave and f is concave then a common ownership allocation, so defined, exists. If f is strictly concave, then the allocation is Pareto suboptimal: hence, the "tragedy of the commons." Each fisher fishes "too much," because he does not take into account the negative externality that his fishing imposes upon others, owing to the decreasing marginal productivity of labor on the lake.

There is one case in which free access does not result in Pareto ineffi-ciency, when the production function is linear, $f(L) = \alpha L$, for some real positive number α. If f is linear, designate the economic environment $\xi = \langle u; \omega; \alpha \rangle$, where $u = (u^1, \ldots, u^n)$ is the profile of utility functions and $\omega = (\omega^1, \ldots, \omega^n)$ is the vector of labor endowments. In a linear environ-ment ξ, the labor that others expend has no effect on the productivity of an additional unit of labor, and so each agent decides how much she wants to work at the effective wage rate of α fish per unit of labor. The Nash equilibrium is efficient.

In a linear economy ξ, the free-access allocation is the compelling can-didate for resource allocation in a mixed economy. For each chooses how much of his privately owned labor to expend on the publicly owned tech-nology, all labor is remunerated equally, and no fisher affects the oppor-tunities of any other.

B.   The proportional correspondence[9]

One might view public ownership of the lake as an institution that emerges when the fishers attempt to resolve the suboptimality of common owner-ship, when the technology is not linear. As well as achieving a Pareto effi-cient allocation, they might also wish to preserve the proportionality of labor to fish in the allocation: for, since all labor is equally productive, it seems fair that each fisher receive fish in proportion to his effort.[10] In a linear economy, these two properties hold at the common ownership solution.

Define a *proportional allocation* ζ of labor and fish, for any environ-ment ξ, as one in which (C1) holds and

(P2) ζ is Pareto efficient.

It is not obvious that a proportional allocation exists for any economic environment ξ. We have:

Theorem 1: *Let* $\xi = \langle u; \omega; f \rangle$ *be an economic environment in which the preferences* u *are monotonic and quasi-concave and* f *is concave. There exists a proportional allocation.*

The proof of Theorem 1 is a fixed point argument. In general there are several proportional allocations for a given convex environment ξ, as

---

[9] For a formal and more general presentation of the results in this section, see Roemer and Silvestre (1993).

[10] One can rewrite the model so that fishers have equal endowments of labor, but their la-bor is of different skill levels. In this case, the private ownership of labor would be inter-preted to imply that fish be distributed in proportion to units of effective labor expended. See Essay 10.

there are generally several Walrasian equilibria in a private ownership economy. Because of the existence Theorem 1, we may speak of the *proportional correspondence,* which chooses for each convex economy ξ its proportional allocations. This is our first proposal for an allocation mechanism that represents the economic consequences of mixed property rights that characterize the economies in question.

Proposing the proportional correspondence as a solution to the problem of resource allocation in a mixed economy is not based upon deducing the laws that govern the behavior of state agencies, or of democratic polities in the act of deciding how to exercise their property rights in a publicly owned asset. Its spirit is more normative. A thoroughly positive solution to the problem would, it seems, require a solution to the many-person bargaining problem of how a society will resolve to use the publicly owned asset, given the preferences and private endowments of its members. In this, the "solution" proposed lacks some of the appeal of the Walrasian solution to resource allocation in a private ownership economy. It can be said, however, that a compelling normative proposal may influence the solution that society adopts. Society may decide that the public and private property rights of individuals require that each be paid in fish in proportion to the labor he contributes to fishing.

In a proportional allocation, the entire product is distributed to the members of society in proportion to their contributions of the private input. There is no "return" to the publicly owned asset, in the sense that there would be were the lake a privately owned asset in a capitalist economy. Of course, the lake remains just as productive as it would be in a private ownership economy, but the accounting is different. Because the proportional allocation is not the free access allocation (except for linear economies), it cannot be achieved without regulation. Nor, in the non-linear case, can it be decentralized, or implemented, by the public authority offering a fixed wage of fish in terms of labor, and accepting all the labor that is offered.

The idea of a proportional allocation can be generalized to economic environments with many goods and firms, which may be either privately or publicly owned. A proportional allocation is defined to be a Pareto efficient allocation in which the outputs from publicly owned enterprises accruing to individuals are proportional in value to their contributions of private inputs, where goods are evaluated at the efficiency prices that support the allocation.

We can gain further insight into the proportional allocation. In an environment $\xi = \langle u; \omega; f \rangle$ where u is a profile of quasi-concave utilities and f is concave, every Pareto efficient solution is achievable as a Walrasian equilibrium with respect to some private distribution of the assets. Is there an initial private distribution of property rights in the "firm" that operates the technology that generates as its Walrasian equilibrium the proportional allocation, when each person retains private ownership of his labor?

Theorem 2: *Let* $\zeta = ((L^1, Y^1), \ldots, (L^n, Y^n))$ *be a proportional allocation for* $\xi = \langle u; \omega; f \rangle$. *Let* $\gamma^i = L^i/L$, *where* $L = \sum L^i$. *Then* ζ *is a Walrasian equilibrium associated with the private ownership economy where each agent owns a share* γ^i *of the profits of the fishing enterprise.*

A proportional allocation has this property: it is as if the public fishing enterprise were privately owned by the fishers, the share of the profits belonging to a fisher being equal to his share of the input contributed.

C. *The Nash dominator correspondence*

Imagine that, before public ownership is adopted in a society whose economic environment is $\xi = \langle u; \omega; f \rangle$, common ownership prevails, that is, the Nash equilibrium allocation discussed in Section 2A. If the fishers meet to solve the tragedy of the commons, it might be proposed that, whatever solution is adopted, each fisher should be at least as well off as he is under common ownership. The gains from cooperation should be distributed to all. Unfortunately, the proportional correspondence does not have this property, in general. However, there is an easily definable correspondence that does.

Let $\tilde{\zeta} = ((\tilde{L}^1, \tilde{Y}^1), \ldots, (\tilde{L}^n, \tilde{Y}^n))$ be a common ownership allocation. Let $\sigma^i = \tilde{L}^i/\tilde{L}$. Let ζ be a Walrasian equilibrium where fisher i is assigned a share σ^i in the profits of the fishing enterprise. ζ is called a *Nash dominator allocation,* because of the following theorem.

Theorem 3: *Let* $\tilde{\zeta}$ *be a common ownership allocation, and let* σ^i *be fisher i's labor share at* $\tilde{\zeta}$. *If* ζ *is a Walrasian allocation derived from private distribution of shares* σ^i *in the public firm, then* ζ *is Pareto efficient and Pareto superior to* $\tilde{\zeta}$.

ζ is Pareto efficient, of course, because it is a Walrasian equilibrium. Call the mapping that associates to each environment ξ its Nash dominator allocations the *Nash dominator correspondence.* It is important to distinguish between the characterization of the proportional correspondence in Theorem 2 and this characterization of the Nash dominator correspondence. In the former, it is as if property rights were distributed to fishers to reflect their share of labor expended in the allocation itself; in the latter, it is as if property rights were distributed to reflect "historical" labor shares, from the era of common ownership.

It is not difficult to generalize the concept of common ownership of some resources and technologies to an economy with many goods and firms, some of which may be privately owned. The analog of the Nash dominator correspondence can likewise be defined. However, the correspondence no longer possesses its essential property, of Pareto dominating the common ownership equilibrium. The possibility of trading privately produced goods against the ones produced on commonly owned technologies destroys that property. This severely limits the usefulness of the Nash dominator mechanism as an implementation of public ownership.

D.   *The equal division correspondence*

A third candidate for an allocation mechanism in a mixed economy is the *equal-division-Walrasian-equilibrium correspondence,* which assigns the Walrasian equilibrium(-a) associated with the private ownership economy in which each fisher owns an equal share in the profits of the enterprise, and his own labor endowment. This allocation is justified by a view that maintains that a person has a right to benefit from the publicly owned asset by virtue of his citizenship, rather than his contribution. Of course, we have:

Theorem 4: *If ξ is an economic environment with quasi-concave utilities and concave technology, then an equal division allocation exists.*

In Roemer and Silvestre (1987), the equal division correspondence is characterized as providing *equal benefits* to all citizens, in the following sense. At the efficiency prices that support an equal division allocation, the difference between the value of the consumption bundle (of leisure and fish) and the value of the initial endowment of leisure is equal for all agents.

As with the first two allocation correspondences, the equal division correspondence can be defined for economic environments with many goods and private firms as well as public ones. It is as if each agent were given her per capita share of the profits of every public enterprise.

If a public firm is characterized by increasing returns to scale, then it is still possible to define an equal benefits allocation which is Pareto efficient, by using the definition of benefits provided above. An equal benefits allocation, however, may fail to exist. In such an allocation there is marginal cost pricing and the firm incurs a loss, which is divided equally among the citizens, whether or not they contribute inputs or consume the output of the public firm. (Similarly, in a firm that has a concave technology, every citizen shares in the profits of the firm, whether or not he has any other economic relationship with the firm.) This might seem to

be normatively unattractive when compared to the proportional allocation, in which only those who trade with the firm are "taxed" to cover the
loss in the case of increasing returns. If a firm with increasing returns to
scale trades at marginal cost prices (as it does in an equal benefits or proportional allocation), then those who sell labor to the firm benefit from
the high wages it pays, and this seems to justify their sharing in the firm's
loss. Similarly, those who purchase output from such a firm gain from its
low product price. But in the equal benefits allocation, citizens must share
in the loss even if they do not trade with the enterprise.

E.   *The linear equivalent correspondence* [11]

The three conceptions of resource allocation discussed thus far are motivated by static considerations only. Perhaps the simplest kind of dynamic
consideration to introduce as a characteristic of economic environments
is technical change, which, in an environment $\xi = \langle u; \omega; f \rangle$, appears as a
change in f. It seems reasonable to propose as a desideratum in a mixed
economy that no agent suffer as a result of technical progress in a publicly
owned industry. If the technology is publicly owned, all agents should
share in the gains made possible by an improvement in f.

Let F be an allocation mechanism that assigns to each economic environment ξ an allocation, $F(\xi)$. Let $u(F(\xi))$ represent the vector of utilities, in R^n, at the allocation $F(\xi)$. Then this property of an allocation
mechanism can be stated as:

Technological monotonicity axiom: Let $\xi = \langle u; \omega; f \rangle$, $\xi^* = \langle u; \omega; f^* \rangle$,
where for all L, $f^*(L) \geq f(L)$. Then $u(F(\xi^*)) \geq u(F(\xi))$.

For the axiom of technological monotonicity to make sense, we require
that the allocation correspondence F be essentially a function, that is,
that the mapping $u(F(\xi))$ be single-valued in utility space. This is the reason that I wrote above that F choose *an* allocation.

To state the next result, it is necessary to be precise concerning the domain of economic environments. Let Σ^{DR} be the set of all economic environments ξ for n agents, where the profile u consists of quasi-concave,
monotonic utility functions, ω is any nonnegative vector in R^n, and f is a
continuous, increasing function, with $f(0) = 0$ which enjoys nonincreasing returns to scale (i.e., $f(L)/L$ is nonincreasing). Let Σ^{IR} be the domain
defined as above, except that f enjoys nondecreasing returns to scale.
Note that the linear economies $\langle u; \omega; \alpha \rangle$ constitute the intersection of
Σ^{DR} and Σ^{IR}. Let Σ be the class of economic environments with no scale
restrictions on f.

[11] This mechanism is the one described in Essay 10.

I argued in Section 2A that, whatever public ownership in a mixed economy entails, it should at least assign, in the linear economic environments, the free-access allocation. We have the following:

Theorem 5: *There is a unique allocation mechanism, F, that is defined on Σ^{DR}, is Pareto optimal, assigns the free-access allocation on the linear economies, and satisfies the axiom of technological monotonicity. F is called the linear equivalent allocation mechanism.*[12]

Theorem 5 is true as well if Σ^{DR} is replaced by Σ^{IR} or by Σ.

The linear equivalent allocation mechanism acts as follows, on a given economic environment $\xi = \langle u; \omega; f \rangle$. Consider the family of linear economies $\{\xi_\alpha = \langle u; \omega; \alpha \rangle \mid \alpha \geq 0\}$, for fixed (u, ω). We know that $F(\xi_\alpha)$ is the free-access allocation on the linear economy ξ_α. For small positive α, $F(\xi_\alpha)$ is strictly Pareto dominated by some Pareto efficient allocation in ξ. For large enough α, $F(\xi_\alpha)$ strictly Pareto dominates some efficient allocation in ξ. There is exactly one α with the property that $F(\xi_\alpha)$ is Pareto indifferent to some efficient allocation in ξ. Define $F(\xi)$ as that allocation. Alternatively put, the locus $u(F(\xi_\alpha))$ in utility space, as α increases from 0 to infinity, describes a monotone increasing path, which intersects the Pareto frontier of ξ in utility space in one point. $F(\xi)$ is defined as the allocation in ξ that induces that utility allocation.

For an environment ξ that has a nonlinear production function, the free-access (common ownership) allocation is Pareto inefficient. The linear equivalent allocation is so named because it chooses that efficient allocation in ξ that is Pareto indifferent to the allocation that the same agents would have chosen in some linear economy under common and public ownership.

The linear equivalent mechanism is only defined in the one-input-one-output world. This is its serious limitation.

F.   Simulations

These four allocation correspondences were calculated for a collection of two-person economic environments, where the parameters describing the utility functions, the production function, and the endowments of the private good were varied to form an array of 22 economies.[13] Figures 13.1–

---

[12] Proved in Roemer and Silvestre (1987). Essentially the same theorem is proved in Moulin (1987).

[13] Utility functions are $u^1(L, Y) = (\omega - L)^a Y^{1-a}$, $u^2(L, Y) = (1 - \omega - L)^b Y^{1-b}$; the production function is $f(L) = (.5L)^c$. Total labor endowment is normalized at 1, with the first agent's endowment being ω, and the second agent's $(1 - \omega)$. Thus, an economic environment is described by a parameter vector (a, b, ω, c). Twenty-two values of this vector were chosen.

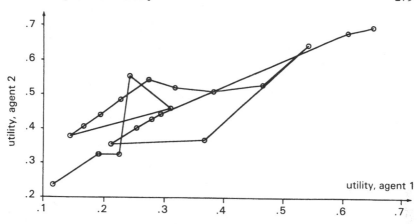

Figure 13.1. The equal division allocation: 22 economies

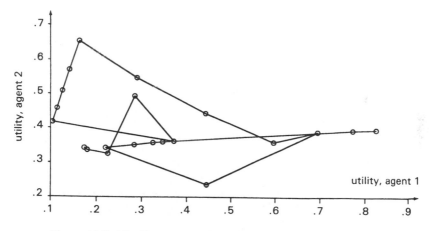

Figure 13.2. The linear equivalent allocation: 22 economies

13.4 plot, for each mechanism, the utility allocation for both agents. There is no particular significance to the choice of the 22 economies in the sample; the plots are useful only insofar as they illustrate the degree of similarity among the mechanisms. Although three of the allocation correspondences are not in general single-valued in utility space, for the chosen economies they are.

Two observations stand out: the equal division allocation is markedly different from the others, and the proportional and linear equivalent allocations are very close to each other in utility space. Indeed, simulations were run with a variety of other specifications for the utility functions,

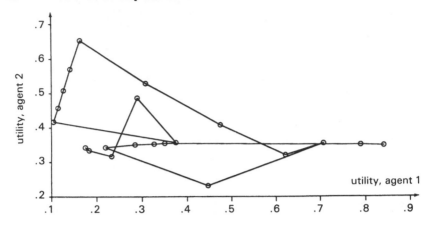

Figure 13.3. The proportional allocation: 22 economies

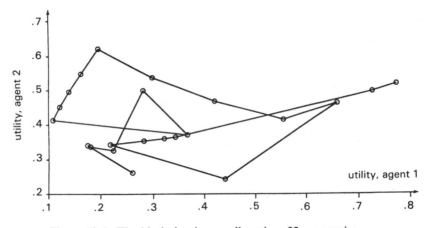

Figure 13.4. The Nash dominator allocation: 22 economies

and the similarity between the proportional and linear equivalent allocations remained. Although the linear equivalent mechanism does not generalize to economies with many goods, we can view the proportional allocation mechanism, which does generalize, as some kind of close proxy for it.

The simulations verify some natural intuitions. In the economies numbered 16, 17, 18, 19, 5, 20, and 21 (read the order of the economies by "following the dots," starting at the endpoint closer to the origin), the second agent has a strong preference for leisure compared to the first agent. In these seven economies, the production function improves steadily, while the traits of the agents remain unchanged. In the proportional allocation, note that the first agent gains a great deal in utility, while the second agent's utility barely changes. Only the first agent gains because of technical progress, as only he invests more labor. In contrast, the equal division allocation gives rise to large utility gains for both agents. The "lazy" agent profits from the labor of "industrious," by virtue of his property right to one-half of the enterprise profits.

G. *Summary*

The considerations that led to the proposal of these four allocation mechanisms as ways of respecting the agents' private property in their labor and their public ownership of the technology, can be summarized as follows. We insist, to begin, that any proposal for resource allocation must be Pareto efficient, and coincide on the linear economies with the free-access allocation. There is, so to speak, one degree of freedom left. We can insist that output be distributed in proportion to input contribution, that every agent gain in the thought experiment that imagines passing from common to public ownership, that every citizen have an equal share in the profits from the public technology, at efficiency prices, or that every agent gain as a result of technical progress as it affects the public technology. These four considerations give rise, respectively, to the proportional, Nash dominator, equal division, and linear equivalent mechanisms.[14] Unfortunately, on the domain of convex economies, these allocation rules all differ. The allocations assigned by these rules coincide only in two cases: when the economic environment is linear, and when all agents are identical (for all i, j, $(u^i, \omega^i) = (u^j, \omega^j)$).[15]

3. Implementation

Do there exist decentralized mechanisms by which planners can implement the proposed allocation mechanisms for a mixed economy that we have discussed? This question can be studied using the theory of implementation of social choice correspondences in Nash equilibrium, due to Maskin (1977, 1985), and the theory of implementation of economic allocation mechanisms in dominant strategies due to Makowski and Ostroy (1992). In the next subsection, I briefly review the former theory in the context of our problem, and then apply it in the the following subsection.

---

[14] The proportional, equal division, and linear equivalent mechanisms are characterized by these considerations, respectively; this is not the case with the Nash dominator mechanism. There are other mechanisms that are Pareto efficient and Pareto dominate the common ownership allocation, though the definition of Nash dominator correspondence has a nice justification in terms of property rights.

[15] Moulin (1990) proposes a different set of axioms and characterizes the proportional, equal division, and linear equivalent mechanisms using those axioms.

A.   *Nash implementation*

The planner faces some economic environment ξ; assume that she knows the technology f, but does not know the profile of individuals' characteristics, (u, ω), which could be drawn from among all possible profiles, as discussed in Section 2. The domain of economic environments she faces we may call $\Sigma^f := \{\langle u; \omega; f \rangle | u$ is a quasi-concave profile, $\omega \in R^n_+\}$. She wishes to implement some allocation correspondence F defined on Σ^f, which assigns to any $\xi \in \Sigma^f$ a feasible allocation in ξ. The planner proposes a game form $G = [S^1, S^2, ..., S^n; \varphi]$ where S^i is the strategy set of agent i, and φ is a mapping that associates to any n-tuple of strategies $s = (s^1, ..., s^n)$ an allocation $\varphi(s) = ((L^1, Y^1), ..., (L^n, Y^n))$ in R^{2n}. The allocation $\varphi(s)$ is not necessarily feasible in ξ, the actual environment, because the planner does not know the true ω. (She can only calculate the true feasible set when she knows ω, as well as f.) Nevertheless, $u^i(L^i, Y^i)$ is defined for each i. Therefore G induces a game among the players, because to each strategy n-tuple s there is associated a utility for each player. We say that G *implements the allocation correspondence* F if, when s^* is a Nash equilibrium of the game described, $\varphi(s^*) \in F(\langle u; \omega; f \rangle)$, where (u, ω) is the true profile of traits. Alternatively, we can insist on the apparently stronger requirement that $\{\varphi(s^*) | s^*$ is a Nash equilibrium of the game$\} = F(\langle u; \omega; f \rangle)$.

The interpretation of G as a method of decentralizing economic allocation is this. G is an institution, a set of rules, which, if followed by the agents, will implement the desired resource allocation $F(\xi)$, for any environment ξ, without the planner having to know their preferences and endowments. The planner's role is, first, to design the game form G. The authority of society must then be invoked to assure that the population participates – that is, that its members announce strategies in S^i. It is presumed that they announce, or arrive at, Nash equilibrium strategies, s^*. The function of the planning agency is to announce $\varphi(s^*)$. Some enforcement procedure is then required to get each agent to offer the labor he is assigned in $\varphi(s^*)$, and to distribute the product as it is assigned in $\varphi(s^*)$. Indeed, one of the serious problems in actual socialist economies is finding an enforcement procedure to do this last part, a problem that is not addressed by this theory.[16]

---

[16] This story may help. The planner knows neither the preferences nor the labor endowments of the fishers. She designs a game that enables her to calculate a social allocation of labor and fish, which, according to construction, is indeed the allocation $F(\xi)$ she wants to implement. But now the fishers must fish the number of hours assigned to them in this allocation. It may be foggy on the lake, and the planner can't see whether the fishers are in fact fishing according to the schedule. The theory of Nash implementation does not address the foggy day problem.

B.   *Implementation of public ownership in Nash equilibrium*

Maskin (1977, 1985) provides a necessary and sufficient condition for the implementability of a resource allocation correspondence in an economic environment, and using this condition, one can check which of the four allocation correspondences proposed as solutions to the allocation problem in a mixed economy can be implemented.

Theorem 6: *The proportional allocation and equal division correspondences can be implemented in Nash equilibrium. The Nash dominator and linear equivalent allocation correspondences cannot be.*

Nevertheless, there is a fairly appealing way to implement the linear equivalent mechanism, due to Moulin (1990), as a subgame perfect equilibrium of a game that the players play in two stages.

Recalling that the Nash dominator correspondence was just one of many correspondences that Pareto dominate the common ownership allocation of ξ, we should inquire whether any member of that class can be implemented in Nash equilibrium.

Theorem 7: *No allocation correspondence that is Pareto efficient and Pareto dominates the common ownership equilibrium can be implemented in Nash equilibrium.*

This theorem has an interesting application to the debate among political philosophers concerning the justification of a private property system. Robert Nozick (1974), the central proponent of the ethical justifiability of capitalist property relations, constructs an argument for private property, which I have translated into the language of allocation mechanisms elsewhere (Roemer, 1989a). The gist is this. Nozick asserts that it is necessary to justify the original private appropriation of natural resources that, in some initial state, were in common use by all. Such appropriations are justifiable, he argues, if and only if the allocation of resources after private appropriation renders every agent at least as well off as he was prior to appropriation. In the present language, an allocation correspondence that summarizes the results of private appropriation from nature is acceptable if and only if it produces an outcome that Pareto dominates the common ownership allocation. If it is the case that such an allocation is efficient, Theorem 7 says that it is not decentralizable in the sense that Nash implementation makes precise. Now Nozick, and other advocates of private property, argue that a virtue of laissez-faire *is* its efficiency: if true, then the premise of Theorem 7 holds, and the impossibility of assuring, by decentralized means, that the outcome satisfies Nozick's proviso, follows. That is, society can never propose a set of rules or a constitution (a game form G) which, if followed by its members, is efficient and always results in Nozick-acceptable private appropriations. Ironically, an interventionist state – one that does more than design a constitution G – is necessary to guarantee the ethical acceptability of private appropriations in an efficient laissez-faire economy! For Nozick, who argues for a minimal state, this must be a problematic conclusion.

The important caveat in the discussion of Nash implementation is the link between practical methods of decentralizing economic activity and the theory of Nash implementation. The agents must be extremely knowledgeable and capable of complex reasoning to play the games that they are required to play in the theory. In particular, (1) each agent must know the traits of some other agents (although the planner need know none of these), (2) each agent must announce a profile of traits for the whole society as his strategy (i.e., the strategy spaces S^i are sets of high dimension),[17] and (3) calculating an agent's optimal strategy is complex. Point (2) is furthermore objectionable in a democratic society, in which a planning agency does not have the authority to compel an agent to report on the traits of others.

The theory of implementation in dominant strategy equilibrium, to which we now proceed, avoids at least problems (1) and (2).

C.   *Implementation in dominant strategies*

Let U be the class of possible utility functions, and $U^* = U \times R^1$. Given an allocation correspondence F defined on Σ^f, is there a game form $G = [U^*, U^*, ..., U^*; \varphi]$, which, with the profile (u, ω), induces a game whose dominant strategy equilibria implement the correspondence, that is, whose dominant strategy equilibria induce under φ the allocations that the correspondence F chooses for the true profile of the economy?[18] We can further ask whether there is such a game in which the dominant strategy of player i is to announce his true characteristics (u^i, ω^i). If so, then objections (1) and (2) raised against the cogency of Nash implementation do not apply here; objection (3) may, as it may still be difficult for the player to calculate that his dominant strategy is to tell the truth. The planner can, however, publicly announce that truthful reporting is the optimal strategy for each agent, and this should help.

[17] Corchón and Ortuño-Ortin (in press) have recently weakened this requirement, so that each agent need only know the preferences of one another.

[18] It turns out that restricting the game form to using the strategy space U^* for each agent is no restriction; if an allocation mechanism can be implemented in dominant strategies with some abstract strategy space for each agent, then it can be implemented with a game form in which the strategy space for each agent is the set of possible traits, U^*.

Dominant strategy implementation is a far more convincing institutional proposal for decentralizing an allocation mechanism than Nash implementation; it is also a far stronger requirement. There is no Pareto efficient allocation mechanism defined on our domain of economic environments (with a fixed, finite number of agents) that can be implemented in dominant strategies. Consider, however, economic environments with a finite number of types of agents, but a continuum of agents of each type. These are called finite-type environments, and can be designated $\xi = \langle u^1, \ldots, u^r; \omega^1, \ldots, \omega^r; M^1, \ldots, M^r; f \rangle$, where M^i is the measure of type i agents. We have:

Theorem 8: *On the domain of finite-type environments, there is a unique allocation correspondence that is Pareto efficient, anonymous,*[19] *and implementable in dominant strategies, the equal-division-Walrasian mechanism.*[20]

Theorem 8 is proved (in an unpublished appendix of Roemer, 1989a) by use of the characterization of dominant strategy mechanisms on finite-type economies provided by Makowski and Ostroy (1992). Anonymity can be viewed as a minimal requirement of fairness. The interpretation is that the unique minimally fair, efficient allocation mechanism that is capable of decentralization in the sense of dominant strategy implementation is the one that requires public ownership of the technology, in the equal-division-of-the-profits sense.

4. Conclusion

Four normative proposals for the resource allocation in a mixed economy, where an input is privately owned and the output is produced on a publicly owned technology, have been offered. Each of the four can be viewed as the economic consequence of defining public ownership by the specification of certain rights to which citizens are entitled. The proportional allocation rule asserts that each citizen has a right to a share of the output from the publicly owned enterprise equal to his share of total input contributed. The equal division allocation asserts that each citizen has a right, by virtue of citizenship alone, to an equal share of the profits of the publicly owned enterprise. The Nash dominator allocation rule results

---

[19] An anonymous mechanism assigns an agent an allocation based only on his traits (u^i, ω^i). If the numbers (or names) of agent-types are permuted, the allocation is similarly permuted. E.g., $F^1(\langle u^1, u^2, \omega^1, \omega^2, f \rangle) = F^2(\langle u^2, u^1, \omega^2, \omega^1, f \rangle)$, etc.

[20] Recall that this mechanism assigns the competitive allocation associated with the endowment structure in which each owns his own labor, and the profits of the public firm are divided equally among agents.

from giving each person the right to a welfare level at least as high as he would have achieved under common ownership property rights over the technology. The linear equivalent rule insists that each person has the right to a (weak) improvement in his welfare when the publicly owned technology improves. Of these four, only two generalize in a satisfactory way to economies with many inputs and many outputs, in which property rights of resources and technologies can be private or public: the proportional allocation rule incarnates a venerable socialist dictum, that each should work according to his ability and be paid according to his work, while the equal division rule has an intellectual heritage in the idea of a property-owning economic democracy, advocated by James Meade (1964).

With regard to the decentralizability of a mixed economy, I think that the existing theory of the implementation of resource allocation mechanisms makes little contribution, because of the complexity of the games that are in general required. The negative results (showing that a mechanism cannot be implemented) are more useful than the positive ones (showing that one can be implemented), for the former at least tell us that there is no hope of decentralization, while the latter tell us that decentralization is possible, but perhaps only with unrealistically optimistic assumptions about the knowledge and reasoning powers of individuals.

Market mechanisms with nonprivate property, the topic to which we turn next, offer more realistic possibilities for effecting income distributions that are more egalitarian than those typical of capitalist economies.

The morality and efficiency of market socialism

I. Moral issues

One can defend the moral legitimacy of the institution of public property in two ways: on grounds of rights and on egalitarian grounds. An argument against public ownership on grounds of rights is presented by Robert Nozick (1974), and rebutted by G. A. Cohen (1985). Nozick's argument is well known and hardly need be rehearsed here. A person has a right to appropriate part of the natural world as his private property, as long as the consequences of the appropriation are such that no one is worse off than he would have been had the property remained in its natural state. In this way, one can conceive of a scenario in which eventually no part of the natural world remains unowned and all objects that are made from it and labor belong to individuals. Cohen responds that Nozick has an implicit assumption that the natural world is, morally speaking, originally unowned and, hence, up for grabs. But why not postulate that, morally speaking, the natural world is originally publicly owned? What would this mean? That no one would have a right to appropriate part of it as his own unless the public so agreed (by whatever decision-making procedure it has). But would not the public approve appropriations if Nozick's condition held, that is, if an appropriation would leave no one worse off – or, to sweeten the pot, let's say if it would leave everyone better off – than before the appropriation? No. The public might only approve the appropriation if it could think of no better way of using the land, say, than the candidate appropriator proposes. Or, it might approve the appropriation only if 80 percent of the gains from the appropriation are distributed to the public and 20 percent to the appropriator, while Nozick would permit the appropriation as long as 1 percent of the gains went to the public.

Cohen's challenge to Nozick, that the natural world in its unexploited state could be viewed, morally speaking, as owned by everyone, is appealing and might be motivated today by a green philosophy. We are all custodians of this planet for future generations of humans and other animals; this custodianship is better served by the planet's being publicly owned than privately owned. One might, then, attempt to ground public ownership of the world in a right of future generations to inherit a world not inferior to the one enjoyed by their predecessors. Nevertheless, I think such a rights-based approach would be less compelling than the egalitarian approaches that I outline next.

Nozickian rights theorists do not accept the premise that justice requires the equalizing of some opportunity or outcome among people, and I will not try to argue for that here. Suffice it to say that there are many arguments in political philosophy that attempt to establish egalitarianism, in some form, as a requirement of justice. Egalitarian theories can be classified in a number of ways; one is according to whether the equalisandum is an opportunity or an outcome. Primary among outcome-equalizing theories is equality of welfare. I do not think anyone defends an unadorned equality-of-welfare theory today, in part because it leaves persons not responsible in regard to their own efforts and ambitions. Richard Arneson (1989, 1990) and G. A. Cohen (1989) come the closest, in their defense of equality of opportunity for welfare and equal access to advantage, respectively. The nonwelfarist egalitarian theories can all be thought of as equality-of-opportunity theories. Rawls advocates equality of primary goods, as such goods are seen as necessary for anyone to realize her life plan. Hence, primary-goods equality establishes an initial condition under which all have equal opportunity to do what is important for them. Ronald Dworkin advocates (although he claims he is only defining, not advocating) equality of resources, where resources are defined in a comprehensive way, to include internal talents. Resources are, of course, things that enable one to achieve some outcome, and hence his is an opportunity-equalizing theory. Amartya Sen advocates the equalization of capabilities of a basic kind rather than primary goods or resources; his criticism against these other theories is that primary goods and resources are in fact only inputs into what everyone needs in order to achieve his life plan, namely, the capabilities to take some basic action (move about, read, etc.), and if two people need different amounts of a primary good in order to be able to move about, then primary-goods equalization will not achieve what opportunity equalization requires.

It is not difficult to argue that public ownership of the means of production will result in greater equality of all the above equalisanda than private ownership of such means will entail. Both the supporters of and detractors from public ownership agree on this. But equality is not the only goal; many believe that equality is trumped by Pareto optimality, in the following sense. Suppose there are two economic institutions, the first of which achieves equality of some equalisandum, while the second achieves an unequal distribution of that equalisandum but in which every-

body has more of it than under the first institution. Most of us would prefer the second institution.[1] And this is the focal point of the debate that
engages people in the world today on the question of public ownership.
Many believe, on the basis of the experience of Communism in the Soviet
Union and Eastern Europe, that public ownership of the means of production produces an allocation of welfare or resources or primary goods
or capabilities that is Pareto inferior to what can be achieved with private
ownership – in the sense that any of these equalisanda can be provided in
greater amounts to all in a capitalist system, perhaps minimally modified
with a welfare safety net, than in a socialist system with public ownership.

Thus, in one sense, one might say that the sixty-four-dollar question is
not about ethics or equity but about efficiency. I believe, however, this is
a false dichotomy. For, as I have posed the issue, the "efficiency" or Pareto superiority of one system over another *is* an ethical issue.

Suppose one is an egalitarian of the type I have described in footnote 1
(i.e., one who views equality as instrumental) and wants to argue for
the moral superiority of socialism over capitalism. There are two general
strategies one might employ. The first is to argue that, although capitalism (with a safety net) may Pareto-dominate socialism with respect to the
provision of material goods, the equalisandum should be something else.
Perhaps socialism dominates capitalism with respect to a self-realization
index or a communitarian index. The second is to argue that capitalism
does not dominate socialism even along the index in which it excels,
namely, the provision of material goods. Most people in the world today
would not be moved by an argument of the first kind. Or, to be more
precise, the failures of the European centrally planned economies to provide enough material goods for their citizens are so severe that people are
suspicious of any argument that admits the inferiority of socialism as a
mechanism for providing materials goods yet claims, nevertheless, that
socialism dominates capitalism for "spiritual" reasons. It is, of course,
logically possible that such a socialism is possible, and that its spiritual
advantages over capitalism would be so great as to compensate for its
inferiority with respect to the provision of material goods.

In what follows, I shall take the second tack, and argue for the feasibility of a socialism that is not inferior to capitalism in terms of the provision

---

[1] Most, but not all, for some view equality per se as a goal. I am more attracted to the view
that equality is merely instrumental for assuring that scarcity is equally shared. Put another way, the goal is not that everyone have the same amount but that everyone have
enough. In most cases, there is not enough for everybody, so equality is a second-best
desideratum. If everybody can have enough, then I think an argument for equality is
much more difficult to sustain. Under conditions of scarcity of the thing to be equalized
(i.e., there is not "enough" for everyone), a distribution, call it *A*, in which everyone has
more than in some equal distribution, *B*, is socially preferred to *B*.

of material goods. Moreover, equality of income (or material goods) will be greater in the socialist variant than under capitalism, and therefore, as an instrumental egalitarian, I argue that the socialist system is morally preferable to the capitalist one. It is not so important that income be the equalisandum – it could be primary goods or capabilities or resources, all of which, I believe, are quite highly correlated with income. Markets, I shall argue, are an essential aspect of such a socialism; my task is to propose a blueprint for market socialism.

II.   A common false inference about public ownership

All commentators on the right, and some on the left,[2] have written socialism's obituary based on the overthrow of the Communist regimes in Eastern Europe in 1989 and the present acute economic and political crisis in the Soviet Union. Among the quickest to toss socialism into history's dustbin are the intellectuals of the Eastern European countries, and this in itself, it would seem, is a powerful argument against socialism. The societies that failed, however, differed from Western capitalism along more dimensions than property rights, and so the experiment carried out in Eastern Europe was not one properly controlled for the variable 'ownership'. In particular, these societies were characterized by

1. noncompetitive (i.e., dictatorial) politics,
2. central administrative allocation of resources (as opposed to reliance on the market), and
3. public ownership of the means of production.

We have observed the failure of the politico-economic mechanism in which 1 + 2 + 3 hold. From this we cannot conclude that any system involving 3 must fail. In particular, the version of market socialism that I shall propose embodies (not 1) + (not 2) + 3. To put the matter less schematically, I conjecture that the failures of Communism are due to its noncompetitive politics and its abjuring of markets, not to its public ownership. (The reader may query whether public ownership is conceivable without a system of central allocation of resources. In what follows I will distinguish between these two characteristics of an economic system.)

I will not attempt to establish this conjecture by a painstaking analysis of the anatomy of the centrally planned politico-economic mechanism, an operation I am not equipped to perform competently. Briefly, I am convinced that it is impossible for an economy, in which literally millions of decisions must be made by a bureaucratic apparatus, to perform efficiently. The argument is well presented by Alec Nove (1983). The non-

[2] See, e.g., Heilbroner (1989).

competitive politics further exacerbate the problems, for without political competition there is no mechanism to prevent government agencies from entering into self-interested pacts with economic units such as firms.

Rather, my argument for the conjecture will be positive in that I will argue for the feasibility and success of a politico-economic mechanism embodying competitive politics, market allocation of most private goods,[3] and public ownership.

III. A blueprint for market socialism

The viability of market socialism depends upon the claim that private ownership of the means of production is unnecessary for the successful operation of a market economy. In the blueprint which I shall now sketch, I attempt to support this claim. But we have, as yet, very little empirical evidence that would enable us to evaluate the claim in a rigorous way. The argument must be, at this point, theoretical.

The market socialism I envisage has these components: firms will be managed by managers whose goal will be to maximize profits, at going prices. That is, the firm manager will try to hire labor and produce output of that variety and quality which will maximize the long-run profits of the firm. Firm managers will either be elected by workers or appointed by boards of directors, about whose composition I will speak presently. What is important, however, is that managers try to profit-maximize. Labor will be hired on labor markets, and wages will be set by supply and demand, in the market. Almost all private goods and services will be allocated on markets, and prices will be determined in these markets. The government will continue to provide public goods, financed by taxation of profits and wages. Certain private goods, such as health services, may also be provided gratis to the population and financed from taxation – but this is nothing new, even for capitalist countries.

There are two socialist aspects to this economy. First, the government will have the power to intervene in the economy to direct the pattern and level of investment. One plank of the platform of a political party, in such a society, will be the direction that investment shall take should it be elected. The desired investment levels and pattern will not be implemented through a command system but by manipulating interest rates at which different industrial sectors can borrow funds from state banks. Thus, if the government's intention is to decrease the production of automobiles, it will raise above the market rate the interest rate at which the state banks lend to automobile firms. People will thus exercise some collective control,

---

[3] Private as opposed to public goods; all economies, capitalist or socialist, must arrange for government intervention in the provision of public goods.

through democratic politics, over the use of savings in society. In this sense there will be public control of the use of the economic surplus, a phrase with a socialist ring. I do not propose that people vote on this particular matter, the composition of investment, because of that ring but because I think that the markets which would be necessary for investment to be allocated in a socially desirable way are necessarily absent (see Sec. IV below for further discussion). This is reflected in the extreme volatility of investment in large capitalist economies, a volatility responsible for the business cycle and therefore, in particular, the rise and fall of unemployment. (What I am saying is less true of small capitalist countries, where the demand for exports can lead the business cycle. But it is substantially the case that the demand for investment goods leads the business cycle in countries like the United States.)

The second socialist aspect of this economy is that the profits of firms will not go to a small fraction of the citizenry but will be divided, after taxes, more or less equally among all adult citizens, taking a form that Oskar Lange (1938) called the social dividend. Thus, a citizen in this society will receive income from three sources: wage income, which will vary depending upon her skill and the amount of time she works; interest forthcoming from savings, which will also vary across households; and the social dividend, which will be, in principle, approximately equal across households. The social dividend will be a form of guaranteed income, or what some European writers have called a universal grant.[4] I prefer not to call it a grant, since it is not a gift, which 'grant' connotes; it is that part of the national income which is not distributed as wages or interest but which belongs to the people as owners of the means of production. Of course, a society such as the one I am describing might decide to distribute profits in some other way to people, such as in proportion to the value of labor they have expended, but I personally would oppose that proposal.

What will taxes be used for in this society? All the usual things: public goods that a government provides, income transfers to those who are unable to work, subsidies to families who cannot earn enough to live decently, and so on. They will also be used to subsidize the government's intervention in the capital market, as follows. Suppose it is decided to encourage several large industries to invest more than they would have at an equilibrium where there was no government intervention. This is accomplished by providing loans to those industries at interest rates lower than the market rate. Such loans are financed by social savings, and citizens receive the market rate on their savings accounts. Thus, the banks

---

4 Van der Veen and Van Parijs (1986).

will collect interest on loans to firms at low rates and must pay out interest to citizens on savings at a higher rate. The ensuing deficit must be financed by the government.[5]

Substantial inequality will continue to exist in this society, due primarily to the differential wages that people will earn and also, to some extent, to their differential savings behavior. What will be equalized is that part of income due to corporate profits. The income distribution will consequently be far more equal than in most, if not all, capitalist economies – even without further intervention to soften the wage differentials that will exist in a competitive labor market.

Why do I include as an integral part of this proposal the stipulation that firm managers maximize profits of the firm? Would it not be better to let workers manage the firms directly? The answer is that the firm belongs to everyone, and every household depends upon each firm as a source of part of its income, via the social dividend. Workers, in any case, should not be able to appropriate the profits of the firm they work in: that would lead to gross inequities across workers. We know, from economic theory, that profit maximization, under the right conditions (which include a competitive environment for the firm) leads to an efficient allocation of resources – that is the main reason to use profit maximization as an instrument. Now profit maximization may lead to some antisocial behavior, and that will have to be regulated. But we have no example of a large economy that has operated successfully without profit maximization as a goal of firms, and my attempt here is to propose a blueprint that is based, as much as possible, on the successes of capitalism, while deviating from capitalism in certain important ways.

These are the main lines of the blueprint. I shall modify it somewhat below. If people continue to work about as hard as they do under capitalism, and technological change takes place about as it does under capitalism, then the two major differences between this kind of market socialism and capitalism are the direction of investment by a political process and a more egalitarian income distribution. What funds were used under capitalism to finance the consumption of capitalists (corporate profits) will here be distributed to all citizens. If capitalists consume a small fraction of national income, as in Norway, then the change in income distribution effected by market socialism will be small. If, as in Brazil, the rich consume 40 to 60 percent of national income, then the redistributive effect would be substantial.

The first question one must ask about this blueprint is, Will it work? There are various levels at which that question can be asked. One is at the

[5] For precise details, see Ortuño, Roemer, and Silvestre (1993).

level of economic theory. Is it possible for a market system to equilibrate an economy in which profits are distributed as I described, and in which the government intervenes in the investment behavior of the economy by manipulating interest rates as I described, if the managers of firms maximize profits, facing market prices, wages, and interest rates? This question is studied in the aforementioned paper by Ortuño, Silvestre, and me (1993). It is indeed possible for the government to achieve any of a large variety of possible compositions of investment for the economy by the setting of discounts and surcharges on the market interest rate; prices in all markets will adjust in such a way that an equilibrium is achieved, in which the demand for each good by consumers is equal to the supply of that good by firms. Furthermore, since managers are maximizing profits, the allocation of goods and labor at equilibrium is constrained Pareto efficient, given the investment vector that the government is implementing. The social control over investment is achieved without setting ten thousand prices, or one million prices – the figure for the Soviet Union varies, depending upon the source. Nor does the center tell any firm what to produce or where to acquire its inputs or where to ship its outputs. All these millions of decisions, supposedly but impossibly made by the planning system in Soviet-type economies, are left to individuals to arrange through markets. Yet by the adjustment of a small number of interest rates, the economy can realize the composition of investment that its planners aim to achieve.

Thus, I do not think that the lessons of the Communist experience include an admonition against planning as such, against the direction of the economy toward preconceived ends. The methods of Soviet planning were ineffective, and worse, because they did not use markets as a way of decentralizing millions of small decisions. Ironically, perhaps, the most effective planning requires the use of markets. What are not planned in this vision of market socialism are the composition of output, the prices of goods, and the distribution of labor; planned is just the composition of investment.[6]

Another level at which the can-it-work question can be asked is, Will the managers of firms be motivated to maximize profits in an economy where firms are not privately owned by investors? Will entrepreneurial spirit be forthcoming? Will technological innovation take place? This is the level at which most economists are skeptical concerning the feasibility of market socialism.

---

[6] We could design an economic mechanism that plans, e.g., the allocation of labor rather than the allocation of investment. We chose to plan investment for reasons discussed both above and in Sec. IV below.

Let us first take up the question of managerial discipline. Stories abound about corrupt and incompetent management of firms in socialist economies. It is wrong to conclude from the observation of firms in a command economy what publicly owned firms would be like in a market economy. Managerial culture in the Soviet Union is demoralized, to say the least; for the main, one can only acquire the inputs one needs by bribery and barter. This culture would be different if inputs and outputs could be bought and sold on markets. But this, of course, cannot be the complete answer to the query. "Bourgeois" finance economics maintains that the only reason that managers pursue the interests of shareholders, which require maximizing profits rather than their own selfish interests, is the threat of losing their jobs. The discipline is provided via the stock market. If a firm is being poorly managed, its profit prospects will darken and its stock price will fall. It will become an attractive target for a take-over by investors who will buy the firm cheap, put in better management, and return the firm to a profit-maximizing program. The stock market has therefore been called the market for corporate control. What mechanism can a market socialist economy use to substitute for the capitalist stock market to keep managers doing their job?

A clue to a possible answer comes from the experience of Japanese capitalism. In Japan, the stock market was relatively unimportant in the economy until recently. Firms are organized into groups, called *keiretsu*. Each *keiretsu* is associated with a main bank, whose responsibility it is to arrange loans for the firms in its group and to monitor the firms' managements. The investment projects proposed by firms are evaluated by the staff of the bank, and in this way the bank is able to monitor the firms' behavior. These main banks also defend firms in their group against take-overs from firms outside the group. This system has been successful (if we take Japanese capitalism as a successful capitalist variant). But there is no market for corporate control in Japan – at least, it does not take the form that it has in the United States, and capital is not directed to its profitable uses via a stock market. This last point is worth emphasizing, for another plank of capitalist ideology is that bureaucrats cannot decide how to allocate capital; that is best done by a stock market, where millions of people express their opinions by voting with their dollars. Yet in Japan, apparently the accountants, economists, and industrial experts working for the big banks are sufficiently savvy to pass good judgment on investment proposals of firms and do the job that supposedly requires a stock market.

Bardhan (1993) has proposed a system wherein firms in the kind of market socialist economy I outlined above could be organized into groups modeled after the Japanese *keiretsu*. Each group would consist of firms whose products are somewhat related – but direct competitors would never be in the same group. Say firms W, X, Y, and Z are in one group, with bank B. Each firm would own some shares of the other firms in the group, and the bank would also own some shares of each firm. The board of directors of a firm would consist of representatives of its shareholders, that is, of the various firms and banks in the group. That part of profits of firm W, say, not going to the bank, the other three firms, or directly to W's own workers would go to the state and would be distributed to all citizens as part of the social dividend. The fraction of firm W's profits going to firms X, Y, and Z by virtue of their ownership of shares of W would constitute a significant other part of the social dividend of the workers of X, Y, and Z. Thus, every worker in the economy would receive his social dividend from two sources: a centralized dividend from the government, comprising a small share of profits of all firms in the economy, perhaps consumed as public goods and services, and a decentralized part, consisting of a fraction of the profits of the other firms in his group. The function of this decentralization is to give firms X, Y, and Z an interest in monitoring the behavior of firm W. In particular, if firm X thinks firm W is not profit-maximizing, then it can sell to the bank its shares of W. This in turn puts pressure on the bank to force W to do better.

Bardhan's proposal is not equivalent to introducing a stock market; it is a mechanism for decentralizing the accountability of firm management to a small number of institutions, in this case, other firms and banks, which are capable of monitoring the management. Complete equality in the social dividend received by citizens would be sacrificed in the interests of creating a mechanism for decentralizing the monitoring of firms.

A word about innovation. Again, it would be wrong to conclude from the experience of firms in command economies that firms that are not privately owned will not innovate. I think that if there is sufficient competition, innovation will occur in these market socialist firms. To the extent that innovation takes place as a consequence of research and development in large firms anywhere, it can just as well take place in a socialist firm.

Now, it might be said that the kind of innovation that will not occur under market socialism will be that of the lonely inventor, who, spurred by the prospect of becoming a multimillionaire, invents a new kind of computer. Under capitalism, these people exist; if they succeed, they form small firms, and are in almost all cases eventually bought out by large firms. If this source of innovation appears important, then I suggest that such private firms be permitted in market socialist economies. They should be nationalized, with proper compensation to the owners, at some given size. The government would buy out the small computer firm instead of

IBM's buying it out. Or the publicly owned IBM could buy out the small firm, subject to the usual antitrust considerations, which will be necessary under market socialism as well. This mechanism should provide almost as much incentive to the entrepreneurial spirit as capitalism provides.[7]

To sum up, I think it is possible to use markets to allocate resources in an economy where firms are not privately owned by investors who trade stock in them with the purpose of maximizing their gain, and that the government can intervene, in such an economy, to influence the level and composition of investment. The principal skepticism about the model I propose concerns the possibility of designing incentives to get managers to maximize profits. My argument against this skepticism is that a similar agency problem exists in modern capitalism, where private owners of firms must induce hired managers to maximize profits. The necessary, and perhaps sufficient, condition for the solution of the agency problem in capitalist corporations is taken, by most finance economists, to be the concentration of large quantities of the firm's stock in the hands of a small number of investors, who therefore have the incentive to spend the resources necessary to monitor the management.[8] (Small investors have no such incentive, because the costs to them of monitoring exceed their expected gains. Of course, they could collectively hire a monitor, but that only shifts the agency problem to one between them and their monitor.) Bardhan's proposal exploits this conventional wisdom and designs a system wherein the ownership of firms is concentrated among several other firms and banks. Because of the significant dependence of workers in one firm on the profits of another firm in its group, via the decentralized formula for the social dividend, each firm has an incentive to monitor the activities of the other firms. Indeed, the board of directors of a firm would consist of representatives of its shareholders and the main bank in its group.

At this point, the skeptical laissez-faire economist will argue that the bankers would not perform their job of pressuring or replacing non-profit-maximizing firm management, because they would not be responsible to shareholders cracking the whip. The chickens of public ownership will always come home to roost, they say, in this form: there is no principal at the end of the sequence of decision makers whose fortune depends upon profit maximization of the firm.[9] To paraphrase the challenge, who will monitor the monitor?

[7] A more careful discussion of the prospects for innovation under market socialism is found in Berliner (1993).

[8] For a debate on the efficacy of the stock market in the U.S. economy as a monitoring device of firm management, see Jensen (1989).

[9] A thoughtful discussion of the issues involved is found in Putterman (1993).

First, there must be constitutional safeguards preventing the interference of the government in the short- and medium-term policies of banks. Banks must act in an environment where economic considerations determine their decisions, not political ones. Thus, if a firm should, for economic reasons, be declared bankrupt, it must not be possible for politicians to prevent its reorganization because of the disruption involved in the lives of workers. Of course, there must be concomitant retraining and relocation programs for workers. Second, the *keiretsu* system will induce banks to monitor carefully firms in their jurisdiction, because the ability to arrange loan consortia for these firms depends on the bank's reputation for running a tight ship. Moreover, new firms will want to join corporate groups whose banks have a reputation for securing loans on good terms for their firms. Thus, a bank that does not perform its monitoring job well will soon find itself losing money and under attack from the firms in its group for not being able to sell their bond issues on good terms. Thus, competition between and political insulation of banks are the aspects of the design that should induce the monitor to monitor.[10]

IV.   The political determination of investment

I wrote above that my advocacy of the political determination of the pattern and level of investment in the market socialist economy is not based upon the Marxist view that "the people should control the use of the economic surplus." In principle, under certain conditions, I do not think that socialism requires that there be popular control of the investment decision in the economy, by which I mean that market determination of investment is not in principle antisocialist. Suppose that we are nonpaternalistic and accept people's preferences for consumption over time as their business. (We do not seek to protect the future selves of citizens from their present selves.) Or we may not be principled nonpaternalists, but we believe that conditions are such that the preferences people have developed reflect their true interests. Suppose that capital markets are perfect, that futures' markets for all commodities under all possible states of the world exist, and that externalities are absent. Then the competitive (market) equilibrium of the economy will be Pareto efficient, which implies, in particular, that no different allocation of investment could make everybody at least as well off, and some better off.[11] On what further grounds might we object to this equilibrium? On equity grounds – but those grounds are limited, as we have already divided corporate profits among households

---

[10] For further discussion of this problem and of the "soft budget constraint," see Essay 15.
[11] This is shown in Debreu (1959), chap. 7.

in an equal way. That is to say, there is no reason left to modify the economy's investment decision as such, although there may be reason to modify further the income distribution the inequality of which now depends mainly on differential wages.

I believe that political control of the investment vector, or the planning of investment, is desirable not as a deep socialist principle but for instrumental reasons.[12] These reasons come under the rubrics of paternalism and market failure.

By paternalism, I do not suggest that the state as a disembodied actor should decide the pattern of investment because people do not know what they need: rather that the person as citizen may decide in the voting booth that she, as consumer, behaves in a way contrary to her real interests. (One might call this intrapersonal paternalism.) When faced with the decision to purchase a refrigerator that does not use chlorofluorocarbon (CFC) technology, the person as consumer may well decide not to. But in the voting booth the same person might decide to authorize the government to subsidize investment in pollution-superior technologies to an extent that will cost her a thousand dollars more in taxes and price effects than otherwise would have been the case. Now, there is one sound economic reason for this apparently contradictory behavior. If the consumer buys the clean and green refrigerator, her act has a minuscule effect on the ozone layer. If, however, a law is passed subsidizing clean refrigeration technology, then everyone must contribute a thousand dollars, and the effect will be substantial. Besides this public-good rationale, however, the behavior of people when voting may be more civically oriented than when purchasing.[13] I am suggesting that the more reliable guardian of a person's true interests may be her civic persona rather than her economic one, a view challenged by George Stigler (1972), who maintains that people only act responsibly when they must bear the costs of their actions. (A citizen's vote is irresponsible because it only makes a difference in the costs she must bear in the infinitesimally likely case that she breaks a tie in the election.)

There are many types of market failure that can motivate the need for political determination of investment. The refrigerator example is the conventional one of an externality. The purchase of CFC refrigerators by

---

[12] In contrast, Roberto Ungar advocates the political control of investment as a deep democratic principle. Despite this difference in motivation, his "rotating capital fund" is one institutional proposal, friendly to my views, for implementing the democratic control of investment. Ungar advocates using both interest rate intervention and rationing to achieve a socially desirable allocation of investment funds. I am indebted to Will Kymlicka for referring me to Ungar (1987), pp. 491–502.

[13] For the rationality of such behavior, see Sen (1977). See also Sunstein (1991).

others affects the ozone layer which I consume. Markets do not induce a socially optimal amount of refrigerators in this case. The political process is one way of resolving the Prisoners' Dilemma that afflicts the market place.

Another market failure which recommends the planning of investment is due to the nonexistence of markets for goods in the future contingent upon the realization of various possible states of the world. It is probably this market incompleteness that explains the volatility of investment in capitalist economies. But there are externalities, as well, that compound the problem of reaching an optimal investment plan because there are missing markets. Makowski (1980) shows that, in the absence of a complete set of markets, the set of goods that a private ownership economy will produce is not a Pareto-optimal set of goods. That is, certain goods which could be innovated will not be, because of the lack of markets, and all would be better off with a set of goods different from what exists at the market equilibrium. Finally, there is the relatively new literature on "endogenous growth," in which it is argued that investment itself increases technological know-how, which then makes possible more rapid innovation and growth.[14] If this is the case, then, even with a complete set of markets, the equilibrium amount of investment will be too low from a social point of view.

V.   Is market socialism just?

It is wrong, in my view, to maintain that any market system, with or without capitalists, allocates resources and incomes justly. What perfectly working competitive markets do is pay people according to the evaluation that other people in society put on their contribution. In a capitalist economy, a person's contribution consists not just of her labor contribution but also of the contribution of her capital. Leftists have usually attacked the justice of the capitalist income distribution on the grounds that capitalists are not the rightful owners of their capital, and hence their receipt of profits constitutes an injustice and, moreover, exploitation of those to whom the capital should rightly belong. The problem with this argument is that it does not go far enough. For I do not think that a distribution of income in which each is paid the value of his labor contribution to the rest of society is just either. For it is surely the case that different people make contributions of very different values to society, due in large part to their differential training. (It is wrong to say, as utopians sometimes do, that the contribution of an unskilled worker is just as valuable to society

---

[14]   Romer (1986).

as that of a physician; it could be if, counterfactually, almost no one had the capacity to be an unskilled worker and almost everybody with no training could be a physician. Value must be measured not, as Marx said, just as the labor embodied in producing the thing but as the total real resource cost that people are willing to sacrifice to make the thing available.)

Under market socialism, people will receive differential wages, and that will reflect their differential economic value to society. But they will not deserve those wages nor be entitled to them, because I do not believe they deserve or are entitled to returns to their arbitrarily assigned genetic compositions and familial and social environments, which largely determine their skills. This is an old Marxist point; in the introduction to the *Critique of the Gotha Program,* Marx wrote of payment according to the value of one's labor as "bourgeois right."

I view the differential wages that will accompany a market socialist system as justifiable for only one reason: they are a by-product of using a labor market to allocate labor, and there is no other known way to allocate labor more efficiently in a large, complex economy than by use of a labor market. Now, there are various ways of decreasing real-income differentials of workers which could be used by a market socialist society – to the extent, of course, that a democratic society condones using them. One practice of the social democracies is to tax income sharply and progressively and to redistribute it by providing some goods, such as health services, on an equal basis to all at no fee.

If some inequality is one undesirable feature of market socialism, a second is, as G. A. Cohen (1991) puts it, that the market "motivates contribution not on the basis of commitment to one's fellow human beings and a desire to serve them while being served by them, but on the basis of impersonal cash reward." Indeed, one should not idealize the behavior of people in a market socialist economy. Firms may advertise deceptively and try, as they do under capitalism, to create in people tastes for goods by exploiting their feelings of insecurity and incompetence. Workers will need unions to protect them from overzealous managers, even if they have the power to remove management. More generally, conflicts between different groups of people based upon their different interests will continue to exist. Environmentalists and workers in the lumber industry will continue to clash. The political arena will be the site of sharp contests.

A remark is required on the position I have taken above on the management of the firm. Worker control of the firm is not an essential part of the blueprint I offer – indeed, it would be in tension with the blueprint if such control would cause the firm to pursue a goal other than profit maximization. One might argue that the control of the workplace is sufficiently important to the welfare or self-realization of workers that the society would be willing to sacrifice income to enable worker control. My instinct is to disagree, but I have no hard evidence to offer. There might be, however, another reason to introduce worker control that I have not pursued here, as I have not discussed in any detail the politics of a market socialist society. Such a society would have to take steps to prevent managers from becoming a class in the political sense, a class that has political power to influence state policy. One check of managerial power might be to stipulate that workers have the power to hire and fire managers. I leave this question open.

Market socialism would dominate capitalism from the point of view of justice, for the reasons outlined in the first section, if it can indeed succeed in significantly equalizing the distribution of income with little efficiency cost, a possibility I have tried to argue is feasible. It is not the only road away from standard capitalism: Scandinavian social democracy may do about as well as market socialism can do in equalizing the distribution of income, and I have not argued that market socialism is intrinsically better for people than social democracy because, for instance, of the nonexistence of a capitalist class in the former.[15] But for many countries in the next fifty years, market socialism might be a desirable option, while social democracy might not be feasible.

---

[15] This is not to say such arguments cannot be made; indeed, a society without capitalists is likely to have quite different politics from a social democratic society. For an economic argument developing this point, see Essay 15, especially Sections 4 and 7.

ESSAY 15

A future for socialism

Introduction

The demise of the Communist system in the Soviet Union and Eastern Europe has caused many to believe that socialism cannot exist, either in the present world or as an ideal. I shall argue that, in both cases, it can: but this requires some revision of what constitutes socialism, for if one thought socialism were coextensive with the Soviet model, then clearly the answer to the two questions would be no. In arguing for my revisionist definition of socialism, I begin by discussing what I believe socialists want – the political philosophy, if you will, of socialism. In Section 2, I ask whether public ownership, as it has been conceived of in the socialist movement, is necessary to realize in a politico-economic system what socialists want, and conclude that it is not. In particular, I claim that the direct control of firms by the state is not necessary for socialist goals. Socialists should be eclectic in their attitude toward property relations: there may be many such relations more amenable to reaching socialism's goals than traditional state ownership of the means of production. In Section 3, I propose an explanation for why the centrally planned economies eventually failed, by virtue of their failure to solve what economists call principal–agent problems, and finally critique and amend that theory. Section 4 discusses how the levels of a number of "public bads" in a society, from pollution to imperialist wars, may be determined by the way an economy distributes aggregate firm profits among its citizens. In particular, I argue that a reorganization of property rights in firms could significantly improve the "quality of life," as it is reflected in the absence of public bads, even before the values of people change so that they exemplify what socialists used to call, in the days before the consciousness of linguistic gender-neutrality, "socialist man." Section 5 (the one somewhat technical section of the essay) studies a general equilibrium model of market socialism. It proposes that a stock market is not inimical to socialist values, that one can be designed that does not seriously compromise egalitarianism, while having beneficial effects on the efficiency of the economy. Section 6 addresses specifically the issue that critics consider to be

303

socialism's Achilles' heel: How can a socialist economy – one in which the unfettered accumulation of profits by private citizens is banned – keep firms efficient and the pace of technological innovation brisk? The principal task is to design a device for monitoring the management of firms, which does not depend upon the highly concentrated ownership of stock.

Section 7 remarks on some consequences for socialist thinking of the desideratum of democracy, and argues that the realization of the goals of socialism adumbrated in Section 1 will be a slow process. It is argued that, nevertheless, the equalization of the distribution of profits will substantially change the character of democracy from its character under capitalism. Section 8 presents what I think are the most serious left-wing criticisms of market socialism. Section 9 offers some brief concluding remarks.

The main non-left-wing – and by this hyphenated adjective, I do not mean right-wing – criticism of market socialism is that it is an oxymoron; more specifically, that markets cannot perform their good deeds without the essentially unfettered right to private property in firms and the corollary right to accumulation of capital. It is this view that I hope successfully to challenge with this essay.

1.   What socialists want

I believe socialists want equality of opportunity for:

(1)   self-realization and welfare,
(2)   political influence, and
(3)   social status.

By self-realization, I mean the development and application of one's talents in a direction that gives meaning to one's life. This is a specifically Marxian conception of human flourishing,[1] and is to be distinguished, for instance, from John Rawls's notion of fulfillment of a plan of life, for a plan of life might consist in enjoying one's family and friends, or eating fine meals, or counting blades of grass.[2] These life-plan-fulfillment activities do not count as self-realization, a process of self-transformation that requires struggle in a way that eating a fine meal does not. One does, however, derive welfare from enjoying one's family and eating fine meals, and so I do attribute value to these activities in the socialist's reckoning, for goal (1) specifies equality of opportunity for self-realization and welfare.[3]

---

[1] See Elster (1985, pp. 82–92) for a discussion of self-realization in Marx, and Elster (1986) for a more general discussion.
[2] Rawls (1971, p. 426).
[3] C. B. MacPherson (1973, p. 4) defines democracy as equal self-realization among citizens; I think this builds too much into 'democracy'.

That equality of *opportunity* for self-realization and welfare is the goal, rather than equality of self-realization and welfare, requires comment. The reader is referred to the discussion in Essay 8.

Suppose that we have clarified what goals (1), (2), and (3) each mean – and I will not here attempt to offer any explication of (2) and (3). The statements of (1), (2), and (3) are still inaccurate. For instance, what socialists really want is not equality of opportunity for political influence, but equality of such at a high level. So (2) should be restated as: socialists want an organization of society which equalizes the opportunity for political influence at a level that is no lower than any other organization of society could achieve as an equal level. Or, in other words, (2) says we should maximize, over all possible organizations of society, the level of opportunity for political influence which can be achieved as an equal level for all. But, similarly, (1) calls on us to choose that organization of society which maximizes the level of opportunity for self-realization and welfare that can be achieved as an equal level for all; and a similar statement holds for (3). It is, however, impossible to maximize three objectives at once. That is, the kind of social organization that maximizes the equal level of opportunity for self-realization may well induce highly unequal levels of political influence.

There are two responses to this problem. The first says: there is a form of society in which all three objectives are maximized simultaneously, when "the free development of each becomes the condition for the free development of all," or some such thing. I think this is an unsubstantiated and utopian claim. The second response says that one must admit the possibility of trade-offs among the three objectives. This, in fact, is what most of us do. For instance, a lively debate has taken place in the socialist movement on the question, Which is primary, democracy or equality? Or, rephrased, is equality of opportunity for political influence more important than equality of opportunity for self-realization and welfare? Socialists have different answers to this question. For example, Western socialists assign more importance to equality of opportunity for political influence than most Soviet socialists did. Some socialists did not support the Sandinistas because of the lack of press freedom and democracy in Nicaragua.

I should remark that I am not sure whether, once the optimal trade-off between equality of opportunity for self-realization, welfare, and political influence has been realized, equality of opportunity for social status need be appended as a desideratum. One may, that is, want the latter equality only insofar as one believes that such equality is a facilitator of the first two kinds of equality. Put in Marxian terms, is a classless society desirable for reasons other than achieving (1) and (2)? I don't know, and leave this as an open question.

2.   Public ownership

Marx located the injustice of capitalism in exploitation, and the source of exploitation in private ownership of the means of production (MP). (There are different opinions concerning whether Marx viewed capitalism as unjust or whether, for him, justice was so much "bourgeois cant."[4] I take the view that, whatever he believed, his argument shows that capitalism is unjust.) He located the crisis-prone nature of capitalism in private ownership of the MP. The Marxist prescription was, therefore, to abolish the doubly guilty private ownership of the MP, which was interpreted by Lenin and the Bolsheviks to require state ownership of the MP. This, in turn, has come to be known as public ownership by most of the world.

What *should* public ownership of an asset mean?[5] That the people have control over the disposition of that asset and its product. There are myriad problems in assessing whether a particular mechanism of popular decision-making in fact empowers the people in such matters; I shall conventionally say that democratic elections in an environment with ample civil liberties constitute popular decision-making. Obviously, this makes public ownership of an asset a rather weak concept, since the public can relinquish its control of an asset, through elections, in a variety of ways. For instance, in Eastern Europe, there are currently many different proposals for what to do about the formerly state-owned firms. Some advocate a distribution of ownership of firms to the people through the dispensation of vouchers, some selling the assets to the highest private bidder, some self-management by workers, some traditional state ownership, some turning over the factories to the management and former nomenklatura who know most about them. Any of these solutions might be chosen by democratic elections in some of these countries, and hence, public ownership would voluntarily pass into some other form of ownership, that is, control would be granted to some person or group. Or consider the following: the government distributes a portfolio of stock in the nation's firms to each young adult at age twenty-one, and permits the person to trade that stock as she wishes during her life, collecting the dividends that her portfolio entitles her to, but forbids her from cashing in any stock. At death, her portfolio returns to the public treasury. Does this arrangement constitute public ownership of the MP? Who controls the disposition of the MP in this case? At some level, the public does, through

---

[4] See, for contrasting positions on this question, Allen Wood (1972), who argues the latter view, and Norman Geras (1986, 1992), who argues the former.

[5] In contrast to the political approach taken here, see the normative approach that J. Silvestre and I have taken, as described in Essay 13.

the granting of portfolios to individuals, and the collection of them at death. But during their lives, citizens would have the power, at least collectively, to influence firms to maximize profits in a way that some might feel resembles capitalism too much be called public ownership. (They would have this influence through selling stock when they thought the firm had poor profit prospects, an action that might force the firm to cut wages, lay off workers, etc.)

My view is that socialists have made a fetish of public ownership: public ownership has been viewed as the *sine qua non* of socialism, which is based on a false inference. What socialists want are the three equalities I enumerated in Section 1; they should be open-minded about what kinds of property rights in the MP would bring about these three equalities. There is an infinite gradation of possible property rights between full, unregulated private ownership of firms (which exists almost nowhere) and complete control of a firm by a government organ. There is no guarantee that the state-control end of this spectrum is optimal for bringing about the three equalities, nor is there a guarantee that any particular democratically chosen disposition of the MP will bring about the three equalities. Therefore the link between public ownership and socialism is tenuous, and I think one does much better to drop the concept from the socialist constitution. Socialists should advocate those property rights in the MP that will bring about a society that ranks highest according to their preferences over the three equalities. One cannot honestly say, at this point in history, that one knows what those property rights must be.

In sum, I view the choice of property rights over firms and other resources to be an entirely instrumental matter, which should be evaluated by socialists according to their various propensities to induce the three equalities with which socialists are concerned. The history of socialism on the question is, very crudely, as follows. Private property, characteristic of capitalism, was abolished, and replaced by public property, which became, under the Bolsheviks, state property. For complex reasons (including bureaucratic ossification and class interest), this form remained dominant for seventy years. The labor-managed-firm property form remained peripheral in the socialist movement. The widest variety of property forms became visible in modern capitalism, not socialism: nonprofit firms, limited liability corporations, partnerships, sole proprietorships, public firms, social democratic property,[6] labor-managed firms, and other forms of social-republican property.[7] The property forms which will best further the socialist goals may involve direct popular control or state control of the means of production in only a distant way.

---

[6] By which I mean private property subject to taxation and regulation of various kinds.
[7] See Simon (1991) for a definition and discussion of social-republican property.

By market socialism, I shall mean any of a variety of economic arrangements in which most goods, including labor, are distributed through the price system, and the profits of firms, perhaps managed by workers or not, are distributed quite equally among the population. By what mechanism profits can be so distributed, without unacceptable costs in efficiency, is the central question.

3.   Why the centrally planned economies failed

The failure of the Soviet-type economies was due to the conjunction of three of their characteristics: (1) the allocation of most goods by an administrative apparatus under which producers were not forced to compete with each other, (2) direct control of firms by political units, and (3) noncompetitive, nondemocratic politics. Noting this, however, does not explain the failures, for we must uncover the mechanism through which these characteristics induced economic failure. In some of my own recent work (Roemer, 1992), I wrote that principal–agent problems were the source of failure of the Soviet-type economies. I now believe that the true story is more complex. In this section I shall first outline the argument of Soviet-type failures based on principal–agent problems, then offer some critical remarks on it, and finally modify the argument.

The contour of the argument is that the three characteristics I just listed conspired to prevent the solution of principal–agent problems which, in capitalist democracies, are successfully solved. Communist societies faced three principal–agent problems: (i) the manager–worker relationship in the factory or the collective farm, (ii) the planner–manager relationship, and (iii) the public–planner relationship. Managers must try to get workers to carry out their production plans, planners must try to get managers to carry out the planning bureau's plan, and the planners, in a socialist regime, are supposed to be agents doing the best they can for their collective principal, the public.

The initial, utopian view of the Bolsheviks, and later of the Maoists in China, was that economic incentives were unnecessary to solve these principal–agent problems, and that a socialist society would instead rely upon the transformation of the person into a "socialist man." In Mao's lingo, all should learn to "serve the people," and not to take those actions which maximize personal security or comfort. If this transformation had occurred, the agency problems would have been greatly mitigated. In the event, most people could not motivate themselves, for a lifetime, by serving only the public good: people responded to their immediate situations much as they do in capitalist societies, by trying to look after their material interests a good proportion of the time.

To be more specific, the *manager–worker agency problem* festered for two reasons: workers had little motivation to work hard if it was virtually impossible to fire them, and there was little incentive to earn more because so few goods were available to buy. Much of the consumption bundle, including housing, was provided directly by the firm and not through the market. Secondly, the *planner–manager relationship* became one where the planners, or politicians, depended on the firms in their regions for income, and so, rather than carrying out plans proposed by the planning bureau, firm managers entered into bargaining relationships with politicians. An instance of this relationship was the "soft budget constraint": political authorities extended loans and tax exemptions to firms that, from the viewpoint of economic efficiency, should not have been extended. This was done in part because, not officially recognizing the existence of unemployment, the system had no mechanism for retraining and rehiring laid-off workers, and also because fulfilling the plan's production quotas was often evaluated independently of the costs entailed in so doing. The path of least resistance for government and planning bureaucrats often consisted in continuing to finance a firm that should have been allowed to die. The third agency problem, between the planners and the public, was supposed to be solved, in theory, by the vanguard role of the Communist Party: "From the masses to the masses" was Mao's theory of the party as agent of the people. But Mao was wrong: political competition, which is required to empower the public, was thoroughly squashed by Communist parties holding state power throughout the world.

What are the analogous principal–agent problems in a capitalist economy, and how are they addressed? The manager–worker problem remains essentially the same; it is solved by using both the carrot and the stick. Arguably, the carrot works better. For instance, job ladders within the firm, with wages increasing as one moves up the ladder, are constructed to give workers an incentive to build a career in the firm. This is a type of "efficiency wage" theory, in which a firm pays a worker more than the worker is willing to accept – or, to be somewhat imprecise, more than the market requires – to bind her to the job. Much of modern industrial relations is concerned with ways of solving the manager–worker agency problem.

Under capitalism, the analogue of the planner–manager agency problem is the *stockholder–manager agency problem*. Managers are supposed to undertake policies which are in the best interest of the stockholders, that is, which maximize profits, or the value of the firm. It is often not in the best personal interest of the manager to do so: he may not want to liquidate an unprofitable branch of the firm, because of the stress involved in laying off the employees; or he may be reluctant to distribute profits as dividends to shareholders, preferring to keep them to finance projects internally, and thus to avoid the scrutiny that a bank would insist upon before approving a loan; or, he may purchase corporate jets for executive travel, and make other lavish expenditures that are not in the stockholders' interest. Different capitalist economies have undertaken quite different strategies to solve this agency problem. It is believed by many finance economists that the stock market and the takeover process are the institutions that force managers to operate firms in the interests of shareholders. If profits decline because of bad management, the stock price of the firm falls, and the firm becomes an attractive target for a takeover. This, it is argued, is the main disciplinary device that induces managers to act in the interests of shareholders.

Japan, however, appears to have a quite different way of creating efficient management. The stock market has been relatively unimportant in Japanese corporate finance. Firms are largely financed by bank loans, and stockholders have little say in corporate decisions. Japanese firms are organized into groups called *keiretsu,* each of which is associated with a main bank that is responsible for organizing loan consortia for the firms in its group. The bank is in large part responsible for monitoring the firm's management. The bank even protects its firms from takeovers. A bank has an interest in running a tight ship so that its *keiretsu* is an attractive one for new firms to join, for if it disciplines unprofitable firms it can easily arrange loan consortia for its *keiretsu*'s members.

What is the analogue of the public–planner agency problem under capitalism? It must be the *public–stockholder agency problem,* except neither capitalist property relations nor culture require the stockholder to be an agent of the public. At this point, the theory of capitalism invokes Adam Smith: stockholders, that is to say firm owners, are directed to undertake those actions which are in the public interest as if by an invisible hand. But the invisible hand only works well under a stringent set of conditions. In practice, modern capitalist societies have developed other institutions where the invisible hand fails: antitrust law, regulation of various kinds, taxation and public expenditures, and so on.

The argument, then, seeks to establish that a combination of markets and political democracy solves capitalism's three principal–agent problems better than dictatorship and administrative allocation solve the three problems in Soviet-type economies.

The skepticism I now have about the validity of this argument is that in the postwar period, from 1950 to 1970, the Soviet-type economies did quite well. Indeed, the Western attacks on these economies were of a markedly different nature from their attacks of the late 1980s. In the earlier period, Western critics of Communism argued that, *despite* its economic success,

Communism was bad for human welfare because of the lack of political freedom.

If, indeed, it is true that for about twenty years in the postwar period, and certainly during the 1930s in the Soviet Union, economic growth was respectable in the Communist economies, then we cannot simply invoke principal–agent problems as an explanation of the failure of those economies in the 1980s. At least the principal–agent argument is not sufficiently fine-grained, for some characteristic of these economies that changed between 1960 and 1985 must be brought into play. I conjecture that what changed was the dependence of the growth in economic welfare on technological change. In the postwar period, economic welfare could grow rapidly without technological innovation, since these economies were in large part devastated by the war, and rebuilding them increased economic welfare a great deal, even without technological innovation (so-called intensive growth). By the 1980s, or perhaps earlier, growth in economic welfare depended much more on the ability of an economy to innovate or to adopt new technologies producing improved commodities. At this, the Soviet-type economies failed dismally, and I think it is misleading to characterize this failure as one due to principal–agent problems, except in the tautological sense that the public was not being well served by its agents, the planners and managers, if the latter were not succeeding in introducing technological change.

To state the issue somewhat differently, it is false to say that sufficient technological change did not occur because some agent was not carrying out some principal's orders. No one gave such orders. The correct statement is that, without the competition that is provided by markets – both domestic and international – no business enterprise is forced to innovate, and without such forcing, innovation, at least at the rate that market economies engender, does not occur. Perhaps even the "forcing" view puts too much emphasis on the incentive question. It might just have been extremely difficult to innovate in the Soviet-type economies, because, for instance, information about commodities on the technological frontier was very hard to come by, because the best engineers and scientists were recruited by the defense sector, and because the Weltanschauung of the system belittled the kind of consumer gratification that is catered to by capitalist enterprise. This contrasts with the principal–agent explanation, which tends to emphasize the view that managers and workers didn't work hard because of a failure of incentives due to the economic mechanism.[8]

The question for socialists becomes, then, whether an economic mechanism can be designed under which technological innovation will take

[8] For other explanations of the Soviet failure, see Murrell and Olson (1991), Major (1992), and Andvig (1992).

place, but in which a characteristically capitalist distribution of income does not come about. More specifically, can competition between business enterprises, leading to innovation, be induced without a regime of private property in the means of production? For, at this point, we have no observations of innovation as a generic multisectoral phenomenon in an economy except when it is induced by competition.[9]

4.   Public bads and the distribution of profits

In Essay 14, I described Pranab Bardhan's market-socialist proposal, and in Sections 5 and 6 below, I will describe a related proposal of my own, based on bank monitoring, but where there is a stock market. One might object that these "managerial" market-socialist proposals will not amount to much: the distribution of profits would be essentially equalized, but profits only account for 10 to 30 percent of national income, and they may account under market socialism for less than that, because some revenue that takes the form of corporate profits in a capitalist system would there take the form of interest payments to banks and their depositors. I believe, however, that the partial equalization of income that takes place in these systems is only part of the story.

Classical arguments against capitalism discuss not only its bad distributional properties, but its generation of what in modern economic parlance are called public bads. A public bad is a feature of a society from which everyone suffers. Public bads are often created by free rider problems: it may be in the interest of each individual to perform a certain action, treating the behavior of others as given, but the collective result is a situation that is worse for everyone than if all had abstained from the action. A classical example of such a public bad is unemployment: it may be in the interest of each individual capitalist to lay off workers, but the collective effect can be to induce a depression in which all capitalists and workers suffer.

There is a class of public bads which have the property that they are inputs into or joint products of the production of firms. Pollution is the prototypical example: it is a joint product of many firms, and has a negative effect on people's welfare. The essential property of public bads in this class is that their presence increases the profits of firms. Other examples are: wars which increase profits, as by lowering the price of imported inputs used by firms; noxious advertising, as by cigarette companies; investment in firms doing business in South Africa; and fast assembly line

---

[9] We do have examples of profound innovation by administrative direction in specific areas – for example, the development of the atomic bomb in Los Alamos, New Mexico, in 1944–45.

speeds, or, more generally, the lack of enforcement of legislation applying to labor and occupational safety and health. All these practices increase profits – and often wages, as well – yet also directly reduce the welfare of the population.

It has also been argued that a highly unequal distribution of wealth is
itself a public bad, as it creates a kind of society that decreases the
welfare of all – most obviously, through the crime that it generates, and
less obviously, through the lack of community that it engenders.

Now any economy must admit some level of public bads. If we allowed
no pollution, we would have no production; there are even some ineffi-
ciencies associated with full employment. There is, however, a socially
optimal level of public bads, a level that best implements the trade-off for
society as a whole between consumption of the public bad and consumption of output.[10] The problem in a capitalist economy is that there is a
very small class of wealthy people who receive huge amounts of income as
their share of the firms' profits, and it is generally in the interest of these
people to have high levels of the profit-increasing public bads. The positive effect from the public bad on the income of members of this class
more than compensates them for the direct negative welfare effect.[11] In
this way, these public bads differ from the example of layoffs and unemployment, in which, hypothetically, even the capitalists suffered a net loss
of welfare. People who stand to gain from them actively fight, through
political activity, for high levels of profit-inducing public bads. The virtue of the market-socialist proposals is that there would exist no small,
powerful class of people deriving gargantuan amounts of income from
profits; hence no class would have such an interest in fighting for large
levels of public bads.

I do not make the blanket statement that, if no class exists which derives huge amounts of income from corporate profits, then low levels of
public bads will be forthcoming. One must examine carefully, through
modeling, the general equilibrium effects of a market-socialist mechanism
that precludes the formation of such a class. I have done some work on
this, which I summarize next.

5.   A market-socialist economy with a stock market[12]

In this section, the model I shall describe is not intended to be a complete description of a market-socialist economy. A number of matters are

---

[10] This assumes that we have a social welfare function.
[11] This is so, even if the rich cannot escape exposure to the public bad, as indeed they often
can.
[12] This section is based on Roemer (1992b), which contains the formal statement of the
model.

ignored, such as investment planning by the state. The purpose of the present model is to analyze one question only, the difference in the level of welfare of citizens that would come about as a consequence of different ways of defining property rights in firms.

I shall describe an economic environment upon which two possible politico-economic mechanisms shall be alternatively imposed, one capitalist, the other market-socialist. The problem is to study the welfare of the population at the equilibrium induced by each mechanism. The environment is described as follows. There is only one good produced, which all people like to consume. There is also a public bad, think of it as pollution, which is a joint product with the good in the technology of firms. One may think of this public bad as an input in each firm's production function, even if, in actuality, it is a joint product of the firm's production process, for the level of the public bad that the firm is allowed to "emit" indeed determines its production function – the higher the permissible level of pollution, the greater the firm's production at a given level of the other input. That other input is the good itself. Thus firms produce a single good using "inputs" of pollution and the good.

There are many citizens, of whom a small percentage are initially rich, and a large percentage are initially poor. This means that, initially, the rich own a large amount of the good, and the poor own a smaller amount. All citizens have the same preferences over consumption of the good, at various times, and of the public bad: utility is increasing in consumption of the good, and decreasing in consumption of the bad. The bad is public because all citizens must consume the same amount of it, namely, the amount emitted by firms. There are a number of firms in the economy. There is also a bank, which accepts deposits and makes loans.

There are three relevant dates at which things happen in the economy, call them 0, 1, and 2. Consumption of the good occurs at dates 0 and 2, and production and consumption of the public bad occur at date 2. Thus, a person's utility function has the form $u(x_0, x_2, z)$, where x_0 is consumption of the good at date 0, x_2 is consumption at date 2, and z is consumption of the public bad at date 2. There is uncertainty in the economy, which takes the following form. There are various possible *states of the world* that may occur at date 2. These states are brought about by events that should be thought of as occurring outside the model. What is relevant for us is that the production function of each firm depends upon the state of the world. Thus, the state of the world might be the weather, and the weather might affect the production of firms, which in this case are farms. Or investors may be uncertain about the technological change that will have taken place by date 2. At date 0, all citizens are supposed to know the probabilities with which the various states will occur at date 2.

At date 0, each citizen owns, as well as some amount of the good which characterizes her as rich or poor, an equal per capita share of every firm in the economy. At date 0, each citizen shall have to make consumption and investment decisions, whose precise nature depends upon the economic mechanism that shall be imposed. At date 1, citizens vote to determine the level of pollution that firms shall be allowed to emit. At date 2, one of the states of the world occurs, following which production takes place, with each firm emitting the amount of pollution that has been determined by vote at date 1. Output of the firms is distributed to citizens, and consumed by them, according to the investment decisions they have made at date 0.

A pictorial representation of the dated nature of events in the economy is presented in Figure 15.1.

Let us now impose a capitalist economic mechanism on this economic environment. This means that there is a stock market at date 0. People initially each own equal shares of all firms, but they can now trade these shares, where the price of a share is denominated in units of the good. Thus, at date 0, a person can purchase a portfolio of stock, using her endowment of stock and her endowment of the good in trade. She also chooses how much of her endowment to consume at date 0, and how much to put in the bank at the going interest rate. (She may, alternatively, borrow from the bank.) She also must contribute to the firm a share of its total investment (which is its input of the good) equal to the share of its stock she has purchased. After elections take place and the amount of the public bad is determined at date 1, and after the state of the world is revealed and production takes place at date 2, the citizen receives a share of output from each firm equal to the share of its stock she has purchased, and also receives her principal plus interest from the deposit she made in the bank at date 0 (or, alternatively, pays principal plus interest on the loan she took). Thus, if, at date 0, citizens can predict the outcome of the vote at date 1, and they face prices for stock of each firm and an interest rate, then they can choose a portfolio and consumption plan that maximizes their expected utility, the expectation being taken over the various states of the world that may occur at date 2. This optimal choice will be the same for every poor person and the same for every rich person, since there are only two types in the economy, but it will, of course, differ between the types.

How does a firm choose its level of investment, the amount of input it shall use in production at date 2? At the equilibrium level of investment for each firm, citizens will purchase its stock in varying amounts. For each firm, either the rich or the poor will end owning more than 50 percent of the stock. Call the group that ends up with more than half the

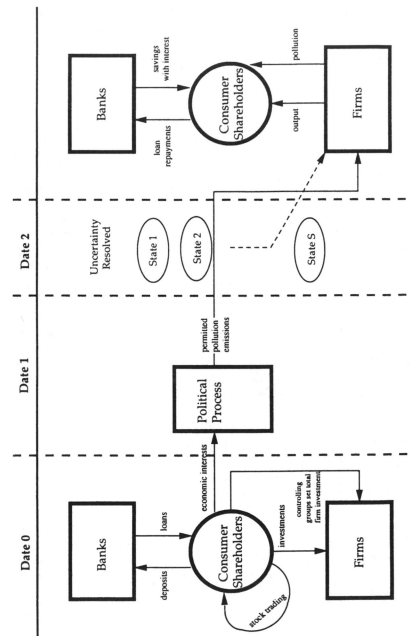

Figure 15.1

stock the firm's controlling group. Then the firm's investment choice must be that which is optimal for its controlling group; that is, there can be no other investment choice that would have enabled its controlling shareholder type to have a higher expected utility.

Finally, we must stipulate how people vote at date 1 on the level of the public bad. Given the investment and consumption choices that people have made at date 0, each has some optimal level for the amount of the public bad. (In this economy with just two types, there is one optimal level of the public bad for the poor and one for the rich.) Recall that increasing the amount of the public bad increases the output firms can produce at date 2, given their investment choices, and because of this, increases the consumption of the good of each citizen at date 2; but, on the other hand, increasing the level of the public bad also decreases utility directly for each citizen. There is, in general, for each citizen type, a level of the public bad which optimizes this trade-off.

A simple theory of voting would stipulate that the outcome of the election will be the level of the public bad preferred by the median voter, or in this case, preferred by the poor, who are in the majority. But this is unrealistic. I shall assume that the political process is sufficiently complex that both the rich and the poor have some impact on the determination of the level of the public bad. As a short-cut to providing a full-fledged theory of this process, I shall simply stipulate that the outcome of the election maximizes some weighted average of the utilities of the poor and the rich, and shall fix the weights used in this average as a characteristic of the political process.[13]

We are now prepared to state the concept of *capitalist politico-economic equilibrium* (CPEE). A CPEE is a set of stock prices for each firm's stock and an interest rate at date 0, a portfolio and consumption choice for each citizen at date 0, an amount of investment for each firm, and an amount of the public bad, such that:

(1)   at that level of the public bad, at those prices and interest rate, and given the investment choice of each firm, the consumption and portfolio choice of each citizen at date 0 maximizes her expected utility;

(2)   given the portfolio choices of each citizen, there is a controlling group for each firm, and the investment choice of the firm maximizes the expected utility for its controlling group, over all possible investment choices, given as well the level of the public bad;

---

[13] I have proposed and studied elsewhere models in which the rich can influence the outcome of elections in which they are in a small minority, through electoral propaganda. See Roemer (1992a).

(3)   the level of the public bad is the outcome of the political process at date 1 (that is, maximizes the appropriate weighted average of the utilities of the rich and the poor), given the portfolio choices of each individual;

(4)   total bank deposits made and total bank loans extended are equal at date 0.

Under suitable restrictions on the preferences of agents and the production functions of firms, a CPEE exists, and we can calculate it for specific choices of those functions.

Next, I describe the market-socialist politico-economic mechanism. It is the same as the capitalist mechanism but for one feature: one cannot purchase stock with the good, but only with coupons. This may be thought of in the following way. Each citizen begins with an endowment of the good, as before, and, say, 1,000 coupons. The prices of the firms' stocks are announced in coupons only. It is illegal to trade coupons for the good; one can only purchase stock of a firm with coupons, and can only sell it for coupons. Thus, each consumer has two budget constraints, one in terms of the good, and one in terms of coupons. The coupon budget constraint states that a person cannot purchase shares valued in excess of 1,000 coupons. The good budget constraint states that total consumption at date 0 plus deposits at date 0 plus amount of the good dedicated to the investment of firms in one's chosen portolio cannot exceed one's initial endowment of the good.

All else is the same as in the description of the CPEE. We can now define a *market-socialist politico-economic equilibrium* (MSPEE) as consisting of a set of stock prices for each firm's stock, denominated now in coupons, and an interest rate at date 0, a portfolio and consumption choice for each citizen at date 0, an amount of investment for each firm, and an amount of the public bad, such that conditions (1) through (4), spelled out in the definition of the CPEE, are satisfied. The only difference is that here prices of stock are denominated in coupons, not in units of the good. Under suitable conditions on preferences and production functions, an MSPEE exists, and, for specific choices of those functions, it can be calculated.

Thus one can, in principle, calculate the expected utilities of the rich and the poor in the equilibria of the two politico-economic mechanisms. I shall report some of those calculations in a moment. But first, let me conjecture, qualitatively, some of the differences that one might expect in politico-economic choices under the two mechanisms. What one should expect to happen in the capitalist mechanism is that the poor will sell a good deal of their initial endowment of firm shares to the rich, who shall pay for them with the good, which the poor shall consume at date 0. This will concentrate the ownership of stock in the hands of the rich, with two effects: they shall constitute the controlling group in most firms, and hence the firms' investment choices will be in their interest; and they shall have a greater interest than the poor in a high level of the public bad, as they own such large fractions of the stock of firms. In the coupon economy, however, the rich are precluded from buying controlling shares of all firms – for shares can only be purchased with coupons, and all citizens have the same initial endowment of coupons. One should expect, then, that at equilibrium the poor will be the controlling group in most firms, as they own the majority of coupons in society. Thus, the firms will choose their levels of investments in the interest of the poor. Furthermore, the rich will derive only a fairly small fraction of their date-2 consumption from the profits of firms, and will not, therefore, desire as high a level of the public bad as they did in the capitalist economy.

All this is conjecture, for the general equilibrium effects can be complicated. The only way to be sure what the welfare effects are in equilibrium is to prove a theorem, or to make some calculations. I have no general theorems at this time, but I report the results of some calculations in Table 15.1.

Table 15.1 presents results from calculating the coupon and capitalist politico-economic equilibria for this economic environment,[14] for values of λ running between 0 and 1, where λ and $(1-\lambda)$ are the weights assigned to the utility of the rich and the utility of the poor, respectively, in the determination of the political outcome, the level of the public bad. Four aspects of the equilibria are reported: the level of the public bad, the utilities of the two types, and total welfare, W, the sum of utilities in society. Let us examine the results for the capitalist economy first. "Median voter" politics occurs when $\lambda = 0$ – that is, when the level of the public bad is the optimal level for the poor voters. As the influence of the rich (λ) increases in the elections, the level of the public bad at equilibrium rises. Intuitively, this occurs because, at all equilibria reported here, the rich end up purchasing a little over 50 percent of the stock of both firms. It turns out that the bank is not used at all, and so the income of the rich (and poor) at date 1 comes entirely from firm revenues. The rich want a higher level of the public bad than the poor because they own a substantial fraction of

---

[14] The utility function of every agent is $u(x_0, x_2, z) = x_0^{1/2} + x_2^{1/2} - z$, where x_0 and x_2 are consumption of the good at dates 0 and 2 and z is consumption of the public bad at date 2. There are 95 poor agents, each endowed with 10 units of the good at date 0, and 5 rich agents, each endowed with 300 units of the good. There are two firms and three states of the world. The production function for firm j in state s is $g_s^j(x, z) = a_s^j x^{c_j} z^{(1-c_j)}$, where $c_1 = .7$, $c_2 = .3$, $(a_1^1, a_2^1, a_3^1) = (5, 13, 30)$, and $(a_1^2, a_2^2, a_3^2) = (9, 13, 16)$.

Table 15.1.

λ	Coupon equilibrium				Capitalist equilibrium			
	$\bar{z}$	u^P	u^R	W	$\bar{z}$	u^P	u^R	W
0	.884	2.46	11.51	291.10	.390	2.44	11.99	292.01
.04	.853	2.46	11.50	291.56	.463	2.45	12.09	292.79
.08	.822	2.47	11.49	291.99	.539	2.44	12.18	293.04
.12	.792	2.47	11.47	292.39	.616	2.44	12.25	292.86
.16	.762	2.48	11.46	292.74	.695	2.43	12.31	292.32
.20	.731	2.48	11.45	293.06	.775	2.42	12.37	291.46
.24	.702	2.49	11.43	293.33	.857	2.40	12.42	290.32
.28	.672	2.49	11.42	293.56	.941	2.39	12.46	288.95
.32	.643	2.49	11.40	293.75	1.03	2.37	12.50	287.36
.36	.614	2.49	11.39	293.89	1.11	2.35	12.54	285.57
.40	.585	2.50	11.37	293.97	1.20	2.32	12.56	283.61
.44	.556	2.50	11.35	294.01	1.29	2.30	12.59	281.49
.48	.528	2.50	11.33	293.98	1.37	2.28	12.61	279.21
.52	.500	2.50	11.31	293.90	1.47	2.25	12.63	276.80
.56	.473	2.50	11.28	293.75	1.56	2.22	12.65	274.26
.60	.445	2.50	11.26	293.53	1.65	2.19	12.66	271.60
.64	.418	2.50	11.23	293.23	1.74	2.16	12.67	268.82
.68	.392	2.49	11.21	292.86	1.84	2.13	12.68	265.94
.72	.366	2.49	11.18	292.40	1.93	2.10	12.69	262.96
.76	.340	2.49	11.15	291.84	2.03	2.07	12.69	259.88
.80	.314	2.48	11.11	291.18	2.12	2.03	12.69	256.71
.84	.289	2.47	11.08	290.41	2.22	2.00	12.69	253.46
.88	.265	2.47	11.04	289.51	2.32	1.96	12.69	250.12
.92	.241	2.46	11.00	288.47	2.42	1.93	12.69	246.70
.96	.217	2.45	10.95	287.26	2.52	1.89	12.69	243.21
1.00	.194	2.44	10.90	285.88	2.62	1.86	12.68	239.65

u^P = utility of the poor.
u^R = utility of the rich.
W = total utility in the population.
$\bar{z}$ = level of public bad.

the firm: each rich person gets a little over 10 percent of each firm's revenue, while each poor person receives about 0.5 percent of each firm's revenue. Thus, increasing the level of the public bad makes a much bigger
difference in date-2 revenue for the rich than for the poor, while they both
suffer the same direct disutility from the public bad. Generally speaking,
as the influence of the rich in the elections increases, the utility of the poor
falls and the utility of the rich rises. This statement is not exactly true,
however – for very small positive values of λ, the utility of the poor rises

with λ, and for λ close to 1, the utility of both agents falls with increases in λ. (The reader will get a feeling for how these apparent anomalies can occur presently, when I discuss the results in the coupon economy.) If one thinks that total welfare is a significant welfare statistic (and one needn't, because utility functions are not necessarily endowed with any interpersonally comparable meaning), then total welfare reaches a maximum at around $\lambda = .08$.

Now, examine the results for the coupon economy. Notice, first, that as the rich gain more influence in the elections, the level of the public bad *falls,* the rich become *worse* off and the poor become *better* off (at least up to a point, around $\lambda = .5$). Indeed, the level of the public bad is lower in the coupon than in the capitalist economy for all $\lambda \geq .20$, and the difference is substantial: e.g., at $\lambda = .52$, the level of the public bad in the coupon economy is about one-third its level in the capitalist economy. Total welfare is greater in the coupon economy for all $\lambda \geq .16$, and the poor (the vast majority of the population, in this environment) are better off in the coupon economy for all values of λ.

Here's the intuition for why the poor become better off as λ rises (up to about .5), an apparently paradoxical phenomenon. It turns out that substantial use of the bank occurs in the coupon economy: the poor borrow and the rich lend at date 0. The rich, who cannot purchase large shares of the firms from the poor on the coupon stock market, end up holding small fractions of both firms. By far the greater part of their income at date 2 comes from revenue from their bank deposits. The rich have little interest in increasing the value of the public bad, because revenues from firms add very little to their date-2 income. The poor, however, depend on firm revenues to pay off their loans at date 2, and so want higher levels of the public bad. Hence, as the rich gain more influence in the political process (increasing λ), the value of the public bad chosen falls. But as it falls, the poor demand to borrow less at date 0, *ceteris paribus,* since they will have less firm revenue at date 1 to pay back loans. This decreases the equilibrium interest rate, an effect that is good for the poor, who are debtors, and hence increases their utility, while the decrease in the public bad decreases their utility. The net effect of these two effects is not easy to predict, and we see that for values of λ less than one-half, the positive utility effect on the poor outweighs the negative effect.[15]

[15] One might argue that a political party representing the rich, and knowing Table 15.1, would advise the rich to reduce their influence in the political process! The rich would be better off abdicating, as it were. (For a discussion of the "abdication theory of the state" in Marx - why it is sometimes in the best interest of the bourgeoisie not to hold state power - see Elster, 1985, pp. 411–22.) But if the influence of the rich in the political process is the aggregated result of the actions of many rich citizens not acting in concert, then the results of Table 15.1 are credible.

In comparing the equilibria under the two politico-economic mechanisms, notice that the poor (who in this specification constitute 95 percent of the population) are better off in the market-socialist equilibrium than in the capitalist equilibrium regardless of the degree of influence the rich have in the elections. This is not a general theorem, but it happens to be true in this model.

To summarize, the market-socialist mechanism prevents a free rider problem from occurring that afflicts the poor under capitalism. In the capitalist economy, it is individually optimal for each poor person to sell the great majority of her initial shares to the rich, which creates a class of rich people who control firms and whose income depends on profits. The rich come to control firms, and through their influence on the political process, a high level of the public bad ensues. Under market socialism, the poor are precluded from liquidating their shares. The poor therefore remain the dominant shareholders, and, as well, the rich turn out to be a force for lowering the level of the public bad. The net effects of these changes are not easy to predict in theory, but we have seen that at least in one example, the poor end up better off in the market-socialist regime.

A final comment on these results is in order. One advantage of having a coupon stock market in real life would be to prevent the poor from selling their shares prematurely to the rich, something one fears might happen if, let us say, firms in a formerly Communist economy were denationalized by distributing shares to all citizens, after which a fully liberalized stock market were opened. Such premature liquidation of one's stock cannot occur in the coupon economy, since liquidation cannot occur. More specifically, this phenomenon could happen in the capitalist politico-economic mechanism if the poor had poorer information than the rich about the probabilities with which the various states of the world occur at date 2. It is important to mention that this does not happen in the model whose equilibria are reported in Table 15.1: there, all agents are equally knowledgeable and rational. So, in real life, one might expect that the difference between the utility of the poor under the two mechanisms would be even greater than it is in Table 15.1.

6. **The efficiency of firms and the rights of capital under market socialism** [16]

At the end of Section 4, I said that the issue for market socialism was whether a politico-economic mechanism could be created under which firms would behave competitively – in particular, in which they would

---

[16] This section is based in part on Bardhan and Roemer (1992).

innovate. As Hayek (1935, 1940) pointed out, and as Kornai (1992, 1993) ramified Hayek's point with the theory of the soft-budget constraint, when the state controls firms, firm managers are to a large extent absolved from responsibility with regard to errors in judgment; more generally, inefficient practices will not generally be weeded out as they are in a competitive market environment. The model of Section 5 does not address this issue at all. That model's purpose was to examine the general equilibrium welfare effects of the different financing mechanisms, under the assumption that the firm manager was a perfect agent of the firm's controlling group. Indeed, technological innovation was not an issue. The purpose of this section is to argue that there are institutions that would force firms to behave competitively in the coupon economy of Section 5.

As in the Bardhan model (Essay 14), firms in the coupon economy would be organized around a fairly small number of main banks, as in the Japanese *keiretsu*. A main bank would be primarily responsible for putting together loan consortia to finance the operations of the firms in its group; it would, correlatively, be responsible for monitoring these firms. The coupon stock market serves two of the three functions of a capitalist stock market: the movement in the coupon price of a firm's stock is a signal to banks and citizens about how well the firm is expected to perform, and it allows citizens to choose how to bear risk. It does not perform the third function, of raising capital, which is here provided by banks. If the coupon price of a firm's stock falls, or more often, before that happens, the main bank would investigate how well the firm is being managed. It has an incentive to monitor the firms in its group effectively, because, by so doing, it keeps its firms profitable, and thereby able to pay back their loans. This gives the bank a good reputation, making it easier for it to continue to raise money to finance the operations of firms in its group.

But why should the bank, which is itself a publicly owned institution, perform its monitoring job well?[17] The principal question is whether the banks would operate with sufficient independence of the state, making decisions about firms using economic and not political criteria. Bardhan and I do not believe that we have a definitive solution to this problem, although we view the following features of the economy as ones which would induce banks to do their job properly.

As Essay 14 explained, there should be, first, constitutional provisions that grant the banks considerable independence from state control. This

[17] I have not specified the control and ownership structure of banks in the market-socialist proposal. I will here suppose that they are publicly owned in the sense that their profits go in large part directly to the state treasury. Their managers, however, would be hired on a competitive managerial labor market, as described below.

would, for example, include guarantees that bank management be evaluated on economic criteria only – that managers be hired on a managerial labor market, for instance, by a board of directors. How should the board of directors of a large state bank be chosen? Robert Pollin (1992) has made a suggestion (in another context): a fraction of the directors should be elected by citizens in the bank's district. This would provide some (although not foolproof) protection against the banks' directors becoming a ruling class who represent the wealthy. Second, the reputational concerns of the main banks' managers should act as an antidote to susceptibility to political pressure. In Japan, even though banks have been closely regulated by the Ministry of Finance, managers exhibit keenness to preserve their reputation as good monitors, and banks compete in seeking the position of main bank for well-run firms. The managerial labor market will not forget if a bank manager forgives bad loans or nonperforming firms too often. Third, incentive features would be a part of the salary structure of bank management. Fourth, the doors of international product competition must be kept open, which would act as a check on laxity of the institutional monitors. Fifth, as Sah and Weitzman (1991) have suggested, before large investment projects begin, banks should make well-publicized precommitments that promise liquidation should the projects' performance at prespecified dates not exceed prespecified levels. The public nature of these precommitments would preclude the soft-budget constraint problems that Mathias Dewatripont and Eric Maskin (1993) have studied, in which it is in the interest of public banks to renegotiate loans on poorly performing projects. Sixth, some significant fraction of the shares of banks should not be held by the government, but by pension funds, insurance companies, and other institutions which would be interested in the banks' profitability, and would act to counter political pressure from the state.

In sum, the banks' independence from political control would be enforced by a series of legal and economic measures; banks would constitute a hard layer of economic accountability between the state and the management of firms. Colin Mayer and his co-authors have argued, in several papers, that a system in which banks monitor firms is preferable to the takeover process as the mechanism guaranteeing firm performance in capitalist economies;[18] there seems ample reason to believe that a similar mechanism can be adapted to a market-socialist economy.

If banks monitor firms aggressively and firms must depend on banks for finance and if the doors to international trade are open, firms will innovate. Under capitalism, innovations are designed in the research-and-development departments of large firms, and also enter the economy

[18] See Corbett and Mayer (1991) and Franks and Mayer (1990).

through the formation of new, small firms. In Bardhan's and my managerial proposals, it is envisaged that many small firms which grow would eventually be bought by large firms in the "public" sector, as happens under capitalism. Or the government might purchase the firm and auction it in the public sector. Perhaps joining the public sector would be a prerequisite to receiving loans from the main banks, or loans at preferential interest rates. There would be a statute requiring nationalization of private firms that reach a given size – a size at which their erstwhile owners would become wealthy from the state's purchase of their firm. Allowing such a private sector should provide almost the same incentives that exist in capitalism for those who form new firms based on innovations. Nationalizing firms at a certain level would prevent the emergence of a class of capitalists capable of influencing politics and economic policy by virtue of its economic control of significant sectors of the means of production.

I must emphasize that I envisage the coupon proposal as a desirable model of market socialism only when the economy can support sophisticated financial institutions and regulation. (For economies at low levels of development, the Bardhan *keiretsu* model is, I believe, superior.) Without a monitoring organ like the U.S. Securities and Exchange Commission, it would be difficult to control black-market transactions in which wealthy citizens purchased coupons from poor citizens with cash. There are other ways that firms can accommodate investors who wish to capitalize their coupon portfolio: some firms could become "cash cows," selling off their capital stock and paying the proceeds out to shareholders as dividends. The coupon price of the shares would eventually fall to zero, but by that time the shareholders would have effectively capitalized their coupon holdings. Cash cows must be prevented by regulation – for example, by limiting dividend payouts to a given fraction of earnings.

Both black-market sales of coupons and cash cows can to a large extent be prevented by the creation of financial instruments enabling those who need a large sum of cash (to start a small business, for example) to get it using their coupon portfolios as collateral. Banks could lend the expected present value of a coupon portfolio to a citizen, taking over the portfolio and managing it during the period of the loan, and servicing the loan with income from the portfolio. If this kind of instrument is used on a large scale, and banks come to control the coupon portfolios of a substantial fraction of the population, one must ask whether the decentralization of economic power, necessary for the decreased levels of public bads as described in Section 4, will be reversed. The answer must be that the banks will be publicly owned, with a fraction of their boards consisting of popularly elected directors. Thus, banks will not represent the interests of a small, wealthy class.

7.   Socialism and democracy

Almost all Western socialists today are democrats; some, such as Samuel Bowles and Herbert Gintis (1986) are interested in socialism principally insofar as it is instrumental for bringing about democracy. I have defined what socialists want as including equal opportunity for political influence, and I shall here be conventional in assuming that democracy is a precondition for such equality, although this assumption is by no means obviously true. It may be more accurate to say that serious disagreements exist with respect to what form of democracy can deliver the desired equality.[19]

A regime of market socialism might well be characterized by its constitution, which would limit the permissible degree of accumulation of private property in productive assets, and perhaps explicitly describe other kinds of property that are (constitutionally) protected. One justification for a supermajoritarian requirement to reverse such provisions is that property relations will not engender long-term planning and, in particular, investment, if they are thought to be easily reversible.

I think it is incontrovertible that a key reform necessary to achieve the three desiderata of socialists is massively improved education for the children of the poor and the working class. Only through education can the difference in opportunities faced by them and the children of the well-off be eradicated; only when skills become less unequally distributed, because of education, will wage differentials narrow significantly. To devote the required amount of resources to this kind of education will require a massive change in outlook of the citizenry of every large, heterogeneous country. Majorities will have to overcome their racism, but more than that, they will have to be won to the position, as John Donne (Devotion 17, 1623) wrote, that "No man is an island entire of itself. Every man is a piece of the continent, a part of the main. . . ." Thus, the implementation of a thoroughgoing socialism in a democracy will take a long time, if it must await such a feeling of community among people.

But I think that a number of the ills of capitalism would probably be cured more quickly, without the prerequisite of this feeling of community, because of the changed economic interests people would have under the various proposals for property redistribution that I have cited. I have outlined how the level of various public bads in a democratic society is the outcome of a political struggle in which different classes fight for their interests. If interests change, then so, in general, will the equilibrium level of public bads. I think that, to some extent, racism and sexism are pub-

---

[19] See Schmitter and Karl (1991) for definitions of democracy, and Riker (1982) for general skepticism concerning the feasibility of democracy.

lic bads of this kind. An old Marxist argument maintains that divisions among the working class – created, for example, by racism and sexism – strengthen the bosses in the struggle against labor.[20] To the extent that this is the case, capitalism may develop mechanisms to foment racism and sexism, for example, by the treatment of minorities and women in the capitalist media. Were profits equally distributed in the population, the public-bad argument of Section 4 implies that such capitalist-inspired fomenting of divisions in the working class would be reduced. I do not ignore the fact that people themselves have racist and sexist ideas, and so one cannot expect changes overnight with respect to these practices. But the change in property relations would dissolve one powerful class interest in the maintenance of discrimination.

A fundamental left-wing criticism of capitalist democracy has been that, as long as capital is in the hands of a small, wealthy class, politics must conform to the needs of that class. (See, for instance, Block 1977; and Przeworski, 1985, p. 42.) With public bank directors popularly elected, and legal provisions limiting the freedom of firms to export capital, the "structural power of capital" over society as a whole would be broken. Those who control capital would not be able to hold society hostage by the threat to exit. In his proposal for reforming capitalism, Block (1992) accomplishes this result by requiring banks' boards of directors to represent a variety of constituencies, including citizens who are not shareholders.

It would be comforting to be able to argue that, once a mechanism for redistributing profits had been put in place, then a feeling of such community would develop that the well-to-do would be willing to sacrifice income in order to fund the kind of educational system necessary to raise massively the opportunities of the many. I do not see the evidence for such a claim. Despite the fact of significant egalitarianism in the European social democracies, that degree of community has not developed there. The ideology of individualism appears to remain quite strong, as reflected in the resurgence of the conservative parties. Despite the norm of egalitarianism that existed to a nontrivial extent in Yugoslavia, the Eastern European countries, and the USSR, we do not see a powerful socialist phoenix rising from the ashes of Communism.

This brings up the question whether the transformation to the "socialist person" will be facilitated by institutions of market socialism, or whether, indeed, such a transformation will ever occur. Every socialist revolution (the Soviet Union, China, Cuba) has had its golden age, a period when a large fraction of the population was motivated to both sacrifice in the

---

[20] For models, evidence, and reference to other literature, see Reich (1981) and Roemer (1979).

name of building socialism and otherwise behave in a cooperative manner. But these golden ages have been quite short; it is not clear whether with continued economic success they would have continued, or whether, independently of economic success, the golden spirit cannot last, because, for instance, it is engendered by a great *change* for the better, rather than a period of *stable* good times.[21]

I therefore remain agnostic on the question of the genesis of the socialist person, and prefer to put my faith in the design of institutions that will engender good results with ordinary people. With such agnosticism, are there nevertheless grounds for believing that market socialism would eventually increase the support for greater investments in public education? Perhaps: again, I will invoke the public-bad argument. To a degree, education of the working class is a profit-increasing public good, and to this degree, it is rational for capitalists to support its financing. It is almost certainly the case that publicly supported education in the United States is at present below this degree, and indeed significant sections of the capitalist class support increased educational funding: U.S. workers would be more productive and could more easily acquire profit-enhancing skills if they could read detailed instruction manuals, as Japanese workers can.[22] What may well be the case, however, is that the optimal degree of working-class education for capitalists is less than the socially optimal degree – after a point, that is, increased public education may have a net negative effect on profits (when the profit taxes needed to finance the marginal educational increment for the working class are more than the profits the increment induces), while it continues to have a large positive marginal effect as a non-profit-inducing public good, via its effect on social culture (in which I include everything from improved television programming to public civility). It is this additional educational increment which, according to the argument of Section 4, a society in which profits are equally distributed is more likely to support through its political process.[23]

The public-bads argument that I have employed here assumes unchanging values; when I have referred to transformation into the socialist person, I refer to changing values. Despite my stated agnosticism concerning the genesis of the latter, I do think that values change as people experience new situations; so if public funding of education increases, first due only to changes in class interests, then experiencing the new equilibrium, where

---

21 Recall Tibor Scitovsky's (1976) view that happiness comes from a change to something different, not a stably good situation.

22 Hashimoto (1992) reports that, in Japan, the Honda training program for workers involves them studying manuals. When Honda set up its U.S. plant, it discovered that workers were unable to learn by reading manuals.

23 To put the argument in the language of Section 4, we would say that, after a point, the *lack* of public education is a profit-increasing public bad.

people are better educated, may well induce a value change, which would then bring about further increases in educational funding. I do believe, however, that value changes occur slowly, and by no means do they always occur in the "right" direction. Albert Hirschman (1982) has argued that values cycle between public-orientedness and private-orientedness. For these reasons, I do not base a blueprint for a socialist future on the coming of the socialist person.

8.   Criticisms of market socialism from the left

There are several powerful challenges to both market socialism based on labor-managed firms and "managerial market" socialism from the left. (I have not discussed the former, better-known type in this essay.) Perhaps the most basic is the claim that some of capitalism's fundamental shortcomings are associated with its competitive nature, and these would be inherited by all varieties of market socialism, relying, as they do, on competition among firms.

Where there is competition, there are losers, and where there are losers, there is often loss of self-esteem. If self-esteem is a (Rawlsian) primary good, and arguably one of the most important, what progress toward human fulfillment would market socialism mark? Now it does not necessarily follow that a society whose economic mechanism requires competition of business enterprises also requires that kind of interpersonal competitiveness whose result is the loss of self-esteem for those who lose. Yet an argument can be made, I think, that competition in the economic sphere engenders interpersonal competition as a more generalized phenomenon in society. But even without such an argument, it must be the case that, as long as markets are used to allocate labor, people will in large part measure themselves by the income they earn. (As a *New Yorker* cartoon quipped, "Money is life's report card.")

Another consequence of competition (besides the self-esteem effect) may be a lack of community. If community is capitalism's essential lack, then market socialism would not mark a qualitative improvement.

Secondly, there is the view, associated with Bowles and Gintis (1986) and Cohen and Rogers (1993) that what is principally valuable about socialism is its extension of democracy into economic life, and accordingly, managerial market socialism, which does not even introduce industrial democracy, is a weak advance at best over capitalism.

The substantive issue posed by these challenges is whether the market-socialist proposals I have outlined represent sufficient advances over capitalism, from the viewpoint of the socialist who is characterized as the triple egalitarian of Section 1, to be called "socialist." I intend market socialism

as a short-term proposal: to wit, as I explain in Essay 14, I do not defend
as just any system in which people receive wages proportional to their
acquired skills. The salient issue is: Does there exist a next step from capitalism approaching the long-term socialist goal which is better than some
variety of market socialism? It will come as no surprise that I believe there
is not, although I have no proof.

I have no objection to further redistribution of income through social
democratic methods – in effect, this means by the provision of more goods
through public financing and its associated system of progressive taxation – but I believe that the Nordic social democratic model requires very
special conditions (a homogeneous population and a strong, unified labor movement). Here, I mention another caveat. In a market economy,
I think people tend to believe they have earned, in the moral sense, what
they receive through selling their talents on the market. (This is closely
related, of course, to the view that market competition engenders a loss
of self-esteem for those who are not economically successful.) This view
is raised to high principle by liberal philosophy of the Lockean variety,
which argues that people have a right to keep that which they make by
their wits and brawn; it is unfortunate that many Marxists misunderstood
the labor theory of value as having similar moral implications.[24] While
modern egalitarian political philosophy is clearly in disagreement with
this liberal view, it is, perhaps, psychologically disassociable from the institution of a labor market. If so, this places a natural limit on the degree
of redistribution that can be accomplished by social democratic methods:
an economic mechanism, at least in a democracy, cannot be stable if it
rewards people in disproportion to what they believe they deserve. Indeed, the current semi-reversion of Scandinavian social democracy to a
less egalitarian capitalism may have this psychological fact as one source.

Thus, the limited degree of equality that I think market socialism can
achieve is due in the main to my skepticism concerning the existence of
alternatives to a competitive labor market for allocating labor in an efficient manner. Indeed, the key to the market-socialist proposals outlined
above is the non-Hayekian view that there is a fundamental asymmetry
between wages and profits as categories of national income: while considerations of efficiency pretty much determine the distribution of wages
among workers, they do not so determine the distribution of profits. This
view is predicated on the estimate that the extreme concentration of profits characteristic of capitalist societies is not due to the possession and
exercise, by the class of wealthy who receive them, of talents that are as
scarce in the population as their remuneration under capitalism would

[24] On this point, see G. A. Cohen (1990a).

seem to imply, or that, although scarce, those talents would nevertheless be exercised, even by their self-interested holders, with substantially less remuneration than they receive under capitalist property relations.

With regard to the left-wing challenges concerning the key role played by competition in the market-socialist models, my response is pragmatic. I think the Soviet experience has shown us that even an authoritarian politico-economic mechanism, *a fortiori* a democratic one, cannot be stable for a society unless it delivers to its members goods of comparable quality to what those in other societies, deemed similar to itself in culture and educational achievement, receive. Thus, socialist politico-economic mechanisms must be capable of innovation at roughly the rate sustained by capitalist ones. As I have argued, we know of no mechanism that can produce an innovative economy except interfirm competition, and it follows that we must limit our investigation to models based upon such competition.

Finally, I offer a defense of the managerial market-socialist model against those who argue that labor management must be a feature of the next step. Contemporary models of labor-managed market socialism all recognize that firms must raise capital from nonmembers, either through a stock market or through bank loans, and this would, to some unknown extent, compromise the autonomy of workers with regard to control of the firm.[25] It is therefore not clear to what extent the managerial and labor-managed proposals for market socialism really differ. My preference for the managerial proposals is based on a conservative principle – that it is best to change features of a system one at a time, if possible.[26] The biological metaphor is apt: an organism with one mutation is more likely to survive than one in which two mutations occur simultaneously. I think it is more important to change the private nature of the financing of firms than the management structure as the first step.

This should not be taken to imply that I unequivocally endorse introducing labor management as the second step after the first step of financial restructuring has been successfully completed. For labor management may make firms too risk-averse, as the authors I have quoted earlier and others recognize.[27] It may, for instance, be socially optimal for firms to take a degree of risk which induces an expectation that each worker will have to change jobs, say, three or four times in her working life, due to a

[25] See Drèze (1993), Weisskopf (1993), and Fleurbaey (1993).

[26] See Murrell (1992) for a characterization of conservatism not as a liberal political philosophy, but as a one-step-at-a-time approach to changing the politico-economic mechanism.

[27] In addition to Weisskopf (1993), Fleurbaey (1993), and Drèze (1993), see Bowles and Gintis (1993).

layoff or bankruptcy. But the individual might well wish to avoid this degree of risk.

9.   Prospects for the future

Writing obituaries for socialism these days has become a popular pastime. It was utopian, they say, to believe a society could be founded on a norm of egalitarianism. Greed is a necessary evil that can be tamed by the right institutions – those of the market, contract law, and private property – to bring about the material conditions enabling human dignity and fulfillment for all.

I am not one to cheer the inglorious end of the Soviet Union, despite what that state had become. Its demise marks a setback for socialism, because, for many hundreds of millions, its existence continued to support the belief that one could more than dream about founding a society based on a norm of equality. And holding that belief is a precondition for struggling to create such a society.

This essay's aim has been to sketch blueprints for a feasible socialism, to provide a basis, once again, for "more than dreaming." I have not, however, engaged in "transitology." Yet for any endstate of a social process to be feasible, some feasible path must exist from here to there. For some tentative transitology, I refer the reader to Roemer (1994, Section 15).

Morale is a key problem for socialists today: to keep the objective point of view, to understand how brief a moment seventy years is in human history, to remember how continuous has been the struggle of humankind against inequality and injustice, and to realize how unsolved on a world scale are those problems that engendered the socialist idea almost two centuries ago. And it is not as if we have not learned from those seventy years: we have learned massively. Those who trumpet the theme that capitalism has won, or that the end of history has come, reveal only their own myopia. (It may have won, but certainly it is too soon to tell. Recall Chou En-lai's wise response to a request to comment on the consequences of the French Revolution: "It's too soon to tell," said he.) There is still ample reason to believe, as Marx once said, that real human history – the history of society that, for the vast majority of people, will eliminate material scarcity as the impassable barrier to self-realization – has not yet begun.

References

Ackerman, B. 1980. *Social Justice and the Liberal State*. New Haven: Yale University Press.

Andvig, J. C. 1992. "Transitions to market economies." Working paper. Norwegian Institute of International Affairs.

Arneson, R. J. 1989. "Equality of opportunity for welfare." *Philosophical Studies* 56, 77-93.

1990. "Liberalism, distributive subjectivism, and equal opportunity for welfare." *Philosophy & Public Affairs* 19, 159-94.

Arrow, K. 1951. *Social Choice and Individual Values*. New Haven: Yale University Press.

Aumann, R. 1985. "What is game theory trying to accomplish?" In K. Arrow and S. Honkapohya (eds.), *Frontiers of Economics*. Oxford: Basil Blackwell.

Bardhan, P. 1982. "Agrarian class formation in India," *Journal of Peasant Studies* 10.

1993. "Risk taking, capital markets, and market socialism." In Bardhan and Roemer (1993).

Bardhan, P., and J. Roemer. 1992. "Market socialism: a case for rejuvenation." *Journal of Economic Perspectives* 6, 101-16.

(eds.). 1993. *Market Socialism: The Current Debate*. New York: Oxford University Press.

Barry, B. 1979. "Don't shoot the trumpeter – he's doing his best!" *Theory and Decision* 11, 153-80.

1989. *Theories of Justice,* vol. 1. Berkeley: University of California Press.

Berliner, J. 1993. "Innovation, the USSR, and market socialism." In Bardhan and Roemer (1993).

Billera, L., and R. Bixby. 1973. "A characterization of Pareto surfaces." *Proceedings of the American Mathematical Society* 41, no. 1.

Binmore, K. G. 1993. "Game theory and the social contract, Part 1." Working paper. Department of Economics, University of Michigan, Ann Arbor.

Blackburn, R. 1991. "Fin de siècle: socialism after the crash." *New Left Review* 185, 5-66.

Block, F. 1977. "The ruling class does not rule: notes on the Marxist theory of the state." *Socialist Revolution* 33, May-June.

1992. "Capitalism without class power." *Politics and Society* 20.

Bös, D. 1986. *Public Enterprise Economics*. Amsterdam: North Holland.

334   References

Bowles, S., and H. Gintis. 1976. *Schooling in Capitalist America.* New York: Basic Books.

1981. "Structure and practice in the labor theory of value." *Review of Radical Political Economics* 12, 1–26.

1983. "The power of capital: on the inadequacy of the conception of the capitalist economy as 'private.'" *Philosophical Forum* 14.

1986. *Democracy and Capitalism.* New York: Basic Books.

1993. "The democratic firm: an agency-theoretic formulation." In Bowles, Gintis, and Gustafsson (1993).

Bowles, S., H. Gintis, and B. Gustafsson (eds.). 1993. *Democracy and Markets: Participation, Accountability, and Efficiency.* Cambridge University Press.

Braithwaite, R. 1955. *Theory of Games as a Tool for the Moral Philosopher.* Cambridge University Press.

Braverman, H. 1974. *Labor and Monopoly Capital.* New York: Monthly Review Press.

Brems, H. 1986. *Pioneering Economic Theory, 1630–1980.* Baltimore: Johns Hopkins University Press.

Brenkert, G. 1979. "Freedom and private property in Marx." *Philosophy & Public Affairs* 8, 122–47.

Brenner, R. 1976. "Agrarian class structure and economic development in preindustrial Europe." *Past and Present* 70, 30–75.

1977. "The origins of capitalist development: a critique of neo-Smithian Marxism." *New Left Review* 104, 25–93.

Brock, H. 1979. "A game theoretic account of social justice." *Theory and Decision* 11, 239–65.

Cohen, G. A. 1978. *Karl Marx's Theory of History: A Defence.* Princeton: Princeton University Press.

1979. "The labor theory of value and the concept of exploitation." *Philosophy & Public Affairs* 8, 338–60.

1981. "Freedom, justice and capitalism." *New Left Review* 125, 3–16.

1983. "More on the labor theory of value." *Inquiry* 26, 309–31.

1983a. "The structure of proletarian unfreedom." *Philosophy & Public Affairs* 12, 3–33.

1985. "Nozick on appropriation." *New Left Review* 150, 89–107.

1986. "Self-Ownership, world ownership, and equality: part 2." *Social Philosophy & Policy* 3, 77–96.

1989. "On the currency of egalitarian justice." *Ethics* 99, 906–44.

1990. "Equality of what? On welfare, goods, and capabilities." *Recherches Economiques de Louvain* 56, 357–82.

1990a. "Marxism and contemporary political philosophy, or: Why Nozick exercises some Marxists more than he does any egalitarian liberal." *Canadian Journal of Philosophy,* Supplementary Volume 16, 363–87.

1991. "The future of a disillusion." *New Left Review* 190 (November–December), 5–22.

1992. "Incentives, inequality, and community." In G. B. Peterson (ed.), *The Tanner Lectures on Human Values,* vol. XIII. Salt Lake City: University of Utah Press.

References

335

Cohen, J., and J. Rogers. 1993. "Associative democracy." In Bardhan and Roemer (1993).

Corbett, J., and C. Mayer. 1991. "Financial reform in Eastern Europe: progress with the wrong model." *Oxford Review of Economic Policy* 7, 57-75.

Corchón, L., and I. Ortuño-Ortin. In press. "Robust implementation under complete local information." *International Journal of Game Theory*.

Dasgupta, P., and P. Hammond. 1980. "Fully progressive taxation." *Journal of Public Economics* 13, 142-54.

Debreu, G. 1959. *Theory of Value*. New Haven: Yale University Press.

Dewatripont, M., and E. Maskin. 1993. "Centralization of credit and long-term investment." In Bardhan and Roemer (1993).

Drèze, J. 1993. "Self-management and economic theory: efficiency, finance, and employment." In Bardhan and Roemer (1993).

Dworkin, R. 1977. *Taking Rights Seriously*. Cambridge, Mass.: Harvard University Press.

1981. "What is equality? Part 1: equality of welfare." *Philosophy & Public Affairs* 10, 185-246.

1981a. "What is equality? Part 2: equality of resources." *Philosophy & Public Affairs* 10, 283-45.

Edwards, R. 1979. *Contested Terrain: The Transformation of the Workplace in America*. New York: Basic Books.

Elster, J. 1982. "Roemer vs. Roemer." *Politics and Society* 11, 363-74.

1982a. *Sour Grapes*. Cambridge University Press.

1985. *Making Sense of Marx*. Cambridge University Press.

1986. "Self-realization in work and politics: the Marxist conception of the good life." *Social Philosophy & Policy* 3, 97-126.

Elster, J., and A. Hylland. 1983. "The contradiction between the forces and relations of production." In J. Elster (ed.), *Explaining Technical Change*. Cambridge University Press.

Elster, J., and J. Roemer (eds.). 1991. *Interpersonal Comparisons of Well-Being*. Cambridge University Press.

Fleurbaey, M. 1993. "An egalitarian democratic private ownership economy." In Bardhan and Roemer (1993).

Foley, D. 1967. "Resource allocation and the public sector." *Yale Economic Essays* 7, 45-98.

1970. "Lindahl's solution and the core of an economy with public goods." *Econometrica* 38, 66-72.

Franks, J., and C. Mayer. 1990. "Corporate ownership and corporate control: a study of France, Germany, and the UK." *Economic Policy* 10, 189-216.

Gauthier, D. 1985. "Bargaining and justice." *Social Philosophy & Policy* 2, 29-47.

1986. *Morals by Agreement*. Oxford: Oxford University Press.

Geras, N. 1986. *Literature of Revolution: Essays on Marxism*. London: Verso.

1992. "Bringing Marx to justice: an addendum and rejoinder." *New Left Review* 195, 37-69.

Grunebaum, J. O. 1987. *Private Ownership*. London: Routledge and Kegan Paul.

Harsanyi, J. 1977. "Morality and the theory of rational behavior." *Social Research* 44, 623–56.

Hashimoto, M. 1992. "Employment-based training in Japanese firms in Japan and in the United States: experiences of automobile manufacturers." Working paper. Department of Economics, Ohio State University.

Hayek, F. A. 1935. "The nature and history of the problem." In F. A. Hayek (ed.), *Collectivist Economic Planning*. London: George Routledge & Sons.

——— 1940. "Socialist calculation: the competitive 'solution.'" *Economica* 7, 125–49.

Heilbroner, R. 1989. "Reflections (capitalism)." *New Yorker* (January 23).

Hirschman, A. O. 1982. *Shifting Involvements: Private Interests and Public Action*. Princeton, N.J.: Princeton University Press.

Howe, R., and J. Roemer. 1981. "Rawlsian justice as the core of a game." *American Economic Review* 71, 880–95.

Hurwicz, L., D. Schmeidler, and H. Sonnenschein (eds.). 1985. *Social Goals and Social Organization*. Cambridge University Press.

Jensen, M. C. 1989. "Eclipse of the public corporation." *Harvard Business Review* (September–October), 61–74.

Kahneman, D., and A. Tversky. 1979. "Prospect theory: an analysis of decision under risk." *Econometrica* 47, 263–91.

——— 1982. "The psychology of preferences." *Scientific American* (January), 160–73.

Kalai, E. 1977. "Proportional solutions to bargaining situations: interpersonal utility comparisons." *Econometrica* 45, 1623–30.

——— 1985. "Solutions to the bargaining problem." In Hurwicz, Schmeidler, and Sonnenschein (1985).

Kalai, E., and D. Samet. 1985. "Monotonic solutions to general cooperative games." *Econometrica* 53, 307–28.

Kalai, E., and M. Smorodinsky. 1975. "Other solutions to Nash's bargaining problem." *Econometrica* 43, 513–18.

Kolm, S. C. 1972. *Justice et Équité*. Paris: Editions du Centre National de la Recherche Scientifique.

Kornai, J. 1992. *The Socialist System: The Political Economy of Communism*. Princeton: Princeton University Press.

——— 1993. "Market socialism revisited." In Bardhan and Roemer (1993).

Kronman, A. 1981. "Talent pooling." *Nomos* 13, 58–79.

Lange, O. 1938. "On the economic theory of socialism." In B. Lippincott (ed.), *On the Economic Theory of Socialism*. Minneapolis: University of Minnesota Press, 1956.

Lensberg, T. 1987. "Stability and collective rationality." *Econometrica* 55, 935–62.

Lindahl, E. 1919. "Positive Losung, Die Gerechtigkeit der Besteurung." Lund. English translation in Musgrave and Peacock (1958).

Lindert, P., and J. Williamson. 1983. "English workers' living standards during the industrial revolution: a new look." *Economic History Review* 36, 1–25.

Loomes, G., and R. Sugden. 1982. "Regret theory: an alternative theory of rational choice under uncertainty." *Economic Journal* 92, 805–24.

Machina, M. 1982. "'Expected utility' analysis without the independence axiom." *Econometrica* 50, 277–324.

1989. "Dynamic consistency and non-expected utility models of choice under uncertainty." *Journal of Economic Literature* 27, 1622–68.

MacPherson, C. B. 1973. *Democratic Theory.* Oxford: Clarendon Press.

1978. *Property: Mainstream and Critical Positions.* Toronto: University of Toronto Press.

Major, I. 1992. "The decay of command economies." Hungarian Institute of Economics, Budapest (processed).

Makowski, L. 1980. "Perfect competition, the profit criterion, and the organization of economic activity." *Journal of Economic Theory* 22, 105–25.

Makowski, L., and J. Ostroy. 1987. "Vickrey–Clarke–Groves mechanisms and perfect competition." *Journal of Economic Theory* 42, 244–61.

1992. "Vickrey–Clarke–Groves mechanisms in continuum economies: characterization and existence." *Journal of Mathematical Economics* 21, 1–35.

Marx, K. 1966. *Capital,* vol. III. Moscow: Progress Publishers.

1973. *The Grundrisse,* ed. Martin Nicolaus. New York: Vintage Books.

Maskin, E. 1977. "Nash equilibrium and welfare optimality." Working paper. Department of Economics, Massachusetts Institute of Technology.

1985. "The theory of implementation in Nash equilibrium: a survey." In Hurwicz, Schmeidler, and Sonnenschein (1985).

Meade, J. 1964. *Efficiency, Equality and the Ownership of Property.* London: Allen & Unwin.

Menger, C. 1954. *Principles of Economics.* Glencoe, Ill.: Free Press.

Mirrlees, J. 1974. "Notes on welfare economics, information, and uncertainty." In M. Balch, D. McFadden, and S. Wu (eds.), *Essays on Economic Behavior under Uncertainty.* Amsterdam: North Holland.

1982. "The economic uses of utilitarianism." In Sen and Williams (1982), pp. 63–84.

Morishima, M. 1973. *Marx's Economics.* Cambridge University Press.

Moulin, H. 1987. "A core selection for pricing a single output monopoly." *Rand Journal of Economics* 18, 397–407.

1990. "Joint ownership of a convex technology: comparison of three solutions." *Review of Economic Studies* 57, 439–52.

Moulin, H., and J. E. Roemer. 1989. "Public ownership of the world and private ownership of self." *Journal of Political Economy* 97, 347–67.

Murrell, P. 1992. "Conservative political philosophy and the strategy of economic transition." *East European Politics and Societies* 6, 3–16.

Murrell, P., and M. Olson. 1991. "The devolution of centrally planned economies." *Journal of Comparative Economics* 15, 239–65.

Musgrave, R. A., and A. T. Peacock (eds.). 1958. *Classics in the Theory of Public Finance.* London: Macmillan.

Nagel, T. 1991. *Equality and Partiality.* New York: Oxford University Press.

Narveson, J. 1983. "On Dworkinian equality." *Social Philosophy & Policy* 1, 1–23.

Nash, J. 1950. "The bargaining problem." *Econometrica* 18, 155–62.

North, D., and R. Thomas. 1973. *The Rise of the Western World.* Cambridge University Press.

Nove, A. 1983. *The Economics of Feasible Socialism*. London: George Allen and Unwin.

Nozick, R. 1974. *Anarchy, State and Utopia*. New York: Basic Books.

Nussbaum, M. 1990. "Aristotelian social democracy." In R. B. Douglass, G. Mara, and H. Richardson (eds.), *Liberalism and the Good*. New York: Routledge.

Ortuño, I., J. E. Roemer, and J. Silvestre. 1993. "Investment planning in market socialism." In Bowles, Gintis, and Gustafsson (1993).

Ostroy, J. 1980. "The non-surplus condition as a characterization of perfectly competitive equilibrium." *Journal of Economic Theory* 22, 183–207.

Parfit, D. 1984. *Reasons and Persons*. Oxford: Oxford University Press.

Pitt, J. No date. "Roemer on dependence." Working paper. Department of Philosophy, California State University at Fresno.

Pollin, R. 1992. "Public credit allocation through the Federal Reserve: why it is needed; how it should be done." Working paper. University of California at Riverside.

Post, D. 1990. "College-going decisions by Chicanos: the politics of misinformation." *Educational Evaluation and Policy Analysis* 12 (Summer), 174–87.

Przeworski, A. 1980. "Material interests, class compromise and the transition to socialism." *Politics and Society* 10, 125–54.

1985. *Capitalism and Social Democracy*. Cambridge University Press.

Putterman, L. 1993. "Incentive problems favoring non-centralized investment fund ownership." In Bardhan and Roemer (1993).

Rawls, J. 1971. *A Theory of Justice*. Cambridge, Mass.: Harvard University Press.

1982. "Social utility and primary goods." In Sen and Williams (1982).

Reich, M. 1981. *Racial Inequality*. Princeton, N.J.: Princeton University Press.

Reiman, J. 1987. "Exploitation, force, and the moral assessment of capitalism: thoughts on Roemer and Cohen." *Philosophy & Public Affairs* 16, 3–41.

Riker, W. H. 1988. *Liberalism against Populism*. Prospect Heights, Ill.: Waveland Press (first published 1982).

Robinson, J. 1966. *An Essay on Marxian Economics*. New York: St. Martin's Press.

Roemer, J. 1979. "Divide and conquer: microfoundations of a Marxian theory of wage discrimination." *Bell Journal of Economics* 10, 695–705.

1981. *Analytical Foundations of Marxian Economic Theory*. Cambridge University Press.

1982. *A General Theory of Exploitation and Class*. Cambridge, Mass.: Harvard University Press.

1982a. "New directions in the Marxian theory of exploitation and class." *Politics and Society* 11, 253–88.

1982b. "Reply." *Politics and Society* 11, 375–94.

1983. "Are socialist ethics consistent with efficiency?" *Philosophical Forum* 14, 369–88.

1983a. "R. P. Wolff's reinterpretation of Marx's labor theory of value: comment." *Philosophy & Public Affairs* 12, 70–83.

1983b. "Unequal exchange, labor migration, and international and capital flows: a theoretical synthesis." In P. Desai (ed.), *Marxism, Central Plan-*

ning, and the Soviet Economy: Essays in Honor of Alexander Erlich. Cambridge, Mass.: MIT Press.

1986. "Equality of resources implies equality of welfare." *Quarterly Journal of Economics* 101, 751–84.

1986a. "Rational choice Marxism." In J. E. Roemer (ed.), *Analytical Marxism*. Cambridge University Press.

1988. "Axiomatic bargaining theory on economic environments." *Journal of Economic Theory* 45, 1–31.

1988a. *Free to Lose: An Introduction to Marxist Economic Philosophy*. Cambridge, Mass.: Harvard University Press.

1989. "Distributing health: the allocation of resources by an international agency." WIDER Working Paper No. 71. Helsinki.

1989a. "A public ownership resolution of the tragedy of the commons." *Social Philosophy & Policy* 6, 74–92.

1992. "Can there be socialism after Communism?" *Politics and Society* 20, 261–76.

1992a. "The strategic role of party ideology when voters are uncertain about how the economy works." *American Political Science Review,* in press.

1992b. "A proposal for denationalization of the state sector when pollution is an issue." Working Paper No. 404. Department of Economics, University of California at Davis.

1994. *A Future for Socialism*. Cambridge, Mass.: Harvard University Press.

Roemer, J. E., and J. Silvestre. 1987. "Public ownership: three proposals for resource allocation." Working Paper No. 307. Department of Economics, University of California at Davis.

1993. "The proportional solution for economies with private and public ownership." *Journal of Economic Theory* 59, 426–44.

Romer, P. 1986. "Increasing returns and long run growth." *Journal of Political Economy* 94, 1002–37.

Roth, A. 1979. *Axiomatic Models of Bargaining*. Berlin: Springer Verlag.

1983. "Towards a theory of bargaining: an experimental study in economics." *Science* 220, 687–91.

Roth, A., and F. Schoumaker. 1983. "Expectations and reputations in bargaining: an experimental study." *American Economic Review* 73, 362–72.

Sah, R., and M. Weitzman. 1991. "A proposal for using incentive pre-commitments in public enterprise funding." *World Development* 19, 595–605.

Samuelson, P. A. 1971. "Understanding the Marxian notion of exploitation: a summary of the so-called transformation problem between Marxian values and competitive prices." *Journal of Economic Literature* 9, 339–431.

1982. "The normative and positive inferiority of Marx's values paradigm." *Southern Economic Journal* 49, 11–18.

Scanlon, T. 1982. "Utilitarianism and Contractarianism." In Sen and Williams (1982), pp. 103–28.

1986. "Equality of resources and equality of welfare: a forced marriage." *Ethics* 97, 111–18.

1988. "The significance of choice." In *The Tanner Lectures in Human Values,* vol. VIII. Salt Lake City: University of Utah Press.

Schmitter, P., and T. L. Karl. 1991. "What democracy is . . . and is not." *Journal of Democracy* 2, 75–88.

Schumpeter, J. 1954. *History of Economic Analysis.* Oxford: Oxford University Press.

Scitovsky, T. 1976. *The Joyless Economy: An Inquiry into Human Satisfaction and Consumer Dissatisfaction.* New York: Oxford University Press.

Sen, A. 1973. *On Economic Equality.* Oxford: Clarendon Press.

1977. "Rational fools: a critique of the behavioural foundations of economic theory." *Philosophy & Public Affairs* 6, 317–44.

1979. *Collective Choice and Social Welfare.* New York: North Holland.

1979a. "Personal utilities and public judgements: or, what's wrong with welfare economics?" *Economic Journal* 89, 537–58.

1979b. "Utilitarianism and welfarism." *Journal of Philosophy* 76, 463–89.

1980. "Equality of what?" In S. McMurrin (ed.), *The Tanner Lectures on Human Values,* vol. I. Cambridge University Press.

1985. *Commodities and Capabilities.* Amsterdam: North-Holland.

1985a. "Well-being, agency, and freedom: the Dewey Lectures 1984." *Journal of Philosophy* 82, 169–221.

1992. *Inequality Reexamined.* Cambridge, Mass.: Harvard University Press.

Sen, A., and B. Williams (eds.). 1982. *Utilitarianism and Beyond.* Cambridge University Press.

Silvestre, J. In press a. "Economic analysis of public ownership." *Investigaciones Económicas.*

In press b. "Public goods and public ownership." *Revista Española de Economía.*

Simon, W. 1991. "Social-republican property." *UCLA Law Review,* 1335–1413.

Steedman, I. 1977. *Marx after Sraffa.* London: New Left Books.

Steiner, H. 1977. "The natural right to the means of production." *Philosophical Quarterly* 27, 41–9.

Stigler, G. 1958. "Ricardo and the 93% labor theory of value." *American Economic Review* 48.

1972. "Economic competition and political competition." *Public Choice* 13, 91–106.

Sunstein, C. 1991. "Preferences and politics." *Philosophy & Public Affairs* 20, 3–34.

Thomson, W. 1983. "Problems of fair division and the egalitarian solution." *Journal of Economic Theory* 31, 211–26.

1991. "Bargaining theory: the axiomatic approach." Manuscript.

Thomson, W., and T. Lensberg. 1989. *Axiomatic Models of Bargaining with a Variable Number of Agents.* Cambridge University Press.

Thomson, W., and H. Varian. 1985. "Theories of justice based on symmetry." In Hurwicz, Schmeidler, and Sonnenschein (1985).

Traven, B. 1973. *The Night Visitor and Other Stories.* New York: Hill and Wang.

Tversky, A. 1981. "Choice, preference, and welfare: some psychological observations." Manuscript. Stanford University.

Ungar, R. M. 1987. *False Necessity.* Cambridge University Press.

Van der Veen, R., and P. Van Parijs. 1986. "A capitalist road to Communism." *Theory and Society* 15, 635–56.

Van Inwagen, P. 1983. *An Essay on Free Will.* Oxford: Oxford University Press.

Varian, H. 1974. "Equity, envy, and efficiency." *Journal of Economic Theory* 9, 63–91.

  1975. "Distributive justice, welfare economics, and the theory of fairness." *Philosophy & Public Affairs* 4, 223–47.

  1978. *Microeconomic Theory.* New York: Norton.

Vegara, J. M. 1979. *Economia politica y modelos multisectoriales.* Madrid: Editorial Tecnos.

Weisskopf, T. 1993. "A democratic-firm-based socialism." In Bardhan and Roemer (1993).

Wolff, R. P. 1981. "A critique and reinterpretation of Marx's labor theory of value." *Philosophy & Public Affairs* 10, 89–120.

Wood, A. 1972. "The Marxian critique of justice." *Philosophy & Public Affairs* 1.

  1981. *Karl Marx.* London: Routledge & Kegan Paul.

Wood, E. M. 1981. "The separation of the economic and political in capitalism." *New Left Review* 127, 66–95.

World Health Organization. 1979. "Allocation of resources between regions." Doc. EB 61/INF.DOC./No. 4. Geneva.

  1979–89. *Proposed Programme Budgets.* Geneva.

  1981. *Development Indicators for Monitoring Progress Towards Health for All by the Year 2000.* Geneva.

  1981a. *Global Strategy for Health for All by the Year 2000.* Geneva.

  1987. *Evaluation of the Strategy of Health for All by the Year 2000.* Geneva.

Wright, E. O. 1982. "The status of the political in the concept of class structure." *Politics and Society* 11, 321–42.

Yaari, M., and M. Bar-Hillel. 1984. "On dividing justly." *Social Choice and Welfare* 1, 1–24.

Index

Abdication theory of the state (Marx), 321n
Able-Infirm case, 206-10
Access-to-advantage equalizing proposal
    (Cohen), 181, 194, 288
Accumulation
    in capitalist economy, 29-31
    in corn-leisure economy, 69, 70
    explained by labor theory of value, 55
    in Karl-Adam model, 81-84
Accumulation model, and elasticity
    condition, 88n
Accumulation theory, 66, 70-72
Ackerman, B., 93
Adam. *See* Karl-Adam model
Adam (shepherd) case, 220, 221
Agent
    "gray area" of, 66
    in Nash implementation, 284
Alienated labor, disutility of, 82
Alienation theory, 66, 79-84. *See also*
    Differential alienation
    Marxian interest in, 94
Allocation mechanism. *See also* Axiomatic
        model
    in Able-Infirm model, 207-8
    with anonymity of goods and equal
        outcomes, 160-63
    for bargaining theory analog of Cohen
        problem, 211
    with cardinal noncomparability axiom,
        173
    with common ownership, 272-73, 275-76
    defined, 207
    for egalitarian models, 150-51
    for environments with named goods, 238
    equal division, 276-77, 279, 281, 285
    with equal outcome but without
        anonymity of goods, 166-67
    implementation, 281-85
    to improve rate of infant survival, 249,
        257-60
    linear equivalent, 227, 277-78, 279, 281,
        286
    in mixed economy, 272-85

Nash dominator, 275-76, 280, 281,
    285-86
    proportional, 273-75, 280, 281, 285
    in public ownership model, 224-25, 227
    for resource (but not welfare)
        egalitarianism, 178
    with weak equity and limited self-
        ownership axioms, 172
    for welfarism, 151
Alternative distribution
    in capitalist game, 24
    defined, 17-21, 40
    to feudal allocation, 23
Ambition, 115
    and will, 180
Ambition-sensitive distribution, 146-47,
    180, 194
*Analytical Foundations of Marxian
    Economic Theory* (Roemer), 1
Ancillary information, 244-45
    irrelevance of (axiom), 247, 255
Andrea. *See* Bob-Andrea model;
    Bob-Andrea talent model
Anonymity of goods. *See* Nameless goods
Anonymity of Goods Axiom, 164-66, 176
Arm's length economic transaction, 105
Arneson, R. J., distributive justice theory
    (equal opportunity), 3, 4, 8, 118,
    180-82, 288
Arrow, K., 199
Auction of labor, perverse outcome, 138-39
Aumann, R., 110
Autonomy, 175n
Axiomatic bargaining theory, inadequacy
    of, 2
Axiomatic model. *See also* Allocation
        mechanism
    for distributing health, 245-50, 255-57
    informational complexity in, 231-42
    of public ownership, 224-29
    for resource equalization, 145, 155-61,
        166-75
    with self-ownership and joint ownership
        of external world, 206-10

343